The European Library.

LIFE OF CARDINAL WOLSEY.

EUROPEAN LIBRARY.

Volumes already Published, 3s. 6d. each:

ROSCOE'S LIFE OF LORENZO DE' MEDICI, CALLED THE MAGNI-
FICENT. Edited by WILLIAM HAZLITT, ESQ. One Volume.

GUIZOT'S HISTORY OF THE ENGLISH REVOLUTION OF 1640.
FROM THE ACCESSION TO THE DEATH OF CHARLES I. One Volume.

DUMAS' MARGUERITE DE VALOIS: an Historical Romance of the
time of the Massacre of St. Bartholomew. One Volume.

ROSCOE'S LIFE AND PONTIFICATE OF LEO X. Edited by
WILLIAM HAZLITT, ESQ. Two Volumes.

LIFE OF LUTHER: written by Himself. Collected and arranged by
M. MICHELET; with Copious Selections from his Table Talk. One
Volume.

LITERARY HISTORY OF THE MIDDLE AGES, FROM THE CLOSE
OF THE REIGN OF AUGUSTUS TO ITS REVIVAL IN THE FIFTEENTH
CENTURY. By the REV. JOSEPH BERINGTON. One Volume.

" This is one of the most valuable works which Mr. Bogue has published in his
European Library, not even excepting ' Guizot's History of the English Revolution.'
What adds to the value of the work is, that it is almost *sui generis :* we know not
where such a complete, and, in the main, just view of the authors and the literature
of Europe, from the decline of Roman learning to its revival about the middle of the
fifteenth century, can be found."—SPECTATOR.

HISTORY OF CIVILIZATION, FROM THE FALL OF THE ROMAN EMPIRE
TO THE FRENCH REVOLUTION. BY F. GUIZOT. Vols 1 and 2. (To
be completed in Three Volumes.)

☞ *The above are the only Editions of* ROSCOE'S HISTORICAL WORKS *in
which the Latin, Italian, and Old French Notes are translated.*

CARDINAL WOLSEY.

FROM THE PICTURE BY HOLBEIN, CHRIST CHURCH, OXFORD.

London. D. Bogue. 86, Fleet Street.

CARDINAL WOLSEY.

BY JOHN GALT.

Third Edition,

WITH ADDITIONAL ILLUSTRATIONS FROM CAVENDISH'S
LIFE OF WOLSEY, AND OTHER SOURCES.

LONDON:

DAVID BOGUE, FLEET STREET.

MDCCCXLVI.

———— " This cardinal,
Though from a humble stock, undoubtedly
Was fashioned to much honour from his cradle.
He was a scholar, and a ripe and good one :
Exceeding wise, fair-spoken, and persuading.
Lofty and sour, to them that loved him not,
But, to those men that sought him, sweet as summer.
And though he was unsatisfied in getting,
(Which was a sin,) yet in bestowing
He was most princely.   Ever witness for him
Ipswich and Oxford !   One of which fell with him,
Unwilling to outlive the good that did it ;
The other, though unfinished, yet so famous,
So excellent in art, and yet so rising,
That Christendom shall ever speak his virtue.
His overthrow heap'd business upon him ;
For then, and not till then, he felt himself,
And found the blessedness of being little :
And, to add greater honours to his age
Than man could give him, he died fearing God."

SHAKSPERE.

ADVERTISEMENT.

THE present is the most complete life of Cardinal Wolsey that has hitherto appeared. Mr. Galt's able work, as originally published, is deficient, occasionally, in those personal and domestic details which give such interest to Cavendish's narrative, but, on the other hand, the latter production is almost entirely wanting in that view of contemporary persons and events which is essential to a due appreciation of the Cardinal's character, or of his influence upon his age and upon posterity. Under these circumstances, it was considered best to adopt the more comprehensive work of Mr. Galt, and to supply the illustrative details, in which it is deficient, from Cavendish. These details I have accordingly appended as foot notes to the pages where I thought they might most fitly be introduced; and the selections thus made are so extensive as to include, I may venture to say, well nigh all that constitutes the peculiar superiority of Cavendish's relation. There is one exception to this arrangement : the finest portion of the great Cardinal's life, at all events, in a dramatic and ethical point of view, is its close—from the hour of his departure for the north, after his first disgrace, up to the hour of his death. This precise period, which in Cavendish occupies a hundred pages of most interesting and precious matter, Mr. Galt has compressed into some half-dozen pages.

I did not feel myself warranted in substituting the narrative of the former for that of the latter, in the body of the work, but I have given Cavendish's account entire immediately after the text, in the Appendix. This Appendix, moreover, will be found to contain a far greater number of Cardinal Wolsey's letters, or rather despatches, than have ever before been brought together; Mr. Galt has some not given in Mr. Singer's edition of Cavendish; the latter has others not printed by Galt; Dr. Fiddes supplies many not given by either: 'To make a fourth, I've joined the other three;' inserting the whole of their various collections; and to save the reader that which I myself found no slightly troublesome task, I have modernized the orthography in each English instance, and have given translations of those foreign documents—Charles V.'s letter to Wolsey, and his grant of the pension, for example—which my predecessors, respecting the virgin dignity of state papers, and their own ease, left in their pristine form. Several of the other letters given in the Appendix, are not to be found in either Galt or Singer.

W. HAZLITT.

Middle Temple, August 1, 1846.

MEMOIR

OF THE

LIFE AND WRITINGS OF JOHN GALT.

To the readers of the Life of Wolsey, some notice of the author, and of his other literary productions, cannot be unacceptable; and for both these topics there are abundant materials. His numerous publications extended over a space of above twenty years, and embraced a great variety of subjects; and he has left an autobiography, which, though composed in disease and disappointment, and consequently breathing a tone of melancholy, is, upon the whole, one of the most candid and unpretending specimens extant of that sort of writing, and therefore one which bears upon the face of it an evident truthfulness. John Galt was born on the 2nd of May, 1779, at Irvine, in Ayrshire. His parents were in a rank of society removed from poverty, but not much elevated in the middle class. They were, however, like most persons similarly situated in Scotland, thoroughly respectable, of great integrity and sound sense; and his mother, in particular, had that turn for keen observation of character, and dry sarcastic humour, which is so conspicuous in many of her son's productions. Like most clever men, he owed to his mother the early impressions which gave tone and colour to his intellect and imagination; whilst from both his parents he derived the far more valuable heritage of an uncompromising though unboastful honesty. This is well illustrated by a little domestic incident, which occurred at a period in his life when he was poor and in debt, and when he would have been relieved, by even a small accession of property, from considerable difficulties. His father died, leaving a will, by which he intended to divide his property equally between his children, subject to a life provision for his widow. By one of those mistakes, so common in testamentary dispositions, the will, in legal construction, would have allowed the whole inheritance to pass to the subject of this memoir. John Galt himself did not hesitate for a moment to take steps for carrying into full effect what he knew to be his deceased parent's wishes; nor did his mother and sister for a moment suspect that he would have hesitated. But he had an intimate and very dear friend, who thought it necessary to warn him, though in delicate and guarded terms, against giving way to the temptation of enriching himself at the expense of his nearest relations. " Well do I recollect (says Galt) the feelings which his letter awakened ; that he, the friend of my youth, should have thought any exhortation necessary !" Certainly, in all this, our author did no more than every honest man must have done, or than most men, perhaps, would have done ; but he did what some who think themselves better than their neighbours would not have done ; and so far the transaction affords a test of principle, which was not belied by Galt's subsequent conduct.

He was initiated into mercantile business early in life, at Greenock, and followed it from the first with exemplary zeal, devoting the intervals of active occupation to studies connected with his pursuit. He tells us that he not only read through, and carefully noted, the *Lex Mercatoria*, but composed a Treatise on Underwriting, a History of early English Commerce, and a History of Bills of Exchange, essays intended for his own use only, and which were never made public. They however indicated an early turn for research, and no doubt tended to give him a facility of composition, which stood him in great stead at subsequent periods.

From Greenock he removed to London, about the age of twenty-five. The proximate cause of this step was his having resented, with great energy and effect, an insult offered, not to himself personally, but to the firm in which he was engaged. The circumstance was not publicly known ; but it gave him a disgust to the place, and led him rashly to seek his fortune in the metropolis, where, after some disappointment, he formed a promising connexion, and carried on business successfully for about three years, when circumstances, in which he was not at all to blame, broke up his establishment, and his house became bankrupt; but the energy and candour with which he acted on the occasion obtained for him the respect of all his creditors. Countenanced by them, and prompted by the activity of his mind, and the sanguine hopes of youth, he embarked, in 1809, for the Mediterranean, in the hope of beating out some new path of commercial enterprise, and it was on this voyage that accident threw him into the company of Lord Byron, whose acquaintance he continued long to possess, and whose life he afterwards wrote.

During the next two years, he visited Sardinia, Malta, Sicily, Corinth, Athens, Hydra, Scios, Ephesus, Smyrna, Samos, Cerigo, Thessalonica, Constantinople, Nicomedia, Widdin, and many other places of note. His chief object was to establish depôts of English goods, for introduction into the continent, in opposition to the insane project of Napoleon for annihilating our commerce, by means of his memorable Berlin and Milan decrees. Mr· Galt's remarks on that subject evince a soundness of judgment, and a grasp of mind not very common in that day, when most men were dazzled with

the splendour of the French victories, or appalled by the threatening aspect
of French power.

After our author's return to England, his occupations were of a very desul-
tory and unsettled nature : at one time he went for some months to Gibraltar,
on a mercantile undertaking : at another time he travelled on the continent ;
afterwards he lived chiefly in London, turning his literary talents to account ;
and among his productions at that period was the *Life of Wolsey*, which
follows the present memoir. But a sudden and unexpected turn of fortune
now occurred to him. He received letters from Canada, appointing him
agent for such of the principal inhabitants as had claims to urge on government for losses suffered during the invasion of the province by the armies of
the United States. They could not have chosen a more zealous or a more
sagacious agent; but every one who has had to do with pecuniary claims on
government, knows how difficult it is to bring them to anything like an
equitable arrangement; what a length of time must be employed ; what
obstacles must be removed ; what arguments must be answered ; and after all,
with the great probability of being turned round on some frivolous or purely
technical objection. Through these difficulties, with persevering firmness,
did Galt work his way : the justice of the claim was formally recognised ;
but still there was a difficulty in finding funds from which the compensation could be made. In 1823, from information communicated by bishop
Macdonnell, Mr. Galt perceived that such a fund might easily be supplied
by the sale of lands belonging to the crown (and called the crown reserves)
in Canada itself. This plan he lost no time in submitting to the secretary
of state for the Colonies, by whom it was favourably received, and eventually
acted upon.

Still a further step was necessary—namely, to find purchasers for the
lands so to be sold; and this, too, was effected by Mr. Galt. He proposed
to an eminent mercantile house in London, to form a company for purchas-
ing and bringing into cultivation the lands in question; they readily ac-
quiesced, and after due communication with government, the *Canada Company* was formed, and Mr. Galt was appointed its secretary. Other means
were afterwards taken by government to compensate the original claimants ;
but under Mr. Galt's direction, 2,384,000 acres were sold, producing in
sterling money 348,680*l.*

Commissioners being appointed to value the lands, the Canada Company
nominated Mr. Galt as one, and he sailed with his colleagues for the province
in 1824. He returned in the following year, when the disputed question of
the clergy reserves was settled; and in 1826, he sailed again as agent of the
Canada Company, to carry into effect the plans which he had suggested to
them. Before we advert to these, however, we cannot but notice the deep
impression made on his mind at this time by the death of his mother. "From
my very childhood," says he, "it had been my greatest delight to please

this affectionate parent, and in consequence, her loss weakened, if I may so say, the motive that had previously impelled my energies. The world, to me, was deprived of one that I was actuated by an endeavour to gratify; and in proportion the charm of life was diminished in its power. But the misfortunes also were weakened in their pungency, and no effort of reason was necessary to convince me that I would suffer less by not having her anxieties to consider. Many years before, I had lost my father; but although few could have stronger claims on the reverence of their children than those to which he was entitled, there is a difference in the filial love which belongs to the father, from that which the child's heart thinks is the mother's due. The one is allied to esteem, friendship, and respect; but the other is a gentle feeling composed of confidence, kindness, and gratitude. The one is more masculine in all its qualities; but the other, without the mind's being able to say wherefore, is at once more durable and more tender."

Mr. Galt's second visit to Canada, though it enabled him to render invaluable services to the company whose agent he was, and services still more important to the province which was the scene of his labours, was to himself productive of mortification and disappointment, of ruined health, and bankrupt circumstances. Yet he sustained these evils manfully, and was cheered at a later period by the incontestable proofs that his conduct had been productive alike of profit to his employers, and of benefit to the Canadians, among whom his name is to this day spoken of with unfeigned respect.

The first vexation that he encountered was from the unfounded suspicions of the local government. His principles, which through life were of a conservative character, had been represented to Sir Peregrine Maitland as republican; and some slight civilities which passed between him and the editor of a democratic newspaper, were construed into proofs that he was disposed to favour rebellion. All this would appear merely ridiculous, were it not that its effects are deeply injurious both to private and public interests, of which unfortunately there are too many, and some very recent examples. The governor of a small colony is often surrounded by parasites, who persuade him that the most legal, moderate, and respectful dissent from his opinions is sedition; and a custom has very generally prevailed among governors of acting on such suggestions, as if they were proofs of guilt; and that, even without letting the suspected person know that he has been accused. Thus Sir P. Maitland complained of Galt privately to the secretary of state, and the complaint was communicated to the directors, who, of course, were prejudiced against their agent, whilst the latter in vain endeavoured to discover the real grounds of that prejudice.

To this was added another and a very different complaint against the unfortunate subject of our memoir. Unfortunately for himself, he had conceived it possible (as indeed it was) to combine with a profitable sale of lands for the Canada Company, a benevolent provision for the thousands of emigrants into the colony from the mother country. His plan was wise, and far seeing. From the nature of it, a considerable outlay was necessary at first, to provide accommodation for the poor labourers, and almost equally poor settlers; but that outlay was so managed, as to ensure eventually not only repayment, but considerable profit to the company; while it laid the foundation of permanent strength and prosperity to the colony. Mr. Galt proceeded on this scheme with his characteristic energy, and of his success, even so early as 1829, the clearest testimony was given by a most intelligent and wholly disinterested witness, Mr. Fellows, a great land agent in the United States. This gentleman having visited the village of Guelph, founded by Mr. Galt, thus speaks:—" Considering the short period of time that has elapsed since the village was founded, and that it is only about eighteen months since it was an entire forest, the number of buildings and the population are proofs of uncommon industry and enterprise." He adds, as his "most decided opinion," that " all the proceedings of Mr. Galt and his assistant, Mr. Prior, have been exceedingly judicious; that *the improvements have been indispensable to the sale and settlement of the company's lands*—that the outlays for mechanics' and labourers' wages are as moderate as is usual in a new and unsettled country—that the sales made, have been at good prices, and the cash payments larger than are usually received from the first settlers in a new tract of land,"—and "that the certificates, contracts, and letters are in very suitable form, and the books are well adapted to exhibit correct and accurate views of the affairs of the company. Upon the whole," concludes Mr. Fellows, " I beg leave most respectfully to state to the company my decided opinion, that Mr. Galt's agency has been conducted with sound judgment, and *a proper regard to economy, and the interests of the company;* and that his proceedings have promoted their best interests; and I believe the company cannot more effectually promote their own views, than by delegating to him the most ample discretionary powers."

Honourable and unimpeachable as was this testimony to Mr. Galt's uprightness and ability, it was met at home by a senseless clamour at the outlay, and the consequent diminution of the dividends. The price of shares fell in the market; and Mr. Galt was superseded! He had to console himself, however, with the recollection that he was not treated worse, nor indeed quite so ill, as the great Columbus, who, for adding a new world to the Spanish empire, was sent home in chains; and if gratitude was not the peculiar feature of the Canada Company, in the nineteenth century, neither was it of the catholic sovereigns, Ferdinand and Isabella, in the sixteenth.

Mr. Galt returned to England poor, with a family dependent on him, and with a broken constitution, but with the pride of conscious integrity. He was even incarcerated by a reverend doctor, one of his oldest acquaintances, and who had been for about forty years a partner with his wife's father; and at length was under the hard necessity of taking the benefit of the Insolvent Act. In mentioning this last mortifying circumstance, he pathetically says : —" This transaction and winding up of my philanthropic dream is stated with as little emotion as possible ; *but it was not so felt.*"

There is something inexpressibly touching in the picture which, for ten years from this period, the truly *noble* spirit of John Galt presents, depending on authorship for the sustenance of himself, his wife, and children, struggling with disease—undergoing no less than *fourteen* successive attacks of paralysis—till his body became a mere wreck, yet still tenaciously clinging to the powers of intellect, and dictating to an amanuensis when he had no longer the power to wield a pen. For the most part, he bore these heavy dispensations with the fortitude of a man and the submission of a Christian ; yet, now and then, he was sadly sensible of his forlorn state ; and in one of those moods he composed lines which cannot be read without emotion :—

> " Hapless, forgotten, sad, and lame,
>   On one lone seat the livelong day,
> I muse of youth, and dreams of fame,
>   And hopes, and wishes—all away !
>
> " No more to me, with carol gay,
>   Shall mounting lark from pasture rise ;
> Nor breezes bland on upland play ;
>   Nor far, fair scenes my steps entice.
>
> " Ah, never more, beneath the skies,
>   The winged heart shall glowing soar ;
> Nor e'er be reach'd the goal or prize ;
>   The spells of life enchant no more.
>
> " The burning thought, the boding sigh,
>   *The grief unnam'd that old men feel,*
> The languid limbs, that with'ring lie,
>   The pow'rless will's effectless zeal.
> All these are mine—and Heav'n bestows
>   The gifts, but still I find them woes."

Whilst the projector and practical benefactor of the Canada Company was thus pining in disregarded misery, the company itself was thriving even beyond his sanguine expectations. His plans, which they had before scouted and condemned, they now directed to be renewed. Shares bought at seventeen pounds were selling at fifty-five, and in little more than one year the shareholders had made above *four hundred thousand pounds !* Galt points to these facts, in no feeling of bitterness ; but, on the contrary, as allaying his sense of personal ruin, by the reflection that his schemes and plans for the good of others were at last fully vindicated. His bodily sufferings terminated at Greenock, on the 11th of April, 1839, when he had almost concluded his sixtieth year.

It only remains for us to take a brief notice of his literary productions. The most original, in his own estimation as well as in the world's, are those which delineate, with the caustic humour and colloquial diction which he derived from his mother, the peculiar habits and manners of the district which gave him birth. The first published of these was the "Ayrshire Legatees," which appeared in Blackwood's Magazine, in 1820 and 1821, and, becoming at once popular, was soon followed by the "Annals of the Parish," and the "Provost." To this class also belong the "Entail," "Sir Andrew Wylie," the "Steam-boat," and the "Gathering of the West;" and all were given to the world within the three years immediately preceding his engagement with the Canada Company.

But he had long before appeared as an author. We say nothing of "The Battle of Larys," and other poetical effusions, which appeared in periodicals; but his first serious attempt at literature was in 1812, in a quarto volume, entitled, "Voyages and Travels, in the years 1808, 1810, and 1811;" which was followed, the next year, by "Letters from the Levant," in octavo. In 1812, too, he wrote "Reflections on Political and Commercial Subjects." These works were in general but ill received, chiefly from defects of style; for they contain many just and shrewd observations, and some which were strikingly anticipative of subsequent events. It is probable, too, that they recommended the author to Dr. Tilloch, the editor of the Philosophical Magazine, and proprietor of the Star newspaper, whose daughter Mr. Galt about that time married. The statistical researches which these productions required, led the author to that remarkable period of our political history which he has ably canvassed in "the Life and Administration of Cardinal Wolsey," a work twice published, (in 1812 and 1818,) and which is now given a third time to the reader.

Wolsey's was not the only life written by Galt. In 1816 he published that of Mr. West, from materials wholly supplied by the worthy president himself. In 1830, he wrote a "Life of Lord Byron," which has been termed coarse and caustic, but which is true, and fair enough. About the same time, he published the "Lives of the Players," an amusing compilation, but making no pretensions to originality.

Soon after his "Ayrshire Legatees," &c., had attracted public attention, he seems to have been tempted (as numberless other writers were) by the example of Sir Walter Scott, to enter on the domain of historical romance. In 1823, he published "Ringan Gilhaize," and the "Spaewife," and at subsequent periods "Rothelan," a tale of the times of Edward III., and "Southenan," of the epoch of the Scottish queen Mary. If the Waverley novels had never appeared, these (especially the first, which marks

with a strong outline the epoch of the Scottish Reformation) would have
been deemed remarkable publications ; but the ground was pre-occupied by
the great magician, and

> "Within that circle none durst walk but he."

Galt was more at home in describing manners and characters which he
had personally witnessed. In 1820, he wrote the "Earthquake," a work
accurately painting Sicilian habits and sentiments, though an extravagant and
ill-constructed story. On this he justly remarks, that our novels of foreign
countries generally contain laudable likenesses of characters and events
that might well enough occur in England, but which resemble the scenery
and society of the lands in which they are laid, much as Tom Jones would
those of Turkey, if the hero were called Hassan Moustapha, or as Roderick
Random might pass for a Greek, if he were baptised Theodosius Phrago-
polus.

His description of Canadian localities and events, and of occurrences and
personages to be met with in the neighbouring part of the United States,
was more easily appreciated, and therefore better relished by the English
public. "Lawrie Todd" and "Bogle Corbet" were, therefore, well received.
In neither of these was there anything, except the names, wholly fictitious.
The writer had in his mind's eye real individuals, specific localities, and
events nearly, if not altogether identical with those which he relates. He
strung them together, too, with no mean skill, and consequently both these
novels were read with avidity, especially by persons who either had con-
nexions in North America, or contemplated visiting those regions themselves. "In fact (says Galt) Bogle Corbet was intended by me to be a
guide book, particularly in the third volume."—"Canada, indeed, must
have altered rapidly if Bogle Corbet be not a true guide to settlers of his
rank."

It is needless, and, indeed, it would be almost endless to, enumerate all
the minor productions of our author, many of them only entitled to favourable criticism in considering the pain, distress, and anxiety under which
they were sent to the press. It may be proper, however, to notice that, in
1812, he put forth a volume of tragedies, one, at least, of which, "The
Witness," was vigorously conceived ; that he at one period wrote in the
"Star," and at another in the "Courier;" and that he concluded his
"strange eventful history" by taking himself as the subject of his pen, in
two distinct works, "The Autobiography of John Galt," 2 vols. 8vo, 1833,
and "The Literary Life and Miscellanies of John Galt," 3 vols. 12mo, 1834.

AUTHOR'S PREFACE.

SEVERAL years ago, while standing in the great quadrangle of Christ Church College, in Oxford, I happened to reflect, that although Cardinal Wolsey was one of the most conspicuous personages of an eventful age, no history of his life had yet been written, which showed the influence of his character in its proper light. Without being aware of the extent of reading requisite for an undertaking necessarily descriptive of the spirit of those times, I began to collect materials for supplying the desideratum at my leisure; and before my departure for the south of Europe, besides volumes of notes and documents, I had composed a narrative; but, as my opinion respecting the manner in which the life of a statesman ought to be written underwent some change during my absence, on my return I was induced to re-model the whole of what I had previously prepared for publication; and instead of a work embracing the biography of other persons, to present one in which the hero should always appear prominent. I now offer it to the public with much unfeigned diffidence; because, although I have endeavoured to render it worthy of some attention, I may be disappointed in my expectation.

To the officers of the British Museum I am under great obligations, for the facility afforded to my researches; and the gentlemen of Jesus College, Oxford, in the politest manner, gave me access to the papers from which Lord Her-

bert compiled his ' History of Henry VIII.' My friend, Mr.
Tilloch, allowed me the use of several very rare and curious
books; but I owe more to his own recondite knowledge
than I could have obtained from any library without a guide,
so learned, communicative, and obliging. I have also had the
advantage of having the sheets revised by Mr. Nichols, of
whose very exact and minute knowledge of English Antiquities
the public are sufficiently acquainted ; and I owe to several
private friends different important hints and interesting suggestions. Nor ought I to omit mentioning, that during my
stay in Palermo I was enabled occasionally to prosecute my
historical inquiries in the magnificent library of the Jesuits
in that capital; and that father Gusta, the librarian, a man of
the most extensive reading, had the kindness to point out the
works that were calculated to afford me information.

With all these aids, and with materials of great magnitude
and variety, it may excite surprise that I should have produced so small a work; and particularly that I should have
omitted many events well known to the most cursory reader
of English history, while I have attached consequence to
minor affairs. But I have endeavoured to imitate the classic
models of antiquity, as I think that it is only the necessary
succession of events which interests posterity; and that many
transactions in which Wolsey was incidentally engaged, belong less to his memoirs than to those of others.

London, 25*th May*, 1812.

CONTENTS.

BOOK I.

BOOK II.

BOOK III.

BOOK IV.

BOOK V.

BOOK VI.

BOOK VII.

LIFE OF CARDINAL WOLSEY.

BOOK I.

EUROPE, during the predominance of the papal authority,
formed, in reality, but one general state, in which the civil
and military institutions were subordinate to the ecclesiastical. The submission yielded to secular superiors, was
modified by the various tenure of feudal property. No
laws existed which the whole of the community conceived
themselves equally bound to maintain, but such as issued
from the apostolical throne. By whatever names the provinces of Christendom were distinguished, empires, kingdoms,

B

or republics, the people and their rulers alike acknowledged themselves subjects of the pontiff. Royalty did homage to superstition; nor was the crown itself allodial, but held of the tiara.

The means by which the papal power was upheld and exercised, were as wonderful as the alleged extent of its prerogatives. A portion of mankind assumed privileges pernicious to the rights of the common race; and the humblest member of that class might aspire to supreme command. As inducements to submission, the priesthood promised, to all who would most slavishly obey its authority, rewards which the vicissitudes of life could not affect. Man surrendered his reason, and yielded a degree of implicit obedience to the pope, such as never existed under any other government. The management of all concerns, in consequence, became entrusted to the officers of his holiness; and in the fulness of the ecclesiastical usurpation, the clergy may be described as constituting the will and mind of the political body.

The long, bloody, and proscriptive wars between the royal families of York and Lancaster, reduced the ancient importance of England as a province of Christendom, and naturally gave a preponderance to military rule over an authority founded on opinion. The restoration of peace and order was favourable to the church; and under Henry VII. the clergy began to recover their wonted influence, and to put forth their former pretensions; but the people, during the civil conflicts, had acquired a military licentiousness of thought, and the church was no longer regarded with the veneration which she had once inspired. In the state, churchmen still attained the highest offices. They were, however, generally regarded as the members of an order, arrogant by the possession of exorbitant privileges, and averse to the social interests of the species. Their conduct was viewed with a distrustful and inquisitorial eye.

The civil wars also operated to the diminution of the personal influence and manorial jurisdiction of the barons. Proscriptions led to changes in the possession of domains. The feudal tenants, accustomed to look upon the hereditary lord of the manor as their natural and rightful superior, viewed his removal as oppression, and considered his successors as usurpers. The ancient ties of connexion between the chiefs and the vassals, were generally relaxed, and, in many instances, entirely dissolved. The nobles were divided into two factions; and as the houses of York and Lancaster alternately prevailed, each faction was, in its turn, doomed to suffer the vengeance of its rival. They found it necessary, also, to be more around the king than when the succession was not disputed:—his friends to maintain his cause—the moderate to avoid suspicion—and his adversaries to watch opportunities of promoting the designs of their own faction. The splendour of the court was thus augmented; but the absence of the nobility from their castles weakened the whole structure of the feudal system which supported the oligarchy, and impaired for ever that formidable power which had resulted from a constant intercourse of affection and authority between the lords and their vassals. The reign of Henry VIII. was not only the most magnificent in the annals of England, but, also, that in which the king exercised the greatest latitude of prerogative, and in which the nobility possessed the least influence. It was later before the full extent of the good, ordained to spring from the evil of the disputed succession, manifested itself among the people.

Although the court presented a scene of gorgeous pageantry unknown in any former period, the personal animosities and fierce altercations of the civil wars had produced among the courtiers rude and turbulent manners. They indulged in a plainness of address, almost as different from the ceremonious courtesy of chivalry, as the easy politeness which has since succeeded. England never exhibited such superb spectacles of knighthood as in the reign of Henry VIII.; but lists and tournaments were no longer regarded as courts of equity, nor the fortune of arms a more accurate criterion of guilt and innocence than the verdict of civil tribunals. All the parade of chivalry was renewed, but the spirit had departed with the circumstances which had called it forth. To profess the sentiments which it had anciently inspired, was not, indeed, ridiculous,* but the vows and pageants which added a gallant dignity to unlettered valour, ceased to be objects of serious concern; and were only imitated for the amusement of the king.

* Cervantes was not born till the year 1547, nor Don Quixote published in Spain till 1605.

The civil wars were not more favourable to the advancement of learning, than to the authority of the nobility and
clergy. During the reign of Henry VI. polite literature had
made some progress. His pacific disposition had led him to
foster the arts which contribute to the pleasures of life; but
from the date of his dethronement they began to decline, and
the universities ceased to recognise the muses. What was
called philosophy consisted in the agitation of logical subtle-
ties, founded, commonly, on mere verbal distinctions, which
sharpened, without informing, the understanding. The
general notion entertained of science was, of something infi-
nitely beyond ordinary uses. It was wrapt up in language
almost as mysterious as the Egyptian hieroglyphics; and
nothing less was expected from it than a knowledge of future
events, and the power of conferring wealth and immortality.[1]
In these vain pursuits, many important facts, it is true, were
ascertained; but they were passed over unheeded and un-
valued. Divinity was the only study that tended to advance
the progress of the public mind; and the art of printing
favoured the prevalent bias of the age, by multiplying the
materials and excitements of controversy.

Besides the civil wars, exterior events had contributed to
alter and expand the views of the English nation. The
riches which Portugal had obtained by exploring the passage
to India, inspired Spain with adventurous emulation; and
her enterprises were recompensed by the attainment of a new
world. This great achievement roused throughout Christendom a similar spirit.* Avarice overcame ambition in the
councils of princes; and sovereigns and subjects, alike eager
to participate in the golden regions of the west, promoted the
moral independence of man, by cultivating the means of commerce. A new order was, in consequence, destined at this
era to arise in society, by which, in time, the policy of nations,
the motives of war, and the modes of rule, were to be radically
changed. Hitherto, the power of our kings had depended
on their territorial possessions, and the influence of our nobles,
on the breadth and fertility of their estates: but the mercantile order, by gradual accumulation, has since attained an

* Henry VIII. was the first English king who established a navy. Ships,
before his time, were hired from the merchants. The Trinity house was
instituted in 1512.

ascendancy in the realm equal to that of the clergy and nobility, and reduced to its subserviency the prerogatives of the
crown itself. In the reign of Henry VIII. this class had, it
is true, not assumed any recognisable form; but the principles
which, by subsequent development, induced all its importance,
began to affect the designs and treaties of the government.

This state of the clergy and nobility, of manners, and learning, and trade, afforded ample scope for the exercise of an
ambitious, resolute, ostentatious mind. The following narrative is an attempt to delineate the operations of a character
indisputably of this description, and to exhibit a view of the
influential events by which it was governed, in a period full
of great emergencies, and fraught with changes affecting the
interests, perhaps, of the whole human race,—a period which,
like the present momentous age, may be regarded as one of
those vast occasional eddies in the mighty current of human
affairs, by which homes and inheritances are overwhelmed
and swept away, but which, as the violence subsides, never
fail to leave behind inestimable riches for the use and improvement of society.

Thomas Wolsey was born at Ipswich, in the month of
March, 1471.* His father,† though of mean condition, pos-

---

* Parish registers were not instituted in England till 1535.

† By some it has been said that he was a butcher, but the foundation
for the assertion nowhere appears. The zealous biographer of the cardinal,
Mr. Grove, made two journies to Ipswich for the purpose of obtaining information there respecting him, but the whole fruit of both expeditions was
ascertaining the name of Wolsey's father, and that he was a man of some
substance. Cavendish simply describes him as "an honest, poor man."
His will, published by Dr. Fiddes, from the Registry at Norwich, and
given by Mr. Singer, runs thus :—
  "In the name of God, Amen. The xxxi. day of the month of September,
in the year of our Lord God 1496. I, Robert Wulcy, of Ipswich, whole of
mind and in good memory, make my testament and my last will in this wise.
First, I bequeath my soul to Almighty God, Our Lady Saint Mary, and to
all the company of heaven ; and my body to be buried in the churchyard of
Our Lady Saint Mary of Newmarket. Also, I bequeath to the high authorities of Saint Nicholas of Ipswich, 6s. 7d. Also, I bequeath to the painting
of the archangel there, 11s. Item, I will that if Thomas, my son, be a priest
within a year next after my decease, then I will that he sing for me and my
friends by the space of a year, and he for to have for his salary 10 marks ; and
if the said Thomas, my son, be not a priest, then I will that another honest
priest sing for me and my friends the term aforesaid, and he to have the
salary of 10 marks. Item, I will that Joan, my wife, have all my land and

sessed some property. Persuaded of the apt and active genius of his son, he sent him early to school, and destined him for the service of the church. Wolsey, at the age of fifteen, was a student in Oxford, and had already obtained the degree of bachelor of arts, which procured him at the university the name of the boy-bachelor. Few, so young, with all the advantages of rank and affluence, attained, in that age, academical honours.[2] Continuing to prosper in philosophy, he was elected a fellow of Magdalen college, appointed a tutor of the school,[3] and entrusted to educate the three sons of the marquis of Dorset. The proficiency which the young noblemen made under his tuition, and his own conversational accomplishments, displayed while passing the Christmas holidays with their father, procured him the patronage of the marquis, who afterwards rewarded him with the rectory of Lymington, in Somersetshire.*

He was at this time bursar of Magdalen college; but having, without a sufficient warrant, applied the funds to complete the great tower of the buildings, he found himself obliged to resign. The tower is one of the ornaments of Oxford, and may be regarded not only as a specimen of his taste in architecture, but as a monument of that forward spirit, and intrepid disrespect of precedents, which he so amply manifested in greater affairs.

His disposition, frank and social, often led him to scenes and enjoyments unbecoming the grave regularity of the ecclesiastical profession. He had not resided long at Lymington before he was found concerned in the riots of a fair in the neighbourhood; for which one of the justices of the peace

tenements in the parish of Saint Nicholas in Ipswich aforesaid, and my free and bond lands in the parish of Saint Stoke to give and to sell. The residue of all my goods not before bequeathed, I give and bequeath to the good disposition of Joan, my wife, Thomas, my son, and Thomas Cady, whom I ordain and make my executors, to dispose of for me as they shall think best to please Almighty God, and profit for my soul; and of this, my testament and last will, I ordain and make Richard Farington supervisor, and he for to have for his labour, 13s. 4d., and if the said Richard deserve more, he for to have more of Joan, my wife. Item, I bequeath to Thomas Cady, my executor aforesaid, 13s. 4d."—The name in Lodge's Portraits is spelt *Wuley;* in Smith's Book of Autographs it is also *Wuley,* and there are said to be two unpublished letters extant, bearing the signature so spelt.—W. H.

* He was instituted Oct. 10, 1500.

subjected him to disgraceful punishment.* Whether this was just or inconsiderate, it could not but serve to render his local intercourse irksome. He therefore removed from Lymington, and was received as one of the domestic chaplains of archbishop Dean. At the death of that prelate he went to Calais, where sir Richard Nanfan, then treasurer, appointed him to manage the business of his office. In this situation Wolsey conducted himself with so much discretion, that sir Richard was induced to exert his influence to procure him promotion, and succeeded in getting him nominated one of the chaplains to the king.

Wolsey, when he obtained this situation, possessed many of those endowments which, at court, are often more advantageous than virtues. He spoke and acted with a generous assurance; and that superiority of deportment which, in the glare of his full fortune, was felt so like arrogance, seemed then only calculated to acquire and secure respect. In the performance of his duty, he had frequent opportunities of improving the impression of his exterior accomplishments; and his advancement accompanied the development of his talents. The abbot of the rich monastery of St. Edmund appointed him to the rectory of Redgrave, in the diocese of Norwich; Fox, bishop of Winchester, who at that time held the privy seal, and sir Thomas Lovell, then chancellor of the exchequer,

---

* Fiddes says that he was put in the stocks; but Cavendish merely says, that sir Amias Paulet "laid him by the heels." Mr. Singer observes: "the ground for the assertion as to the stocks and the disorderly conduct at a fair, seems to rest upon no earlier authority than that of sir John Harrington. Store represents Wolsey as the injured party:

"'Wrong'd by a knight, for no desert of mine.'"

"And being there for that intent, (the being ordained,) one sir Amias Paulet, knight, dwelling in the country thereabout, took an occasion of displeasure against him, but upon what ground I know not; insomuch that he was so bold as to set the schoolmaster by the heels during his displeasure, which affront was afterwards neither forgotten nor forgiven; for when the schoolmaster mounted so high as to be lord chancellor of England, he was not oblivious of the old displeasure most cruelly ministered to him by sir Amias, but sent for him, and after a very sharp reproof, enjoined him not to depart out of London without licence first obtained, so that he continued in the Middle Temple the space of five or six years, who afterwards lay in the gate-house next the street, which he re-edified, and sumptuously beautified all over, on the outside, with the cardinal's arms, his hat, his cognizance, and badges, with other devices, in so glorious a manner, as he thought thereby to have appeased his old displeasure." —*Cavendish.*

also distinguished him by their friendship.* They thought
that his uncommon capacity might be usefully employed in
affairs of state; and, accordingly, while the treaty of marriage
was pending between the king and Margaret the dowager of
Savoy, they proposed him as a fit person to be sent to her
father, the emperor Maximilian, on that business. The king
had not before particularly noticed Wolsey; but, after con-
versing with him on this subject, he was satisfied with his
qualifications, and commanded him to be in readiness for the
embassy.

The court was then at Richmond, from which Wolsey proceeded, with his despatches, to London, where he arrived about
four o'clock in the afternoon. He had a boat waiting, and in
less than three hours was at Gravesend. With post-horses,
he got, next morning, to Dover, reached Calais in the course
of the forenoon, and arrived the same night at the imperial
court. The emperor, informed that an extraordinary ambassador had come from England, immediately admitted him; and
the business being agreeable, was quickly concluded. Wolsey,
without delay, returned. He reached Calais at the opening
of the gates; found the passengers going on board the vessel
that brought him from England; embarked; and, about ten
o'clock, was landed at Dover. Relays of horses having been
provided, he reached Richmond the same evening. Reposing
some time, he rose, and met the king as he came from his
chamber to hear the morning service. His majesty, surprised,
rebuked him for neglecting the orders with which he had been
charged: "May it please your highness," said Wolsey, "I
have been with the emperor, and executed my commission, to
the satisfaction, I trust, of your grace." He then knelt, and
presented Maximilian's letters. Dissembling the admiration
which such unprecedented expedition excited, the king inquired if he had received no orders by a pursuivant sent
after him? Wolsey answered, that he had met the messenger
as he returned; but, having preconceived the purpose for

* "Wolsey had not only the address and good qualities necessary to the
acquisition of such friends, but also retained them to the last. The affection
of Bishop Fox is apparent in the last letter which he wrote to him; and sir
Thomas Lovell's esteem was manifested to the close of his life, for he leaves
him in his will ' a standing cup of golde, and one hundred marks in golde.' "
—Singer.

which he was sent, he had presumed, of his own accord, to supply the defect in his credentials, for which he solicited his majesty's pardon.* The king, pleased with this foresight, and gratified with the result of the negotiation, readily forgave his temerity; and, commanding him to attend the council in the afternoon, he desired that in the meantime he would refresh himself with repose. Wolsey, at the time appointed, reported the business of his mission with so much clearness and propriety, that he received the applause of all present; and the king, when the deanery of Lincoln became vacant, bestowed it on him unsolicited.†

It has been alleged that bishop Fox, in order to counteract the power of the earl of Surrey, who then monopolized almost the whole favour and patronage of the crown, was induced to promote, and avail himself, of Wolsey's rising genius. Whatever were his motives, it may be inferred, that the personal merits of Wolsey were beginning to awaken the envious apprehensions of that sordid race, who ascribe the prosperity of others to any cause rather than to the efforts of ability, and to whom talents form a matter of offence.

Wolsey had not long been dean of Lincoln, when Henry VII. died (22 April, 1509), and was succeeded by his only surviving son, then in the eighteenth year of his age. The claims of the rival families of York and Lancaster were united in the person of Henry VIII. He also inherited from his father greater treasures than any English monarch had ever before enjoyed. Nor was he less distinguished by the gifts of nature than by those of fortune. His figure was eminently handsome; his spirit courageous; and his temper, though hot and arbitrary, disdained the practice of equivocation. During the life of his elder brother, prince Arthur, he was intended for the church; and to the effects of this design historians

---

* Storer makes the cardinal describe his mission very prettily :

> " The Argonautic vessel never past
>   With swifter course along the Colchian main,
> Than my small bark, with fair and steady blast,
>   Convey'd me forth, and reconvey'd again.
>   Thrice had Arcturus driv'n his restless wain,
> And heav'n's bright lamp the day had thrice reviv'd
>   From first departure, till I last arriv'd."

† He was collated Feb. 2, 1508.

have ascribed his erudition, and the personal share which he took in the controversies of the Reformation. He delighted in magnificent spectacles, and was passionately fond of equestrian and athletic exercises—amusements to which the princes and nobles of England have ever been partial. At his accession he was calculated, by his person and manners, to attract the admiration and affections of the multitude; and by his knowledge and capacity to obtain the esteem and indulgence of the discerning few. By the judicious advice of his grandmother, he selected for ministers those counsellors of his father who were the most respected for their caution and wisdom.* And no money being required from the people, the affairs of the kingdom were managed with discretion and popularity. The state of Europe was also, at this time, auspicious to the prosperity of England.

The emperor Maximilian, with a view to secure to his family Burgundy and the Netherlands, which he held only in right of his wife, courted the alliance of the young king. His advances were favourably received; for it was thought that Henry VII. had not acted with his usual perspicuity by acquiescing in the cession of those opulent territories to a potentate, already the greatest in Christendom; and that their entire annexation to the dominions of Austria ought still to be resisted. Lewis XII., of France, was at war with several of the Italian states, and was endeavouring to incorporate with his kingdom Bretagne, which he had obtained by marriage with the heiress; a marriage which Henry VII. was equally blamed for having suffered to take place without opposition. Ferdinand of Aragon, who, by marrying Isabella of Castile, and by repelling the Moors from Grenada, became sovereign of all Spain, had reasons no less powerful for maintaining an intimate alliance with England. His daughter, Katherine, was the queen of Henry VIII. The inducements which had led to this connexion were strengthened by uncertainties in his political relations with the French king, and by peculiar circumstances in the matrimonial condition of Katherine. She had been first married to her husband's elder brother. After his death, a questionable licence had been obtained from the

* Lord Herbert remarks, that there was no lawyer in this administration-

pope, and under it her second marriage was completed.
James IV., of Scotland, had married Henry's eldest sister.
At the close of the late reign a slight coolness had, however,
arisen between the courts of Edinburgh and London, occasioned by the preference which Scotland, according to ancient
policy, gave to the views of France; but no serious hostility
was apprehended, and the congeniality between the characters
of the two monarchs seemed likely to draw them into particular friendship.

No schism had yet, to any apparently dangerous extent,
disturbed the concord of Christendom. Savonarola, who had
ventured to attack the enormities of the papal administration
of Alexander VI., was destroyed at Florence. By his death
the seeds of a reformation, similar to that which afterwards
spread with such rapidity in Germany, were, in Italy, totally
exterminated. The inhabitants of that branch of the Alps
which stretches towards the Pyrenees had, indeed, separated
themselves from the church of Rome; but they were a simple
people, and held little intercourse with the rest of Christendom. In Bohemia, a few followers of John Huss and Jerome
of Prague, preserved, rather than asserted, their principles.
In England, from the days of Wickliffe, many had disliked
the Roman pretensions, but they were in general of humble
rank, unconnected, and only united in enmity against the
ignorant and luxurious clergy.*

At this period Wolsey was in the thirty-eighth year of his
age. Although a priest, he frequented the entertainments of the
young courtiers, of which he partook with the gaiety of secular freedom. One of his Oxford pupils had succeeded to the
marquisate of Dorset, and was an intimate companion of the
king. In his company, Wolsey probably obtained opportunities of studying the temper and inclinations of his master,
and of recommending himself to his serious favour by the
knowledge of public affairs which, in the midst of pleasure
and dissipation, he dextrously took occasion to display. Riches
and honours flowed upon him. In the first year of Henry he
received a grant of lands and tenements in London, was ad-

---

* Henry VIII. was the first king of England who had any correspondence
with the Swiss.

mitted to the privy council, and appointed almoner.* Soon after, the king gave him the rectory of Torrington, made him canon of the collegiate church of Windsor, and registrar of the order of the Garter. Archbishop Bambridge appointed him to be a prebendary in the cathedral of York (1512), where he was soon advanced to the deanery. And the pope, informed of his increasing ascendancy over the monarch, allowed him to hold benefices to the amount of two thousand marks annually, though consisting of more than three parochial churches, if a precedent for such a dispensation could be found in the records of England. But no particular office in the state was committed to his charge until after the French war (in 1513), of the origin and principal events of which it may not be improper to give a brief relation.

The restless and turbulent Julius II., in the prosecution of his ambitious temporal designs, had involved himself in continual quarrels with several of the Italian states, and by his imperious conduct had produced a rebellion even in the consistory itself. The cardinals who disapproved of his violence, and whom he had excommunicated, called a council, which was formed at Tours, under the protection of Lewis XII. They resolved that the sentence of excommunication against them was void; and that a monitory message should be sent to the holy father, in hope of inducing him to act with more moderation and justice. They also agreed, that, in the event of their message being contemned, he should be called before a general council. Julius despised their admonition, and treated their message with contempt. They, in consequence, proceeded to give effect to their resolutions, and summoned him to appear at Pisa. Until this decisive step, the emperor sided with the schismatic cardinals; but as they had begun to manifest an undue predilection to the interests of France, he availed himself of it to separate from the confederacy, and to join the pope.

---

* "The king gave him the house at Bridewell, in Fleet Street, which had belonged to sir Richard Empson, but had merged to the crown by its late owner's attainder. It appears to have been a princely dwelling, for in the present an orchard and twelve gardens are enumerated as belonging to it. The grant bears date in 1510. The property stood upon the ground now occupied by Salisbury Square and Dorset Street, its gardens reaching to the banks of the river."—*Singer*.

Julius, in the mean time, finding that the forces which Lewis had sent into Italy, for the ostensible purpose of supporting the cause of the cardinals, but in reality to make conquests for France, were making rapid progress, anxiously endeavoured to gain the assistance of England. For this purpose, as a mark of high favour, he sent to the king a golden rose, with the papal benediction, and a letter filled with complaints against the unfilial aggressions of Lewis. In this letter he employed every topic of persuasion that he thought likely to influence the young, ardent mind of Henry. He invoked by the mercies of Christ, by the merits of his own famous ancestors, and by his duty to the church, to join in the league against the French and cardinals, offering the distinguished honour of declaring him the chief and protector.

Independently of the gratification which Henry received from the pope's letter, and the mark of distinction which accompanied it, ambition prompted him to seek an opportunity of signalizing himself. Bearing the title of king of France, he was desirous of asserting the rights which that title implied. Besides personal considerations, there were public and more solid reasons to authorise a war with France. Lewis heightened the dissension between the pope and the cardinals for his own particular advantage. It was suspected that his enmity to Julius arose from a wish to place a creature of his own in the apostolical chair, and, therefore, it was thought not only pious, but also prudent policy for England to interfere, in order to prevent the violation of the church, and the aggrandizement of her ancient rival, by the acquisition of new territories in Italy. The English ministers, therefore (1512) decided on war. An embassy was sent to Lewis, requiring him to desist from hostilities. He disregarded the request. A herald was then dispatched in form to declare the ancient claims of the English kings to the crown of France, and to demand restitution of Normandy, Guienne, Anjou, and Mayne, as the patrimonial inheritance of Henry. War ensued. The king resolved to invade France in person, in conjunction with Maximilian.* The commissariat of the army destined for this great undertaking was

* The English monarch landed at Calais in June, 1513.

committed to Wolsey. The office was certainly little consonant to his profession and former pursuits, but it was his character to be equally fit for every kind of business, and the
duty was performed to the satisfaction both of the army and
of the king.

The forces amounted to fourteen thousand men. Being
joined by the imperialists, they proceeded to invest Terouenne
in Artois, a town defended by a deep ditch, bulwarks, and
heavy ordnance. The king soon after arrived at the camp,
where the emperor, assuming the red cross of St. George,
received a hundred crowns a day as the soldier and vassal of
Henry. Terouenne was not at first so closely invested but
that on the side towards the river Lys, a way was left open
by which succours might be thrown in. The French resolved
to avail themselves of this advantage. Accordingly, Lewis,
who lay at Amiens with about twenty thousand men, sent
forward a large detachment of cavalry; but before they had
reached the scene, the allies had drawn their lines closer, and
debarred all access to the town. The French abandoned
their enterprise and retreated. When they thought themselves out of danger, some, impatient of heat, took off their
helmets; others dismounted from their horses, and the whole
fell into a state of disorder that invited surprise. In this
condition they were surrounded by a party sent in pursuit of
them. Though they boasted of possessing many of the best
warriors of France, the rout and confusion became irresistible.
The duke of Longueville, Bayard, Fayette, Clermont, and
Bussy d'Ambois were made prisoners in the pursuit. This
singular encounter received the appropriate appellation of the
Battle of the Spurs.* Terouenne immediately surrendered,

---

* Father Daniel, in his account of this battle, gives an interesting and
characteristic anecdote of Bayard. The chevalier, with only fifteen men at
arms, fighting as he retreated, gained a bridge, over which only two troopers
could pass abreast. On this post, he repulsed a detachment of the imperial
cavalry; but a party of English archers getting to his rear, he told his
soldiers that it was proper they should surrender, to avoid the destructive
effects of the arrows. While waiting, for this purpose, till the enemy could
come up, observing, at a short distance, a man at arms of the combined forces,
resting, fatigued, at the foot of a tree, with his helmet on the ground, he
instantly rode to him. " Surrender, cavalier," cried Bayard, " or you are a
dead man." The astonished gentleman at once resigned his sword. " I am
captain Bayard," added the chevalier, "and I now surrender myself your

and the king, with the emperor as his vassal, made a triumphal
entry on the 24th of August, 1513. Maximilian then left
the army, and Henry, having ordered the fortifications to
be levelled, laid siege to Tournay. Though the town was
of no great extent, the peasantry, by flying to it for shelter,
had increased the population to no less than eighty thousand
souls. Famine soon followed; a capitulation was therefore
inevitable, and the king of England was speedily admitted to
the sovereignty. A new bishop had lately been nominated to
the see, but not installed. Henry, conceiving that he had
acquired by conquest a right to dispose of the bishopric, gave
it to Wolsey, a proceeding contrary to the rules of the church,
and which afterwards occasioned much vexation and trouble
to them both.

While the army lay before Terouenne, the Lion of Scotland, in his herald's garb, arrived in the camp, and demanded
an audience of the king. The purport of this ceremonious
message was to obtain reparation for injuries alleged to
have been suffered by the Scots, with a provisionary declaration of war if satisfaction was refused.[4] Justly considering that James was instigated to this measure by the French,
who were anxious that war should be declared by Scotland
in order that the English army might be withdrawn from
France to defend the kingdom at home, Henry returned a sharp
and reproachful answer. " Now," said he to the herald,
" we perceive the king of Scots, our brother-in-law, and your
master, to be the same sort of person that we always took
him to be. Notwithstanding his oath, his promise on the
word of a king, and his own hand and seal, to his perpetual
dishonour and infamy, he intends in our absence to invade

prisoner. Take my sword; but on condition that it shall be restored, if, in
going to your camp, I shall happen to be insulted." Bayard, after staying
in the camp several days, grew anxious for new enterprises, and requested
the man at arms to procure him liberty to return to the French camp.
" Where is your ransom, chevalier?" answered the man at arms. " And
where is yours?" replied Bayard, " for you are my prisoner." The controversy that ensued was referred to the kings at arms, but they had no law for
such an extraordinary case: appeal was therefore made to Henry and Maximilian, who decided in favour of Bayard, and he was permitted to return into
France. It may be inferred from this occurrence, that, in those days, prisoners,
on account of their ransoms, were still considered as belonging to the soldiers
who took them. I was not aware that the practice had continued so late.

our dominions, an enterprise which he durst not attempt were we there in person. But he has not degenerated from the qualities of his ancestors, who, for the most part, ever violated their promises, nor observed their contracts farther than pleased themselves; therefore, tell your master that he shall never be embraced in any league in which we are a confederate; and also, that, suspecting his intentions, and justly, as the deed shows, we have left behind us one able to defend England against him and all his power. We have provided for this; and he shall not find our realm so defenceless as he expects. Tell him that we are the very owner of Scotland which he holds of us by homage; and since, contrary to his bounden duty as our vassal, he presumes to rebel, we shall at our return, with the help of God, drive him from the kingdom." The Lion, astonished and abashed at this lofty and impassioned address, replied: " As the natural subject of king James, I am bound to deliver boldly whatever he commands; but the orders of others I cannot, nor dare I say to my sovereign. Your highness's letters may declare your pleasure, for how can I repeat such expressions to my king?" Henry, assenting to the propriety of the objection, ordered the herald to be entertained according to the usages of chivalry, and summoned a council to consider the message of the Scottish king, and the answer which it might be expedient to return. The result was a letter to James, in effect the same as the verbal declaration to the Lion, who, after receiving a liberal largess, left the camp, and proceeded by the way of Flanders to take his passage to Scotland. While he waited for a favourable wind, the fate of his master was consummated in the fatal battle of Flodden, an event which the Scottish nation have never ceased to deplore in the finest strains of their poetry and music.[5]

The war had commenced by the earl of Hume crossing the borders with his clan and other forces, to the number of seven or eight thousand men. Sir William Bulmer, who had been apprised of this inroad, posted his troops in ambush among the deep broom of Tillfeild, and defeated the Scots as they returned encumbered with booty. Meanwhile, king James was collecting the whole power of Scotland; and the earl of Surrey, entrusted with the defence of England, marched to Alnwick. The Scottish king approached towards the Cheviot hills, the ancient scene of the hostile exploits of the two nations, and Surrey, being reinforced, advanced to meet him where he had encamped on the heights of Flodden. The Scots were greatly superior in numbers to the English, and equal in valour, skill, and discipline. But numbers, and bravery, and skill weighed light in the balance against the fixed and heavy destiny of the Stuarts. For, by one of those extraordinary and infatuated errors so frequent in the history of that unfortunate family, the king left the high ground, and his army was in consequence totally defeated and ruined in the hollow below. Towards the evening, he was discovered fighting with undaunted constancy in the vortex of the battle. His standard was soon after struck down. Tossed like a wreck on the waves, it floated and disappeared. James, desperate by inevitable ruin, rushed into the thickest throng of the spears and arrows, and was never seen to return. Next morning, a body was found which so strongly resembled the king, that it was considered as his. Surrey ordered it to be embalmed, and it was sent to the monastery of Shene; but, as James had died under a sentence of excommunication,* the rites of Christian burial could not be performed without permission from the pope. The news of the victory was communicated to Henry by the earl of Surrey, and to Wolsey by queen Katherine.† From her letter, it appears that Wolsey enjoyed the bosom confidence of his master, and therefore may be regarded as participating in his intentions, and influencing both the man and the king.

The intelligence of this signal triumph was received by Henry with great exultation; at the same time, he was

* The treaty, by the violation of which James was excommunicated, is signed by Andro of Murray. Rymer's Fœdera, xiii. 261. It was ratified by James himself, at Edinburgh, 28th November, 1509. Ib. 268.

† In looking over a book of old papers, in the British Museum, I found the following memorandum, written on the back of the return of a muster roll of an officer in the camp of Terouenne. It was probably made when the news of the victory arrived.

"The kinge of Scotts was fownd, slayn, by my lord Dakers, in the fronte of his batayll, and also the lord Maxwell and his brother the lord Harryes, erle Crauford, who is knowen, and the kynge of Scotts body is closed in lede and be kept till the kynges pleasure is knowen in Barwicke, and were slayn xi or xii m. Scotts beside them that were slayn in the chase, and iii bisshops, and of Englishmen but iii c. p'sonys slayn."

deeply affected by the death of James. He applied immediately to the pope to revoke the sentence of excommunication, in order that the body might be interred in St. Paul's,
in London, with the honours and solemnities due to the
remains of so august and gallant a knight. The dispensation
was readily granted; but doubts arising whether the Scottish
king was actually slain, and it being reported that the body
found on the field of battle was not really his, the funeral
was never performed. The corpse which Surrey brought
from Flodden was seen, long after, lying in a waste room in
the monastery to which it had been conveyed.

The Scottish nation, astonished and afflicted by so great
a calamity, scarcely made any preparations for the defence
of the country; but the English government had the magnanimity to grant peace without stipulating for any advantage.
This unprecedented liberality had the effect of forming a
party, among the Scottish chieftains, favourable to England,
and averse to the policy which had for so many ages involved
their country in the projects and misfortunes of France.

After the taking of Tournay, Henry returned home, with
all that could recommend a sovereign to the affections of a
proud and martial people. He had maintained, on the plains
of France, the ancient renown of England. The regency had
been still more victorious; and the people, in the full enjoyment of prosperity, exulted at so many proofs of national
pre-eminence.

Soon after the king's return, the bishopric of Lincoln happened to become vacant, and it was given to Wolsey; who,
in taking possession, found his wealth augmented by the
moveables of his predecessor.* He had been scarcely in-
vested† with this new honour, when York also became
vacant, and he was advanced to the archiepiscopal dignity.‡

---

* He had been previously nominated by the king, bishop of Tournay.—
Cavendish.

+ He was consecrated on the 26th of March, 1514.

‡ " After which solemnization done, and he being in possession of the
archbishopric of York, and *Primas Angliæ*, thought himself sufficient to
compare with Canterbury; and therefore erected his cross in the court and
in every other place, as well in the presence of the archbishop of Canterbury
and in the precinct of his jurisdiction, as elsewhere. And forasmuch as
Canterbury claimeth superiority and obedience of York, as he doth of all
other bishops within this realm, forasmuch as he is *Primas totius Angliæ*,

In the mean time, pope Julius II.[6] (1 February, 1513,) the incendiary of Christendom, had died, and was succeeded by the celebrated Leo X., who, with more urbanity of temper, was no less zealous in asserting the pretensions of the church. He opposed the ambition of France with undiminished vigour, and cultivated the friendship of England by the same arts as his predecessor. On ascending the apostolic throne, he consecrated a cap and sword, and sent them addressed to Henry as the most Christian king. This title, being peculiar to the French monarchs, was received by Henry as an omen and assurance of ultimate success in establishing his claims to the crown of France.

But the conduct of Maximilian and Ferdinand in the war had dissatisfied the English government. Lewis, apprized of this change, secretly made overtures of peace. The conti-

and therefore claimeth, as a token of an ancient obedience, of York to abate the advancing of his cross in the presence of the cross of Canterbury; notwithstanding, York, nothing minding to desist from bearing of his cross in manner as is said before, caused his cross to be advanced and borne before him, as well in the presence of Canterbury as elsewhere. Wherefore, Canterbury being moved therewith, gave York a certain check for his presumption; by reason whereof there engendered some grudge between Canterbury and York."—*Cavendish*.

Some remarks upon a plurality of bishoprics having been made by Dr. Robert Barnes, in a sermon on the 24th December, 1525, at St. Edward's church, in Cambridge, certain articles were drawn out from the sermon, upon which the doctor was called to make answer before the new cardinal. Barnes has left us a description of this examination. The sixth of the articles was as follows : " I will never believe that one man may be, by the law of God, a bishop of two or three cities, yea, of a whole country, for it is contrary to St. Paul, who saith: *I have left thee behind, to set in every city a bishop.*

" I was brought before my lord cardinal into his gallery," says Dr. Barnes, " and there he read all mine articles, till he came to this, and there he stopped and said, that this touched him, and therefore he asked me, if I thought it wrong that one bishop should have so many cities underneath him? unto whom I answered, that I could no farther go than St. Paul's text, which set in every city a bishop. Then asked he me, if I thought it now unright (seeing the ordinance of the church) that one bishop should have so many cities ? I answered that I knew none ordinance of the church, as concerning this thing, but St. Paul's saying only. Nevertheless, I did see a contrary custom and practice in the world, but I knew not the original thereof. Then said he, that in the Apostle's time there were divers cities, some seven mile, some six mile long, and over them was there set but one bishop, and of their suburbs also : so, likewise, now, a bishop hath but one city to his cathedral church, and the country about is as suburbs to it. Methought this was far fetched, but I durst not deny it."—*Barnes' Works*, 210. *Singer.*

nuance of hostility afforded him, indeed, no prospect of advantage. Two of his principal frontier towns were taken, the flower of his army were prisoners, and the remainder dejected with many defeats. His trustiest confederate, James, was no more; and the administration of Scottish affairs had devolved on Henry's sister, Margaret, the queen dowager. He was himself old, and unable to undergo the fatigue of longer waging war against the three greatest princes in Europe, combined with the pope, who had abandoned him to the vengeance of all Christendom as an odious schismatic. He therefore became desirous of reconciliation with his enemies.

The duke of Longueville, a prisoner at the court of London, was authorized to negotiate with the king. Lewis being a widower, the overtures commenced by a proposal of marriage between him and Mary, Henry's younger sister. The offer was honourable to the nation, and Wolsey exerted himself to accomplish the match. The negotiation, secretly managed, was completed before the Spanish or imperial ambassadors were aware that it was even in progress. Henry was allowed to retain Tournay; was to be paid a million of crowns, arrears of tribute due to his father and himself; and his sister was to enjoy a jointure as large as that of any former queen of France.

The princess, conducted to Paris, was received with every external demonstration of welcome (9 October, 1514). In the bloom of life and beauty, Mary united to the spirit of her brother, and her sister Margaret, a delightful and gay irreverence for the ceremonious distinctions of her rank. In the decay of old age, Lewis, incapable of enjoying the blandishments of his young queen, was teased and disturbed by the sallies of her vivacity. The attendants who came with her from England were dismissed; even the lady who had been recommended by Wolsey and her brother to assist her with advice, was not allowed to remain. The revelries, however, of the wedding were scarcely over, when she was released from her bondage by the death of Lewis (1 January, 1515,) who was succeeded by Francis I.

Mary, soon after this event, informed her brother, that having once married for his pleasure, she would now again for her own; and that, rather than be controlled, she was resolved to become a nun. The duke of Suffolk was the object of her partiality, and she did not affect to conceal her passion. He had been sent to condole with her on the death of her old husband; and she told him, unless he resolved to marry her in four days, he should not have a second offer. The attachment seems to have been known in France before the death of Lewis; for Francis, on the day of the duke's first audience, informed him, that it was understood he had come to Paris in order to marry the dowager.

A singular incident occurred at this juncture, which served to show how popular the opinion of Wolsey's excessive influence over the mind of Henry had become. An enthusiastic friar went from London to Paris, and obtaining an audience of Mary, told her gravely, it was rumoured in England that she intended to marry the duke of Suffolk. " Of all men," said the friar, " beware of him; for I can assure you that he and Wolsey have dealings with Satan, by which they rule the king for their own ends." The marriage, however, was speedily performed. Henry was offended at the indecorous precipitation of the widow; but his anger was not inveterate: the interference of Wolsey easily persuaded him to forgive the gallant presumption of his own particular friend, and the juvenile levity of a favourite sister.

In the forty-fifth year of his age, (22 December, 1515,) Wolsey was advanced to the rank of cardinal,* and was installed in Westminster Abbey, with circumstances of pomp seldom exceeded at the coronations of kings.† About the

* Wolsey, in his endeavours to obtain the pall, had relied much on the assistance of Adrian, bishop of Bath, himself a cardinal, then the pope's collector in England, but residing at Rome, and acting by Polydore Virgil, his deputy. Adrian being either unable or unwilling to render the expected service, Wolsey, conceiving that he had been betrayed, seized upon the deputy-collector, Polydore, and committed him to the Tower, where he remained, notwithstanding repeated remonstrances from the court of Rome, until the elevation of Wolsey to the cardinalate procured his liberty. " This will account for the unfavourable light in which Wolsey is placed in Polydore Virgil's History."—Singer.

† A highly characteristic circumstance preceded the installation. " Yet, by the way of communication, ye shall understand that the pope sent him the hat as a worthy jewel of his honour, dignity, and authority, the which was conveyed hither in a varlet's budget, who seemed to all men to be but a person of small estimation. Whereof York being advertised of the baseness of the messenger, and of the people's opinion and rumour, thought it for his honour meet, that so high a jewel should not be conveyed by so simple a messenger; whereof, he caused him to be stayed by the way, immediately

same time, the great seal was given to him for life, with the dignity of chancellor of the realm.* Henceforth he may be regarded as the dictator of England; for, although the king appeared afterwards personally in every important transac-

after his arrival in England, where he was newly furnished in all manner of apparel, with all kind of costly silks, which seemed decent for such an high ambassador. And that done, he was encountered upon Blackheath, and there received with a great assembly of prelates, and lusty, gallant gentlemen, and from thence conducted and conveyed through London, with great triumph."—*Cavendish.*

* " Now he being in the chancellorship, and endowed with the promotions of archbishop and cardinal *De Latere,* thought himself so fully furnished, that he was able to surmount Canterbury in all jurisdiction, and with power to convoke Canterbury and all other bishops and spiritual persons to assemble at his convocations wherever he would assign, and to take upon him the correction of ministers and matters within their jurisdictions ; and he visited all spiritual houses within their dioceses, and he had all manner of spiritual ministers there, as commissioners, scribes, apparitors, and all other necessary officers, to furnish his courts; and did present what ministers he pleased wherever he liked throughout the realm and dominion. Then he had two great crosses of silver, whereof one was of his archbishopric, and the other of his Legacy, borne before him wheresoever he rode or went, by two of the tallest and comeliest priests that he could get in the realm.

"And to the increase of his gain, he had in his hand the bishopric of Durham, and St. Albans *in commendam :* when Dr. Fox, bishop of Winchester died, he did surrender Durham to the king, and took Winchester to himself. He had also, as it were, *in farm,* the bishoprics of Bath, Worcester, and Hereford, for the incumbents of these were foreigners, dwelling abroad, and who permitted the cardinal to have their benefices for a convenient yearly sum. He had also attending upon him men of great possessions, and for his guard the tallest yeomen in the realm.

"And for his household you shall understand that he had in his hall, three boards kept with three several officers : that is to say, a steward that was always a priest, a treasurer that was ever a knight, and a comptroller that was an esquire; also, a cofferer, three marshals, two ushers in the hall, besides two almoners and grooms. Then had he in his hall-kitchen, two clerks, a clerk-comptroller, and a surveyor over the dresser, and a clerk of the spicery, which kept continually a mess together in the hall. Also, he had in the hall-kitchen two cooks, and labourers and children, twelve persons ; two yeomen of the scullery, two yeomen of the pastry, with two other pastelayers under the yeomen. Then had he in his own kitchen a master cook, who went daily in velvet or satin, with a gold chain, besides two other cooks, and six labourers in the same room. In the larder, one yeoman and a groom ; in the scalding-house, a yeoman and two grooms ; in the scullery, one yeoman and two grooms ; in the butlery, two yeomen and two grooms ; in the pantry, two yeomen, two grooms, and two other pages ; in the ewry, as many ; in the cellar, three yeomen, two grooms and pages ; in the chandery, two yeomen ; in the wafery, two yeomen ; in the wardrobe of beds, the master of the wardrobe, and twenty persons beside; in the laundry, a yeoman, and a groom, and three pages ; there were two yeomen purveyors and one

tion, the cardinal had acquired such an ascendancy, that the emanations of the royal will were, in fact, only the reflected purposes of the minister.

groom purveyor; in the bakehouse, a yeoman and two grooms; in the wood-yard, one yeoman and a groom; in the garner, one yeoman; in the garden, a yeoman and two labourers; porters at the gate, two yeomen and two grooms; a yeoman of his barge; and a master of his horse; a clerk of the stables, and a yeoman of the same; a farrier, and a yeoman of the stirrup; a muleteer and sixteen grooms, every one of them keeping four geldings.

" Now will I declare unto you, the officers of his chapel, and singing men of the same. First, he had there a dean, a great divine, and a man of excellent learning; a repeater of the choir; a gospeller; an epistoler; of singing priests, twelve; a master of the children; twelve singing children; sixteen singing men. In the vestry, a yeoman and two grooms, besides divers retainers, that came thither at principal feasts.

" As for the furniture of his chapel, it passeth my weak capacity to declare the number of the costly ornaments and rich jewels that were occupied in the same. For I have seen in procession about the hall forty-four copes of one settle, worn, besides the rich candlesticks, and other necessary ornaments to the furniture of the same.

" Now you shall understand that he had two cross-bearers and two pillar-bearers. In his great chamber and in his privy chamber, all these persons: the chief chamberlain, vice-chamberlain, a gentleman usher, besides one of his other chamber, he had also twelve ushers and six gentlemen waiters; also, he had nine or ten lords, who had each of them two or three men to wait upon him, except the earl of Derby, who had five men. Then had he gentlemen cup-bearers, and carvers, and sewers, and of the privy chamber, forty persons; six yeoman ushers, eight grooms of his chamber, also an almoner who waited daily at his board at dinner, twelve doctors and chaplains, a clerk of his closet, two secretaries, and two clerks of his signet.

" And for that he was chancellor of England it was necessary to have officers of the chancery to attend him for the better furniture of the same; first, he had a riding clerk, a clerk of the crown, a clerk of the hamper, a chafer. Then had he a clerk of the check, as well upon the chaplains, as upon the yeomen of the chamber. He had also four footmen, garnished with rich running coats, whenever he had any journey. Then he had an herald-at-arms, a sergeant-at-arms, a physician, an apothecary, four minstrels, a keeper of his tents, an armourer, a director of his wardrobe, an instructor of his wards, and a keeper of his chamber. He had also daily in his house the surveyor of York, a clerk of the green cloth, and an auditor of York. All these were daily attending, down-lying and up-rising. And at meat he had eight continual boards for the chamberlains and gentlemen officers, having a mess for the young lords, and others for the gentlemen. Besides these, there was never an officer, or a gentleman, or other worthy person with him, but he kept some two or three persons to wait upon them, and all others with him at the least had one, which did amount to a great number of persons. In all 180 persons."—*Cavendish.**

---

* The edition of Wordsworth says, 800; Mr. Singer's, 500.

BOOK II.

WHEN Wolsey was appointed prime minister of England, the
affairs of Europe were rapidly advancing towards a new epoch,
and society was pregnant with great events. The intercourse
among the different nations was every day becoming more
active and multifarious. Besides the concerns of peace or of
war, the interests of commerce began to press upon the attention of statesmen; venerable doctrines were falling into disrepute; and the circulation of knowledge, extending by the art
of printing, rendered it no longer possible to misrepresent

the effects of political actions. The proclamation of occurrences at the market crosses of the towns, and the promulgation of new laws in the parochial churches, were the only means by which the English people were anciently informed of the proceedings of their government. The conduct of those, therefore, who had the management of public affairs, must have been flagitious indeed, when it was incapable of being disguised. But, at this period, state delinquencies could no longer be practised with impunity. The press had multiplied the illuminating agents of truth. It was not enough, that the minister should study to please only the sovereign and his parasites: the people also expected to be gratified, and generally in things obnoxious to the court. This alteration in the ancient system of rule, little as it was at first perceivable, has since insensibly obliged the ministers of England to study the will of the nation more than the predilections of the nobles and of the king.

Francis I., with the usual titles of the French monarch, assumed, at his succession, that of duke of Milan; having a double claim to the duchy, as the heir of the house of Orleans, which had pretensions to the inheritance, and as comprehended in the investiture which had been made according to the treaty of Cambray. Succeeding to the means of asserting his claim, he early resolved to make it good; and to vindicate the glory of France, which had been tarnished in the enterprises of his predecessor. In the prosecution of this design, his success rendered it doubtful whether England ought to permit the farther aggrandisement of her rival. Frequent rumours, also, of stratagems for the recovery of Tournay irritated Henry, who was vain of his own conquest, and were regarded as the precursors of actual aggression. An extraordinary council was, in consequence, summoned to deliberate on the state of Christendom, and the existing relations with France; and Wolsey opened the business by recapitulating various causes of complaint which the king had against the conduct of Francis.

" Several English vessels have been plundered by the French cruizers; and indemnity," said he, "cannot be obtained. Rich property, belonging to the king's sister, is withheld on evasive pretences. The duke of Albany has assumed the regency of Scotland, and Francis supports him, contrary to an express agreement, and in contempt of the will of the deceased sovereign, by which the queen had been appointed regent; an appointment confirmed by the pope. The usurpation of Albany is dangerous to the king's nephew, James V., for he is suspected of aspiring to the throne, and has induced the nobles to take an oath of allegiance to himself, inciting them to enmity against England. Nor is the personal conduct of Francis such as becomes the honour of a king. He openly protects Richard de la Pole, a fugitive English traitor. But if all these distinct and palpable grievances be not sufficient to induce England to interfere with the proceedings of France, prudence, prospectively considering the effects of the conquests in Italy, requires that they should not be permitted to extend. The existing circumstances, however, do not call for actual war. It is not necessary that the blood of England should be shed; but the French must be compelled to act justly, and to restrain their appetite for dominion. By assisting the pope and emperor with money only, the objects of a wise and anticipating policy will be effectually attained."

In opposition to the proposal of Wolsey it was urged, that to recommend the violation of treaties was a strange doctrine. When just causes arise for the dissolution of compacts, the injured party ought to protest against the aggressor, before proceeding to war. If any other course is allowed, the law of nations must be sacrificed, and the transactions of kingdoms become destitute of integrity. The conduct of the French king may have been justly represented, but his actions are capable of a different explanation; and it is necessary, therefore, to examine them with circumspection. He entertains Richard de la Pole generously; but whether because he is an English traitor, or only a volunteer seeking employment, seems, at least, doubtful. To the interference of Francis with the affairs of Scotland, it is easy to apply an adequate remedy. If Albany be dangerous to the rights of James V. and his mother, let the king protect them; but seek not by subsidies to kindle into fiercer strife those remote wars, of which the issue is unknown. It may be different from what he fears.

The allegations of Wolsey did not justify actual hostilities, but they furnished a sufficient pretext for the measure he proposed. The pope and emperor were, apparently, unable to resist the progress of the French arms. If Henry showed himself partial to their side, Francis might be induced to agree to terms favourable to the independence for which they contended. The violation of public engagements, by frank or by secret dealing, is undoubtedly contrary to all the theoretical principles of morality. But the guilt of the governments, whose designs and practices render such violations expedient, is deeper than the delinquency of those whom they provoke to the crime. France had not, perhaps, really transgressed the terms of any existing treaty, but she had so acted that England could no longer, with safety, remain neutral. The duration of national contracts is always contingent. The circumstances of a government may become so changed, as to make it, virtually, no longer the party which originally contracted. If France had acquired dominion which she did not possess at the time of concluding her treaties with England, while the condition of England was in no respect altered, the jealousy of national independence warranted the English to seek the reduction of the French power. The great, the only, duty of governments is to preserve the interests of their subjects; nor can any alteration arise in the affairs of other states, which they ought to regard with indifference. The counsellors, unable to discriminate the practical morality of nations so clearly as Wolsey, were satisfied, that the relative condition of France and England called for an alteration in the conduct of the latter; and a system of menacing neutrality was, in consequence, adopted.

The war in Italy, between the emperor and the French king, was prosecuted with various success.* Maximilian, in order to draw Henry into a more available alliance than the degree of countenance which the council had adopted, proposed that the French should be dispossessed of Milan, and that it should be feudally annexed to the English crown. This proposal, like all his schemes, was not without a show of plausibility. He conceived that a barrier for the protection of Italy would thereby be formed, which France could not afterwards force, without incurring the hostility of England. Henry's right to several provinces of France was

* 1516.

as indisputable as that of Francis to Milan: and this scheme seemed to promise a mode of adjusting their respective claims. Maximilian also offered to resign the empire in favour of Henry; but his character and actions were not calculated to gain confidence. His projects were generally extravagant, and his enterprises never guided by the perseverance and energy requisite to ensure success. The king and cardinal only listened to the proposition with grave civility, and therefore he sought a reconciliation with Francis. This was the more easily accomplished, as a crusade against the Turks was loudly preached throughout Christendom, and the French monarch was represented as the prime cause of all the troubles in the seat and region of the papacy, by which this holy purpose was delayed. It was, indeed, not without rational alarm that the attention of the Christians was turned towards the aggressions of the infidels, and the fierce ambition of the reigning sultan.

The history of Selim may be comprehended in a few sentences. It consists but of battles and crimes. Understanding that his father designed to settle the empire on another son, he rebelled, and, by corrupting the janissaries, obliged him to abandon the throne. To secure his usurpation, he did not scruple to commit parricide. His brother, who had taken up arms against him, was vanquished and put to death, with all the children of the same maternal stock. He subdued the Aladolites, and, descending from their mountains upon Persia, defeated the sophy, and took possession of Touris.[1] Returning to Constantinople, he spent several months in tyranny, and preparations for new aggressions. His avowed object was the complete subjugation of Persia, but he suddenly turned upon the soldan of Syria and Egypt, —a prince of ancient dignity; highly venerated by the professors of the Mahometan faith; powerful by the opulence of his dominions, and by the military order of the Mamelukes, who had maintained their independence, with great lustre, upwards of three hundred years.

The soldanic government was elective; and none were advanced to the dignity of soldan but men who had passed through all the gradations of military rank to the rule of provinces, and the command of armies, and who had uniformly proved their valour and wisdom. The Mamelukes, by whom the soldan was elected, and of whose order he was necessarily a member, were formed from children, originally chosen for the vigour of their appearance, and reared to manhood with frugal diet, and the continual exercise of arms. Their number did not exceed eighteen thousand; but such was the excellence of their skill and management, that all Egypt, Syria, and many of the neighbouring nations, submitted to their sway; and they had sometimes proved victorious over the numerous Ottoman armies.

Selim subdued this formidable state, and consigned many of the members to ignominious deaths, as if the defence of their independence had been a municipal crime. When he had made himself master of Cairo, the Christian princes were not alarmed without reason. With vast resources, audacious courage, he united an enthusiastic desire of transmitting to posterity a heroic name. He read the actions of Alexander and Cæsar, and repined at the inferiority of his own exploits. Indefatigable in the improvement of his soldiers, and continually augmenting his navy, Christendom attracted and modified his schemes. The rumour of his success, and the dread of his designs, agitated the pontifical court. Prayers resounded in all the churches of Rome. Leo edified the faith of the populace by walking barefoot in the processions, and the aid of human helps and means was solicited directly, as well as by the agency of the saints.

Briefs were addressed to all Christian princes, admonishing them to lay aside their particular quarrels, and, with united hearts and hands, to carry war into the dwellings of the infidel. Consultations were held with travellers acquainted with the countries, the dispositions of the inhabitants, and the forces of the Turkish empire; and a wide and general arrangement of all the array of Christendom was planned, and communicated to the provincial governments of the pope. The emperor, with the horse and foot of his dominions, was to proceed by the Danube, and through Bosnia, towards Constantinople. The French king, with the armies of France, Venice, and the other Italian states, accompanied by the Helvetic infantry, was to transport himself from Brindisi to Greece, a country full of Christians eager to revolt from the sultan. The kings of Spain, Portugal, and England, uniting their fleets at Carthagena, were to sail directly to the Dardanelles, while the pope in person proceeded from Ancona, to join the forces as they invested Constantinople. Against such a coalition, there was good cause to hope that Selim would be unable to defend himself; and a crusade thus intended to cover the sea and land could not fail to have a speedy and triumphant end. In the meantime, a tax was levied on all Christians, and voluntary contributions were earnestly solicited to promote the undertaking.

Preparatory to the execution of this great project, Leo enjoined a truce on all his secular vassals, for five years, under penalty of the most grievous censures; and cardinals, of distinguished address, in order to further the business, were appointed legates to the different courts. Campeggio was sent to London. But he was informed at Calais that he must remain there, until cardinal Wolsey was joined with him in the commission. This obstacle removed by compliance, he landed in England. As his retinue was mean, and himself not opulent, Wolsey sent him twelve mules, and a quantity of scarlet cloth, in order that the pomp of his entrance into the metropolis might, in some degree, correspond with the importance attached to his mission. The rational few may ridicule the artifices of ostentation; but the numerous commonality cannot easily conceive that magnificence does not possess an intrinsic moral value; nor how things on which their superiors in knowledge bestow so much attention, may not deserve respect. In every town through which Campeggio passed, he was greeted with great veneration. On Blackheath, he was met by a train of prelates, nobles, and gentlemen. The clergy of London received him in the borough, with all their processional paraphernalia. The livery of London lined the streets; the lord mayor and aldermen humiliated themselves before him; and sir Thomas More, in the name of the city, welcomed his arrival in a Latin oration. Such expressions of devotion to the pontifical government afforded Campeggio the highest delight. But, unfortunately, as the procession passed through Cheapside, a mule became restive, and threw the whole pageantry into confusion. The trunks and coffers, which had been covered with the scarlet gift of Wolsey, and which the people piously imagined were filled with precious presents to the king, and pardons and indulgences for all their own sins, were thrown down, and bursting open in the fall, discovered a ludicrous collection of the crumbs and scraps of beggary. This unexpected disclosure of ecclesiastical imposition turned the whole triumph of the day into contempt; and Campeggio, as he proceeded towards the palace, was a mortified object of scorn and derision. The motives of his mission were also rendered abortive by the death of Selim. The immediate cause of danger being removed by this event, the projected crusade was abandoned, and the Christian potentates turned their thoughts again to the modes and means of over-reaching each other.

The imperial dignity had hitherto been greater in name and title, than in substance and effect; but nature and fortune seemed combining, at this juncture, to realise all its claims and pretensions to supremacy. Maximilian was far advanced in life, and the settlement of the empire occupied his thoughts. Charles, his grandson, had succeeded to the crown of Spain (23rd January, 1516). By raising him to the imperial dignity, a larger extent of dominion would be subjected to the control of the Austrian family, than any monarch had enjoyed since the removal of the Roman government from Rome to Constantinople; for, with his hereditary kingdoms, this young prince had succeeded to a new world. Maximilian, with this view, began to canvass the electors. Francis perceived that the union of the Spanish and imperial powers would be highly dangerous to his kingdom; and therefore, in order either to oppose the election of Charles to the empire, or to assist in the wars that were likely to arise in the event of his success, he endeavoured to gain the friendship of Henry.

The French nation has always had the sinister wisdom to employ personal inducements in their diplomatic transactions; by which, though they may not as yet have uniformly succeeded in corrupting the integrity of those with whom they dealt, they have, generally, obtained many national distinctions, which are better estimated by the feelings than by the judgment of mankind.* Francis, aware of the ascendancy

* The diplomatic inferiority of the English is of a very ancient date. William Tindall, in his *Practices of Popish Prelates*, says, that "the Frenchmen of late days made a play, or a disguising, at Paris, in which the emperor daunced with the pope and the French king, and wearied them; the king of England sitting on a high bench, and looking on. And when it was asked, why he daunced not, it was answered, that he sate there but to pay the minstrels their wages only: as who should say, we paid for all men's dauncing."—Wordsworth.

that Wolsey had acquired over his master, was persuaded of the advantage that might arise from obtaining his favour. For this purpose, he sent to London the admiral of France; a man of excellent address, who was not long in making an agreeable impression on the mind of the cardinal. He lamented that his master had lost the friendship of so eminent a person, and dextrously hoped, that, as he was anxious to recover, he might again obtain it. The flattery of such advances, from so great a monarch, had due effect. To acquire Wolsey still more decidedly to his interest, Francis affected to consult him concerning the various emergencies of his affairs. Henry was acquainted with the process of this secret adulation; but it only served to convince him of the superior talents of his minister. " I plainly discover," said the king, " that you will govern both Francis and me;" and he intimated, by his manner and approbation, that he thought him qualified.

The first effects of this diplomatic courtship was the formation of a league between England and France, (2nd October, 1518.) The principles on which it was founded, and the objects it embraced, served as the basis of the general treaties of the English government for a long period. The treaty itself may be regarded as one of the fundamental statutes of that great code, which, till the era of the French revolution, continued to be the laws and constitution of the community of the European nations. It was enacted, if the expression may be used, that, between the two sovereigns, their successors, and subjects, perfect peace and amity, by sea and land, should subsist; and that they should be the friends of the friends, and the enemies of the enemies, of one another. All their respective allies were included in the league. It was declared, that if the dominions of either of the principal contracting parties were at any time invaded, the aggressor should be required by the other to desist, and make reparation; which if he refused to do within the space of a month from the date of the admonition, the confederates were to declare war against him. If rebellions happened to arise in any of their respective states, none of the confederates were to interfere, unless foreign princes had been the cause; in which case their forces were to be all united against the aggressors. It was also declared, that none of the confederates should suffer their subjects to bear arms against the other's, nor retain foreign troops in their service; and that all persons accused of high treason should not be received within their respective territories, but that after twenty days' warning they should be obliged to depart.

The object of this league was to preserve the then relative state of the different nations, and to anticipate the consequences that might ensue by the election of Charles to the empire; but it is chiefly worthy of note as being an alteration in the constitution of Christendom; for the pope was admitted a party, and thereby became amenable to a secular tribunal constituted by the members of the confederation. Nor could he violate his engagements to them, without becoming subject to the penalties and forfeitures which were provided to ensure stability to the league. This was the first grand political error of the pontifical government; and from this epoch the power of the papacy has continued to decline. Charles and Maximilian, as well as Leo X., having acceded, Henry naturally became the arbiter in the disputes that afterwards arose among the confederates; for, secure in his insular dominions, he was not immediately exposed to their conflicts, and could only be indirectly affected by the continental revolutions. The effects, therefore, of this important measure were, under the management of Wolsey, calculated to exalt the dignity of England, and to render her the judge of the neighbouring states.

Besides the general league, a treaty of affinity and alliance was at the same time negotiated between Henry and Francis. The French had never ceased to grudge the loss of Tournay;* schemes to recover it occupied their minds; and in these negotiations the restitution formed a primary topic; nor was it untimely introduced. The expense of the fortifications began to be felt in the exchequer; and the bishop-elect had

---

* This place the king had but little comfort of, being always in fear of surprise. The cardinal had again another time, in the month of May, whether in the year 1514 or 1515 I know not, intelligence brought him by a friar, whom he had employed as a spy, of a sudden attempt intended to be made on the place: of which the cardinal and the council, from the palace at Hampton-court, wrote to sir Richard Jernigan, now the king's lieutenant there, as certain news. This was wrote the 9th of May, and such speed was made, that, on the 11th, at night, the said lieutenant received it."—Strype's Eccl. Mem. i. 11. ed. 1733.

D

appealed to the pope against his dispossession by Henry.
Either by the secret influence of France, or the negligence of
the English minister at Rome, he obtained a bull, authorising
him to use coercive means, and to claim the aid of the inhabitants to accomplish his installation. Henry was justly
incensed when he heard of this, and wrote to his agent,
Adrian,* in terms of unsparing reproach against Leo. " The
bull," said he, " is an exorbitant grant, and the pope may
very well think, that neither I nor my officers, soldiers, or
subjects, will obey processes and sentences contrary to justice.
The bull is contrary to the laws of God and man, justice and
reason, and it is a great dishonour to the pope to have acted
so indiscreetly."† This curious letter, though composed in
the affluent style of the cardinal, appears, by the fierceness of
the expressions, to have been dictated by the king himself.
It is, also, a satisfactory voucher that there existed weighty
political reasons for the restoration of Tournay, without the
necessity of supposing, with the contemporary historians,
who had not access to the state papers, that Wolsey was
bribed. Henry had, it is true, intended to keep Tournay as
a perpetual trophy of his campaign, but subsequent events
seemed tending to make it the cause of controversies derogatory to his dignity. To get rid of it without compromising
his honour was, therefore, judicious policy. But the real
motives of the resolution could not with propriety be stated
to the public; and those which the cardinal assigned were
certainly not satisfactory. He represented that Tournay lay
so far from Calais, that, in war, it would be difficult to keep
the communication open. " Being situated on the frontiers of
France and the Netherlands, it is exposed to the assaults of
both. The inhabitants are insubordinate and averse to the
English, so that even in peace a large garrison is necessary
to preserve it, and the expense is greater than the utility and
value of the place." A treaty was, in consequence, concluded, by which Tournay was agreed to be restored to
France, and the princess of England, Mary, to be held as

* This prelate bequeathed a palace in Rome to the king of England,
which was afterwards called the English palace. It is now possessed by
the Colonna family.—Fiddes, 171.

† Fiddes's Coll. No. 4.

betrothed to the dauphin.* The debateable city was given as her dowry; and, in the event of the marriage not being completed, it was again to be surrendered to England. As Henry had made expensive additions to the citadel, Francis engaged to pay him six hundred thousand crowns, in twelve yearly payments. It was also stipulated, that a pension of twelve thousand livres should be granted to Wolsey, as an equivalent for the revenues of the bishopric, which he agreed to resign. And to ensure the faithful performance of these engagements, Francis contracted to give eight noble hostages, and to recal the duke of Albany from Scotland, where his presence was disagreeable to Henry, and thought dangerous to the rights of the queen and her children. It was likewise arranged, that the courts of France and England should, next year, hold a friendly meeting on the plains of Picardy.

When the treaty was ratified, the cardinal gave orders to the officers of Tournay, to sell the provisions and the materials which had been collected for the new fortifications. He enjoined them to put all things in order, that when the French commissioners arrived, the city might be resigned with ease, and without suspicion of indirect dealing. He also commanded all vagabonds to be put out of the town, and every man to discharge his debts. Thus maintaining the national integrity by fulfilling the engagements undertaken for the public, and enforcing the performance of individual contracts. Nor was he negligent of his own private rights. He employed an honest priest, who became afterwards a distinguished diplomatist, to collect the arrears of the episcopal income, and the business was managed with mercantile sagacity. The disregard of pecuniary concerns is sometimes an infirmity, but oftener one of the many affectations of genius. But contempt for trifles is very different from the anxious particularity of avarice, and the negligence that entails privations. No man can be dishonoured by the strict administration of his personal affairs, but the neglect of them is both shameful and injurious. The plea of public employment should not screen him from the imputation of private delinquency.

In the beginning of the year 1519, died Maximilian, who,

* There was something ludicrous in this article, for the dauphin was not then born, but the queen was with child.

D 2

by his bustling projects, had so long wasted the strength of the empire in fruitless wars. His intrigues for securing the succession to Charles were not complete. Francis, therefore, immediately declared himself also a candidate for the vacant throne, openly professing himself the rival of the Spanish king. "It is honourable to both," said Francis, "to desire an increase of dignity. Let neither, therefore, suppose himself wronged by the pretensions of the other, but, like two young lovers emulous for a lady's favour, strive, each in his own way to recommend himself." *

Francis was then in the twenty-ninth year of his age, gallant, ingenuous, and accomplished. He was formed to command the affections of a polished people; but a degree of self-willed impetuosity, and a libertine disregard of engagements, deformed these amiable qualities. In his transactions as a sovereign, more feeling, rivalry, and personal profligacy appeared, than is usually met with in the conduct of kings. His opponent, Charles, was, in many respects, different; and in natural endowments, perhaps, his inferior. His mind was sedate and reflecting, more embued with the sinister prudence of private life, than with the magnanimity which dignifies a monarch. He was at this time only nineteen, but his head was cool and wary; and he already practised artifice by the suggestions of natural propensity, with the ease and confidence of a statesman grown hoary in dissimulation. Not only sordid in making bargains, he always endeavoured to obtain remote advantages unperceived by those with whom he dealt. If Francis, sometimes, found himself over-reached, and refused to fulfil his treaties, Charles was, as often, obliged to sustain the self-wounding sting of disappointed cunning.

The conduct of Henry towards the two rivals is involved in some degree of obscurity. The policy of England, from this period, and during the remainder of Wolsey's administration, varied so often, and so suddenly, that contemporary historians found it easier to accuse the cardinal of being alternately bribed by the Imperial and French courts, than to comprehend the scope of his views. It is the fate of statesmen to be denied the respect due to their merits, until

* Guicciardini, lib. xiii.

their plans are surveyed from the heights of posterity. But the hope of obtaining justice at last enables the man, conscious of great purposes, to persevere in his course, undismayed by the clamours of the multitude, the malice of tyrants, and the commotions and anarchies of the world. When the kings of France and Spain became competitors for the imperial crown, their respective qualifications could not but render it difficult to determine what system the English government ought to pursue. The union of France with the empire would constitute a power destructive to the independence of other nations. The hereditary dominions of Charles, added to the imperial, would form a more extensive monarchy, but less compact than the other. For Spain was shaken with intestine war, and Hungary exposed to the menaces of the Turks. The doubtful balance, in the English council, settled in favour of Charles; but so lightly, that it was easily disturbed. A policy of prospective considerations could not be adopted. Wolsey could only endeavour to render his master arbiter to the rival kings, by sometimes favouring the one, and sometimes the other; seldom acting as the decided friend of either. In the subsequent wars, when Charles or Francis alternately gained the ascendancy, Henry sided with the loser, and the weight of England restored the equilibrium of power.

Charles was elected emperor, and Francis, notwithstanding the gallantry of his professions, could not disguise his chagrin. The pains of mortification felt like the wounds of injury. Though only disappointed, he acted as if he had been wronged. The advantages of his alliance with Henry were duly estimated, and he spared neither flattery, presents, nor promises, to cement the friendship of Wolsey. He empowered him to arrange the formalities of the great meeting of the courts of France and England; an event which Charles contemplated with apprehension, and endeavoured to anticipate, by previously visiting Henry, as he lay at Canterbury, preparatory to passing over to Calais. The king was secretly apprised of his coming; indeed, the visit had been undertaken at the suggestion of the cardinal, who, having been solicited to frustrate the interview with the French sovereign, said that he thought Charles might come himself, and discuss with Henry the impolicy of the meeting.

About ten o'clock at night, the emperor, under his canopy of state, landed at Dover, with the queen of Aragon and his principal nobility. He was welcomed on shore by the cardinal, and conducted to the castle. The mingled blaze of torches, arms, and embroidery, brightened the faces of a vast multitude, as he ascended the heights; and the flashing of the ordnance from the battlements afforded, at short intervals, a momentary view of the cliffs below, and the English and Imperial navies at anchor. Henry, informed of his arrival, hastened to meet him, and next morning they proceeded together to Canterbury, at that time one of the finest cities in England. The cathedral contained the relics of the audacious Becket, and was famed through all Christendom for its riches. In every place it was illuminated with the lustre of precious stones; and the shrine of the papal champion was so embossed with jewels, that gold was the meanest thing about it. The cardinal and the clergy received the king and the emperor at the gates, and led them to the church, where mass was performed, and fresh riches added to that immense treasure which the devout folly of ages had heaped together. Charles was afterwards introduced to the queen, his aunt. His constitutional gravity was noticed at the evening banquet, and flatteringly ascribed to the appearance of the dowager of France, the wife of Suffolk, then the most beautiful and sprightly woman of the age, and to whom it had been, at one time, proposed that Charles should be affianced. After enjoying three days of revelry, and having obtained a promise that Henry would not enter into any engagement with Francis prejudicial to him, he sailed from Sandwich for Flanders on the same day that the English court passed from Dover to Picardy.* It has been alleged that Charles, during this visit, endeavoured to acquire the favour of Wolsey, by promising his influence to procure him the papacy; but no serious effect could be expected from such a promise, if it was made, for Leo X. was in the prime of life, and many years younger than the cardinal.

The meeting of the courts of France and England is the most sumptuous event in the records of magnificent spectacles. The two kings were in the flower of life; the attendants were

* May 30, 1520.

selected from the most famous and high-born of the rival
nations; and such was the profusion of riches, emulously exhibited, that the place of meeting, between Ardres and
Guisnes, has since continued to be called "the field of gold."
Temporary palaces, exceeding in splendour the regular abodes
of the monarch, were prepared in England and carried to the
scene. The walls of the chambers and galleries were hung
with costly arras, and the chapel was adorned with everything
that could increase the gorgeous ritual of popery. The French
king inhabited pavilions of golden tissue, lined with blue velvet, embroidered with the lilies of France, and fastened with
cords of silk, entwisted with cyprian gold.—But kings, by
their greatness, as well as by their duties, cannot long continue together. The prodigal pomp of Henry and Francis
lasted only fourteen days. No political discussion of influential consequence took place. The interview was only the
final and collective exhibition of those pageants of chivalry
which had so long interested the admiration of Christendom.
A treaty was, indeed, concluded, but it only declared that
Francis, after discharging the outstanding debt due from
France to England, should yearly pay at Calais, one hundred
thousand livres, until the marriage between his son and the
daughter of Henry was solemnized. This was, probably, a
kind of feudatory acknowledgment personally to Henry, for it
was to continue payable throughout his lifetime. It was also
agreed, that the differences relative to Scotland should be left
to the arbitration of the cardinal and the mother of Francis.
Although this treaty is the only documentary evidence of
business, the interview afforded opportunities for studying
the characters of the French statesmen, highly important to
such a man as Wolsey. He never afterwards appears to have
trusted the government of Francis, or to have considered
France fit to be allied to England, except when she was in a
reduced condition, and when there was some chance that
necessity and the prospect of advantage would ensure fidelity.

Before returning home, Henry visited the emperor at
Gravelines; and Charles, next day, with his aunt Margaret,
regent of the Netherlands, returned this courtesy to the English court at Calais, where the shows of the field of gold were

* Rymer's Fœdera, June 6, 1520.

renewed, with new decorations. An amphitheatre, eight hundred feet in compass, which was constructed for the occasion, deserves particular mention, as a proof of the taste and splendour of the age. The ceiling was painted in imitation of the fabrics of antiquity, and, like them, it was adorned with statues and pictures. But the tilts and masques were interrupted by a furious storm, which extinguished above a thousand of the candles, and defaced the thrones prepared for the princes. During this visit, Henry endeavoured to persuade Charles to accede, as emperor, to the league of London, to which he was already a party, in his capacity as king of Spain. But whether already contemplating the amount of his means, and wishing to be considered as free, or really regarding his former accession as sufficient, admits of controversy. Procrastination was one of Charles's maxims; and, on this occasion, he could avoid, without refusing, the proposition. In the end, however, he consented that his first accession should remain obligatory on him as emperor.

It is of little importance to inquire on what pretexts Francis and Charles engaged in those terrible wars which so long after laid waste their dominions, and afflicted their subjects. The cause was their personal rivalry. The fervent propensities of the French king instigated him to be the aggressor. He meditated revenge for the success of Charles in the election; he was ambitious of renown; he saw his kingdom circumscribed and invested by the jurisdiction of the man who had overtopped his destiny; and he could not refrain from war. But the league of London made it expedient that he should not appear to be the first to violate the peace; for in that case, the king of England and his allies would be obliged to assist the emperor. There were, however, in the situation of Charles, allurements to hostilities which Francis could not withstand.

On the same day that Charles was crowned at Aix-la-Chapelle, Soliman was inaugurated at Constantinople; and, in the astrological language of the time, it was remarked, that they had a similar ascendant. For Charles was the eleventh emperor from Albert, in whose time the dominion of the Ottomans commenced, and Soliman was the eleventh sultan of that race. The French government, from the ambition and activity of Soliman, expected that he would afford ample employment to the German forces. The Spaniards, uneasy at the promotion of their king to the imperial dignity, aware that, in consequence, his residence would rarely be among them, became discontented. Foreigners, to the exclusion of natives, had been promoted to offices in the state; and, like aliens in all nations, they studied only their own emolument. When Charles departed to be crowned emperor, the people openly rebelled, assembled the Junta* to redress their grievances, and prepared to defend themselves and the rights of their country against the foreigners, but without infringing their allegiance to the king. Francis, actuated by revenge and hope, and the temptation of these circumstances, sent an army into Navarre, and allowed one of his vassals to commit depredations in Luxemburg. Charles claimed the interference of Henry, according to the terms of the league; and an embassy was, in consequence, sent from London, by which Francis was required to desist from hostilities. The invasion of Navarre proving disastrous, he complied; but war had commenced, and the emperor finding his means equal, at least, to his difficulties, was not disposed to lay aside his arms. Francis, therefore, in his turn, as a member of the league, also appealed to England; and stated, that he could not avoid war, as the imperial armies were constantly augmenting. The king answered, that he had resolved to remain neutral in the quarrel; but offered to be umpire in the dispute, and, for this purpose, if Charles and Francis would send plenipotentiaries to Calais, Wolsey should meet them there, and act in his name, as arbitrator. The proposal was accepted, and the cardinal went to the place appointed.†

Before the congress was opened, the cardinal visited the emperor at Bruges.‡ Charles received him in person, about

---

* Guicciardini, lib. xiii.   † August, 1521.

‡ " After he was thus furnished, in manner as I have before rehearsed unto you, he was sent twice on embassage to the emperor Charles V. . . . For divers urgent occasions touching his majesty, it was thought fit that about such weighty matters and to so noble a prince, the cardinal was most meet to be sent on such embassages; and he being one ready to take the charge thereof upon him, was furnished in every respect most like a great prince, which was much to the honour of his majesty and of this realm. For first he proceeded forth, like to a cardinal, having all things correspondent; his gentlemen, being very many in number, were clothed in livery coats of crimson velvet of the best, and chains of gold about their necks;

a mile from the town, and entertained him thirteen days, as the vicegerent of the English king. Every night his livery was served by the officers of the emperor with an entertainment, which consisted of caudles, wine, sugar, and manchet; differing little in its circumstances and jollity from the ancient custom of welcoming the new year. Wolsey, at all times susceptible of the flattery of honourable treatment, could not but feel himself gratified; and his necessary ackowledgments of politeness were interpreted by the French as proofs of his disposition to comply with the wishes of the emperor.

The first point to determine was, which of the sovereigns began the war, for the king of England was bound to aid the injured. Wolsey could not but consider Francis as the aggressor. The minister of Charles, accordingly, made proposals not calculated to be accepted. The French, also, offered terms equally inadmissible. After spending ten days in fruitless altercation, the cardinal declared, that he saw no way of reconciling the parties. Francis, indeed, though he had appealed to Henry, and consented that Wolsey should be the arbiter, had really no wish to remain at peace. For even

and his yeomen and all his mean officers were clad in fine scarlet, guarded with black velvet one hand in breadth. Thus furnished, he was twice sent to the emperor, in Flanders, then lying at Bruges, who did most nobly entertain him, discharging all his own charges, and his men's ; there was no house in the town of Bruges, wherein any of my lord's gentlemen were lodged, or had recourse, but that the owners of the houses were commanded by the emperor's officers, upon the pain of their lives, to take no money for anything that the cardinal's men did take of any kind of victuals; no, although they were disposed to make costly banquets, further commanding their said hosts that they should want nothing which they honestly required, or desired to have.

" Also the emperor's officers went every night through the town, from house to house, where any Englishman had recourse or lodged, and served their delivery for the night, which was done in this manner : First, the officers brought into the house a cast of fine manchet bread, two silver pots of wine, a pound of sugar, white lights and yellow lights, a bowl of silver and a goblet to drink out of, and every night a staff torch. This was the order of their livery every night. And then, in the morning, when the officers came to fetch away their stuff, they would account for the gentlemen's costs the day before. Thus the emperor entertained the cardinal and his train during the time of his embassy. And that done, he returned into England with great triumph, being no less in estimation with the king than he was before, but rather much more, for he increased daily in the king's favour, by reason of his wish and readiness to do the king's pleasure in all things."—*Cavendish.*

while the congress was sitting, he permitted the duke of Albany to depart for Scotland;* although he was bound, by word and treaty, not to connive at any of his proceedings, which were held to be averse to the interests of Henry's sister and her family.

Having failed to adjust the difference between the rival monarchs, the cardinal, acting upon the principles of the great league of London, proposed and concluded a treaty conducive to a crusade, which was then projected, in order to draw the minds of mankind from various anticlerical notions, by which they began to be affected. And because no expedition could be undertaken against the Turks until the pride of France was repressed, the pope, the emperor, and the king of England, agreed to the following articles: "When Charles passes to Spain, Henry shall give him convoy through the channel, with leave to land in England, and honourable entertainment while he remains there. When Henry passes to Picardy, Charles shall, in requital, do similar service. If, before the end of the current year, peace be not established between the pope, the emperor, and the French king, or if the French king begin the war afresh, Henry shall, on the arrival of Charles in England, declare himself against Francis. In this event, the English fleet, having conveyed the emperor to Spain, shall return and infest the coasts of France; and the pope shall send forth his curse, and incite the secular arm of the Christians against Francis. Between Charles, Henry, Leo, and the Medici family, with their several confederates, a reciprocity of protection shall be undertaken. And, in order that they may avail themselves, as well as the French, of the mercenaries of Switzerland, it is agreed, that the inhabitants of the Alps be permitted to remain neutral. The secular contrahents undertake to maintain the papal pretensions within their respective territories, and within any conquests that they may make during the war. When the ambition of France is curbed, the Turks shall be attacked; and no treaty shall, in future, be signed by any of the contrahents prejudicial to the league of London." It was also agreed, that, although the princess of England was betrothed to the dauphin of France, yet, for the public good of Christendom, she might be married

---

* He reached Edinburgh on the 30th October, 1521.

to the emperor; and the pope agreed to dispense with the obstacles of their affinity.* Before the ratification of this treaty the pope suddenly died.

Few men have attained so much fame by so little effort as pope Leo X. His station, equanimity, and affable demeanour would, without talent, have secured him the admiration of mankind; yet his mental endowments were such as, without the factitious aids of rank and manner, might have ensured the respect of the wise, and esteem of the virtuous. But indolence overgrew his nobler faculties, and induced such a poverty of moral honour, that he died an object of pity to the good, and of contempt to the libertine. His private life was disgraced by sensual vice; but the incense of poetical adulation has veiled it in delightful obscurity. His public conduct was stained with crimes; but they have lost their hideousness by the elegance with which they have been recorded. His reign is glorious to Italy, and memorable to the world; but the halo of immortality that surrounds his name was formed by the genius of others, and the obligations of posterity are owing to the errors of his government. It was his destiny, however, to appear at an important epoch, and he will always be regarded as the auspicious harbinger of the great intellectual day.

* Lord Herbert, 108.

BOOK III.

State of the church in England in the age of Leo X.—Proposed ecclesiastical reform by Wolsey—Vices of the pontifical government—Sale of indulgences—Impolitic measures pursued by Leo—Popularity of Luther—Spirit of controversy excited among all ranks of people—Henry's book on the seven sacraments—Wolsey aspires to the tiara—Objections of the consistory—Circumstances which prevented his election—Adrian elevated to the papal dignity—Trial and execution of the duke of Buckingham—Designs of the French faction in Scotland—Proceedings of Francis in violation of the league of London—Remonstrance of Wolsey to the French ambassador—Preparations for war—Science of political economy scarcely known in the time of Wolsey—Difficulties of levying money for the exigencies of the war—Changes arising from the decay of the feudal system—Policy which connected Scotland and France—Second visit of the emperor to England—Treaty of Windsor—Wolsey constituted arbiter of the differences between the two sovereigns—Measures of the cardinal—Convocation and Parliament summoned—Procures from the clergy a vote of ten per cent.—His overtures with the Parliament not so successful—Complaints of the people—Wolsey's reply to a deputation of the merchants of London—Revolution in Denmark—Christern solicits aid of England—Death of pope Adrian—Overtures of Wolsey to procure the papacy—Giulio de Medici chosen—Rebellion of the duke of Bourbon—His character.

IT is the peculiar quality of legitimate ambition to urge its subjects to make themselves illustrious by beneficial actions. The love of distinction alone is but a perishable vanity, and without the ennobling energy of benevolence, the passion of adding kingdoms to kingdoms is only avarice, and the achievements of conquerors are but crimes. The reputation of statesmen is never venerated, unless connected with institutions of perennial utility. Nor is success always the criterion of merit, for sometimes the motives, as seen in the means of enterprise, so unequivocally indicate honourable intentions, that fame follows even failure and defeat. In the biography, therefore, of eminent men, it is proper to keep in view the peculiar qualities of their ambition, in order to determine whether they are entitled to the respect of posterity, or ought to be classed with those ephemeral characters who are only solicitous of contemporary distinction.

In the age of Leo X., the church had in England, as elsewhere, attained the extremes of her prosperity and power. Her sins and luxuries could not be exceeded, nor longer endured. The monasteries, exempted from regal and episcopal jurisdiction, and possessing, generally, the privilege of sanctuary, their inhabitants did not languish for the want of any species of voluptuous enjoyment.* The doctrine of purgatory supplied them with ample resources. The mortmain laws but feebly restrained the profusion of post-obital piety. To prevent the total alienation of the lands to the priesthood, primogenitureship, entails, and various other pernicious limitations in the descent of property, were contrived. Blended with the feudal system, these checks on ecclesiastical usurpation became the basis of the laws which still regulate inheritance; and they are the sources of those peculiar restraints on territorial wealth, by which the claims of creditors and the operations of equity are frustrated. The church, not content with the rich accumulation of legacies, invented the doctrine of the intercession of saints, and the legends of miraculous relics, and found them wonderfully efficacious in ridding Christian people of their wealth and gems. Reason and fancy were equally repressed. Sometimes, it is true, the dramas, exhibited in the cathedrals, emanated a feeble ray of poetical genius in the midst of the most obscure logomachies; but it only served to make the surrounding darkness visible.[1] All was gloom, and fraud, and sin, and mystery, and shame.

Henry VII., perplexed by the different pretenders to the throne, and particularly by the followers of Perkin Warbeck taking refuge in the churches and abbeys, applied to Julius II. for a bull to correct the abuse of sanctuary in England. His holiness, solicitous of the king's friendship, granted the request; and the bull issued on that occasion is the first on record, by which a limit was put to a general privilege of

* Burnet, 21.

the church.* To disclose the whole turpitude of the ecclesiastical abodes of England, and to propose a system of gradual reformation, was reserved for cardinal Wolsey. Perceiving that the tendency of opinion might undermine the papal structure, unless effectual means were adopted to restrain the licentiousness of the clergy, he obtained a bull, which conferred on him a legatine right to visit all the monasteries of the realm, and to suspend the pontifical laws in England, at discretion, during a whole year. His motive, at first, for seeking this commission, was to reduce the swarm of monks, who, from the days of the Saxon kings, had continued to multiply.† He regarded them as consuming locusts, a reproach to the church, and wasteful to the state; and he resolved to convert their habitations into cathedrals and colleges, with the view of restoring the clergy to the mental superiority which they anciently possessed over the people. The rumour of an innovation so terrible alarmed all the ecclesiastical orders. Their clamour was loud, incessant, and almost universal. Every levity that the upstart reformer had committed was brought before the public, and magnified to the utmost; and, as if it could diminish the worthlessness of his brethren, it was alleged to be little less than monstrous, that a man so prone to the pleasures of life himself, should abridge the sensualities of others. Those who were free from the reprobate inclinations with which the priesthood were charged in the bull, exclaimed against the generality of the charge, and the criminals were enraged at the prevention and punishment of their infamies.

* 19th June, 1504.
† The extant accounts of the ancient British monks are very imperfect; they are sufficient, however, to show that the number was very great, and obedient to the bishop of Caerleon, as all the monks of the early ages of the church were to their bishops, according to the canons of the council of Chalcedon. During the ravages of the Danes, they were so much reduced, that the order was almost destroyed, and their houses rendered everywhere desolate, till king Edgar was persuaded to restore them. He erected forty-seven monasteries, which he intended to increase to fifty, the jubilee number; and, from that period, monkery continued to thrive in England. In his reign the celibacy of the clergy was established; for those who refused to part with their wives were then expelled from their livings, by Dunstan, archbishop of Canterbury, Ethelwald, bishop of Winchester, and Oswald, bishop of Worcester. The exemption of the monasteries from episcopal and regal jurisdiction, did not, however, fully prevail until some time after.

By virtue of his commission, Wolsey, as legate, instituted a court, which he endowed with a censorial jurisdiction over the priesthood. It was empowered to investigate matters of conscience, conduct which had given scandal, and actions which, though they escaped the law, might be found contrary to good morals. The clergy furnished abundant employment to this inquisitorial institution; and as the fines were strictly levied, and the awards sternly executed, it enhanced their exasperation against the founder.

The same causes which had induced Wolsey to attempt a reformation in the manners of the English ecclesiastics, had, in other parts of Christendom, been long operating to produce similar effects. From the election of Alexander VI. the venality and vices of the pontifical government became notorious; and the wars which occupied the hearts of the holy fathers from that era had exhausted the papal treasury. Leo X., finding the ordinary revenues of the popes insufficient for the demands of his political designs and magnificent amusements, had, in order to raise money, recourse to many fraudulent artifices. Among others, he revived those by which Urban II., towards the close of the eleventh century, incited Christendom to arm for the recovery of Palestine. His first attempt was rendered abortive by the death of sultan Selim; but, as all flesh is prone to the enjoyments of sin, Leo thought that the sale of indulgences would prove a lucrative trade. Auricular confession was one of the great secrets by which the church attained and preserved her exorbitant domination; and it had been rendered completely effectual by the episcopal appointment of confessors, who were selected on account of their bigotry and devotion to the ecclesiastical cause. Sinners often felt the hardship of this regulation, and trembled to reveal the instigations of young desire, and the levities of youthful blood, to an austere and sanctimonious old man. Leo, therefore, thought that freedom in the choice of confessors would be a great comfort to sinners. Licences to choose them were accordingly sold; but the measure only tended to facilitate the progress of schism and apostasy. Those who had begun to suspect the validity of the papal pretensions, and to doubt the efficacy of ecclesiastical mediation, took for their confessors priests who were inclined to their own opinions. The chiefs of the church, in consequence, were neither so early nor so well informed of the propagation of heresy as formerly, and the danger was far advanced before measures could be taken to procure abortion. The horrible outrages on humanity which were afterwards committed, only served to make the catholic priesthood for ever detestable.

But although the licences for choosing confessors would have gradually accomplished the diminution of the antichristian usurpations, it is probable that, without the conjunction of other more immediately decisive events, the Reformation, which commenced by the secession of Luther, would not have so speedily taken place. The first outcry of that arrogant expounder of the benevolent texts and precepts of Christianity, was directed rather against abuses in the sale of warrants to sin, than against the principle on which they were sold. Even after he had been provoked to assail the papal sacraments, he showed himself still so much inclined to maintain exclusive prerogatives to the clergy,* that it may be fairly questioned whether his rebellion against the pope was inspired by religious integrity or by carnal revenge. Luther belonged to an order of strolling friars, who were employed to sell the indulgences in Germany, but who lost this advantage by a grant which Leo X. made of the profits arising from the sins of Saxony, to his sister Magdalen and her husband, a bastard of pope Innocent VIII. Punishment, among the vulgar, is considered as the proof of guilt; and things tolerated by statutes and practice are rarely suspected of being wrong. The serviceless pensioners of the church, the sisters and bastards of her princes and ministers, never conceived that frauds on mankind collectively were of the same degree of moral turpitude as if they had been practised against individuals. Persons who would have repelled with indignation any proposal to swindle their neighbour, and would have punished, with feelings of just indignation, the practices of vulgar felons, made no scruple of dilapidating the stock of public wealth.

* His consent that the landgrave of Hesse should marry two wives was, at least, a questionable dispensation. It may very fairly be said, either to have originated in a motive to gain the landgrave fully to his will, or to have been the beginning of new ecclesiastical dogmas, which circumstances afterwards frustrated.

E

Magdalen and Cibo appointed an imprudent agent, who employed the Dominicans instead of the order to which Luther belonged, and they so glutted the market, that the trade of indulgences was ruined for ever. Powers for delivering souls from purgatory were openly staked in gaming-houses, by the inferior miscreants who acted as brokers for the sister of the holy father; and indulgences of the most odious description were sold in taverns and bagnios.* It was, therefore, not surprising that the conscientious, as well as the discontented subjects of the pope, should openly proclaim the abuses of the apostolical government. The advocates of existing customs exposed, in vain, the turbulent self-sufficiency of the reformers; and recalled to remembrance, with what constancy of virtue their ancestors had reared and supported that venerable frame of things, which a reprobate generation, actuated by a strange phrenzy, was rushing to destroy. They forgot that the misconduct of advocates never can impair the principles of a cause. But institutions are only improved by the pressure of external compulsion. Reformations may be ascribed to the wisdom of particular men; but they are the effects of remote causes, and extorted because the public will not endure the corruptions that render them desirable. The ecclesiastical machine was rotten. It could no longer perform its wonted functions, and a new one, suitable to the improved knowledge of the age, was indispensable. The manners of the workmen could neither affect the materials of the old, nor the design of the new. Among the reformers were many virtuous characters; haters of corruption for its own sake, and professors of Christianity for a recompence not of this world: nor can it be denied that the church of Rome contained many members equally blameless; but the plunderers of shrines, and the burners of heretics, were not of this description.

By the plan of ecclesiastical reformation which Wolsey adopted, the interference of the people was anticipated in England. His legatine authority made him head of the church; and, as chancellor and chief minister, he possessed the efficient power of the executive government. Hence the reformation, being undertaken by him, seemed to emanate

* Guicciardini, lib. xiv.

from the crown; and the nation was saved from those dreadful tumults which attended the overthrow of popery in other countries, and which, though they were provoked by the bigotry of prelates and statesmen, were not the less criminal against society.   The treasures and the costly fabrics of the monks should have reverted to the commonwealth, when their original destination ceased, and the alteration of opinions had superseded their utility.   But the incendiary and selfish proceedings of the fathers of protestantism must be regarded as having been necessary, and the good which resulted from their destructive system has expiated their guilt.   The measures pursued by the pope, contrasted with those of Wolsey, show the superiority of the cardinal's character to much advantage.   Leo, instead of endeavouring to amend the errors and vices of the church, punished those who exposed them. But the flames of persecution aided, as it were, the light of truth, and still more strikingly illuminated the atheistical atrocities of the Vatican.   Luther was cited to Rome, suspended from preaching, and excommunicated; but these resolutions only served to magnify his importance, and to interest the people in his fate.   The spirit of controversy, in consequence, seized on all ranks, ages, and sexes, to such a degree, that extraordinary celestial aspects, which happened to be then observed, were alone supposed adequate to produce an effect so general and wonderful; and it has been remarked, that while the shrines were broken in Europe, the altars and idols of Asia and the new world were also shaken and overthrown.

Henry caught the enthusiasm of the age, and Wolsey was ordered to apply to the pope for authority to permit the perusal of Luther's prohibited writings to such as desired it, for the purpose of refuting their errors.   Leo readily complied; and, in due season, the king brought forth his book on the seven sacraments; a work which the clergy, of course, extolled as the most learned under the sun.   The author was compared to Solomon, and magnified for wisdom above all Christian princes that had ever existed.   When the book was presented to the pope, he made no scruple of saying, that he held it equal to the works of St. Jerome and St. Augustine; and, with the concurrence of the consistory, he bestowed the

E 2

title of Defender of the Faith* on Henry, and all his successors, for ever. But though the king, in the management of
his argument, may have shown himself an able divine, and
superior in the vigour and propriety of his style, the force of
his reasoning, and the learning of his citations;† yet, as the
friar addressed himself to the common sense of mankind, the
practical effects of their writings were very different. Whether Wolsey actually assisted in the composition of Henry's
book is doubtful. That he was acquainted with its progress,
and consulted with respect to the execution, is probable.
The number and extent of his public trusts, certainly, formed
sufficient employment for all his time; but as the uncommon
elasticity of his mind enabled him to pass, at once, from one
kind of business to another, with extraordinary facility, he
might, occasionally, perform the part of a friendly critic,
without having any particular share in the regular labour of
the work.

At the death of Leo X., Wolsey aspired to the tiara. How
this ambition should ever have been regarded as something
very iniquitous is difficult to understand. It is the means
used to procure the gratification, and not the passion, which
make ambition criminal. But though he was eminently
qualified for the papal dignity, the Italian cardinals had strong
objections to him on account of his country and character.
They regarded all foreigners as barbarians,‡ and dreaded to
admit into the consistory any person from those distant provinces of Christendom where Rome was regarded as the asy-
lum of all that was holy, harmless, and undefiled. He had
therefore to contend with the impediment arising from this
prejudice, and with the two formidable factions, the imperial
and French, which divided the conclave. A still stronger
objection, though one that was felt, but could not be discussed,

* Fiddes mentions, that it appears from a charter of Richard II. to the
university of Oxford, that he made use of the title of *the Defender of the
Faith.*—Page 285.

Fuller says, in his Church History, " There went a tradition that Patch,
the king's jester, perceiving the king very jocund one day, asked him the
reason, and when the king told him it was because of his new title, *Defender
of the Faith,* the jester made this arch reply, ' Prithee, good Harry, let thee
and me defend one another, and let the faith alone to defend itself.' "—
Rapin, i. 749, note 3, folio ed.

† Collier's Eccl. Hist. ii. 17.   ‡ Guicciar. lib. xiv.

arose from his known endeavours to curtail the licentiousness of the clergy. But it may be proper to consider, generally, the public circumstances which, undoubtedly, ministered to prevent his election.

Besides the personal qualifications of the candidates, it was natural for the conclave to consider the political interests which they were likely to affect. Both the French and Imperial factions could not but perceive, that the election of Wolsey would tend to form a third party, with aims and interests different from theirs. The menaces of the sultan, and the insurgency of the Spaniards, rendered Charles, notwithstanding the geographical extent of his territories, barely a match for Francis, whose rounded, compact, and populous dominions enjoyed entire tranquillity. The kingdom of Henry, though scarcely equal to some of the emperor's provinces, was yet, by its insular situation and prosperity, not inferior in the balance of power to either. The elevation of Wolsey to the papacy would therefore, probably, in the opinion of the cardinals, have given an undue preponderance in favour of England; especially if his character was taken into the estimate, and character has always great weight in the estimates of contemporary politicians. His vast pride, that lofty self-confidence which admitted of no control, was a topic of detraction throughout all Europe. His country made him obnoxious to the French and imperial factions, and his exposure of the ecclesiastical corruptions had not rendered him acceptable to the general body of the priesthood. At the death of Leo, it was obviously not the interest of the French to promote a man whose views and principles were inimical to Francis; and it was more for the advantage of the imperialists to choose one of their own party, than such a man as Wolsey. Although opposed to each other, they were united against him. It was therefore natural, that, in order to get rid of Wolsey, and since they could not agree upon choosing a decisive character from among themselves, they should fix upon one who, by his age and neutral qualities, was not likely to essentially impair their respective influence. The event took place accordingly. After the conclave had been closed longer than usual, and when there was no likelihood of terminating the election in favour of the original candidates, a new one was proposed,— Adrian, the tutor of Charles; a man of moderate propensities, and so far advanced in life that he could not reasonably be expected to live long. He was immediately elected. His elevation was, in fact, the effect of a tacit compromise among all parties; his age and character compensating for the advantage which the imperialists were likely to gain by the event. As the election was unanimous, the cardinals, with their usual impiety, ascribed it to a special interference of the Holy Ghost, who was wont, they said, on such occasions, to inspire their hearts.* Whatever Wolsey may have privately felt at being disappointed of the honour to which he had aspired, the result did not alter the political policy which he had previously adopted. Nor is there any proof extant that he did not concur in opinion with those who suggested the expediency of electing the emperor's tutor. Besides, his disappointment must have been palliated by the consideration, that Adrian was a foreigner, and that, by choosing him, the door, which had been long shut on the transalpine clergy, was again opened to them, as well as to the natives of Italy. It could not fail to be remarked, that the objection of his country would weigh less at the next vacancy, the prospect of which, by the infirmities of the new pope, was not very distant. It has been alleged, that Charles did not exert himself on this occasion for the advancement of the cardinal, as he had promised; but the contrary is the fact.† It is true that his own tutor was preferred; but there is little reason to believe that it was by his particular interference. The views and motives of the French and imperial factions, in choosing Adrian, seem sufficiently obvious.

In the meantime, the domestic administration of the cardinal had been troubled with an unhappy event, the trial and execution of Edward Stafford, duke of Buckingham. He was descended from a daughter of Thomas of Woodstock, the sixth son of Edward III.; and, consequently, as all the legitimate heirs of the five elder brothers, but the mother of the king, had been cut off in the civil wars, he was next in line of blood to the crown, in the event of Henry VII.'s family be-

---

* Guicciardini, lib. xiv.

† Charles certainly did write to his ambassador at Rome, to solicit the cardinals to elect Wolsey to the papacy. There is a letter of his to this effect, dated 30th December, 1521, in the Cottonian Library, Vitellius, b. iv. No. 103.

coming extinct.* But his chance of rightfully ascending the throne was very remote; for besides the princess Mary, then heir apparent, the dowagers of France and Scotland had each several children, and, as well as the king, had the hope and prospect of more. The notion, however, had taken possession of his imagination; and the fatality that has uniformly attended the possessors of the title of Buckingham, a title ever famous in the political factions of England, allured him to commit improprieties which indicated treasonable wishes. His revenues were ample, his expenditure liberal, and, flat- tered by his inferiors, he mistook the deference paid to the accidents of fortune, for assurances of future royalty. With- out any of those strong and steady talents which are at once the causes and the means of ambition, he was deeply imbued with the fatalism which attends that imperial passion, and he pried into the undeveloped secrets of time with a weak and feminine solicitude. The lordliness and lofty genius of the cardinal, overtowering all the courtiers, mortified his pride, and rebuked his pretensions. He grudged that a man of mean birth should enjoy so much authority; and he hated him for being qualified to maintain it. This antipathy was the nar- row jealousy of aristocratic arrogance, exasperated, probably, by the contempt with which it was retaliated.†

* The following is the genealogy of Buckingham from Edward III.

Thomas duke of Gloucester.

Earl of Buckingham==Eleanor Bohun, d. 1397.

Ann==Edmund, earl of Stafford.

Humphrey duke of Buckingham.

Humphrey died vita patris.

Harry, beheaded 1485, father of Edward.

† The origin of Buckingham's hatred of Wolsey has been ascribed to various occurrences; but I think it more likely to have arisen from that indescribable antipathy which may have been produced by the character of the cardinal operating on the pride and rash temperament of the duke. The incidents which are said to have caused their quarrel, I regard only as occurrences which served to publish the animosity of Buckingham. Some

Among other things which the duke complained of in the administration of the cardinal was, the expensive meeting of the courts of France and England. He represented it as a theatrical show, by which Wolsey only desired to exhibit to the world his influence over the two kings; but, being ordered to attend, he had prepared for the voyage with the magnificence suitable to his rank and fortune. Happening to be ready before the court, he went forward to his estates in Kent, and dismissed his steward for having vexed and oppressed the tenantry. A short time before his departure from London, his son-in-law, the earl of Surrey, appointed viceroy of Ireland, had proceeded to Dublin.* It is necessary to notice this circumstance particularly; because, it has been alleged, that Surrey was sent purposely out of the way, that Wolsey might the more easily accomplish his machinations for the ruin of Buckingham, although it was chiefly on the evidence of the steward that he was found guilty.

In the spring† following the interview of the kings, and about twelve months after Surrey had been sent to Ireland, Buckingham was accused of treasonable practices; arrested, and frequently examined; he was impeached, and ordered for trial. That he was fairly dealt with in the process cannot be

have said, that the duke, holding the basin and towel to the emperor and the king at Canterbury, was enraged at the cardinal for also attempting to wash his fingers while he held it. But this anecdote is not well authenticated, and is told in several different ways. Besides, those who lay stress on it, must exculpate Wolsey for having resolved on the overthrow of Buckingham when he sent Surrey to Ireland, as the earl had departed for Dublin before the court removed to Canterbury, when this quarrel should have taken place.

There is another story which seems to illustrate the character of the duke. One of the king's sworn servants having, without leave, removed into the service of Buckingham, was, on refusing to return, imprisoned by order of Wolsey; and being accused of this demeanour in the Star-chamber, and before the king in person, was found guilty, and obliged to return to his duty. Buckingham construed this proceeding into a personal affront, and never after ceased from reviling the cardinal's administration.

* April, 1520. It has been regularly alleged, from the days of Polydore Virgil to those of Rapin, that Surrey was sent to Ireland in order that he might be out of the way when the ruin of the duke was determined. But the fact appears to be, that the earl of Surrey was sent to Ireland a year before the arrest of Buckingham, and some time previous to the discharge of the servant, by whose evidence his desires were disclosed.

† 1521.

denied. The duke of Norfolk, father of his son-in-law, was appointed great steward for the occasion; nor have the other members of the court, which consisted of a marquis, seven earls, and twelve barons, ever been mentioned as actuated against him by any questionable motive. But witnesses might be suborned, and the court, though of the purest integrity, might hear such assertions in evidence, that sentence against the victim could not possibly be avoided. This, however, has never been alleged. It has never been asserted that the witnesses were false, although the execution was considered as a severity which the actual aggression did not merit. He was convicted on charges which, in an age credulous of astrological predictions, and at a time when the calamities of the York and Lancaster wars were fresh in every memory, appeared much more heinous than can be conceived, without reference to the period in which they were made. The turpitude of crimes depends on the state of the public feelings when they happen to be committed. The amount of wrong does not constitute the degree of the guilt of evil actions; but the result of the estimate which society makes of the probable issue of tolerating such actions. The hideousness of guilt consists in its consequences, as Sin is made horrible by the voluminous and loathsome length of her extremities.

It was proved against Buckingham that he had declared, before the birth of the princess Mary, that he considered himself, if the king died without issue, as heir to the crown; that he did many things which evinced a traitorous ambition, finding fault with the conduct of Henry VII., and murmuring against the existing government; that he had dealt with a fortune-telling monk concerning his chance of succeeding to the throne; and, having confidence in the predictions, had courted popularity; that he said to his dismissed steward, if he had been committed to the Tower on account of one of the king's servants, who had entered without leave into his household, and who had been convicted of contumacy in the Star-chamber, he would have played the part his father meant to have acted against Richard III., when he entreated to be brought into his presence. He would have stabbed the king as he affected to kneel in homage; and, in telling these words, he grasped his dagger, and swore fiercely; and it was also proved that he had said, if the king died he would have the rule of the realm in spite of all opposition.

Such is the essence of the charges on which he was arraigned. His consultations with the monk had taken place many years before, and seem to have been brought forward with a view to show how long he had cherished unlawful notions. Norfolk, in pronouncing the horrible sentence of high treason, wept bitterly. " My lord," replied Buckingham, " you have spoken as a traitor should be condemned, but I was never one;" and, turning to the other members of the court, he added, "I wish you no harm for what you have done to me. May God forgive you my death, as I do! To the king I will not sue for life; but he is a gracious prince, and more good may come from him than I deserve." He then requested the prayers of the court, and, being conducted out of the hall, was conveyed to the Tower. Owing, probably, to the state of the tide at London bridge, he was landed at the Temple stairs, and carried through the city. Treason, though of all crimes the most dreadful, is yet, by something either in its magnitude or its resemblance to the gallant enterprises of war, never considered with those sentiments of detestation that acts of inferior guilt inspire. And a condemned man, whatever may have been his offence, is always an object of compassion. In carrying the duke through London, the pity of the spectators would have been excited, even although his attendants had not solicited their prayers; especially as he had not actually perpetrated any palpable crime. The lamentations, therefore, which accompanied his condemnation and execution,* is rather a proof of the generosity of the people and of his own popularity, than evidence of innocence, or of the Machiavelism ascribed by contemporary historians to the cardinal.

After Wolsey's unavailing attempt to reconcile Francis and Charles, it was expected that the French faction in Scotland, at the head of which was the duke of Albany, would, according to the ancient policy of that kingdom, endeavour to disturb the tranquillity of England, while Henry embarked in the war against France. This was rendered the more probable, as queen Margaret, in consequence of a domestic dis-

* 17th May, 1521.

agreement,* had detached herself from the English party, and openly declared, that she was accessory to Albany's return.† Prompt measures were, therefore, necessary to frustrate the designs which the regent of Scotland unequivocally meditated. The warden of the marches was, accordingly, commanded to pass the borders,‡ and to proclaim, that the Scots in less than a month, should desist from their predatory inroads and warlike preparations. The regency of Scotland disregarded the admonition, and the duke, with a numerous army, advanced towards the borders. But the barons and chieftains, though they had agreed to protect the frontiers of their own country, refused to molest the land and subjects of England. Albany was, in consequence, obliged to propose a truce, and to allow his army to disperse. Thus disappointed, he suddenly returned to Paris, in order to concert new measures with Francis, who, though menaced on all sides by the confederates, continued assiduous in the execution of the plans which had, originally, induced him to violate the league of London.

Francis had ordered the goods, debts, and persons, of the English in Bourdeaux to be arrested;§ an aggression which greatly astonished the inhabitants of London, and quickened the indignation with which his conduct had greatly inspired the government. The cardinal, instantly on receiving the news, sent for the French ambassador, and expressed with the utmost acerbity his opinions of Francis and his government,‖

* The duke of Albany had certainly been recalled to Scotland by a large party in the state. The queen herself had invited him. After the battle of Flodden, she had married the young earl of Angus, who proving an unfaithful husband, she had endeavoured, by the means of Albany, to procure a divorce; and among other causes that she alleged for seeking this indulgence, was a report that king James had not been killed in the battle, but was alive at the period of her second marriage. Henry disapproved of this proceeding, and came to high words with his sister, who answered him in a letter of no small pith and spirit. Francis certainly connived at the return of Albany into Scotland; but there is no evidence which distinctly proves that he directly instigated it. On the contrary, Albany, it appears, was openly invited to assume the regency of Scotland.

† Rapin, 750. ‡ 8th Feb., 1522. Stow, 515.
§ 6th March, 1522.
‖ " Laid sore to his charge." The cardinal appears to have been in the practice of doing this to the foreign ambassadors, whenever he was displeased with the conduct of their courts.

in being the first promoters of the league of London, and the first who had violated its engagements. " Francis," said Wolsey, " gave his word to the king, when they met in Picardy, that Albany should not be allowed to return to Scotland; and yet he has sent him there. What sort of a fellow must your master be?" The ambassador was then ordered to keep his house; and all the French and Scots in London were indiscriminately thrown into prison. This summary retribution was immediately followed by other decisive acts of hostility; and orders were issued to ascertain the population and resources of the kingdom, preparatory to the calling forth of all its power.

The science of political economy, which has been so amply elucidated in the course of the eighteenth century, was scarcely known in the time of Wolsey. Whatever was raised from the people, for the service of the state, was regarded as so much subtracted from the wealth of the nation. The vital energy which arises from the general interchange of money, commodities, and skill, was, like the circulation of the blood,* then very imperfectly known. Nor was it understood that the impoverishment, occasioned by wars, proceeds as much from diminishing the number of productive labourers, as from the expenditure of treasure. It was not the custom for armies to act only against armies in those days, but to practise that system of levying contributions, which the French have, with so much success, resorted to in these. Whenever a country was invaded, all within the reach of the invader was subjected to his use. The inhabitants would have beheld, with as much astonishment, the enemy paying for provisions, as the soldiers would have heard with indignation an order denying them the privilege of plundering. By the feudal obligations, those expenses which constitute the main expenditure of nations, fell immediately on the possessors of the soil, before the encroachments of the clergy had attached to the church the richest domains, and made it no longer possible for the secular orders to bear the whole charge alone. The ecclesiastics being ex-

---

* Dr. Harvey did not discover, but only demonstrated the circulation of the blood. Among many other notices of a knowledge of its motion in different writings, Brutus says to Portia, that she was
" As dear to me as are the ruddy drops
That visit my sad heart."—*Julius Cæsar.*

empted from personal service, it became customary for the kings of England to solicit them for pecuniary aids. But the laymen were still bound to furnish arms and soldiers. The public works also were, in those days, not constructed at the expense of the royal revenues, but were either paid for by local taxes, or executed by a proportional number of labourers and mechanics drawn from different parts of the kingdom. The civil and judicial offices were independent of the crown, and attached to the soil. Property, which is the basis of political power, was anciently in England the legal and constitutional criterion of capacity.[2] In proportion to the opulence of an estate was the extent of the possessor's authority. The disbursements of the exchequer were, consequently, on account of the royal household, except when armies were transported to the plains of France: on these occasions, the preparations for the fleet rendered it necessary to solicit benevolences, or gifts, from the priesthood, and all other willing and loyal subjects. But this precarious resource was inadequate for the exigencies of that wide and extended war which Henry had resolved to wage, in conjunction with Charles and his other allies, against Francis. The duty, therefore, which the cardinal had to perform was the most ungracious that could fall to the lot of any minister. Taxation was regarded, in some sort, as a heresy in state dogmas; and that complex machinery by which so much of the vast revenues of England is now collected from the raspings and friction of industry, was not then invented. Nor were the objects of the war obvious to the multitude, while its burdens were greater than any other which the English nation had ever before maintained.

When the feudal system was in its vigour, it set bounds to the ambition of kings. For, although it enabled them to resist aggression with more expedition than any military arrangement that has yet appeared, it prevented them from combining with so much effect as the later institution of standing armies. It was only calculated for defensive operations. The limited time which the vassals were bound to attend the chieftains, accoutred and provided for the field, was too short for the execution of great schemes of conquest, though sufficient to frustrate invasions undertaken by feudal armies. But as the system itself fell into decay, forces were

formed, with commanders distinct from the possessors of the
land, before any material change took place in the relative
condition of the provincial states of Christendom. The
change, arising from the decay, first began to show itself in
leagues offensive and defensive; for the preservation of which,
troops, ready for the field, became requisite, and for their
maintenance the obligations of knight-service were• com-
muted for money. As the feudal system sunk, the financial
rose; and the means were taken from the people of defend-
ing themselves, and placed in the hands of the military order.
Hence, nations which formerly would have required the
efforts of ages to overcome, have, in these days, been con-
quered by regular armies in a single battle. Under the
financial system, that country which can support the largest
standing force must necessarily prevail. But during the
ancient state of the European nations, the farther an invading
army advanced, its means of annoyance diminished, while
those of its opponents increased. The case is different when
the contest lies between two regular armies: the inhabitants
of the invaded country are defenceless; they trust to their
military order, and when it is vanquished, they are subdued.
The rule becomes transferred to the victors, and the people,
destitute of those standards of local champions, around which
their ancestors were wont to rally with invigorated hopes,
even after repeated defeats, submit without resistance to the
decrees of their new masters. This state of things can only
be abrogated by the renunciation of coalitionary projects;
and by each nation constituting within itself a system of
defence commensurate to its population. It is difficult to
understand on what principle of natural justice one government should link its fate to that of another. For what are
called the common causes of nations, those in which different
states with distinct interests and opposite sentiments unite
and war against any other particular state, must necessarily
be unjust, because the very object of their coalition is only
contingent. Such contracts, however, as the league of London, which, perhaps, ought to be regarded as the grandest
monument of the comprehensive mind of Wolsey, are of a
different nature. They are, in some degree, to nations, what
public statutes are to persons; and their tendency, as was
shown in the appeal to Henry, and in the meeting of the

congress at Calais, is manifestly to constitute a tribunal, to which nations may refer their complaints against the encroachments of one another.

Scotland, by her alliance with France, always reckoned, in the event of war with England, on a powerful diversion being made in her favour, by the proximity of the English continental dominions to the territories of the French kings. And France, in her turn, being continually exposed to the pretensions of the warlike Plantagenets to her whole crown, calculated on a similar advantage from the borders of Scotland, against the very body itself of the English monarchy. This reciprocity of policy formed a strong connexion between the courts of Paris and Edinburgh; and nothing, prior to the marriage of James IV. with the daughter of Henry VII., occurred to impair its utility. But that marriage, and the magnanimity of England after the calamitous fall of James at Flodden, with the relationship of his children to Henry, opened the affairs and politics of Scotland to the influence of the English cabinet. Wolsey availed himself of this circumstance; and the ministers of Queen Elizabeth perfected the systematic interference which he so successfully commenced. Improbable as it ought to be, that persons belonging to that high class which is particularly entrusted with the sacred custody of the honour and independence of their country, should, for selfish purposes, enter into a corrupt correspondence with the minister of a foreign state, there are numerous documents extant which prove the venality of Scottish peers and prelates, and their subserviency to cardinal Wolsey. From the period of the battle of Flodden, and the meeting of the congress at Calais, a greater predilection towards England was formed within the bosom of Scotland than had existed since the time of Edward I. From the date of the battle, the French influence began to decline. During the cardinal's administration it was rendered almost nugatory; for when it did happen to succeed to a certain extent, its schemes, by some secret skilful management, suddenly dissolved in the moment of parturition, and disappointed the hopes of those who had conceived them.

The time which the emperor had fixed for his second visit to England, and for which he had made stipulations in the treaty concluded by Wolsey at Calais, was now arrived. A number of persons of the first rank were, in consequence, sent to attend him across the channel; and the cardinal, with a sumptuous train of ecclesiastics, received him again at Dover.* The king, as on his former visit, met him in the castle, and thence conducted him to the palace of Greenwich. On Whitsunday, he went to St. Paul's with the court; and the cardinal performed the service with a degree of ostentatious pomp never surpassed by the popes themselves. Two barons held the basin and towel before the mass; two earls after the gospels; and two dukes served him at the last lavation. When Charles was soon after instituted a knight of the garter, he received the sacrament with Henry; and they vowed, together, kneeling at the altar, to maintain inviolate a treaty which had been previously drawn up, and which, from the place of ratification, was called the treaty of Windsor.

By this contract it was declared, that hostilities having arisen between the emperor and the French king, they had, as contrahents of the league of London, applied to the king of England, who, to compose their differences, had sent cardinal Wolsey to Calais, and it was proved that the aggressions had first been committed by the French. Wolsey failing to effect a reconciliation, and Francis having violated his faith to Henry by sending the duke of Albany to Scotland, and also by molesting the English trade, it was agreed that Charles and Henry should unite in the prosecution of the war against France: and, in order to render their alliance the more effectual and permanent, it was likewise agreed, that Charles should, in due time, be married to the princess Mary, or forfeit five hundred thousand crowns if he failed in this engagement. The daughter of Henry had formerly been betrothed to the unborn heir of Francis, but the occurrence of war had dissolved that contract. The most remarkable article, however, in the treaty of Windsor, is an agreement on the part, respectively, of the two sovereigns, to constitute cardinal Wolsey judge and arbiter of their differences; and they empowered him to pronounce the sentence of excommunication on the first that infringed the articles of the contract.†

* May 26, 1522.   † Lord Herbert, 118.

During the emperor's residence in England, Henry set no limits to his munificence; a continual succession of those gorgeous entertainments in which he himself so much delighted, afforded to his guest opportunities of practising that meretricious affability which captivates the affections of the vulgar; while he secured by gifts and vails a lease of the good will and praise of the courtiers. Surrey was recalled from Ireland to be employed in the war. It was alleged, that between him and Wolsey there was a secret antipathy. If this was the case, the conduct of the cardinal was certainly magnanimous towards this courageous and decisive man. He kept him employed in situations of the highest trust, and enabled him to acquire that lofty renown which still exhibits him to posterity as one of the greatest warriors that England ever produced. He was, at this time, appointed admiral of the combined English and imperial fleet, from which, while the emperor was with the king, he made two descents on the coast of France, and returned with much booty. He afterwards conveyed the emperor to Spain with a fleet of one hundred and eighty men of war, the largest that had ever before departed from the shores of England.

It has been said* that, although Charles appeared to treat Wolsey with so much deference, one of the objects of his visit was to ingratiate himself more intimately with Henry, and to acquire an interest in his affections beyond the influence of the favourite. But this is not probable. The visit had been concerted by Wolsey himself, and nothing had occurred which could induce the emperor to expect, or to desire, a change in the councils and system of England. It is true that, at this period, the active genius of the cardinal was felt throughout all Europe; and that he arrogated a degree of mastery over the particular affairs of England, which the constitution was not supposed to have vested, even then, in the prerogatives of the crown. But Henry, always fervent in his attachments, was proud of the great qualities and zeal of his minister, and alike regardless of the insinuations of envy, the venom of malice, and the craft of diplomatic depravity. He had too much discernment not to perceive the blemishes of Wolsey's character, his surpassing ostentation, pride of superiority, and

* Godwin's Annals.

F

love of luxury;* but these specks were lost in the lustre of his general merits.

Surrey, after conveying the emperor to Spain, landed on the coast of France a force of about seven thousand men, who plundered the town, and destroyed the ships, in the harbour of Morlaix. Having re-embarked, he came to Cowes, in the

* " . . . . Now must I declare the manner of his going to Westminster Hall in the term time. First, when he came out of his privy chamber, he most commonly heard two masses in his chapel; and I heard one of his chaplains say since (that was a man of credit and excellent learning,) that what business soever the cardinal had in the day time, that he never went to bed with any part of his service unsaid; no, not so much as one collect, in which I think he deceived many a man. Then going into his chamber again, he demanded of some of his servants if they were in readiness, and had furnished his chamber of presence, and waiting chamber. He being then advertised of this, came out of his privy chamber about eight of the clock, ready apparelled in red, like a cardinal; his upper vesture was all of scarlet, or else of fine crimson taffeta, or crimson satin ingrained. His head-pillion scarlet, with a black velvet cap, and a tippet of sables about his neck, holding in his hand an orange, the meat or substance thereof being taken out, and filled again with a part of a sponge, full of vinegar and other confections against pestilent airs, the which he most commonly held to his nose when he came to a press, or when he was pestered with many suitors. And before him was borne the broad Seal of England, and then the cardinal's hat, by some lord or some gentleman of worship, right solemnly. And as soon as he was entered into his chamber of presence, where there were daily attending on him as well noblemen of this realm, as other worthy gentlemen of his own family, then cried the gentlemen-ushers that went before him bareheaded, ' On, masters, before, and make room for my lord!' Thus went he down the hall, with a serjeant-at-arms before him, bearing a great mace of silver, and two gentlemen carrying two great plates of silver. And when he came to the hall door, there his mule stood trapped all in crimson velvet, with a saddle of the same.

" Then there were attending him, when he was mounted, his two cross-bearers, his two pillar-bearers, all upon great horses all in fine scarlet. And so he marched on, with a train of gentry, having four footmen about him, bearing every one of them a poleaxe in his hand. And thus passed he forth, till he came to Westminster, and there alighted, and went in this manner up to the chancery, stayed awhile at a bar, made for him beneath the chancery, and there he communed sometimes with the judges, and sometimes with other persons. And then he went up to the chancery, and sat there till eleven of the clock, to hear suits and to determine causes. And from thence he would go into the Star Chamber, as occasion served him; he neither spared high nor low, but did judge every one according to right.

" Every Sunday he would resort to the court, being then at Greenwich, with his former rehearsed train and triumph, taking his barge at his own stairs, furnished with yeomen standing upon the bayls, and his gentlemen

Isle of Wight, where he conferred the honour of knighthood on several officers who had signalised themselves in that exploit;* for the practices of chivalry still prevailed, and knights in arms were qualified to elect the distinguished soldier on the field.

The war, in the meantime, against Francis, was resolved to be prosecuted at all points. Orders were issued to ascer-

within and about, and landed at the Three Cranes, in the Vintry, and from thence he rode upon his mule with his crosses, his pillars, his hat, and his Broad Seal carried before him upon horseback, along Thames-street, until he came to Billingsgate, and there he took his barge, and so went to Greenwich, where he was nobly entertained of the lords in the king's house, being there with staves in their hands, as the treasurer, comptroller, and many others, and so conveyed into the king's chamber. After dinner he went home again in like triumph."—*Cavendish.*

It was made one of the articles of impeachment against him, " That by his outrageous pride he had greatly shadowed a long season his grace's honour." Art. xliv. Sir Thomas More, when speaker of the House of Commons, noticing a complaint which had been made by the cardinal, that nothing could be said or done in that house, but it was presently spread abroad, and became the talk of every tavern or ale house, " Masters (says he) forasmuch as my lord cardinal lately laid to our charge the lightness of our tongues for things uttered out of this house, it shall not, in my mind, be amiss to receive him in all his pomp, with his maces, his pillars, poleaxes, his crosses, his hat, and the great seal too; to the intent that if he find the like fault with us hereafter, we may be the bolder from ourselves to lay the blame on those which his grace bringeth with him."—*Roper's Life of Sir Thomas More*, p. 21, edit. 1817. Sir Thomas More, also, in his Apology, written in the year 1533, reflects severely upon the change introduced among the clergy, through the cardinal's means, in the luxury and sumptuousness of their dress.—*Works*, p. 892.

The pulpit, likewise, constantly raised its voice against him. Doctor Barnes, who was burnt in Smithfield, in the year 1541, preached, in St. Edwards' church, in Cambridge, a sermon, for which he was called to appear before the cardinal. This was a part of their dialogue, as it is related in Fox:—" What, master doctor, (said the cardinal,) had you not a sufficient scope in the scriptures to teach the people, but my golden shoes, my poleaxes, my pillars, my golden cushions, my cross, did so sore offend you, that you must make us *ridiculum caput* amongst the people ? We were jolly that day laughed to scorn. Verily it was a sermon more fit to be preached on a stage than in a pulpit; for at the last you said I wore a pair of *red* gloves. I should say *bloody* gloves, (quoth you) that I should not be cold in the midst of my ceremonies ;" and Barnes answered, " I spake nothing but the truth out of the scriptures, according to my conscience, and according to the old doctors."—*Fox's Acts*, p. 1088.

The following curious passage from Doctor Barnes's " Supplication to

---

* Holinshed, 874.

tain the full strength of the kingdom. An exhibition was made of all the arms; the number of persons above the age of sixteen was reckoned; and the names of the lords of manors, as well as of all the beneficed clergy, were taken. Aliens were, at the same time, obliged to register with the magistrates an account of their families, their professions, and the occasion of their residence in England. The result enabled

the King," printed by Myddleton, in 12mo, without date, is probably more correct than the exaggeration of the good old martyrologist. It opens to us, as Doctor Wordsworth justly remarks, some part of the philosophy upon which the cardinal defended the fitness of that pomp and state which he maintained. " They have *baculum pastolarem* to take sheep with, but it is not like a shepherd's hook, for it is intricate and manifold crooked, and turneth always in, so that it may be called a mace, for it hath neither beginning nor ending, and it is more like to knock swine and wolves in the head with, than to take sheep. *They have also pillars and poleaxes,* and other ceremonies, which no doubt be but trifles and things of nought. I pray you what is the cause that you call your staff a shepherd's staff? You help no man with it? You comfort no man? You lift up no man with it? But you have stricken down kings and kingdoms with it; and knocked in the head dukes and earls with it. Call you this a shepherd's staff? There is a space in the shepherd's staff for the foot to come out again; but your staff turneth and windeth always inward and never outward, signifying that whosoever he be that cometh within your danger, that he shall never come out again. This exposition your deeds do declare; let them be examined that you have to do with, and let us see how they have escaped your shepherd's hook. But these be the articles for the which I must needs be a heretic; nevertheless all the world may see how shamefully that I have erred against your holiness in saying the truth. My lord cardinal reasoned with me on this article; all the others he passed over, saving this and the sixth article. Here did he ask, ' If I thought it good and reasonable that he should lay down his pillars and poleaxes, and coin them?' Here is the heresy that is so abominable,—I made him answer that I thought it well done. ' Then,' said he, ' how think you, were it better for me, (being in the honour and dignity that I am,) to coin my pillars and poleaxes, and to give the money to five or six beggars, than for to maintain the common wealth by them as I do? Do you not reckon,' quoth he, ' the common wealth better than five or six beggars?'—*Singer.*

" His house was always resorted unto, like a king's house, with noble and gentlemen, coming and going in and out, feasting and banquetting all ambassadors, and other strangers right nobly. And when it pleased the king's majesty, as many times it did, he would, for his recreation, resort unto the cardinal's house, against whose coming they wanted no preparation or goodly furniture, with victuals of the finest sort that could be had for money or for friendship. Such pleasures were here devised for the king's delight, as could be invented or imagined; banquets set with masques and mummers, in such costly manner, that it was glorious to behold. There wanted no damsels meet to dance with the masquers, or to garnish the place for the time with a variety

the cardinal to know the extent of his resources; and, in order to avail himself of them, the convocation and parliament were summoned to meet.

The convocation of the clergy anciently consisted of two chambers like the parliament. In the upper, sat the arch-bishops, and mitred abbots; and in the lower, the deans with the inferior graduates. With the king's writ for calling the

of other pastimes. Then were there divers kinds of music, and many choice men and women singers appointed to sing, who had excellent voices. I have seen the king come suddenly thither in a mask, with a dozen masquers, all in garments, like shepherds, made of fine cloth of gold, and silver wire, and fine crimson satin, engrained, and caps of the same, with vizards, and sixteen torch-bearers, besides their drummers and others attending on them with vizards, and clothed all in satin; and before his entering into the hall, you shall understand that he came by water to the water-gate, without any noise, where were layd divers chambers and guns, charged with shot, and on his landing they were discharged, which made such a rattling noise in the air, that it was like thunder; it made all the noblemen, gentlemen, and ladies to muse what it should mean, coming so suddenly, they sitting quietly at a banquet, in this sort. You shall understand that the tables were set in the chamber of presence, covered, and my lord cardinal sitting under his cloth of state, and having his service all alone; and there was there set a lady and a nobleman, and a gentleman and a gentlewoman, throughout all the tables in the chamber on the one side, which were made all joining, as it were, but one table; all which order was done by my lord Sands, then lord-chamberlain to the king, and by Sir Henry Guilford, the comptroller of the king's house. Then, immediately after this great shot of guns, the cardinal desired the lord chamberlain to see what it did mean, as though he knew nothing of the matter; they then looked out of the window into the Thames, and returning again, told him that they thought that they were noblemen and strangers, arrived at the bridge, and coming as ambassadors from some foreign prince. With that said the cardinal: ' I desire you, because you can speak French, to take the pains to go into the hall, there to receive them into the chamber, when they shall see us, and all these noble personages sitting merry at our banquet, desiring them to sit down with us, and take part of our fare.' Then went they incontinently into the hall, where they received them with twenty torches, and conveyed them up into the chamber with such a number of drums and flutes as I have seldom seen together at one time and place. Then, at their arrival into the cham-ber, they went two and two together, directly before the cardinal, where he sat, and saluted him very reverently. To whom the lord chamberlain, for them, said: ' Sir, forasmuch as they are strangers, and cannot speak English, they have desired me to tell you that having an understanding of this, your triumphant banquet, and that there were assembled such a number of fair dames, could do no less, under the supportation of your grace, than to view as well their incomparable beauty, as to accompany them at mum-chance, and after that to dance with them, so to beget their better acquaintance; and, fur-thermore, they require of your grace licence to accomplish this cause of

parliament, an order was sent to the archbishops to summon the convocation, but the day of meeting was not mentioned in the royal order. The clergy, affecting to be independent of the crown, did not choose that it should appear that they were particularly controlled in the assembling of the convocation. The will of the king, as to the day of meeting, was, in consequence, privately communicated to the archbishops, who, in

their coming.' Whereupon the cardinal said he was willing, and very well content that they should do so. Then went the masquers, and first saluted all the dames, and then returned to the most worthiest, and there opened a great cup of gold, filled with crowns and other pieces, to cast at. Thus perusing all the gentlewomen, of some they won, and to some they lost. And having viewed all the ladies, they returned to the cardinal with great reverence, pouring down all their gold, which was above two hundred crowns. 'At all!' quoth the cardinal, and casting the dice, he won it, whereat was made great joy. Then quoth the cardinal to my lord chamberlain : ' I pray you go tell them, that to me it seemeth there should be a nobleman amongst them, that better deserves to sit in this place than I, to whom I should gladly surrender the same, according to my duty, if I knew him.' Then spake my lord chamberlain to them in French, and declared my lord cardinal's words, and they rounding (whispering) him again in the ear, the lord chamberlain said unto my lord cardinal : ' Sir,' quoth he, ' they confess that among them is such a noble personage, whom, if your grace can point out from the rest, he is contented to disclose himself, and to accept of your place most willingly.' With that the cardinal, taking a good avisement, went amongst them, and at the last, quoth he : ' It seemeth to me that the gentleman with the black beard should be he ;' and with that he rose out of his chair, and offered the same to the gentleman with the black beard, with the cup in his hand. But the cardinal was mistaken, for the person to whom he then offered his chair, was Sir Edward Neville, a comely knight, and of a goodly personage, who did more resemble his majesty's person, than any other in that masque. The king, seeing the cardinal so deceived in his choice, could not forbear laughing, but pulled down his vizard, and Sir Edward Neville also, with such a pleasant countenance and cheer, that all the noble estates there rejoiced. The cardinal desired him to take his place, to whom the king made answer, that he would first go and shift him ; and thereupon went into the cardinal's bedchamber, where was a great fire prepared for him, and there he new apparelled himself with rich and princely garments. And in the king's absence, the dishes of the banquet were clean taken away, and the tables covered again with new and perfumed cloths, every man sitting still, until the king's majesty, with his masquers, came in among them, every man new apparelled. Then the king took his seat, under the cloth of estate, commanding every man to sit still, as they did before. And then came in a new banquet before his majesty and the rest, of two hundred dishes, and more, of wondrous costly meats and devices, and so they passed the night in banquetting and dancing until the morning, which much rejoiced the cardinal to see his sovereign lord so pleasant at his house."—*Cavendish.*

their writs, informed the subalterns of their respective provinces when and where to assemble. On this occasion, Wolsey, by virtue of his legatine superiority, regulated the convocation. The clergy met according to the summons of the archbishops in St. Paul's, London; but the cardinal obliged them to adjourn their meeting to Westminster abbey,* where he explained to them the causes which required their attention and deliberation.

He expatiated on the obligations which the church lay under to the king, for suppressing the schism which was likely to have arisen in the days of Julius; but particularly for that excellent book which he had written in defence of the faith, and which they had all so becomingly declared to be inestimable. "Now," said the cardinal, "as he is engaged in a war with the French king, who has sent the duke of Albany into Scotland to invade England from that quarter, it is proper that his clergy should show the sincerity of their gratitude; and prove themselves sensible of the happiness of having such a sovereign, by granting him something, as much beyond all precedent, as they have affirmed that he has transcended all kings;" and he concluded by proposing, that they should engage to pay him yearly, for five years, a sum equal to the tenth part of their incomes. The opulent prelates of Rochester and Winchester opposed the motion. They represented it as an unheard-of extortion, which it was not possible for the clergy to pay and live. Wolsey, however, was not daunted. By practising the common modes of managing deliberative bodies, by corrupting some, and contriving occasions of absence for others, he secured a majority of votes, and, in the end, was victorious. All natives who held benefices were to pay ten per cent. and all foreigners twenty per cent. A few celebrated men were placed on a footing with the natives, among whom Erasmus and Polydore Virgil were mentioned with distinction. This is a singular fact, and proves the estimation in which the characters of those eminent authors were then held. But the general host of ecclesiastics regarded the conduct of the cardinal, on this occasion, as scarcely less tolerable than in the institution of his legatine court; and they were only content to pacify their indignation

* 8th May, 1523.

by obtaining an exemption of their means from secular investigation; an exemption which, having been stipulated, was,
probably, not originally intended to have been allowed.

In the parliament the cardinal was not so successful. The
members of that venerable body, obliged, by the rated valuation of their lands, to provide proportioned quantities of the
materials of war, in common with all the other lay proprietors,
and having no means of indemnity for their individual contributions, either in colonial or revenue offices, or contracts,
or army promotions, or any of those numerous modes of
recompensing themselves for their share of the public burdens,
by which, in later times, such miracles in finance have been
performed, were not so easily swayed by the energy of the
minister's eloquence. The commons chose Sir Thomas More
for their speaker.* When the customary ceremonies at the
opening of parliament were over, the cardinal, attended by
several of the peers and prelates, bearing a verbal message
from the king, entered the house, and addressed the speaker
on the expediency of granting supplies adequate to the vigorous
prosecution of the war. When he had retired, a long debate ensued, which terminated in a resolution to grant only
half the sum demanded. Wolsey, on hearing this, went a
second time to the house, and requested to hear the reasons
of those who opposed the motion. But the speaker informed
him, that it was the order of the house to hear, but not to
reason, except among themselves. The cardinal then repeated what he had before said on the subject, and endeavoured
to convince the members that what was required for the
public service, ought not to be considered as subtracted from
the wealth of the nation.† The war, however, being one of

* April 15, 1523. Sir Thomas More, on this occasion, when introduced
as speaker, addressed the king to the following effect. " I am both wanting
in wit, learning, and discretion, to speak before so great a prince. Phormio,
your majesty must well know, desired Hannibal to attend his lectures, which
he consented to. But, when Hannibal was come, Phormio began to treat
of chivalry; upon which he immediately called him a fool, for presuming to
teach him, who was master of the art of war. So, in like manner, if I should
speak before your majesty of learning, and ordering of the commonwealth,
your highness being so well warned, and of such prudence and experience,
might justly say to me as the great Hannibal said to Phormio."

† There is an anecdote told of the king on this occasion. Hearing that
the commons were likely to object altogether to the grant, he sent for one of

policy, and not in revenge for injury received, nor to avert any visible danger, the commons were resolute, and only granted about five per cent. on certain incomes for five years, instead of double that sum, as the minister had requested.*

But even the reduced grant was loudly complained of, and the people universally repined that their means and properties should be subject to the investigation of the collectors of the tax. Deputations from the merchants of London waited on the cardinal, and begged him to consider, for God's sake! that the richest merchants were often bare of money in war; and they entreated that they might not be sworn as to the value of their property, for the valuation was necessarily doubtful, and many an honest man's credit was better than his substance. "To make us swear," said they, "will expose us to commit perjury." "The dread of committing perjury," said Wolsey, calmly, "is, at least, a sign of grace; but you should give the king some proof of your loyalty. You see what costly armies are preparing for France and Scotland; and these he cannot maintain unless you give him assistance, and we know that you can afford to do it very well. On Saturday next I will, therefore, send a person to receive estimates of your means: and let such of you as have more credit than property, come privately to me, and I will take care that he shall not be injured." The merchants departed, muttering against the minister, who, as he had threatened, sent his secretary to St. Paul's, to receive the estimates of the citizens, without oaths.

During these transactions with the convocation, the par-liament, and the people, a remarkable event occurred, which

the members, Edward Montagu, the ancestor of the dukes of that name, and, maternally, of the present dukes of Marlborough and Buccleugh; and, upon his kneeling, exclaimed, "Ho! will they not suffer my bill to pass?" and, laying his hand on Montagu's head, added, "Get my bill passed to morrow; or else, to-morrow, this head of yours shall be off."

* The grant was two shillings in the pound on the income from estates of the annual value of twenty pounds and upwards; one shilling on the in-come of estates of the annual rent of forty shillings, and not exceeding twenty pounds; and a groat a head on every one upwards of sixteen years of age. It was, after the second visit of the cardinal, agreed that estates of fifty pounds rental, and upwards, should pay three shillings in the pound. This sum, like the grant of the clergy, was payable in five years, but not annually.

claimed the particular attention of Wolsey, and enabled him, as in the business of the income tax, to afford a precedent for future ministers in revolutionary times. The crown of Denmark was not then hereditary. The inheritance was limited to one family, but the son was not regularly the successor of the father.* The monarchy was elective, but it was requisite that the candidates should be of the royal family. The prerogative of election was also limited to a certain number of persons, and the heir was chosen during the lifetime of the king.† This form of constitution prevailed, anciently, over all the northern nations of Europe; nor was the law confined to crowns, but extended over all the inferior orders in the state of the gothic nations.‡ It preceded the law of tenures; and, when the feudal system was fallen into decay, some remains of it could be traced in the customs of tanestry, which, even in the time of queen Elizabeth, existed in those parts of Ireland to which that system had never been extended. Christiern II. who married the emperor's sister, Isabella, and niece to the queen of England, was, at this time, king of Denmark. During the life of his father, and while only seven years old, he had been elected to succeed to the crown. Whether this was considered by the electors as a favour which entitled them to impose new restrictions on the royal prerogatives, or that the old king, with a view of laying the foundations of a regular hereditary

* This accounts for the circumstance of Hamlet, in Shakspere's tragedy, not succeeding to his father. His uncle must have been chosen successor in the life-time of the father.

† The constitution of Sweden was, anciently, of the same description as that of Denmark, and Christiern had previously forfeited his right to the crown of Sweden also. The history of the revolutions in Sweden, ascribed to Vertot, commences by stating, that it continued an elective monarchy till about the middle of the fourteenth century. " For although," says the author, " the children and nearest relations of the deceased monarch were usually advanced to the throne, the order of birthright was sometimes neglected, and the succession was always determined by choice. By virtue of this right of election, the Swedes oftentimes claimed a power to depose their sovereigns, when they encroached upon the liberty and privileges of the nation. The royal authority was confined within very narrow limits; for the king could neither make war nor peace, and much less raise money or soldiers, without the consent of the senate, or of the estates assembled."

‡ See Pinkerton's Enquiry into the ancient History of Scotland. The Goths thought the line of blood more regular by the mothers than the fathers.

succession in his own family, had conceded that his son should be more limited in power than his predecessors, is of no importance to ascertain; but Christiern, after his accession, thought, as the restraints upon him were greater than customary on the kings of Denmark, and having been incurred without his consent, that he was not bound to abide by them. Instead, however, of resigning the crown, as he, therefore, ought to have done, he so acted that the electors were obliged to declare that he had violated the conditions on which he held it. In consequence, they proclaimed the throne vacant, and elected his uncle into the sovereignty.

Christiern left the country, with his family, and took refuge in the Netherlands, expecting, from the powerful relations of his wife, such assistance as might enable him to recover the throne. They afterwards came over to England, and were received by the court with the distinction due to them as the near relations of the queen. Upon his soliciting aid, however, the cardinal advised him to repair, without delay, to his patrimonial dominions, and try, by beneficial conduct, to recover the good opinion of the Danes, and a reconciliation with his enemies in Denmark. He assured him that Henry and Charles would use their best persuasion, both by letters and ministers, to the electors, the new king, and the influential lords of the realm, to procure his restoration; and that, out of the respect which Henry had for Isabella, his niece, he would, as an inducement, offer to guarantee to the Danish states the reformation of those abuses of which they complained, and for which they had deposed him. The cardinal also added, that the English residentiary at Rome should be immediately instructed to apply to the pope for his interposition, by briefs and exhortations, in order to accomplish the restoration. "But if these fair and equitable means fail of effect, then others shall be tried. For it is disreputable," said he, "to reason and good sense, that a prince should, by the wilfulness of his lords and commons, be expelled from his kingdom, without having first given an answer to a statement of their grievances." With these assurances, Christiern departed, and Wolsey immediately concerted the means for realizing the expectations that he had cherished; but, in the end, the cause was necessarily abandoned.

The Danish revolution not being followed with any effect on the affairs of Europe, with which Wolsey was particularly engaged, is chiefly remarkable on account of the insight which it affords to the cardinal's political notions. His expressions on the occasion are, indeed, so extraordinary, considering his situation, and the period in which he lived, that if he had not, under his own hand, furnished the record, they might justly be questioned, having never before been particularly noticed by any historian. In the reign of Henry VIII. the right of blood does not appear to have been considered as essential in the succession; for he was allowed to dispose of the crown by will, and actually excluded his eldest sister's heirs from the right of succeeding.* The English constitution, indeed, appears generally to have very distinctly recognised the supreme and ultimate authority of the people, and to have held the monarchs entitled to the throne only so long as they fulfilled their engagements. The opinion of Wolsey as to the obligation of kings, and the power of lords and commons, is now an acknowledged maxim, both in the theory and practice of the constitution.

While the preparations for the war were vigorously undertaken by Henry, Adrian, who had filled the papal throne with more innocence and less talent than either Julius or Leo, having ineffectually endeavoured to reconcile the belligerent potentates, was induced to break from the neutrality which he had assumed at his election, and to become a member of the confederacy against Francis. But he had not long done this, when he fell sick and died.† The cardinal, on being informed, immediately wrote to the king, who was then on one of his country excursions, and solicited his assistance, and also his influence with the emperor, to procure the papacy. In the event of Wolsey not succeeding, the English government were desirous that Giulio di Medici should be preferred; and, from the sequel, it appears that a reciprocity of advantage had been previously concerted between the rivals, in the event of either being elected.

---

* There is a singular pamphlet written by one Ed. Davies, for the express purpose of proving that Henry VIII. was an example of a patriot king. The author does not attribute the conduct of the monarch to personal feelings, but to public principles.

† 14th Sept. 1523.

The cardinals at Rome, after spending fifty days in the conclave, were not likely to come to any decision; so that the Holy Ghost was again obliged to interfere, and the election, of course, was unanimous. Giulio was chosen, and assumed the title of Clement VII. It has been, almost uniformly, since alleged, that Charles had particularly engaged to use his utmost influence to promote Wolsey to the apostolical dignity; but there is no allusion to any such engagement in their correspondence on that subject. The previous understanding, however, between Giulio and Wolsey, is less equivocal; for as soon as possible after his election, the pope appointed the cardinal legate for life, and conferred on him all the papal pretensions over England which he could alienate; sanctioning, in every other respect, the measures which he had adopted for the reformation of the clergy within his jurisdiction. The character of Clement for talent stood high in the world. During the pontificate of his kinsman Leo, he had been intrusted with the chief administration of the papal affairs, and had acquired the reputation of being ambitious and innovating, which raised at his election a general expectation of great changes. The world, however, was mistaken: many of the measures which had been attributed to him, were suggested by the more capacious, but indolent, Leo. He was, in fact, but an ordinary man, in whom the constitutional qualities of gravity, temperance, and assiduity, were more remarkable than the faculties which originate and direct superior speculations.

About the period of Adrian's death, the duke of Bourbon, high constable of France, declared himself in rebellion against his king. Private animosities had long rendered him adverse to Francis; and the English and imperial cabinets, aware of his disposition, incited him to the decisive step which he took at this time. The price which they at first offered for his treachery had been rejected; but an accumulation of petty circumstances enhanced his resentment, and the terms being made more acceptable, he was induced to enter into the service of Charles. Bourbon was a plain and gallant soldier; his enmity to Francis arose from the frankness of his nature, and the want of that dissimulation which, while it degrades the man, rarely fails to exalt the courtier. In the outline of his talents he resembled Surrey, then the hero of England; but, with all the qualities which recommended him to the affections of his companions in danger, Bourbon was deficient in self-control. The principles of loyalty were, in that age, weak among military men, and renown in arms was a higher aim than patriotism. Though Bourbon must ever be regarded as a traitor to his country, his crime, in the opinion of his contemporaries, admitted of a liberal construction.

BOOK IV.

Agitated state of the public mind—Failure of the campaign against France—
Ravages of Surrey in Scotland—Clement VII. refuses to accede to the
league of Calais—The imperialists rescue Milan—Operations of Bourbon in Provence—The French recover Milan, and invest Pavia—Wolsey's view of the state of Europe—Secret mission to him from Louisa,
regent of France—Conduct of the imperial minister—Embassy of France
to England—The negotiation frustrated—The Venetians propose a league
to the pope, which he declines—Henry determines to invade France—
Suspends his purpose—Measures of the cardinal—Francis conveyed
prisoner to Spain—Preparations for war in England—Ambassadors sent
to Charles—Peace proclaimed—Treaty of Madrid—Exchange of Francis
for his sons—Distracted state of Italy—War in Hungary—Successes
of Solyman—Capture of Rome—Measures of Henry against Charles in
consequence of this event—Wolsey sent ambassador to Francis—Proceeds to France—His address to his household at Calais—Meeting with
Francis—Removal of the court to Compeigne—Three treaties concluded
—Importance of the third treaty—Charles orders the pope to be set at
liberty—Heralds from France and England demand and obtain audience
of the emperor—His replies—Discontents of the people at the prospect
of a new war—Wolsey now at the meridian of his fortune—His income
equal to the royal revenues—Magnificence of his house—Splendid
entertainment given by him at Hampton-court to the French commissioners.

THE administration of Wolsey presents now a various and
busy scene. The principal characters have been introduced;
and the secret movements and circumstances which, in the
end, conspired to hasten the catastrophe, have all been un-
folded. The narrative of future transactions will therefore
proceed rapidly; and in the detail of the military events, only
those incidents shall be noticed which serve to illustrate the
state of society, and the peculiarities of individuals. The
active operations in the field, and the eager controversies of

the Reformation, excited the public mind to an impassioned degree, and the imaginations of men were infected with fearful predictions. Astrologers denounced deluges and devastations; but the deluges were the blood of mankind, and the devastations proceeded from the sword.*

In the autumn of 1523, the duke of Suffolk was appointed to the command of an army sent to invade France, and joined the count de Bure, in Picardy.† Francis was at Lyons, on his way to Italy, when informed of the invasion, which, by the junction of the English and imperialists, was more formidable than he had previously reason to expect. The allies, leaving the fortified towns unassailed, marched directly towards Paris. The whole kingdom was astonished. All the troops hurried to the capital. The recruits, then ascending the Alps, threw aside the hopes of their enterprise, and hastily returned to protect their homes: but a premature winter proved more efficient than preparations dictated by consternation and fear. The allies were compelled to halt ; their provisions became exhausted, and the cold was so intense that no creature could withstand its severity. Wolsey, however, was desirous that the troops should still keep the field, and, by the practice of an evasive warfare, deter Francis from reinforcing his army in Italy. But the privations of the ill-provided imperialists were so extreme, that the officers consented that the soldiers should disband themselves; and Suffolk, in consequence, sending his men into winter quarters, returned to England without having accomplished any other object than suspending the march of the reinforcements destined to strengthen the French army in Italy. The miserable and helpless condition of the imperial troops made a deep impression on the mind of the cardinal; and he expressed himself on the failure of the campaign as if he thought the emperor undervalued the exertions of England, or calculated on supporting his army at her expense.

The earl of Surrey had been ordered from the fleet, and sent to command the troops on the borders of Scotland. The

---

* Many provident persons ascended to high places, and watched with anxious awe for the second flood. The abbot of St. Bartholomew's, in Smithfield, built a house at Harrow-on-the-Hill, for the retreat of himself and brethren.

† 20th Sept. 1523.

records of his operations present an awful picture of that unsparing desolation which so long spread a lonely barrier of
heaths and moors between the habitable tracts of the sister
kingdoms. During the summer, he ravaged all the Merse
and the dale of Tweed, leaving neither castle, village, tree,
cattle, nor corn. The inhabitants abandoned the country
to the marauders: some fled into England in the most calamitous state of distress. The bread which they craved,
instead of repairing their strength, was devoured with such
rapacious hunger, that it only hastened their death. Among
other places that suffered severely, Jedburg, then much larger
than Berwick, was taken, and the fortifications thrown down.
On the night of the sack, a party of the English horses, lying
in or without the camp, were seized with some unaccountable
panic, and ran about in all directions. The soldiers started
to arms. The flames of the burning town threw a wild and
troubled light on the tumult. The imaginations of the men
were filled with superstitious fears; and Surrey, in giving an
account of the affair to Wolsey, says, that seven times that
night spirits and terrible sights were visible.*

Clement, after his election, refused to accede to the league
of Calais, and declared his intention of remaining neuter in
the quarrels between Charles and Francis. At this time
Bourbon commanded the imperial army in Italy. The
emperor, designing to draw supplies from the Italian powers,
with whom he was allied, as he did from England in the
campaign in Picardy, left Bourbon and the troops without
money. This sordid craft obliged the general to levy a contribution on the inhabitants of Milan, which, with other
money that he secretly persuaded the pope and Florentines
to lend, enabled him to take the field in the spring of 1524,
with about five and thirty thousand men. The French army
was as much impoverished as the imperial; a band of the
mercenary Swiss, finding they were not likely to be paid,
having deserted, the French general resolved to repass the

* The expense of the operations in France and Scotland drained the exchequer, and the cardinal was obliged to call for a premature advance of
part of the subsidy, which had been granted by the convocation and parliament. The sum which he thus required was called an anticipation. As
the term had hitherto been unknown in the language, and the war was unpopular, the people thought they paid too dear for learning it.

mountains. Hearing of his retreat, Bourbon pursued. Between the imperial van and the rear of the fugitives, several interesting skirmishes took place, but the French crossed the Alps without coming to a general battle. The Milanese towns, however, in which they had left garrisons, readily surrendered to the imperialists.

The duchy of Milan being thus rescued, Charles refused to invest Francisco Sforza with the dukedom, although he had previously acknowledged his claim. This, with other manifestations of a grasping nature, inspired the pope with apprehension, and he suspected that the emperor meditated against Italy the same designs which Francis had been compelled to relinquish. The papal nuncio at the court of London was, in consequence, instructed to attempt the reconciliation of France and England. But Henry, at this period, cherished the hope of giving substantial validity to his title of king of France; and Wolsey did not consider the presumptuous nation yet sufficiently humbled. The papal mediation, therefore, failed, and new arrangements were concerted with Charles for the vigorous prosecution of the war. Calculating on success, they resolved that Provence and Dauphiné should be erected into a kingdom for the duke of Bourbon, who was to hold it in fee of Henry, and that the other provinces should be restored to the English crown, with the exception of Burgundy, which was to be appropriated to Charles. The emperor engaged to furnish a powerful army to reduce Provence ; and to the maintenance of this force, England agreed to contribute a hundred thousand crowns monthly, unless the king himself invaded France with his own troops in person.

Bourbon, continuing to prosecute his successful pursuit, entered Provence, took possession of Aix, and laid siege to Marseilles. The garrison, being previously reinforced, gallantly resisted; and Francis, advancing rapidly, raised the siege. It was now the end of autumn, and the imperialists, in turn retreating, the French followed to recover Milan. Bourbon, aware of the design of Francis, made surprising exertions. Having reinforced Pavia, and taken all the precautionary measures which the hurry of retreat permitted, he continued to retire upon Italy. The French, soon masters of the town of Milan, proceeded to invest Pavia. Francis, deficient in military genius, forgot that success in war, as in all human undertakings, depends upon the undivided application of means; and occupied his attention with objects that ought only to have been contingent. He detached a large body of troops towards Naples, by which the strength of his army before Pavia was essentially reduced; but as it was still superior in number to the garrison, he continued the siege.

The condition of the Scottish government at the close of the year 1524, and during these motions in Italy, was truly deplorable. Faction violated patriotism; and the nation seemed devoted for so easy a prey to her neighbour, that it is difficult to account for the forbearance of the English government, at this time, upon any other principle, than that Henry regarded Scotland rather as the private estate of his sister's family, than as the rival of England. A kind of domestic interest pervades the public correspondence of the two courts, and this intimacy and affection promised to become closer, by a proposition from the Scots to unite their young king, James V., to his cousin Mary, the English heiress. Charles, alarmed when he heard of the matrimonial proposal from Scotland, although secretly negotiating a marriage for himself with the princess of Portugal, sent ambassadors to London, in order to request that Mary might be delivered to him, according to the terms of the treaty, by which they were regarded as affianced. His affairs at this time were far from prosperous in Italy; and Solyman, the sultan, obtaining possession of Belgrade, menaced Hungary, and seemed to be rapidly opening a passage into the very bosom of Christendom. It was also reported that the pope had allied himself with the French king, so that at this period the emperor, when he regarded the situation of his affairs in Italy, and the ambition of the Turks, had reason to be anxious to preserve his alliance with Henry entire. Nor were the politics of England less unclouded. The conduct of the emperor had not been satisfactory. The Spaniards, eloquent in words, were dilatory in action; and the cardinal, in his correspondence, could not disguise his contemptuous opinion of their sober and dribbling wars. The behaviour of the pope was greatly suspicious. It was rumoured that the republic of Florence, and the Tuscan territory, were to be converted into a kingdom for the Medici, and to be called Etruria. The minds of men were agitated

G 2

with polemical controversies ; all was obscure, ominous, and perplexed.

At this epoch, Wolsey made a masterly view of the moral and political state of Europe, which he requested the English minister at Rome to lay before the pope. He represented, in strong terms, the evils that must inevitably ensue to Christendom, if his holiness, while the opinions of Luther infected every country, studied, as was reported, only the selfish aggrandizement of his own family and kindred. He set forth the example of disinterestedness which the English king had shown to all princes, in suspending his private rights and pretensions to France, in order to promote the general welfare of the Christian world. He pointed out the confidence which had been given to his holiness; and the expectation cherished, that his pontificate would prove renowned, by the removal of abuses, and the renovation of the papal dignity, which had been so visibly stricken by the wrath of Almighty God, since the heads of the church had become parties in the projects of secular princes. He warned his holiness not to offend the emperor, in whose dominions the Lutheran heresies were so rife; and expatiated on the damage and detriment which the papacy must suffer, if the French king succeeded in his notorious designs; for not only the imperial dominions, but also England, and, in the end, possibly even France herself, might renounce the apostolical authority, to the everlasting shame and dishonour of Clement.

The part which Henry had taken in the wars was exceedingly disagreeable to his own subjects. They murmured at the requisite taxes, and that Bourbon, a Frenchman, should be, in some measure, employed by their king; nor could they conceive in what manner the interests of England were to be promoted, either by the subjugation or the rescue of Italy, a remote country. The conduct of Charles also dissatisfied the merchants. His cruizers molested their vessels; and he had raised the price of English money in his dominions, by which the value of their commodities was depreciated. The king himself began to be dubious of the emperor's integrity; and the whole tenour of the cardinal's correspondence, at this period, indicates distrust, while he suggests many expedients for bringing the war to a speedy conclusion. Louisa, the mother of Francis, having been appointed regent of France during the absence of her son, being apprised of the altered disposition of the English cabinet, sent a monk* secretly to Wolsey, to ascertain how far an offer of peace was likely to prove acceptable. But the monk being unauthorized to propose any basis of negotiation, the cardinal said, shortly, that if the French government was sincere in its desire for peace, it should deal more frankly, and send persons of more consequence and with fuller credentials, to Charles, as well as to Henry. The monk begged to be informed, what the king of England might demand for his part. "The whole realm and crown of France," said the cardinal, "with Normandy, Gascoigne, Guienne, and other dependencies, his rightful patrimony, so long withheld by the French kings. What have you to say that he should not have all his claims?" The monk answered, that he was not instructed to speak on such matters, but he would relate to the regent what had passed, and he thought she would send ambassadors, properly accredited, both to the emperor and to the king of England. Although this interview lasted only about half an hour, and the monk, immediately after, was conveyed out of the kingdom, it was not so secret but that some notion of its purport spread abroad, and, like all other rumours, received various additions, and underwent several transformations, in the course of repeating.

The imperial minister, De Praet, a man who scrupled not to aggrandise the reputation of his abilities at the expense of others, and of truth, had frequently, in communicating to his master the details of his transactions with the cardinal, represented, as the results of his own address and skill, those measures in the war which were suggested and planned within the English cabinet. Wolsey was informed of this diplomatic artifice, and marked, by his contemptuous manner, how much he despised the man. The ambassador was irritated by this treatment, and vindictively misrepresented to his government the conduct of the cardinal, and particularly with respect to the mission of the monk; of which, instead of sending a fair statement of the facts, he transmitted a garbled account of the popular rumour; but the clandestine manner

* Giovanni Gioachino Passano, a Genoese; afterwards called Seigneur de Vaux.

which he took to send these perfidious dispatches led to the exposure of his despicable character.

One evening, soon after the French emissary had been with the cardinal, a ward and watch of citizens, as was then frequently the custom, happened to be held in the city and environs of London. About midnight, a man on horseback was seized by one of the patrol, on the road to Brentford; and being questioned as to his journey, he answered so equivocally, that he was carried to the guard-house, where he was searched, and the imperial minister's dispatches were found concealed in his clothes. The watchmen, unable to read the address of the packet, carried it to an attorney's clerk, who belonged to their party, and the seal being broken, he found that it contained letters written in cipher. The clerk gave it to the king's solicitor, who was also on guard that night. He, conceiving that the letters must, necessarily, be of importance, delivered them to Sir Thomas More, who lived at Chelsea, and belonged to another company of the nightly watch. Next morning Sir Thomas gave them to the cardinal in the court of chancery. Wolsey, it would appear, was acquainted with the imperial ciphers; for, on looking into the letters, he perceived that others, of a similar tenour, had been sent in the course of the preceding day. He therefore ordered all the packets of the imperial minister to be stopped, and brought to him: and he commanded the ambassador to confine himself to his house, transmitting, along with the disreputable writings, a circumstantial account of the real transactions of the English government, to be laid before the emperor, in order to show how much his confidence had been misplaced; and to warn him of the danger that might ensue to the mutual amity of the two courts, by employing such unprincipled and mischievous men.

In consequence of what had passed between the monk and the cardinal, the regency of France sent a public embassy to open a negotiation; but, before they had presented their credentials, tidings arrived in London of the defeat and captivity of their king at Pavia, an event which filled all Europe with consternation. The French garrisons in Italy abandoned their posts. The troops, spared from the battle, fled in amazement. The often-contested duchy of Milan was restored to the imperialists. The Italian states, seeing the emperor thus in the possession of his rival, and apprehending, by his conduct to Francesco Sforza, that he was infected with the ambition of being sole monarch, prepared to confederate for mutual defence. The Venetians proposed a league to the pope; but Clement, dreading to incur the vengeance of the imperial arms, refused their offer. The maritime state, however, with a courage worthy of freedom, determined to hazard all, rather than incur the consequences of seeing the house of Austria without a rival. In London, the destruction of the French army, and the captivity of the French king, afforded at first the liveliest pleasure. Henry boasted of his intention to proceed directly to France; and the people exulted in the idea of seeing the projects of the Edwards and their fifth Harry realised.

But the preparations ordered for the invasion were scarcely commenced, when messages came, from all parts, that gave such a description of the arrogance of the imperialists, and the conduct of the emperor, in attempting to appropriate entirely to himself all the fruits of the victory, that the king suspended his purpose. He was convinced that the balance of power was overthrown; that it was barely possible for him to maintain the proud eminence on which he had hitherto stood; and that the events which he thought so favourable to the accomplishment of his wishes, menaced him, in fact, with a more subordinate fortune than the kings of England had ever known. It is seldom that any man can sway the current of national affairs; but a wide and earnest system of action never fails to produce results which resemble the pre-expected effects of particular designs. The cardinal, in conjunction with the Italian states, promptly adopted a course of policy which had for its object the restoration of the balance of power. The imperial ambassador was therefore permitted to quit his confinement, and to leave the kingdom; while it was secretly intimated to the court of Paris, that the king of England had determined not to avail himself of the unfortunate and defenceless state of France.

The first intelligence of the defeat at Pavia filled the French nation with despair and sorrow. The people imagined and expected every calamity which fear could suggest and adversity render probable. They bewailed the captivity of their king—their nobles also prisoners, or slain in the battle—and they deemed their misfortunes irreparable. The realm was exhausted of treasure; environed with mighty armies; and the noise of the terrible preparations of the English king resounded continually in their ears. The government was in the hands of a woman; the princes were still children; and the soldiers were destitute of leaders:—all seemed combined to denote their subjugation. But the mother of Francis possessed a firm and majestic mind. Though his letters informed her that all was lost, but life and honour, she exerted her spirit in the midst of the general consternation, and roused the ministers to perform their duty.

Francis was conveyed in his own gallies to Spain; and his voyage was cheered by the hope that, when brought into the presence of Charles, he should easily negotiate his freedom; at least, that his treatment would resemble the magnanimous entertainment which his ancestor had received at the court of England in the time of Edward III. The emperor did indeed give orders to receive him with the courtesy due to his rank; but this generosity was of short duration. Francis had not been long upon the Spanish territory when he was conveyed a close prisoner to the castle of Madrid, allowed no honourable pastime, and deprived of the expectation of seeing Charles. The keen sense of indignity, disappointment, and misfortune, pressed upon his mind, and reduced him to such a low, despondent state, that the physicians despaired of his recovery, unless the emperor would have the humanity to visit him with some assurance of freedom. Charles had received the news of the victory of Pavia with Tiberian hypocrisy. He forbade among his subjects all demonstrations of joy, and affected to be impressed with sentiments which were not natural, nor such as he could feel. The peculiar malady of Francis disconcerted his craftiness. He had not decided in what manner to act; and the death of the captive would render the victory comparatively fruitless. But he was admonished, that he could not comply with the suggestions of the physicians without setting Francis free, or without incurring the disgraceful imputation of having desired the preservation of his life only to satisfy his own avarice. Sovereigns are not bound by the predilections of men; but it is an essential part of their duty to ennoble the topics of human admiration by the grandeur of their generosity. Charles, however, though at this period only in the twenty-fifth year of his age, had survived the disinterestedness of youth, and despised the unprofitable heroism of chivalry. He visited Francis; seated himself, with unfelt kindness, beside his couch; and, by the practice of fraudulent compassion, renovated the hope and life that were on the point of expiring.

The system of preparation which was formed in England for the vigorous prosecution of the war, and which Henry, on receiving the news of Francis's defeat, had exultingly ordered to be directed against France, were continued, in order to provide for the consequences which were apprehended from the conduct of the emperor. But the expense had already greatly exceeded the sums voted by the convocation and parliament: in consequence, it was resolved to levy an extraordinary contribution,* under the name of a benevolence. Commissions were accordingly issued to all the shires, requiring the sixth part of every layman's, and the fourth part of every churchman's, plate and coin, to be delivered for the king's use. The rage which the publication of this exorbitant stretch of prerogative excited against the king and the cardinal, made it soon evident that the expedient could not succeed. On this occasion the citizens of London were again conspicuously reluctant. Several public meetings of the members of the corporation were held, with-

* There seems reason to think, but I have not ascertained distinctly the fact, that this contribution had reference to the grant of the parliament and convocation, and was founded on them. For among Masters's MS. collection in the library of Jesus college, Oxford, I met with the following note: " 1525. The dukes of Norfolk and Suffolk write to the cardinal, that the commons lay all the blame on him ; and that, if any insurrection follow, the quarrel shall be only against him. The cardinal writes to the same, that it is the custom of the people, when anything miscontents them, to blame those that be near about the king ; and, when they dare not use their tongues against their sovereign, they, for venting their malice, will not fail to give evil language against the council. . . . . . It seems this amicable grant was a modification of a greater grant, which the commons first condescended to, and after got it part reduced."

Henry VII., in the year 1489, obtained a similar kind of grant from parliament. " Which kind of levying money was first devised by king Edward the fourth. King Henry, following the like example, published abroad, that by their open gifts he would measure and search their benevolent hearts and good minds towards him, so that he that gave most should be judged to be his most loving friend ; and he that gave little to be esteemed according to his gift."—Holinshed, fol. 771.

out coming to any decision. Wolsey became impatient. He
sent for the mayor and aldermen, and demanded if they really
meant to execute their commission? because if they did not,
he would himself claim the benevolence. A counsellor, whom
the magistrates had brought with them, observed that, by a
statute of king Richard III., benevolences could not be
exacted. "Your grace," said he, "may, no doubt, obtain
something from individuals; but it will either be by the dread
of your power, or the hope of your favour." The cardinal
replied, that he was surprised to hear any precedent alleged
from the usurpation of Richard. "But, my lord," said this
firm and intrepid citizen, "many of his laws are excellent;*
and they were all sanctioned by parliament, which exercises
the authority of the whole realm." In the deliberations of
the common council of the city, it had, prior to this meeting,
been resolved that the aldermen should severally apply to
the respective wards for the benevolence; the lord mayor,
therefore, hearing that benevolences were contrary to law,
and observing the cardinal tacitly assenting to the truth of
the counsellor's remark, fell on his knees, and entreated that
the resolution, since it appeared to be illegal, might be re-
scinded. "I am content so far," said Wolsey, "but what
will you and the aldermen here give?" "Pardon me, my
lord," answered the mayor, "were I to promise, personally, any
grant, it might cost me my life;" alluding to the indignation
it might occasion in the city. "Your life!" observed the cardinal, "that is, truly, a marvellous fine word for your loyalty!
Will the citizens put it in jeopardy? If they dare to do so,

---

* The English nation is indebted for its best laws to the frequent usurpations of those who attained the throne to the prejudice of the lineal heirs.
The laws of William I. and II. regulate the descent, and define the rights, of
territorial property to this day. The basis of Magna Charta was laid in the
concessions with which Henry I. conciliated the people to his usurpation of
the rights of his elder brother. John, who murdered the heir to the crown,
granted the Magna Charta. Henry IV., who deposed Richard II., endeavoured to reduce the exorbitant cormorants of the church. Richard III.
abolished the prerogative of applying directly to the people for money. In
Oliver Cromwell's time, the principles of the navigation laws were first
established. The faction who accomplished the revolution of 1688 procured, by William and Mary, the establishment of protestantism. And the
bringing in of the Hanoverian family defined the privileges of the king
more explicitly than they had ever been before. Nations are the better now
and then for having an usurper.

they shall certainly feel the king's power. My lord mayor, let you and your citizens, if you be displeased with anything in this demand, respectfully, and in a proper manner, come to me, and I will endeavour to procure you satisfaction. In the mean time, collect the money, and place it where you think it may be safe, that, if the king shall not happen to need it for the war, it may be returned to the contributors."* From the tenour of this conversation, it is evident that the cardinal was apprized of the difficulty of his situation with the people; and also, that there was some indisposition, the effect of the emperor's policy, in the government to prosecute the war.

The murmurs in the metropolis were trifling, compared to the vehement discontent which prevailed in other parts of the kingdom. Some of the commissioners were intimidated from their duty, and others exasperated the people by intolerable insolence. The duke of Suffolk had, in his county, succeeded in persuading many of the wealthy manufacturers to comply with the wishes of government; but when they returned to their homes, crowds assembled, and riotously attacked them. The duke ordered, in consequence, the constables to seize all the warlike weapons in private houses, which enraged the multitude still more. The alarm bells were rung, and about four thousand men appeared in arms, threatening with death all the abettors of the benevolence. Suffolk hastily summoned the gentlemen of the county, ordered the bridges to be broken, and requested Surrey, who, by the death of his father, was now duke of Norfolk, to come to his assistance. As the restoration of tranquillity, rather than punishment, was the object, Norfolk, on his arrival, rode up to the insurgents, and with that manly affability which is always found connected with great talents of every kind, and which constitutes one of the chief ingredients of a general's character, he endeavoured to pacify their anger, and advised them to retire. " Poverty and necessity," they exclaimed, " have incited and led us on, and without redress, as we can but die, we will not disperse." He entreated them still to return quietly to their homes and callings, and assured them that Suffolk and himself would speak in their behalf to

* Lord Herbert, 162.

the king. At length the ringleaders surrendered, and were taken to London; and the rest, in token of repentance, went with halters round their necks to the abbey of St. Edmund, and having done this penance, peacefully dispersed. The rumour of these discontents and insurrections had in the meanwhile alarmed the king, who, having ordered the privy councillors to meet in the cardinal's palace, indignantly addressed them to the following effect: " By whose authority have the commissions for the benevolence been so rigidly enforced? It was not my intention to ask anything contrary to law; I must therefore be informed by whose advice this grievance has been committed." Each of the counsellors endeavoured to exculpate himself, but Wolsey answered, " That when it was deliberated in what manner the money for the public exigencies should be levied, the whole council and the judges of the land agreed that any benevolence might be sought by commission. For myself, I take God to witness that I never desired to oppress the people; but since every man lays the blame from him, I will take it on myself, and answer to the clamour of the nation!" There was so much honest magnanimity in this speech, that it appears to have sensibly affected the king, who immediately said— " Some of you did tell me that England was never before so opulent, that no trouble would arise from this demand, and that every man would freely give at my requesting. The truth, I see, is otherwise, and therefore there shall be no more of this vexation. Let letters instantly be sent to the shires, to stop this unhappy business." Letters were sent accordingly, in which it was declared that the cardinal had authorized the commissions, sanctioned by the opinion of the judges, and the general sentiment of the king's council; and that at his intercession they were again recalled. The leaders of the Suffolk insurrection, after this, were taken from prison to the Star Chamber, where the cardinal, presiding, rebuked them sharply for their offence. He placed before their imaginations the havoc and ruin that they might have entailed on themselves and others; " but his majesty," said he, " notwithstanding the greatness of the crime, is pleased to pardon, provided that securities are found for future good behaviour." The prisoners answered that they had no sureties to offer. " Indeed!" replied the cardinal; " then my lord of Norfolk here will be one for you, and as you are my countrymen, I will be the other." And they were dismissed from the bar, and returned cheerfully home. Thus terminated a series of transactions which might have filled the nation with calamities, and thus a rebellion was quelled, without bloodshed in the field, or that wasteful retribution which the judicature on such occasions is too strongly prone to exercise.

In order to ascertain how far Charles actually entertained those ambitious and unjust designs which the Italian states conceived they had reason to fear, ambassadors were sent from London to demand from him an immediate fulfilment of the terms of his different treaties with Henry. They were instructed to urge, that as the war had been made at the common expense of the two monarchs, their sovereign should participate in the fruits of the battle of Pavia; and therefore, in treating with Francis, it ought to be stipulated that those provinces of France which were considered as the rightful inheritance of the English kings, should be restored to Henry. If this could not be obtained by negotiation, then Charles should invade France from the Spanish frontiers, while Henry entered by the way of Picardy; and that both should continue the war until the king was satisfied. As it was agreed in the treaty of Windsor that each should deliver up to each other all the usurpers of their respective rights, it was required, that on the same day in which the princess Mary, the bride betrothed of the emperor, was consigned to his ministers, the French king should be delivered to English officers. The ambassadors were also instructed to say, that the emperor ought the more readily to comply with their king's wishes in these things, for, being contracted to the heiress of his crown, all the advantages would in the end devolve on himself. The validity of these requisitions Charles could not dispute; but it was evident, from their extent, that they constituted only a diplomatic stratagem, by which the obloquy of failing in the engagements would fall upon him. To the application of the ministers he returned a general, and of course an unsatisfactory answer.

Meanwhile, ambassadors came from Paris, and were received with great distinction and much compassion by Henry. In their interview with Wolsey they were, however, treated more according to the deserts of their government.* He represented to them how perfidious the conduct of France had been; how unsteady to her engagements; and, but for the gracious intentions of his master, how abject she must become. They replied, with the characteristic humility of Frenchmen in distress, "If we have offended, surely you have punished us severely. Our towns have been sacked, our people slain, our country desolated, and brought low in misery, we sue for peace." With ambassadors so humble it was not difficult to negotiate; but the design of the cardinal was not to reduce France, but to restore the equilibrium of Europe, the great purpose and aim of all his political undertakings. The treaty concluded, in consequence, was singularly generous. It was, in fact, a defensive league between the two nations. Henry engaged to procure the deliverance of Francis; two millions of crowns, payable in twenty years, by annual instalments, were accepted for the debts and tribute due from France to England; and a bond for a hundred thousand crowns was given to Wolsey, in consideration of the arrears of the pension due to him for the bishopric of Tournay, and the loss that he might incur by a rupture with the emperor, as he held at this time the bishoprics of Placentia and Badajos, in Spain, besides a pension from Charles himself. The arrears due to the king's sister, the dowager of France, were also to be paid, and her jointure to be regularly continued. The regency of France further engaged that Albany should not return to Scotland during the remainder of the minority of James V.† The treaty arranged was duly ratified by the king,‡ and peace was proclaimed, in terms flattering to the national pride.

---

* Holinshed, 887.

† The circumstance of a bond being given to the cardinal for so large a sum as a hundred thousand crowns, has been held as a proof of his corruption. But when the amount of the arrears of his pension is considered, and the revenues which he derived from Spain, and which there was every probability, at that time, would be arrested, there will be no reason for this opinion. Besides this, it was the practice of the age, on the occasion of concluding treaties, to give large presents, and often benefices, to the ministers, who were commonly ecclesiastics. Cardinal Campeggio got from Henry VII. the bishopric of Salisbury, and the king's agent at Rome, cardinal Adrian, was bishop of Bath.

‡ At Moor, in Hertfordshire, 30 August, 1525. The terms in which the

The effects of this treaty renovated the spirit of the French nation. The Italian states acquired additional confidence in the measures which they had adopted, to prevent the aggressions of the imperialists; and England maintained herself more firmly than ever, on the lofty eminence on which she stood among the nations of Europe. Charles, alarmed by the extent of the confederacy that was rising against him, and by the progress of the Turks in Hungary, hastily concluded, contrary to the advice of his ministers, the treaty of Madrid with Francis. The first article in the execution of this impolitic engagement was, the exchange of the French king, which ought, certainly, to have been the last, as the terms were such as the French nation was not likely, willingly, to fulfil; although the children of the king were to be delivered as hostages.

The dauphin and the duke of Orleans, on the day appointed for the exchange, were brought to Bayonne, by the regent, their grandmother, and the officers of state. Francis was at the same time conveyed to Fuenterabia, a small town on the sea-coast, between the province of Biscay and the duchy of Guienne. Accompanied by two persons of high rank, and surrounded by cavalry, he was conducted to the river which separates the frontiers of France and Spain. The princes of France, with their attendants, arrived at the same time on the opposite side. The banks were crowded with spectators. In the middle of the stream lay a vessel at anchor. No person was permitted to be on board. Francis, with the two imperial officers, and eight men, armed with short weapons, entered a barge, and were rowed towards the vessel. At the same moment his children, similarly attended, also embarked. The spectators were silent. The boats reached the vessel. The king and the princes were put aboard. The children

previous truce was proclaimed are singular, and perhaps without precedent. " Forasmuch as the lady regent of France, mother unto the French king, by consent of the princes and peers of the seignorial, and others of the council of the same, hath on the behalf of the French king, and of the three estates of the realm of France, sent unto the king's highness honourable ambassadors, sufficiently authorized to sue, require, and labour for peace ; and the same, under honourable conditions and offers, to conclude with the king's highness, if it so shall stand with his gracious pleasure," &c. &c. Harleian Collection, No. 442, No. 27, page 55. 15 August, 1525.

passed across the deck without speaking to the boat which
their father had quitted.* He looked at them; sighed deeply;
hastily sprung into theirs, and was rapidly conveyed to his
own kingdom, and welcomed with shouts and acclamations by
his soldiers and subjects. An Arabian horse, provided for
the purpose, stood ready caparisoned on the strand. Francis
vaulted into the saddle, and exultingly exclaimed, as he
galloped away: " I am again a king!"†

As all Europe expected, Francis was not long in convincing
Charles that the treaty of Madrid was never intended to be
fulfilled. The resolution taken, pretexts for delay were easily
found; and no opportunity was lost by which the French
thought they could reduce the ransom of their princes. The
emperor, enraged, insisted upon the terms of the treaty; but,
in the meantime, Solyman, the sultan, was advancing upon
Hungary. Italy was full of uproar and war. England
alone, of all the Christian nations, enjoyed, in her insular protection, the blessings of peace. In the invasion of Hungary,
Lewis, the king, was killed, while flying from the Turks,
after a defeat as fatal as the battle of Flodden had been to
Scotland. Ferdinand, the brother of Charles, in right of his
wife, sister to Lewis, succeeded to the throne, and a truce
was concluded with Solyman. But John Lepuse, governor
of Transylvania, pretending that the majority of the Hunga-
rian nobles had chosen him for their king, complained to
several of the Christian princes of Ferdinand's usurpation.
Solyman, foreseeing the confusion that would arise from this
rivalry, prepared to renew the invasion. Ferdinand, fearful
of the consequences, sent ambassadors to England, and im-
plored the assistance of Henry his uncle. But as the English
government attributed the progress which the sultan had been
allowed to make, wholly to the ambitious warfare which the
emperor still continued to wage, the embassy proved abortive.
The ministers were told, that as the brother of their master
would not agree to any reasonable terms of accommodation
with Francis, the princes of Christendom could not unite
against the infidels, and that Solyman must of course prevail.

* Lord Herbert says, they kissed their father's hand; page 184.
† Holinshed says, that the exchange took place on the 18th March, 1526;
but the bonds and letters of thanks and gratitude to the king and cardinal
of England were dated at Bayonne on the 17th.

It could not, indeed, be expected, that while Charles pursued only his own schemes of aggrandizement, to the manifest destruction of the balance of power, that England, protectress of the balance, would virtually abet his designs in Italy, by assisting Ferdinand.

But before any decisive measure had come to maturity for the restoration of the French princes, an event happened in Italy still more alarming to all Christendom than the battle of Pavia. Clement, who, after that battle, had declined to unite with the Venetians, finding his hope of making better terms for himself frustrated, had, at length, joined them and the other Italian states in a league which was called by his name, and of which the king of England had been declared the protector. Bourbon, in consequence, resolved to seize the city of Rome, not only to punish the pope, but to indemnify his troops for the hardships and privations which they had long suffered. Leaving unmolested the army which the leaguers had collected in Tuscany, he marched directly to the metropolis; and encamping on the meadows, near the Tiber, he demanded, by the sound of trumpet, permission to pass through the city to Naples. The pope was astonished, and defenceless. The whole of his guards were with the army in Tuscany; and he had only his anathemas to resist the imperial soldiers. The Roman populace, however, felt a glow of the spirit of their ancestors: menials, grooms, and mechanics, voluntarily formed a boisterous, but animating, array; while the rich and the noble retired into their mansions, hoping, by such pusillanimous neutrality, to be respected by the conquerors;* thus serving to demonstrate, that the bold and sturdy vulgar, who have only lives to hazard, are ever the faithful guardians of their country, as they are of freedom. Clement, infatuated by terror, without attempting to negotiate, refused the summons. At break of day, the army, which might be compared to gaunt and famished wolves surrounding a fold, rose from the meadows, and advanced towards the city. A thick mist concealed the temples of Rome, and overshadowed the ancient monuments of her military glory. The imperialists advanced under it in silence. In the same moment that the resolute but undisciplined mul-

* Guicciardini, lib. 18.

H

titude on the walls discovered their approach, the assault began. Bourbon, to animate his men, seized a scaling ladder, and, running forward, was shot, and fell dead on the earth.* The prince of Orange flung a cloak over the body, and called on the soldiers to revenge the death of their general. For two hours the citizens defended themselves with a courageous constancy not unworthy of the Roman name; but one of those sudden panics, to which undisciplined volunteers, of the bravest individual spirit, are always liable, suddenly seized them, and they fled from their posts, abandoned entirely to fear. The pope, attended by the cardinals and other high personages, was in the chapel of the Vatican, standing at the altar, in anxious dread of the event. The shrieks and cries of flying women and children were heard without. The rites of religion were suspended. The noise rose louder and louder. The clash of arms, and the tumultuous sounds of fighting and vengeance drew nearer and nearer. The trembling prelates looked at one another; and the pope, hastily gathering up the folds of his robes, ran precipitately, followed by the spectators, to the castle of St. Angelo. The city became the victim of the rage and sensuality of the assailants. The shrines were broken, and the bones of holy men were scattered with derision in the streets. The German soldiers, tainted with the principles of Luther, were conspicuously active in the profanation. The effigy of the pope was burnt as antichrist. But it was not on the senseless objects of superstition that the licentiousness of the soldiers was chiefly manifested. During the pillage, a furious passion for gaming took possession of their minds.† Some, loaded with plate and treasure, were seen running to where their companions sat at dice, and staking their whole spoil on a throw, lost it, and returned instantly to pillage more. The dastardly nobles, shut up in their houses, endeavouring, from the windows,

---

* By Benvenuti Cellini, it is said.

† Those pious Presbyterians, who inveigh against cards as the devil's books, are little aware that they were an instrument in the great work of the Reformation. The vulgar game about that time was the devil and the priest; and the skill of the players consisted in preserving the priest from the devil, but the devil in the end always got hold of him. The Scottish game of *catch honours* is possibly a reformed method of the popish practice; and is dull and stupifying, by having lost the waggery about the *de'il and the minister.*

to ransom themselves and their families, were obliged to treat with every gang of plunderers, until they had nothing left to offer; and then they were compelled to witness and endure the calamities and the shame which they had vainly hoped to avert. Private mansions were not the only scenes of slaughter and sensual fury. The convents were burst open, and the miserable nuns violated in the midst of corpses and blood. The lamentations of those who despaired of escaping, or were made loathsome to themselves, only served to instigate to new crimes. Some of the soldiers, in the momentary glut of appetite, with a wild hope of obliterating their guilt, set fire to the theatres of these dreadful tragedies, and consumed victims and violators together. The soldiers were not the only criminals. The citizens joined in the carnival of sin; and horrible desires were openly gratified, with applause, in the midst of murders, and the putrefactions of death.

All Christendom was filled with horror and grief. Henry vowed immediate vengeance against Charles, whom he regarded as the cause of transactions such as had never before disgraced the Christian character, and of calamities, such as Rome, in all the vicissitudes of her eventful fortune, had never before suffered. Nor was the cardinal* less eager to avenge what had happened, or to avert what might ensue. It was apprehended that a vast sum would be levied on all the members of the church for the ransom of the pope and the papal city, and that privileges would be extorted derogatory to the pontifical supremacy and the independence of Christendom. To anticipate these consequences, prompt and comprehensive measures were necessary. A council was summoned, and the flagrant proceedings of the imperial army, as well as the conduct of the emperor, were immediately considered. When his circumstances rendered him scarcely a match for the French king, he became a contrahent in the league of London; and when that league was violated by the French, the English government performed all its engage-

---

* The cardinal ordered prayers to be said for the pope, and all people to fast four days in the week; but few fasted, for the priests said their commands were to exhort the lay people, and not to fast themselves. But the lay people said the priests should fast first, for the very cause of the fasting was for a priest; few, however, of either fasted.—*Hall.*

ments and obligations. But immediately after the battle of Pavia, when Charles conceived himself master of the continent, and no longer under any necessity of depending on the aid of England, he assumed an insolence of demeanour which he had never before manifested. In his letters to Henry his uncle, he laid aside the customary courtesy and equality with which he had formerly addressed him, and assumed the consequential style of a superior. He treated Francis, while in his possession, more as a culprit vassal of his own, than as a prisoner of war; and could it be expected, that, master of the capital of Christendom, and of the pope's person, his ambition would be repressed? It was therefore determined, that a convention should immediately be concluded with Francis, which should have for its object the deliverance of Clement; and that, for this purpose, Wolsey should proceed immediately to France, in order to arrange the terms, and to concert the measures essential to give it effect.* The objects of this embassy being deemed peculiarly solemn, the preparations were unusually magnificent. The cardinal left London accompanied by many peers and prelates, with a train of above a thousand servants, and eighty waggons loaded with baggage and treasure.† When he passed through Canter-

---

* " At the last, as you have heard, divers of the great states and lords of the council, with my lady Anne (Bullen,) lay in continual wait to spy a convenient occasion to take my lord cardinal in a snare. Therefore they consulted with the cardinal, and informed him, that they thought it a necessary time for him to take upon him the king's commission, to travel beyond the seas, and by his wisdom to compass a present peace amongst these great princes and potentates, encouraging him thereto, and alleging that it was more meet for his wisdom, discretion, and authority, to bring so weighty a matter to pass than any other within this realm; their intent was no other but to get him from the king, that they might adventure by the help of their then chief mistress, to deprave him unto the king, and in his absence bring him into his disgrace, or at the least to be in less estimation; and so the matter was handled that the cardinal was commanded to prepare himself for the journey, which he took upon him, but whether willingly or not, I cannot say."—Cavendish.

† " When all things were concluded and provided for this noble journey, he advanced forwards in the name of God. . . . Then marched he forward out of his new house at Westminster, through all London, (3rd July, 1526), over London bridge, having a great many of gentlemen, in ranks of three before him, in black velvet coats, and the most part of them with chains of gold about their necks. And all his own yeomen, with the noblemen's and great men's servants, all in orange tawny coats, with T. C., for Thomas,

bury, prayers were performed in the cathedral for the deliverance of the pope from his miserable captivity; and during the chanting of the pathetic orison* prepared for the occasion, Wolsey, convinced of the instability of his own grandeur, and touched with a presentiment of his fall, was observed to weep tenderly.

The narrative of the cardinal's journey and progress in France strikingly displays his love of magnificence, and the splendour of the age; but the details are more interesting to the antiquary than to the historian. Still, however, it contains circumstances worthy of selection, as they serve to illustrate his domestic character, and the decision of his mind in public affairs. When his equipages were landed at Calais, and while the French court was coming to meet him, he ordered all his household into his presence, and addressed them to the following effect:—"I have called you hither, to declare unto you, that I would have you consider both the duty you owe unto me, and the good will I semblably bear unto you for the same. Your intendment of service is to further the authority I have by commission from the king, which diligent observance of yours I will hereafter recommend to his majesty, as also to show, from the nature of the Frenchmen, and withal to instruct you what reverence you shall use to me for the high honour of the king's majesty; and to inform you also how you shall entertain and accompany the Frenchmen when you meet at any time. Concerning the first point, ye shall understand that, for divers weighty affairs of his grace's, and for more advancement of his royal dignity, he hath assigned me in this journey to be

Cardinal, embroidered upon them, as well upon his own servants' ceats, as upon all the rest of the gentlemen's. His sumpter mules, which were twenty and more in number, and all his carriages and carts and other of his train, had passed on before. He rode very sumptuously like a cardinal, on his mule, with his spare mule behind, and a spare horse, the trappings of crimson velvet, with gilt stirrups. And before him he had his two great silver crosses, and his two pillars of silver, the king's broad Seal of England, and his cardinal's hat, and a gentleman carrying his balances, otherwise called his cloak bag, which was made of fine scarlet, all embroidered very richly with gold. Thus he passed through London, as I said before, and all the way in his said journey he was thus furnished, having his harbingers in every place before him, who prepared lodgings for him and his train."— *Cavendish.*

* " Sancta Maria, ora ! pro papa nostro Clemente."—*Cavendish.*

his lieutenant. What reverence therefore belongs to me for the
same, I will show you. By virtue of my commission and
lieutenantship, I assume and take upon me to be esteemed
in all honours and degrees of service as unto his highness is
meet and due, and nothing to be neglected by me that to his
state is due and appertinent; for my part, ye shall see, that I
will not omit one jot thereof. Therefore, one of the chief
causes of your assembly at this time is to inform you, that
you be not ignorant of your duty in this. I wish you, therefore, as you would have my favour, and also charge you all,
in the king's name, that you do not forget the same in time
and places, but that every one of you do observe his duty to
me, according as you will, at your return, avoid the king's
indignation, and deserve his highness' thanks; the which I
will set forth at our return, as each of you shall deserve.
Now to the second point:—The nature of the Frenchmen is
such, that at the first meeting they will be as familiar with
you as if they had known you by long acquaintance; and
they will converse with you in their French tongue as though
you knew every word; therefore, use them in like manner, and be as familiar with them as they are with you: if
they speak to you in their natural tongue, speak to them in
English, so that, if you do not understand them, no more
shall they you;" and he added, turning facetiously to one of
his gentlemen, who was a Welshman: " Price, speak thou
Welsh to them, and I doubt not but thy speech shall be no
more diffuse and obscure to them than is French to thee.
But I pray you all, let your entertainment and behaviour be
according to all gentleness and humility, that it may be reported, after our departure, that you were gentlemen of good
behaviour, and that all men may know you understand your
duties to your lord and king, and to your master: Thus shall
you not only obtain to yourselves great recommendations and
praises, but also greatly advance your prince and country."
From Calais he went towards Amiens. Francis having, as a
mark of his singular esteem, and by the title of his dearest
and great friend, empowered him to pardon all criminals but
those who had been guilty of high treason, rape, and sacri-
lege; the cardinal exercised the royal prerogative of mercy
in the different towns through which the embassy passed,
and the inhabitants entertained him with Latin orations and

triumphal processions.* When he had arrived within a short distance of the city, word was brought that Francis and the court were advancing to meet him. He immediately alighted, and entering a small chapel which stood on the road side, he arrayed himself more sumptuously than usual, and his mule was at the same time caparisoned with gold and crimson velvet. By the time he was again mounted, the king, with his guards,† had come very near. The cardinal only advanced a little way, and then stopped. Francis, surprised, sent forward one of his attendants to inquire the reason. Wolsey said that he expected to be met half way. The messenger returned, and the king advancing, the cardinal also came forward, and, both alighting at the same time, embraced in the midway between their respective retinues. Francis having placed Wolsey on his right, and each English gentleman and attendant being marshalled with a Frenchman of equal rank, the procession, extending nearly two miles in length, proceeded to Amiens. After spending a few days there, the court removed to the castle of Compiegne, which had been previously partitioned, one division being appropriated for the French, and the other for the English.

The business, which had been preluded with so much grandeur, now seriously commenced. Wolsey, during the discussions, was frequently irritated by the chicanery of the French ministers. One evening, while Francis himself was present, he lost all patience, and, starting from his seat, said to the French chancellor, indignantly: "Sir, it becomes not you to trifle with the friendship between our sovereigns; and if your master follow your practices, he shall not fail shortly to feel what it is to war against England;" and he immediately left the room; nor could he be persuaded to resume the discussion, until the mother of Francis had entreated him to return. The objects of his mission, by this bold and sin-

---

* Notwithstanding all this public pomp and deference, the cardinal in private suffered several little mortifications. In every place where he lodged he was robbed of something valuable; and he met with a hieroglyphical admonition to humility, by a representation, one morning, on his window, of a cardinal's hat with a gallows over it.—*Stow.*

† The guard of tall Scots that attended the French king on this occasion, were more comely than all the others.—*Cavendish.*

gular diplomatic artifice, were speedily brought to a conclusion. Three several treaties, forming a league offensive, defensive, and of affinity, were concluded. The first related to a marriage between the princess of England and the duke of Orleans,—the emperor, by marrying the princess of Portugal,* having left her free. The second concerned the affairs of Francis and Charles, the deliverance of the French princes, and the restoration of the duchy of Milan to Sforza. In the event of Henry declaring war against Charles, Francis agreed that the English merchants should enjoy, in the French ports, the same privileges that they enjoyed in the imperial dominions. The third treaty, was, however, the principal; and, both as the object of the embassy, and as the parent of events which have not, perhaps, even at this day, ceased to operate, deserves to be particularly noticed.

It declared, that while the pope remained a prisoner, no summons for a general council of the church should take effect within the dominions of France and England; and the two kings engaged respectively, that their clergy should publicly protest their detestation of any such convocation. It was also declared, that any commandment, sentence, bull, letter, or brief, proceeding from the pope in his present situation, tending to the prejudice of the French or English nations, or to the legatine authority of cardinal Wolsey, should not be obeyed, but that the bearers of them should be punished; and that during the captivity of the pope, whatsoever the cardinal, in conjunction with the other prelates of England, assembled by the king, determined in the ecclesiastical affairs of the English, should, when sanctioned by his majesty, be valid and obligatory. The like was settled by the French. Thus was a radical alteration made in the constitution of Christendom. Leo X., by becoming a party to the league of London, had degraded the pope to an equality with the secular princes. But this treaty openly declared, that even in ecclesiastical affairs, the political authority was to be supreme, and Henry afterwards maintained the principle with his characteristic vigour.

Charles, when informed that the pope was his prisoner,

* 2nd January, 1526.

and aware of the amazement which the pillage of Rome had diffused throughout Christendom, endeavoured to traffic with the temper of Henry. He sent him a letter, in which the excesses of the soldiery were palliated; and, affecting to doubt what should be his own conduct in so difficult a crisis, artfully solicited advice. To the different foreign ministers at his court he was equally plausible, but gave no satisfaction before the terms of the treaties between France and England were known. Then, in order to avert the consequences, he offered to the French and English ambassadors, to give up those stipulations in the treaty of Madrid which the French nation had resolved not to fulfil; and he sent orders to the prince of Orange, who, after the death of Bourbon, commanded the imperialists in Rome, to set the pope at liberty; but to take care that from a friend he might not be able to become an enemy. This oracular order puzzled the prince exceedingly; who, being unable to expound it himself, called a council of war. The plain and blunt soldiers who composed the council, having wasted a long time in vain perplexity, at length decided that in a case so abstruse the main point should be secured. They accordingly stripped the pope of all he had, or could procure;* and turned him out of the

---

* The money which at this time Clement was obliged to borrow, in order to satisfy the extortions of the officers, occasioned the first institution of public funds; that species of financial resource which, during the eighteenth century, attracted so much of the attention of the statesmen and political economists of Europe, and which, in this country, is the great object of the care and solicitude of ministers. The money was borrowed at ten per cent. interest. In order to pay the interest, and to liquidate the principal, the *luoghi di monte* were formed, which, under Sextus V., was reduced into a complete system.

The pope has in his disposal a great number of posts or employments, particularly in the Roman datary, which at that time, and till very lately, were extremely profitable to the occupiers. They are all during life ; and Sextus ordained, that as the occupiers dropped off, their employments should, for the future, be sold at certain fixed prices to any that would offer for them. He formed a curious table, or tariff, for this purpose, which was never to be exceeded; and the prices were so moderate, as to leave a very considerable profit to the purchasers. These employments are called vacabili, because they are vacable or transferable from any occupier under sixty years of age to another, though of inferior age. The sums received from the sales of these vacabili were to form a sinking fund for the extinction of the national debt, which was to be paid off at certain periods, and in certain proportions.

castle, as the best way of executing the emperor's instructions.

Before any advantage could be taken of the politic moderation which Charles had assumed, on learning the result of Wolsey's embassy to France, heralds from France and England arrived,* and, with the customary ceremonies of the age, demanded an audience of the emperor. Their request was granted. Charles ascended his throne, and being surrounded by his officers and nobles, the heralds were admitted. Over their left arm they carried their armorial mantles, and making three low obeisances, approached the foot of the throne, where the English king at arms claimed protection and entertainment in a speech to the following effect. " According to the laws and edicts, inviolably guarded by the Roman emperors, your predecessors, and by all other kings and princes, we, in the name of our respective sovereigns, have come to declare important matters; and therefore we beseech your majesty, out of your benign clemency, to afford us, agreeably to those laws and edicts, security and honourable treatment, while we wait your answer; and, afterwards, to grant us safe conduct till we return to the lands and lordships of our masters." The emperor having assented in the customary form to this request, the French herald then stepped forward, and said, " Because your imperial majesty will not agree to equitable terms of peace; nor pay your debts to the king of England;† nor set the pope free ; nor leave Italy in quietness; the king, my lord and master, commands me to declare, that he and his brother the king of England must henceforth treat you as an enemy; and from this day forward he will keep no contract for your profit and advantage : but he will exert against you and your subjects all the annoyance of war, until, upon fair and honest terms, you restore his sons; set the pope free; pay the king of England; and leave in tranquillity all his allies and confederates : forty days respite are allowed to enable your subjects to withdraw from his dominions, and he requires the like for his subjects in yours." The herald then put on his mantle; and

* 11th November, 1527.

† Charles, having married the princess of Portugal, forfeited to Henry, by not marrying his daughter, five hundred thousand crowns, according to the stipulations of the treaty of Windsor.

the emperor replied, " I perfectly understand what you have said on the part of the king your master; but I am surprised by this defiance; for he is my prisoner, and not eligible to send me a defiance. He has made war with me long, and never did this before; but I trust in God that I shall be able to defend myself. No one regrets what has happened to the pope more than I do: it was done without my knowledge, and yesterday I received letters that he has been set at liberty. As for the sons of your king, it is not my fault that they are not free; I hold them in pawn, and he should redeem them.* And as to what you say concerning my uncle the king of England, he is not well informed of these affairs; otherwise he would not have sent me this message: I will myself write to him the whole truth. I never refused the payment of my debts, and I will act as I am in justice bound. But if he will make war, I must defend; and I pray God that I may have no greater occasion to make war on him than he has received from me." The English herald then answered : " The king, my supreme lord, considers peace necessary to the Christian world, that the princes may combine to resist the Turk, who has already taken Belgrade, and expelled the knights of St. John from the isle of Rhodes; and that the heresies and schismatic sects, which have lately arisen, may be repressed. But your commanders and army have sacked the city of Rome; taken our holy father prisoner; put the cardinals to ransom; sacrilegiously profaned the churches; slain with the sword

---

* The mean and sordid spirit of Charles and the Spanish government, was fully shown in the treatment which the helpless children of Francis received. They were consigned to the custody of a stupid superstitious wretch, a marquis of the name of Virlanga, and imprisoned in the castle of Pedracu. A French officer, who was sent to visit them, found them in a dark dirty room, playing with dogs and dolls, and neglected in their persons. They had forgotten all their native language, and he was obliged to make use of an interpreter. How different was this from the entertainment which James I. of Scotland received while a prisoner in England! The officer presented them with new clothes, which the marquis would not allow to be put on, until first tried upon the bodies of other boys; for he believed that there were witches in France who could transport, through the air, any one whose bodies were touched by their ointments. Lord Herbert, in speaking of this circumstance, endeavours, in words without meaning, to give another reason for the conduct of Virlanga; but the notion was not peculiar to that despicable Spaniard,—it was common to the age.[1] (See Appendix.)

religious persons of all descriptions, till the air and the earth have been infected,* and the wrath of Heaven has come down demanding reparation. The debates and contentions between you and the French king are the roots and causes of these evils; and my sovereign has in vain proposed to you terms of reconciliation. These things, with those that have been related by the French herald, have induced him to adopt an ultimate resolution. He has concluded a league with Francis and other confederates, to constrain you, by force of arms, to act with equity; and I am authorised to offer, once for all, the conditions which have been already proposed." He concluded the defiance with the proposal of forty days' respite. Having put on his mantle, the emperor answered to the same effect as he did to the other herald; and afterwards wrote a long representation, in which he recapitulated many circumstances of complaint which he had against the government of Henry, and particularly against the cardinal.† — England gained nothing by the wasteful wars in which she had embarked, chiefly on his account: Charles endeavoured to appropriate all the fruits of the battle of Pavia to himself, in despite of positive stipulations by treaty: and by the sack of Rome, the frame of Christendom, of which Henry was the declared champion and defender, was nearly overthrown.

Wolsey, after his return from France, on opening the Michaelmas term, addressed the judges and the other eminent persons then assembled upon the subject of his embassy, and the treaties which he had concluded with Francis, stating that such was the reciprocity and friendship established between the two kingdoms, that they would, in future, appear but as one monarchy. But the nation could not understand how it was for their advantage that the king should become so familiar with their old and deadly enemy, and abandon his own nephew, for whose behalf he had so urgently asked them for money; and they had ceased to feel much interest in the fate of the pope. The merchants foresaw the loss of their trade with Spain and the Netherlands, and doubted if all the advantages which might be derived from the opening of the French ports would be an equivalent.

---

* At this time a pestilence raged in most parts of Europe.
† Lord Herbert, 218.

A new war was also probable; and the people, unable to
comprehend the views of the cardinal, but witnessing his
ostentation and arrogance, began to be infected by the discontents of the nobility and ecclesiastics, whom he had mortified
by his talents, and offended by his justice. Wolsey had, indeed, attained the meridian of his fortune. In every transaction abroad, his name was mentioned and his influence felt.
The learned and the artists of all countries came trooping to
his gates, and the kingdom resounded with the fame of his
affluence and the noise of the buildings which he was erecting
to luxury and knowledge. His revenues, derived from the
fines in the legatine court, the archbishopric of York, the
bishopric of Winchester, and the abbey of St. Albans, with
several other English bishoprics which were held by foreigners,
but assigned to him at low rents for granting them the privilege of living abroad, together with his pensions from Charles
and Francis, the emoluments of the chancellorship, the
revenues of the bishoprics of Badajos and Placentia, in Spain,
with rich occasional presents from all the allies of the king,
and the wealth and domains of forty dissolved monasteries,
formed an aggregate of income equal to the royal revenues.
His house exhibited the finest productions of art which such
wealth could command in the age of Leo X. The walls of
his chambers were hung with cloth of gold, and tapestry still
more precious, representing the most remarkable events in
sacred history,* for the easel was then subordinate to the
loom. His floors were covered with embroidered carpets,
and sideboards of cypress were loaded with vessels of gold.
The sons of the nobility, according to the fashion of the

---

* The subjects of the tapestry consisted of triumphs, probably Roman;
the story of Absalom, bordered with the cardinal's arms; the petition of
Esther, and the honouring of Mordecai; the history of Samson, bordered
with the cardinal's arms; the history of Solomon; the story of Susannah
and the elders, bordered with the cardinal's arms; the history of Jacob, also
bordered; Holofernes and Judith, bordered; the story of Joseph, of David,
and of St. John the Baptist; the history of the Virgin; the passion of
Christ; the Worthies; the story of Nebuchadnezzar; a pilgrimage—all bordered. His chapel had three organs, and was ornamented with statues of
St. John, the Virgin, the Mother and Child, St. Matthew, St. Anthony, St.
Barbara, and pictures made of inlaid wood and ivory. Some of these latter
kinds of pictures were, in that age, made in a very superior style. A cata-
logue of part of his furniture is in the British Museum.

age, attended him as pages,* and the daily service of the household corresponded to the opulence and ostentation of the master.

The entertainment which the cardinal gave at Hampton Court to the French commissioners† who were sent to ratify the league, offensive and defensive, exceeded in splendour every banquet which had before that time been exhibited in

---

* Hume speaks of the young nobility wearing the cardinal's livery as if such a thing had not happened before, and was peculiar to his household. " Some of the nobility," says the philosophical historian, " put their children into his family, as a place of education ; and, in order to ingratiate them with their patron, allowed them to bear offices as his servants." It was, however, the practice of the time, and of some antiquity. " A custom which had been introduced in former ages, seems in this (Henry VIII.) to have been carried almost beyond credibility: it was that of retaining in the houses of the nobility the sons of their superior dependents, where their educations were completed, who, with a numerous retinue of servants, were all known by the badges of their lord." *Dallaway's Enquiries into the Origin and Progress of Heraldry in England*, p. 186. Whiting, abbot of Glastonbury, who was contemporary with Wolsey, retained young noblemen. And Gavin Douglas, the celebrated bishop of Dunkeld, who was also a contemporary of Wolsey, mentions that he learnt the dialect which he makes use of in his poetry, when he was a page. *Ellis's Early English Poets*, vol. i. p. 397. And Douglas was a son of old Bell-the-Cat, earl of Angus, a man who was not likely to have allowed his sons to serve as pages had not the custom been common. The practice, in fact, continued till the reign of Charles I. Dr. Fiddes mentions that, in his time, the then earl of Stafford had a letter of instructions written by the earl of Arundel, in the year 1620, for the benefit of his son William, then in the house of the bishop of Norwich, in which he says, " You shall, in all things, reverence, honour, and obey my lord bishop of Norwich, as you would do your parents, esteeming what he shall tell or command you, as if your grandmother of Arundel, your mother, or myself, should say it ; and, in all things, esteem yourself as my lord's page ; a breeding which youths of my house, far superior to you, were accustomed to, as my grandfather of Norfolk, and his brother, my good uncle of Northampton, were both bred as pages, with bishops."

† " Then was there no more to do but to make preparation of all things for the entertainment of this great assembly at Hampton Court, at the time appointed. My lord cardinal called before him all his chief officers, as stewards, treasurers, comptrollers, and clerks of his kitchen, to whom he declared his whole mind touching the entertainment of the Frenchmen at Hampton Court, to whom he also gave command neither to spare for any cost, or expense, or pains, to make such a triumphant banquet, as the guests might not only wonder at it here, but also make a glorious report to the great honour of our king and this realm. Thus having made known his pleasure, to accomplish his commandment, they sent all the carriers, purveyors, and other persons, to prepare all they could for love or liking, for

England. Two hundred and eighty beds, with furniture of
the costliest silks and velvets, and as many ewers and basins
of silver, were prepared for the guests. The halls were
illuminated with innumerable sconces and branches of plate.
Supper was announced by the sound of trumpets, and served
with triumphal music. But the master was not yet come.
He had been detained late in London, and the dessert, which

my lord's friends. Also they sent for all expert cooks, and cunning persons
in the art of cookery in London, or elsewhere that might be gotten to beau-
tify the noble feast, then the purveyors provided, and my lord's friends sent
in such provision that it was a wonder to see it. The cooks they wrought
both day and night in many curious devices, where was no lack of gold,
silver, or any other costly thing. The yeomen and grooms of his ward-
robes were busied in hanging the chambers with costly hangings, and furnishing the same with beds of silk, and other furniture for the same in every
degree. Then my lord sent me, being his gentleman-usher, and two other
of my fellows, to foresee all things, touching our rooms to be richly garnished, wherein our pains were not small, but daily we travelled up and
down, from chamber to chamber, to see things fitted. Then wrought joiners,
carpenters, painters, and all other artificers needful, so that there should be
nothing wanting to adorn this noble feast. There was carriage and re-car-
riage of plate, stuff, and other rich implements, so that there was nothing
lacking that could be devised or imagined for the purpose. There were
also provided two hundred and eighty beds, with all manner of furniture to
them, too long to be here related.

" The day assigned to the Frenchmen being come, they were ready
assembled at Hampton Court, before the hour of their appointment, wherefore the officers called them to ride to Hanworth, a park of the king's within
three miles of Hampton Court, there to spend the time in hunting till night,
which they did, and then returned, and every one of them was conveyed to
his several chamber, having in it a good fire, and store of wine, where they
remained till supper was ready.

" The chambers where they supped and banqueted were adorned thus :
—First, the great waiting chamber was hung with a very rich cloth of
arras, and so all the rest, some better than others, and furnished with
tall yeomen to serve. There were set tables round about the chambers,
banquetwise covered ; also a cupboard garnished with white plate, having
also in the same chamber, to give the more light, four great plates of silver,
set with lights, and a great fire. The next chamber was the chamber of
presence, richly hanged also with the cloth of arras, and a sumptuous cloth
of estate, furnished with many goodly gentlemen to serve. The tables
were ordered in manner as the others were, save only the high table was
removed beneath the cloth of state, towards the midst of the chamber.
There was a cupboard with six desks of plate, garnished all over with fine
gold, with one pair of candlesticks of silver and gilt, that cost three hundred
marks, with lights of wax in the same. The cupboard was barred about,
that no man could come very near, for there was great store of plate to use

consisted of figures, castles, and cathedrals, in confectionary, with all the emblems of ecclesiastical pomp and the pageants of chivalry, was on the tables when he entered, booted and spurred. Having welcomed the guests, he called for a golden bowl filled with hippocras; the French commissioners were served, at the same time, with another, and they reciprocally drank to the health of their respective sovereigns. He then retired to dress, and returning speedily to the company, exerted those convivial talents which had first contributed to his attainment of this excessive grandeur. The Frenchmen doubted which most to admire, the mansion, the feast, or the master. Wolsey felt exultingly gratified, and the measure of his greatness could hold no more.

besides. The plates that hung on the walls to give light, were silver and gilt, with wax lights.

" Now were all things in readiness, and supper fit; the principal officers caused the trumpets to blow, to warn all to supper. Then the officers conducted the French noblemen where they were to sup, and they being set, the service came up in such abundance, both costly and full of devices, with such a pleasant noise of music, that the Frenchmen, as it seemed, were wrapped up in a heavenly paradise. You must understand that my lord cardinal was not there all this while, but the French *Monsieurs* were very merry with their rich fare and curious cates and knacks; but before the second course, my lord cardinal came in, booted and spurred, suddenly amongst them, and bade them *proface* (*proficiat*, may it do you good). At his coming there was great joy, every man rising from his place, whom my lord cardinal caused to sit still and keep their places, and being in his riding apparel, called for his chair, and sat him down in the midst of the high table, and was there as merry and as pleasant as ever I saw him in my life. Presently after came up the second course, which was above a hundred several devices, which were so goodly and costly, that I think the Frenchmen never saw the like. But the rarest curiosity of all the rest, they all wondered at, which indeed was worthy of wonder, were castles with images in the same; Saint Paul's church, the model thereof; beasts, birds, fowls, personages most excellently made, some fighting with swords, some with guns, others with cross-bows, some dancing with ladies, some on horseback with complete armour, jousting with long and sharp spears, and many more strange devices, which I cannot describe. Amongst them all I noticed there was a chess-board of spices, with men to the same, and of good proportion; and because the Frenchmen are very expert at that sport, my lord cardinal gave the same to a French gentleman, commanding that there should be made a good case to convey the same into his country."—*Cavendish.*

BOOK V.

State of Ireland—Character of the Irish—Feudal system—Election of chieftains—Tanistrie—Origin of yeomanry—Brehon law—Ireland as often subject to military rule as to civil discipline—Laid waste during the civil wars of Henry VI.—State on the accession of Henry VIII.—The earl of Kildare deputy of Ireland — His administration — Summoned to England on charges of misdemeanour—The earl of Ossory appointed deputy—Acquittal of Kildare—Again summoned to London—His defence —Its effect on the cardinal — The Reformation — Anarchy in France after the death of Charlemagne—Efforts of the priesthood to restrain it—Preaching of Peter the Hermit—Intercourse caused by the crusades —Revival of literature in Italy — Changes produced by it—Wolsey's design in reforming the church—First general result of the Reformation —Wolsey more the patron of literary institutions than of men of genius —Literature of the reign of Henry VIII. and of the age of Elizabeth —Progress of the ornamental arts in Italy—State of literature and arts in Scotland—College of physicians founded—Low state of medical science prior to that event—Wolsey a patron of national instruction—Proposes to found public lectures at Oxford—The laws of that university submitted to him for revisal—Cambridge adopts the same measure—Progress of learning—Wolsey founds and endows Christ-church college, Oxford— Project by which he proposed to furnish its library—Wolsey lays the foundation of a public school at Ipswich—Estimate of his acquirements as a scholar—Projects an institution to be founded in London for the study of law—The courtiers and clergy jealous of his influence.

It may still be said, as in the days of queen Elizabeth, that Ireland seems reserved by Almighty God for woes which shall come by her upon England. Causes intrinsically similar to those which agitated that unfortunate country in the age of Henry VIII., have stained the annals of the present reign* with blood. The terrible constancy with which the people have reviled, for more than six hundred years, the English system of rule, must be ascribed to the effect of something

* That of George III.

I

vicious in that system. Nor can this be denied. By calling
the descendants of the English who settled in Ireland subsequent to the time of Henry II. Protestants, and the aboriginal
inhabitants Catholics, the relative condition of the people will
appear to have continued unaltered since that epoch; and yet,
in all the series of the ministers who have successively ruled
England, will it be found that any one of them has pursued a
wiser policy than that of cardinal Wolsey?

The earliest authentic descriptions of the Irish represent
them as a frank, kind-hearted people, much under the influence of the imagination, enthusiastic in all their passions
and pursuits, amorous, fond of renown, delighted with war,
generous to the distressed, and hospitable to friends and
strangers. When polished by education, they excel in the
convivial fascination of wit and humour, and they are the
most eloquent of all the modern nations. The lower classes
are faithful and affectionate where they form attachments, but
the strength of their passions makes them lax in their
morality. They have little ambition, the consequence of
ignorance, and they entertain for their masters sentiments
that would become the humility of an inferior cast. The
men are well formed, tall, and clear complexioned, and the
women are more remarkable for the symmetry of their arms
and limbs than for the beauty of their features. In the days
of Campion, the men wore their hair cropped close, leaving
on their forehead a large tuft,* which they thought added to
the manliness of their countenance; and in the present age
the same fashion has been revived. To their national
customs the Irish have always been strongly attached, valuing
antiquity more than utility. In the time of Wolsey, those
who were skilled in the delicacy of their native language
affected to be enraptured by the allusions and apophthegms of
the bards and jesters. The chieftains retained tale-tellers,
who invented stories for their amusement; and the delight
which the nation has always received from wonderful tales
has drawn upon Irishmen the imputation of being credulous.†

* They called it their *glibbe.*
† In the sixteenth century, a remarkable class of adventurers, called carrows, who followed no other profession but cards, was entertained among
them. These carrows, being commonly well-born, but without patrimony,
gleaned a livelihood by passing, in quest of play, from house to house among

The feudal system was never generally established in Ireland. The English adventurers in the expedition of Henry II. doubtless received their portions of his conquest on the condition of rendering military service; but he only subdued a small part of the kingdom, and the ancient usages retained, beyond the English bounds, in the reign of Henry VIII., much of their primitive peculiarity. The aboriginal Irish law of territorial inheritance was, probably, similar to what prevailed in the northern parts of Europe, before the feudal system was established. It seems to have been an early offset from the more ancient and patriarchal rule of clanship. The territorial heir was not, as in Scotland, among the clans, the military successor of his father; nor, as in feudatory states, the superior of the inhabitants of his domain. For, when a commander happened to die, the people resorted to a known appointed place, in order to choose another leader; and the relation of the deceased who was most admired for his hardihood and exploits was generally preferred, without reference to his degree of consanguinity. When the election was declared, the successful candidate was placed on a stone consecrated by the use of ages for that purpose. It commonly stood on the top of a hill, and had a foot engraved on it, alleged to be the form of that of the first commander of the district to which the stone belonged.* While standing on the stone, the chief took an oath to preserve all the customs of the country, and the rights of the tanist, or territorial heir. A wand was then delivered to him by an officer appointed for that part of the ceremony; and, on receiving it, he descended from the stone, and, turning thrice round, backwards and forwards, completed his inauguration. The military command being thus distinct from the possession of the land, domains in Ireland were said to be regulated by tanists; and to this peculiarity, and the usages attached to it, the mul-

the gentry. To such an infatuated degree were they devoted to this thriftless commerce, that they have sometimes pledged their clothes; and, when stripped to the skin, have lain by the highways trussed in leaves and straw, inviting the passengers to a game on the green, at which, having nothing else to stake, they put to hazard the glibbs on their foreheads, their nails, and even their limbs and members, to be lost or redeemed at the courtesy of the winner.—*Campion.*

* The ancient practice of crowning the Scottish kings on the black stone of Scoone was derived, no doubt, from a similar practice.

titudinous funerals of the Irish populace, and their custom of
assembling in crowds on raths and hills to discuss their public
grievances, may be distinctly traced.   The origin of an evil
which still severely afflicts the nation may also be attributed
to those ancient customs; although the causes which serve
to prolong that evil cannot now be ascribed to the exercise
of popular rights.   Under the feudal system, the landlord was
induced to cultivate the affection of his vassals, that he might
himself the more eminently perform his military service.   He
allowed them, in consequence, not only to acquire independent property, but to obtain an interest in the soil.   As the
system fell into decay, the descendants of those vassals who
had judiciously managed the favours of their chief, gradually
formed the yeomen—a class of men which, as it exists in
England, is the most truly respectable of the human race.
But the tanistry proprietor, having no motive to study the
predilections of his tenants, sought only to increase his income; and, accordingly, even while the feudal system and
practices were still in some degree of force in the neighbouring kingdoms, it was considered as a great misfortune to Ireland that the lands were let at rack-rents from year to year,
and often only during pleasure.

Among other usages which, in the days of Wolsey, stinted
the improvement of the Irish, the Brehon law deserves to be
particularly noticed.   By it all crimes seemed to be estimated
only as injuries done to the individuals who suffered; and, as
such, were considered as eligible to be compromised at the
option of the injured.   The widow might compound with the
murderer of her husband; the son with his father's; and, in
all the varieties of offence, delinquents were not responsible
to the public, but only to the offended.   This singular tradi-
tionary rule of right, in principle so different from the divine
and civil laws, is the strongest proof that can be adduced of
the originality and antiquity of the Irish nation.   The progress of jurisprudence tends to take criminal prosecutions
out of the hands of individuals, and to vest them in the hands
of public ministers: perhaps even in civil actions it has the
same tendency; at least, the expense of obtaining legal satisfaction in England has become so enormous, that many men
submit to considerable losses, rather than incur the charges
of the lawyers; and it has been found necessary to authorise

the justices of the peace to decide those small suits of creditors which are supposed to affect the claims and dealings of the labouring class. But the progress is slow, and the abolition of opinions, which have become habitual notions, like those which relate to the principles and forms of judicial proceeding, requires long patience and diligent perseverance. It has been the peculiar destiny of Ireland, owing to the exclusive distinction which England has always made between the two great classes into which she has held the inhabitants, never to have been so steadily treated as to enable her people to acquire those regular habits which result from a long continued administration of uniform law. Ireland has been as often exposed to the hardships of military rule as she has enjoyed the benefits of civil discipline. After the invasion of Henry II., and prior to the contest between the families of York and Lancaster, some progress was made in subjecting the subjects within the English pale to the laws of the sovereign. But at the unhappy revolution by which Henry VI. was deposed, many of the nobility, and other influential persons of English origin, came over to this country, and took a part in the civil wars: and the wild Irish, as the inhabitants beyond the pale were called, burst in upon the civilized, and laid waste their cultivation; so that when Henry VIII. came to the throne, scarce a trace of it remained. The popular feuds and animosities were exasperated to the utmost. The subjects of English extraction enjoyed all the public distribution of power, while the aboriginal race, by far the most numerous, sustained the contumelious treatment of an inferior religious order, and were deemed incapable of enjoying the beneficence of jurisprudence.* Continual insurrections, midnight ravages, and frightful assassinations, were the consequence. The alarm was nightly sounded; and the mischief arising from a divided people was considered as a reason for perpetuating the distinctions that produced it.

When Wolsey was appointed prime minister, Gerald Fitzgerald, earl of Kildare, was deputy of Ireland. His father, earl Thomas, for more than thirty years, had enjoyed the same trust, and, in the course of that time, the power of the

---

* Sir John Davies, in the year 1612, published a curious tract on this subject. It is worthy of being reprinted at the expense of the Irish nation.

family had been much augmented; but his contentions with James Butler, earl of Ormond, had proved mischievous to the prosperity of the country. In the great debate of the York and Lancaster question, they had taken opposite sides; and, by that means, spread in Ireland calamities similar to those which ravaged England. Kildare embraced the cause of the York family, and Ormond that of the Lancaster. After the death of earl Thomas, Gerald was appointed deputy, and some steps were taken to improve the condition of the Irish people. His administration commenced, indeed, favourably to the interests of his country, and he reduced the inhabitants, if not into subjection, at least into awe. In order to end the feud between the Geraldines and the Butlers, he matched his sister Margaret with Pierce Butler, earl of Ossory, whom, at the decease of earl James, the rival of his father, he assisted to rescue the earldom of Ormond from the usurpation of a bastard. Whether, in the mode or means of accomplishing this, he had exceeded the limits of his authority, and put forth a vigour beyond the law, or was falsely accused, is not very clear; but he was called by the cardinal to England in order to answer, before the privy council, to charges of misdemeanour.* His successor was Surrey, whose administration has been already alluded to, and who was still more distinguished than Gerald Fitzgerald, by efforts to advance the authority of the laws, and to improve the judicature.

One day, as Surrey sat at dinner in the castle of Dublin, he was informed that the clan of O'more was up in great force, and violating the English pale. The troops were immediately ordered out, and, headed by himself, proceeded to attack them. An incident which took place in this affair is singularly characteristic of the men and of the times. The mayor of Dublin, John Fitzsimons, raised a party of volunteers, and, next morning, joined the lord lieutenant. The O'mores, as the king's forces approached, divided themselves into companies; one of which, understanding that the baggage, dragging behind, was slenderly guarded, passed into the rear of the citizens, and attacked the guard, among which were some of the lord lieutenant's men, who instantly fled.

* 1521.

The baggage, thus deserted, would have been captured, but for the bravery of a relation of the mayor, Patrick Fitzsimons, a stout and resolute youth, who manfully compelled the rebels to retreat. Having himself killed two, he cut off their heads, which he carried with him to the mayor's tent. The soldiers who had fled so dastardly, conceiving that the baggage must have been lost, told their lord that Patrick Fitzsimons ran away, and that the rebels were too numerous for them to resist. The earl went instantly to the mayor in a passion, and told him that Patrick was a cowardly traitor in deserting his duty. "What am I?" cried the youth, starting out of the pavilion in his shirt, with a bloody head dangling in each hand; "My lord, I am no coward; I stood true while your men gave me the slip; I rescued the baggage, and these are the tokens of my manhood," throwing down the heads. "Sayest thou so, Fitzsimons?" cried Surrey, pleased with his spirit, "I cry thee mercy, and, by Saint George, I would to God I had been with thee in that skirmish." He then called for a bowl of wine, and drinking to the volunteer, rewarded his valour. Soon after this insurrection, which was speedily quelled, war being proclaimed against France and Scotland, Surrey was recalled home, and appointed to the army on the Scottish borders.[*] His valour, integrity, and good humour established his reputation as a statesman among the Irish, by whom he was long after remembered with affectionate esteem.

The earl of Ossory, who had married Margaret Fitzgerald, was next appointed deputy. In the meantime, Kildare was acquitted in England, and, having married a sister of the marquis of Dorset, returned to Ireland. Notwithstanding the marriage of Ossory, the Geraldines still hated the Butlers; and his administration was, in consequence, so troubled by their disputes, that it was deemed necessary to send commissioners[†] from England to endeavour, by civil means, to restore the public tranquillity. The result of their inquiries proving disadvantageous to Ossory, he was deposed, and Kildare reinstated in the lieutenancy. At their return, they brought with them a Fitzgerald, who, during Ossory's admi-

_____
[*] 1523.

[†] Sir Anthony Fitzherbert, one of the justices of the Common Pleas; Ralph Egerton; Dr. Denton, dean of Lichfield.—*Holinshed*, 883.

nistration, had murdered an Irish privy counsellor, for keeping a record of the excesses of the Geraldines. While the murderer, after his condemnation, was led, with a halter round his neck, and a taper in his hand, slowly, through the streets of London, towards the place of execution, a pardon was obtained for him. The cardinal was vexed by this unexpected, and, as he thought, injudicious, interposition of the regal mercy; and his chagrin, though occasioned by the love of justice, was construed into an opinion that he was hostile to the blood of the Geraldines.

Ossory, mortified by his removal from the government, directed his spleen against the means and measures of his successor, who indeed was not scrupulous in his mode of ruling, but often furnished matter of just complaint, with respect to his treatment of the subjects, and particularly in the non-performance of his duty towards his cousin the earl of Desmond, who had entered into a treasonable correspondence with the French king, and afterwards with the emperor. Ossory, in consequence, lodged information against Kildare, and he was a second time summoned to London. The charges, at first, were not supposed to be of a very heinous nature, and he was allowed to leave his brother deputy during his absence. In the course, however, of the investigation, other circumstances of a more serious kind were discovered, and when he was subsequently brought before the privy council, the cardinal assailed him with much asperity; but he replied with admirable shrewdness, and that bold familiar eloquence peculiar to his countrymen. Wolsey began by saying, "I know well, my lord, that I am not the fittest man at this table to accuse you, because your adherents assert that I am an enemy to all nobility, and particularly to your blood. But the charges against you are so strong that we cannot overlook them, and so clear that you cannot deny them. I must therefore beg, notwithstanding the stale slander against me, to be the mouth and orator of these honourable gentlemen, and to state the treasons of which you stand accused, without respecting how you may like it. My lord, you well remember how the earl of Desmond, your kinsman, sent emissaries with letters to Francis, the French king, offering the aid of Munster and Connaught for the conquest of Ireland; and, receiving but a cold answer, applied to Charles, the emperor. How many letters, what precepts, what messages, what threats, have been sent to you to apprehend him, and it is not yet done. Why? Because you could not catch him? nay, my lord, you would not, forsooth! catch him. If he be justly suspected, why are you so partial? If not, why are you so fearful to have him tried? But it will be sworn to your face, that to avoid him you have winked wilfully, shunned his haunts, altered your course, advised his friends, and stopped both ears and eyes in the business; and that, when you did make a show of hunting him out, he was always beforehand, and gone. Surely, my lord, this juggling little became an honest man called to such honour, or a nobleman with so great a trust. Had you lost but a cow or a carrion of your own, two hundred retainers would have started up at your whistle to rescue the prey from the farthest edge of Ulster. All the Irish in Ireland must have made way for you. But, in performing your duty in this affair, merciful God! how delicate, how dilatory, how dangerous have you been! One time he is from home; another time he is at home; sometimes fled, and sometimes in places where you dare not venture. What! the earl of Kildare not venture! Nay, the king of Kildare; for you reign more than you govern the land. When you are offended, the lowest subjects stand as rebels; when you are pleased, rebels are very dutiful subjects. Hearts and hands, lives and lands, must all be at your beck. Who fawns not to you, cannot live within your scent, and your scent is so keen, that you track them out at pleasure." While the cardinal was speaking, the earl frequently changed colour, and vainly endeavoured to master himself. He affected to smile; but his face was pale, his lips quivered, and his eyes lightened with rage. "My lord chancellor," he exclaimed, fiercely, "my lord chancellor, I beseech you, pardon me. I have but a short memory, and you know that I have to tell a long tale. If you proceed in this way, I shall forget the half of my defence. I have no school tricks, nor art of recollection. Unless you hear me while I remember, your second charge will hammer the first out of my head." Several of the counsellors were friends of the earl; and, knowing the acrimony of the cardinal's taunts, which they were themselves often obliged to endure,* inter-

* Skelton, who was the Peter Pindar of his day, gives the following ludicrous description of the cardinal, in a satire for which he prudently took refuge in the sanctuary of Westminster Abbey:—

fered, and entreated that the charges might be discussed one by one. Wolsey assenting to this, Kildare resumed. " It is with good reason that your grace is the mouth of this council; but, my lord, the mouths that put this tale into yours are very wide, and have gaped long for my ruin. What my cousin Desmond has done I know not; I curse him for holding out so long. If he be taken in the traps that I have set for him, my adversaries, by this heap of heinous charges, will only have proved their own malice. But if he be never taken, what is Kildare to blame more than Ossory, who, notwithstanding his high promises, and having now the king's power, you see, takes his own time to bring him in. Cannot the earl of Desmond stir, but I must advise? Cannot he be hid, but I must wink? If he is befriended, am I, therefore, a traitor? It is truly a formidable accusation! My first denial confounds my accusers. Who made them so familiar with my sight? When was the earl in my view? Who stood

"Our barons are so bold,
Into a mouse hold the wold
Run away and creep ;
Like as many of sheep
Dare not look out a dur,
For dread of the mastiff cur ;
For dread of the butcher's dog,
Would worry them like a hog.
For if this cur do gnar,
They must all stand afar,
To hold up their hand at the bar.
For all their noble blood
He plucks them by the hood
And shakes them by the ear,
And brings them in such fear,
He baiteth them like a bear,
Like an ox or a bull.
Their wits, he saith, are dull :
He saith they have no brain,
Their estate to maintain ;
And makes to bow the knee
Before his majesty.

"Judge of the king's laws,
He counts them fools and daws ;
Sergeants of the coif eke,
He sayeth they are to seek,
In pleading of their case

At the Common Pleas,
Or at the King's Bench ;
He wringeth them such a wrench,
That all our learned men,
Dare not set their pen
To plead a true trial
Within Westminster-hall.
In the Chancery where he sits,
But such as he admits,
None so hardy are to speak.

"He saith, 'Thou huddy peak,
Thy learning is too lewd,
Thy tongue is not well thew'd
To seek before your grace,
And only in this place.'
He rages and he raves,
And calls them canker'd knaves.
Thus royally he doth deal,
Under the king's broad seal.
And in the chequer he them checks,
In Star chamber he nods and becks,
And beneath him they're so stout,
That no man of them dare rout,
Duke, earl, baron, nor lord,
But to his sentence must accord ;
Whether he be knight or squire,
All must follow his desire."

by when I let him slip? But, say they, I sent him word. Who was the messenger? Where are the letters? Confute my denial. Only see how loosely this idle gear of theirs hangs together! Desmond is not taken. Well! Kildare is in fault. Why? Because he is. Who proves it? Nobody. But it is thought; it is said. By whom? His enemies. Who informed them? They will swear it. Will they swear it, my lord? Why, then, they must know it. Either they have my letters to show, or can produce my messengers, or were present at a conference, or were concerned with Desmond, or somebody betrayed the secret to them, or they were themselves my vicegerents in the business : which of these points will they choose to maintain? I know them too well, to reckon myself convicted by their assertions, hearsays, or any oaths which they may swear. My letters could soon be read, were any such things extant. My servants and friends are ready to be sifted. Of my cousin Desmond, they may lie loudly; for no man here can contradict. As to myself, I never saw in them so much sense or integrity, that I would have staked on their silence the life of a good hound, far less my own. I doubt not, if your honours examine them apart, you will find that they are but the tools of others, suborned to say, swear, and state anything but truth; and that their tongues are chained, as it were, to some patron's trencher. I am grieved, my lord cardinal, that your grace, whom I take to be passing wise and sharp, and who, of your own blessed disposition wishes me so well, should be so far gone in crediting these corrupt informers, that abuse your ignorance —of Ireland. Little know you, my lord, how necessary it is, not only for the governor, but also for every nobleman, in that country, to hamper his uncivil neighbours at discretion. Were we to wait for processes of law, and had not those hearts and hands, of which you speak, we should soon lose both lives and lands. You hear of our case as in a dream, and feel not the smart of suffering that we endure. In England, there is not a subject that dare extend his arm to fillip a peer of the realm. In Ireland, unless the lord have ability to his power, and power to protect himself, with sufficient authority to take thieves and varlets whenever they stir, he will find them swarm so fast, that it will soon be too late to call for justice. If you will have our service to effect, you must not bind us always to judicial proceedings, such as you are blessed with here in England. As to my kingdom, my lord cardinal, I know not what you mean. If your grace thinks that a kingdom consists in serving God, in obeying the king, in governing the commonwealth with love, in sheltering the subjects, in suppressing rebels, in executing justice, and in bridling factions, I would gladly be invested with so virtuous and royal a state. But, if you only call me king, because you are persuaded that I repine at the government of my sovereign, wink at malefactors, and oppress well-doers, I utterly disclaim the odious epithet, surprised that your grace should appropriate so sacred a name to conduct so wicked. But however this may be, I would you and I, my lord, exchanged kingdoms for one month. I would, in that time, undertake to gather more crumbs than twice the revenues of my poor earldom. You are safe and warm, my lord cardinal, and should not upbraid me. While you sleep in your bed of down, I lie in a hovel; while you are served under a canopy, I serve under the cope of heaven; while you drink wine from golden cups, I must be content with water from a shell ; my charger is trained for the field, your gennet is taught to amble; while you are be-lorded and be-graced, and crouched and knelt to, I get little reverence, but when I cut the rebels off by the knees." This spirited retaliation touched the cardinal's pride to the quick ; and it was evident that he restrained his passion with the greatest difficulty. The counsellors, gratified in seeing him so treated, would have laughed, but they had not the courage. As Kildare was neither to be trifled with nor brow-beaten, and the evidence was not direct enough to stand the test of so shrewd a mind, Wolsey rose from the table, and the earl was detained until better proofs could be produced. Surrey, who had succeeded to the title of Norfolk by the death of his father, became bail for Kildare to the whole extent of his estate and life.* The earl, being afterwards pardoned, returned home.† During the remainder of the

* 1527.

† There is a story told of Kildare, but it seems so imperfectly authenticated that I have omitted it in the text. It is reported that he was found guilty of treason, and, being in the Tower a prisoner, was one evening amusing himself at some game of pastime with the lieutenant, when a mandate came from the cardinal for his execution. The earl, suspecting some

cardinal's administration, Ossory continued deputy, having superseded the brother of Kildare, who had been left in the government when that nobleman was summoned to England. He was a man of mean qualifications ; but, by the assistance of his wife, he ruled with vigour and utility.   The countess was a woman of surprising majesty of demeanour; august in her understanding; possessed of masculine fortitude; and of wisdom fit for a sovereign. But the merits and virtues of her character were chilled and overshadowed by the vast pride peculiar to her family. The O'Neals and O'Connors, excited by the Fitzgeralds, disturbed the government of her husband; but the annals of Ireland, during the lieutenancy of Ossory, as well as in the transactions already related, afford evidence honourable to the administration of Wolsey.

The Reformation, next to the preaching of the apostles, is one of the most important occurrences in the history of human affairs. Prior to the reign of Henry VIII., the doctrines of the gospel had not very obviously affected the public transactions of the world. It was only opinions and principles, surreptitiously concealed under the Christian name, that really guided the policy of rulers, and the conduct of men.* The ritual of the church differed but little from that

foul play, persuaded the lieutenant, who, by right of office, had access to the king at all times, to go and ascertain whether his majesty was privy to the warrant.   The king, who admired the character of Kildare, is said to have been greatly astonished at the presumption of the cardinal, and to have forbade the execution. But the story is altogether exceedingly confused, and there is no trace of Kildare having been at all tried. Besides, the warrant could not have been issued without the sign manual ; and the cardinal was not charged in his impeachment with ever having attempted to exercise an authority so illegal, as to send forth a warrant for execution, without having obtained the king's consent and signature.

* See Middleton's letter from Rome.   There is a curious history connected with this celebrated performance. In the year 1667, a book was printed, in French, at Leyden, which had been translated into English, under the title of " The Conformity between Modern and Ancient Ceremonies." The translator says, the original is so scarce, that, though conversant in large well-furnished libraries, he never met with but two copies ; and he, therefore, conceived, that the impression may have been bought up by the Roman priesthood ; a mode of assassinating truth which they often practised. However, it would appear, that certainly more than two copies did exist in this country : for the motive which led him to make the translation arose out of the great popularity of the letter from Rome by Conyers Middleton. That learned doctor of divinity, in his preface to his work, says,

of the pantheon; but the distinguishing characteristics of
saints and demi-gods indicated, that some change had taken
place in the notions of mankind.   Before the promulgation of
Christianity, the objects of admiration were military achievements; and the actions which entitled to posthumous reverence evinced only superior talents for spreading desolation
and crimes.   But, at the epoch of the Reformation, the same
kind of applause was bestowed on other qualities; and the
men who manifested in their lives the greatest contempt for
the pleasures of sense, were deemed the mirrors of human
conduct.   The change that had taken place in the sentiments
of the world, elevated the priest above the soldier.   But the
attributes of the priest were not those of the Christian, and a
revolution was necessary to display in what the difference
consisted.   The Reformation effected this.   The epoch,
however, has still to arrive, when Christianity shall command

"Many writers, I know, have treated the same subject before me; *some of
which I have never seen*, but those I have looked into, handle it in a manner
so differently from what I have pursued, that I am under no apprehension
of being thought a plagiary, or to have undertaken a province already occupied." But, upon comparing his performance with the translation alluded
to, there certainly never was a more clear case of plagiarism; for there is
nothing at all important in the doctor's letter which is not taken from the
other book, although there are many things in the other book which are not
in the doctor's letter. He has, in fact, being a sort of a classical man, confined himself to the pilfering of the quotations and allusions to the classics.
I should not have noticed this literary fraud, but for a slander which Middleton has propagated against the cardinal. He says, in his dedication to
the bishop of Norwich, after speaking of the effects which the freedom of
printing had in dissolving the influence of the papal spells and superstition,
"In the very infancy of printing amongst us, cardinal Wolsey foresaw this
effect of it, and, in a speech to the clergy, publicly forewarned them, that if
they did not destroy the press, the press would destroy them." Now, this
not only shows the most complete ignorance of the history of Wolsey, but
also of the origin of the church of England, of which the author was a
member; but is as false in statement, as some other passages from his pen.
The truth is, that what Middleton ascribes to the cardinal, was said by the
vicar of Croydon, in Surrey, in a sermon which he preached at Paul's Cross,
about the time that the New Testament was translated. "We must," said
the vicar, "root out printing, or printing will root out us." See *Fox's Acts
and Monuments*, vol. i. page 927. See also *Lewis's History of the Translations of the Bible*, 8vo, edit. page 71.—It is curious to trace the regular
descent of scandal, when it is once sanctioned by an authority. I remember, in reading a book of travels, (I think Barrow's in China,) meeting
with a repetition of the aspersion which Middleton, in his ignorance, has
thrown out on Wolsey.

its proper influence; although the priest, with respect to the Christian, holds now, perhaps, the same relative state that the hero did to the saint in the days of cardinal Wolsey. The history of the church, from the age of Charlemagne to that of Napoleon,—from the full establishment of the papal supremacy to its degradation,—affords a various and impressive theme. It demonstrates the insignificancy of military talents on the destiny of mankind; and mortifies the pride of statesmen, by showing that their influence is small and secondary; and that they are themselves but the implicit agents of deep and general predilections, previously nourished among the public.

After the death of Charlemagne, the kingdom of France fell into great disorder. The barons rose in continual hostility against one another; and that reprobate barbarity, in which the vices of civilization are joined with the atrocities of the savage state, menaced the inhabitants. The priesthood attempted to restrain this ruinous anarchy, and, by enjoining fasts, and threatening excommunications, vainly attempted to oppose the indefatigable spirit of aggression by which it was propagated and maintained. Entreaty and exhortation having failed, recourse was had to stratagem. In the year 1041, Durand, a carpenter, in the city of Puy in Auvergne, had rendered himself remarkable, and a fit instrument for the purposes of the clergy, by the warmth of his religious enthusiasm and the simplicity of his heart. One day, while alone in the fields, a person, who called himself the Redeemer, delivered to him a letter sealed with a representation of the sacred mother seated in a chair, and holding the infant upon her knee; a device not uncommon for the seals of monasteries. The letter was written from Jesus Christ, and addressed to the people, entreating them, for his sake, to suspend their warfare. Durand conceived that he had seen a vision, and he fancied himself commissioned, by divine authority, to be the advocate of peace on earth, and good will to man. The news of the apparition and of the holy letter spread far and wide; and the festival of the Ascension being at hand, the bishop requested Durand to come on that day and to publish his mission in the cathedral. A vast multitude, attracted by the circumstances, filled the church. Among the spectators were two noblemen of the neighbourhood, between whom a

deadly feud had long been cherished, and which had proved
calamitous to all within the scope of their conflicts. Durand
was placed on a high platform in the middle of the congrega-
tion. Animated by the notion of the sublimity of his trust,
he delivered his tale and message with such sincere and
fervent eloquence, that the whole audience presently began
to weep and sigh, and to praise the love and compassion of
Jesus. The hostile noblemen, subdued by benevolent sympathy, embraced each other in token of obedience to the Redeemer's request, and swore on the Evangelists to live in concord and friendship. The attendants followed the example of
their masters. All among the crowd, who had been at variance with each other, renounced their animosities. Badges
of tin, impressed with the figures on the sealing of the letter,
were distributed; and whoever piously assumed them, became immediately converted from malicious propensities, and,
in the presence of those who had done them the greatest
wrong, forgot their revenge, and were filled with charity and
love. The sympathy of this benevolent superstition spread
rapidly over the whole country; and the effects were so singular, so happy, and apparently so miraculous, that the tranquillity which ensued was called the truce of God.*

The success which attended this stratagem suggested the
scheme by which the preaching of Peter the Hermit soon
after was rendered still more influential. The hermit in his
appearance resembled the carpenter. His person was equally
mean and despicable, and his face and look ordinarily wore
the soft and sleepy aspect of idiocy; but he possessed a
glowing mind, an eloquent tongue, and when animated by the
topics of his subject, his countenance beamed with astonishing
energy, his eyes flashed with the rapture of inspiration, and
none could withstand his call to arise and rescue the holy
sepulchre. The consistory, perceiving the enthusiasm which
his active zeal had kindled throughout Christendom, contrived
the means of giving it the semblance of miraculous effect. A
council was summoned to meet at Clermont, where many
princes and nobles, prepared by art, and influenced by the
general passion, met the pope, who exhorted them to assume
the cross, and to exert their powers and faculties for the

* Favyn's Theatre of Honour.

deliverance of the Holy Land. The priests, tutored for the occasion, and the seculars, predisposed by the preaching of the hermit, at the conclusion of the pope's oration exclaimed, that God willed all to undertake the enterprise, and therefore they resolved to obey. On the same night their resolution was known, it is said, throughout Christendom; a circumstance then believed to have been effected by supernatural agency, but easy of explanation, when the regular correspondence among all the papal officers and the predetermined result of the council are considered.

The holy war lasted nearly two hundred years; in the course of which a great intercourse arose between the remote parts of Christendom and those places which still retained relics of the grandeur of Rome and the learning of Greece. The chiefs and vassals of the west in their march to Palestine, were surprised by the view of arts and manners of which they had never heard. At their return they related their adventures and the wonders that they had seen. Knowledge was in consequence disseminated. Sometimes they brought with them specimens of the productions of those strange and splendid regions, and the exhibitions of rarities excited a general desire to possess them. The spirit of commerce was awakened; and the intercourse which had been opened by the crusades was, after the war, continued, in order to gratify the demands of the opulent. The revival of literature in Italy sprung from this commerce, and books became an important branch of trade. As the documents of antiquity were multiplied, the oral traditions of the clergy fell in estimation, and a more precise and authentic style of learning was established. This affected the respect previously paid to the assertions of the priests. Many things devoutly received on ecclesiastical authority were found very differently stated in the works from which it was alleged that they had been derived; and forms and doctrines, considered essential to Christianity, were discovered to have been of later growth, the corrupt engraftings of ancient error. This moral change was quickened to political effects by the pontificates of Alexander VI., Julius II., and Leo X.; and the progress of the Lutheran heresies showed that the foundations of the papal structure were, in the days of Wolsey, deeply undermined.

The church was a government of opinion; and the cardinal

K

saw that the clergy would be compelled to resign their influence over the affairs of mankind, unless they could recover that relative superiority of knowledge by which, in ruder times, they had acquired the ascendancy. What stood, in his mind, as the church of Christ, was the pre-eminence of the priesthood. In the consequences of the Lutheran opinions he did not affect to value the precepts, but only the damage and detriment which might ensue to the papal power and dignity, were the priests to declare themselves independent of each other, and consequently dissolve that mighty confederacy which had so long ruled and enjoyed the world. His system of ecclesiastical reformation is, therefore, less remarkable for its effects on the progress of knowledge than on account of its objects. The aim of his designs was, to obtain for the priesthood generally the same kind of influence which the institutes of Loyola afterwards so wonderfully ministered to procure for the famous society of the Jesuits. It was calculated to render them entitled to possess superiority, although directed to preserve their exclusive privileges. The tendency of human affairs is, perhaps, towards the formation of a system, in which power shall be possessed by right of intellectual attainment; at least, since the period of the Reformation, there seems to have been a gradual converging of the elements of such a system. The influence of the literary character has been evidently augmented; and the unity of sentiment that is publicly propagated by the press, in some degree approximates to the effect of the systematic correspondence of the papal clergy. The first general result of the Reformation was, the transfer of the political power possessed by churchmen into the hereditary class.* The necessary

* The effect which the progress of society in this country has had in the choice of ministers of state, would afford a curious subject of investigation. In the rude and early times, when war was the business of the people and the study of the rulers, the ministers were men who had proved their capacity in the field of battle. After the different kingdoms of the heptarchy were consolidated under one crown, and when the clergy had obtained access to the secrets of men's minds and a separate establishment, the ministers were generally ecclesiastics. On the abrogation of the papal authority, the nobility succeeded to the power and emolument of state administration : but they, in turn, seem also destined to make way for the lawyers. The military rulers disciplined the people into order and subordination; the clergy reduced into a system (keeping in view the advancement of their own class)

consequence of this has been, that as much of the detail of ruling depends upon an accurate knowledge of law and the principles of equity, the hereditary class should either be distinguished by superior legal information, or it should employ, as agents and ministers, persons so distinguished. And accordingly it will not be disputed, that in all protestant nations the lawyers have superseded the clergy in the administration of police and the rules of life, in which the substance of political power really consists.

Erasmus, with his accustomed sycophancy towards the prosperous great, describes the cardinal's table, surrounded by the wise and learned of the age, as furnished with stars which threw a glorious brightness;* but it does not appear to have been frequented by any person—with the exception, perhaps, of sir Thomas More, whose works continue to amuse posterity. The object of Wolsey was to produce a general effect; and the history of his patronage of literature relates,

---

those maxims and regulations by which the military preserved submission and obedience; and the nobility, less numerous than the clergy, and more interested in the concerns of the people, have improved and extended, though still with reservations to their own advantage, the laws and usages which their ecclesiastical predecessors introduced.

* Sir Thomas More gives a caricatured description of the cardinal at his table. "It happened one day, that he had, in a great audience, made an oration, wherein he liked himself so well, that at his dinner he sat on thorns till he might hear how they that sat with him might commend it. And when he had sat musing awhile, devising, as I thought, upon some pretty proper way to begin, at last, for the lack of a better, he brought it even bluntly forth, and asked us all how well we liked the oration. But when the problem was once proposed, till it was full answered, no man, I ween, ate one morsel more; every man fell into so deep a study for the finding of some exquisite praise. For he that should have brought out but a vulgar and a common commendation, would have thought himself shamed for ever. Then said we our sentences by row as we sat, from the lowest unto the highest, in good order, as it had been a great matter of the common weal in a right solemn council. He that sat highest, and was to speak, was a great beneficed man, and not a doctor only, but also somewhat learned indeed in the laws of the church. A wonder it was to see how he marked every man's word that spake before him; and it seemed that every word the more proper it was, the worse he liked it, for the cumberance he had to study out a better to pass it. The man even sweat with labour, so that he was fain in the while to wipe his face."—Sir Thomas, although he speaks of the personage so bepraised as a great man of Germany, evidently meant Wolsey. The caricature is, however, more disgraceful to the guests than to the patron.

in consequence, more to institutions than to men of genius.
In this respect, as in his political measures, he differs advan-
tageously from Leo X.; but he is not so fortunate in his
reputation. His name is not connected with those of poets,
historians, and artists—but how many men, the pride of
England, and the ornaments of the species, may trace the
origin of their best attainments to the institutions and efforts
of Wolsey? The breadth and solidity of his designs and
undertakings for promoting knowledge entitle him to be
placed very high, if not pre-eminent, among the patrons of
learning. He was, in the emphatic sense of the term, a
statesman, and his munificence to literature was not bestowed
on individuals, but distributed with a general liberality for
the perpetual benefit of the realm. The mind is disposed to
contemplate this part of his policy with unmingled satisfaction, and notwithstanding the overweening ostentation of his
household and deportment, the aim with which he reformed
the laws of the universities, founded colleges, and procured
eminent professors to alter the stagnant state of learning,
entitle him to be considered as animated by that noble ambition which has immortality for its motive, the improvement
of mankind for its means, and the gratitude of posterity for
its reward.

The fine arts are the offspring of literature, which, in
civilized nations, always receives some new tincture and
modification from every general calamity. The interest
excited by public misfortunes gives rise to the details of historians, and their narratives furnish incidents and materials
for the descriptions of the poets, from whom the imitative
artists derive their subjects. In the reign of Henry VIII.,
particularly during the administration of Wolsey, scarcely a
single work of fancy was published; but the chronological
compilations of that period are still the great quarries of
English history.[1] It was not before the age of Elizabeth that
the records of the civil wars produced their full moral effect;
and the taste induced by the wonderful poets and authors of
her time contributed to excite that extraordinary pruriency
for the arts which rendered the early part of the reign of
Charles I. so illustrious. The second age of English literature followed in a similar manner the agitated period of the
Revolution; but the characteristics of the works of genius

produced in the reign of queen Anne showed that the public mind was imbued by another class of writers than the historians of the country. In the time of Charles II., many causes combined to make the nation desirous of forgetting the transactions of the commonwealth. The study of the classics of antiquity had been preferred to that of the historians of the preceding civil wars, and, in consequence, the style and sentiments of the Augustan age became imitated in the reign of Anne. The necessary effect of this was visible in the arts as well as in literature. The intricate and exuberant architecture of the ancient cathedrals, corresponding to the capricious and luxuriant effusions of the aboriginal authors, was superseded by an imitation of the Roman models, the style of which corresponded with the simplicity of the pruned productions of the press, and a general excess of polish almost obliterated originality.

The proficiency which nations make in the ornamental arts is always proportioned to the prosperity of their domestic circumstances. Italy, prior to the invasion of Charles VIII. of France, enjoyed a long period of felicity and repose, which the gravest historians have described with the warmth of poetical enthusiasm. The hills, cultivated to the summits, emulated the fertility of the valleys. The cities vied with antiquity in the elegance of their edifices. The countless ministers of superstitious sovereignty, bearing tribute to Rome, enhanced the flow of general wealth by the generosity of their expenditure; and commerce poured her copious horn, filled with the riches of all nations, into the lap of Florence, of Genoa, and of Venice. Like the illustrious arrangement of ancient Greece before the conquests of Alexander, the country was divided into many small states. The division exposed the whole to the hazard of subjugation from without, but the equilibrium within afforded to each a happy portion of domestic security. The inhabitants of all degrees lived in comparative fellowship — artists were the companions of nobles, for the nobles were merchants, and fostered the arts to increase the profits of trade. The general opulence bestowed the means of granting leisure to the studious to design, and to the mechanical to execute, while genius, by the activity of competition, was incited to retouch and improve its creations. The state of England at that time was far otherwise.

The civil wars were raging in all their fury. The multitudes, withdrawn from labour to arms, from producing to destroying, increased the toil to the remainder, and the public wealth was dilapidated by the reciprocal havoc of the rival families. During the administration of Wolsey, a respectable degree of prosperity was recovered; but the only funds which could be allotted to promote knowledge were monopolized by the church. All the superfluity of industry, which might have procured sustenance for genius, was appropriated to support the indolence of the clergy. It was therefore only by diminishing the number of the monks, and by inducing the other ecclesiastics to become active, that the great intellectual qualities of the English nation could be developed. While Leo X. was enjoying the fruits of the autumn of Italian genius, Wolsey was labouring where the spring had scarcely disclosed a single blossom; but a rich and various harvest has since amply justified the liberality of the preparation and his confidence in the soil.

Warton, in speaking of the state of poetry in the reign of Henry VIII.,* observes, that the marriage of a princess of England with a king of Scotland must have contributed to improve the literature and arts of the Scottish nation. But the observation is unphilosophical, and contrary to historical fact. If diplomatic correspondence and the occasional visits of courtiers have any effect on the progress of nations, the English were more likely to have been indebted to the Scots;†

---

* " The marriage of a princess of England with a king of Scotland, from the new communication and intercourse opened between the two courts and kingdoms by such a connexion, must have greatly contributed to polish the rude manners, and to improve the language, literature, and arts of Scotland."—*History of English Poetry.*

† In the year 1515, one of Sir David Lindsay's comedies was acted at the court of Scotland. I have not been able to find that, during the whole public life of Wolsey any secular dramas in English were exhibited in England. The princess Mary performed in a Latin comedy, which was got up at Greenwich, for the entertainment of the French commissioners sent to ratify the treaty concluded by Wolsey for the extrication of the pope. Dr. Berkenhout mentions, in the preface to his Biog. Brit., that about the year 1110, one Geoffrey, a schoolmaster in Dunstable, wrote a drama called St. Katherine, which the doctor, considering as a play, says that it carries the authentic history of the English theatre two hundred years higher than that of any other modern nation. But I conceive that we ought to reject the ecclesiastical performances from the history of the stage ; and the title

for the court of Edinburgh possessed, at that time, several professors of elegant literature that rivalled in taste and propriety of phraseology even the Italian poets, while that of London was only a dormitory to cumbrous divines. But the literature of nations is rarely improved by the alliances of princes, and seldom promoted by the munificence of courtiers. Which of the great authors of England was indebted for opulence to the patronage of the sovereigns? With the exception of the vain and presumptuous Louis XIV., there is not an instance on record of a monarch who regarded the fostering of knowledge as a part of his regal duty; and for many years a distinguished literary character at the levees of a British king has been almost as rare as the phœnix of the poets among the birds of Egypt; and yet the literature of the nation has certainly not declined.* It was the personal predilections of James IV. of Scotland which drew around him

of St. Katherine implies that it was a monkish exhibition. In the reign of Richard I., Seneca's tragedies, and some other Latin dramas, were translated into English by Henry, a monk of Hyde Abbey. Lord Berners, who died in 1532, was one of our earliest dramatic poets. I have not been able to meet with any of his works; and those of Lord Morley, who was almost his contemporary, are supposed to be lost.

* Unless the king himself have an unaffected predilection for the arts and sciences, the court is not more favourable to the improvement of knowledge, than the universities of Oxford and Cambridge under their existing constitutions. A century has elapsed since either of these great seminaries has possessed, as a resident member, perhaps it may be added produced, one man of influential genius; one who has improved the public taste, or extended the horizon of science. In men of learning, and men whose talents have been strengthened by the reflections of others, undoubtedly the universities of England have not been less prolific, even in proportion to the superior opulence of their endowments, than those of any other country; but persons versed only in books are not entitled to be classed with those men who, by the activity of their genius, and the novelty of their notions, affect the mass of the public mind, and change its bias and motion. It can never, indeed, be admitted, that the granting of emolument to the professors of definite and enacted opinions will promote the essential interests of reason and literature.

There is a list of the most remarkable of the recent offspring of Oxford and Cambridge, among the notes of Dr. Parr's celebrated Spital sermon. It is undoubtedly a splendid list of able characters; but which one of them all is entitled to the epithet of a man of genius, in the proper meaning of that term? which of them can be considered either as the head of his class, or the founder of a school?—a Sir Isaac Newton, a Milton, a Dryden, an Addison, an Adam Smith, or a Franklin?

the poets of his country ; and the ecclesiastical bent of
Henry VIII. operated in a similar manner to fill the court of
England with theologians. Hence the origin of the peculiari-
ties of English and Scottish literature in the time of cardinal
Wolsey.

The College of Physicians, which was founded in the year
1518, was the first national institution which the cardinal
patronized for the improvement of knowledge. Prior to that
event the state of the medical science was very low in
England. It was only remarkable for ingenious hypotheses,
unsupported by the evidence of facts, and for a credulous
faith on astrological influence[2] equally visionary. The kingdom, particularly London, had been often visited by a most
destructive pestilence, the sweating sickness: a disease which
was deemed peculiar to the English climate, but which has
since been happily eradicated. The infected died within
three hours after the first symptoms, and no cure could be
found. The administration of justice was suspended during
its continuance, and the court removed from place to place
with precipitation and fear. Half the people in some parts
of the country were swept away, and the principal trade
practised was in coffins and shrouds; but even that, in the
progress of the plague, was generally abandoned. At London,
vast sepulchral pits were prepared every morning, into which
the victims were thrown promiscuously. The only sounds in
the city during the day were the doleful monotony of un-
ceasing knells, and the lamentations of the tainted, deserted
by their friends, crying from the windows to passengers to
pray for them. The door of almost every house was marked
with a red cross, the sign that the destroying angel had been
there; and all night, as the loaded wheels of the death-wagons
rolled heavily along, a continual cry was heard of " Bring out
your dead." To discover a remedy, or some mode of avert-
ing the recurrence of this terrible calamity, the king, at the
suggestion of Dr. Linacre, was induced to establish the
College of Physicians: among others mentioned in the charter
as the advisers of this beneficial institution, Wolsey is particularly mentioned.

The cardinal was several years minister before he came
forward conspicuously as the patron *of national instruction.
He had been previously the Mecænas of individuals; but the

history of his munificence to literature relates chiefly to public institutions. The character of his mind fitted him to act happily only with wide and prospective considerations. The warmth of his temper, and the pride of conscious greatness, however high his aims, and noble his motives, rendered him harsh in familiar intercourse, and unqualified to acquire the affection of those men of endowment and knowledge whom ostentation invited to his house, and affluence entertained. The court happened to be at Abington in the year 1523, and a deputation of the heads of the colleges being sent from Oxford to pay the compliments of the university, the queen was afterwards induced to visit that city, accompanied by Wolsey. They were received with the customary ceremonies; and the cardinal, in reply to the oration which was addressed to him, declared, that he had the interests of his parental university much at heart, and that he was desirous of substantially evincing his filial attachment. He accordingly proposed to found certain public lectures, and offered to undertake the revisal of the statutes, which were at variance in tenour with one another, and adverse in spirit to the prosperity of learning. These proposals were gladly received, and letters on the subject were without delay sent to the chancellor, archbishop Warham. This jealous and captious old man was sensibly affected by everything that tended to the aggrandisement of Wolsey; and therefore, although he could not possibly object to the instituting of the lectures, he strenuously opposed the plan of committing to him the revision of the statutes. In the end, however, he was constrained to yield his personal antipathy for the public advantage; and the senate in full convocation decreed, that the laws should be placed in the cardinal's hands to be corrected, reformed, changed, or expunged, as he in his discretion should think fit.* Cambridge soon after adopted the same measure, and even exceeded Oxford in adulation. The address voted on the occasion declared, that the statutes were submitted to be modelled according to his judgment, as by a true and settled standard; for he was considered as a man sent by a special order of divine providence for the benefit of mankind. In order to evince still more the unlimited extent of this con-

* Fiddes, 179 and 180.

fidence, the senate conferred on him the power for life of
legislating for the university; and proposed to honour his
memory with perpetual yearly commemorations.* These acts
of homage, in themselves remarkable proofs of the ready subserviency of public bodies to the existing powers, are worthy
of observation, as they form an important era in the history
of English literature. From the date of the revisal of the
statutes by cardinal Wolsey, the progress of popular learning
and the improvement of the language were rapid and extraordinary in the universities; in which, prior to that epoch,
there was scarcely a member distinguished by any proficiency
in practical knowledge. They were inhabited only by men
who had dozed into corpulency over the ponderous folios of
scholastic divinity; and it was probably less on account of
any advantage that was expected to arise to the public from
improving her statutes that Cambridge addressed the cardinal
with such idolatrous adulation, and invested him with such
supreme power, than the hope of inducing him to prefer her
for the seat of a college, which it was then rumoured he intended to build on a plan of the greatest magnificence. It is,
however, but justice to add, that Cambridge very early
became a candidate for his patronage; for when he was only
bishop of Lincoln she offered him her chancellorship, which
he declined.

When he had instituted at Oxford the lectures of which he
had given notice during his visit with the queen, he proceeded with the design of Christ Church college. The foundations were laid† soon after the news arrived in London of
the battle of Pavia. This noble edifice stands on the site of
a priory, the brotherhood of which had for a long time given
such scandal by their profligacy, that the design of dispersing
them, and of converting their revenues and buildings to the
uses of learning, had been entertained several years before.
The preamble of the patent, by which the king assigned to
the cardinal the property of the monasteries dissolved by
virtue of his legatine commission, and destined for the support of his lectures and college, highly commends his administration of the national affairs; and declares that, in consideration of his having so ably sustained the weight of the govern-

* Fiddes, 187.   † March 20th, 1525.

ment for several years, the grant was made as a testimony to
posterity of the sense entertained of his services.   By a draft
of the statutes written by Wolsey himself it appears, that the
permanent members of the college* were intended to consist
of a dean, a subdean, sixty canons of the first rank, and forty
of the second, thirteen chaplains, twelve clerks, and sixteen
choristers, with professors of rhetoric, medicine, philosophy,
mathematics, Greek,† theology, and law, besides four censors
of manners and examiners of the proficiency of the students,
three treasurers, four stewards, and twenty inferior servants.
A revenue was set apart for the entertainment of strangers,
the relief of the poor, and the maintenance of horses for
college business.   The architectural design of the building
was of corresponding magnitude; and had it been completed
according to the plan of the founder, few royal palaces would
have surpassed it in splendour and extent.   The project by
which he proposed to furnish the library was worthy of the
general design.   He took measures to obtain copies of all the
manuscripts in the Vatican,‡ in addition to the ordinary
means of procuring books.[3]

Soon after his return from the great embassy to France,
he laid the foundations of a public school at Ipswich, his
native town.   It was intended to be a preparatory seminary
for the college, similar to the school at Winchester founded
by William of Wickham, and to that at Eton by Henry VI.;
both of which were instituted with the same relative view to
their respective colleges in Oxford and Cambridge.   The
funds appropriated for the support of this institution were

---

* " The cardinal's college was one of the first seminaries of an English
university that professed to explode the pedantries of the old barbarous philosophy, and to cultivate the graces of polite literature."—*Wharton's Hist.
of English Poetry*, vol. iii. p. 3.

† At this period a great contest arose in the university of Oxford, respecting the modern pronunciation of the Greek language.   The opponents
of the new style called themselves Trojans; they had a Priam, a Hector, a
Paris, &c.   But what was at first merely jocular, became the cause of serious
quarrel.   The students felt the rivalry of the ancients, whose names they
had assumed, and the Isis was disturbed with taunts that might have
frightened the Scamander.   The pulpit became, as it were, a tower of Ilium;
for a pious priest took an opportunity of declaiming, with the rapture of
Cassandra, against all Greek and Latin literature.   At length the cardinal,
like Jupiter, interposed, and the Greeks, as of old, were victorious.

‡ Fiddes, 306.

chiefly drawn from the revenues of dissolved monasteries. The town had, before that time, a free grammar school endowed with certain property vested in the hands of the magistrates, who at the cardinal's request judiciously assigned it to the new school, the more extensive purposes of which superseded the utility of continuing the other. He ordered a grammar to be prepared for the use of the students, wrote a prefatory address, in which he speaks of the institution as designed to promote the education of British youth,—an expression that seems to indicate something like an expectation of an ultimate union of the crowns of the island. This is, perhaps, the only literary production of Wolsey entitled to be considered as a publication. His acquirements as a scholar were, indeed, rather proofs of the generality and vigour of his talents, than evidence of the extent of his intellectual powers compared with those of others. The length and fulness of his public dispatches, and the variety of circumstances which he comprehends within the scope of his topics, entitle them to be regarded, in many instances, as dissertations on the events and proceedings of the time. His style, at once powerful, circumstantial, and diffuse, conveys so ample an exposition of his meaning, that he never fails to fill the mind of the reader with a complete conception of what he aims to produce. His sentences are sometimes involved, and often indefinite; but he pours forth such an amazing breadth of explanation, that the general effect is irresistible. In this respect the character of his eloquence may be compared to a large stream flowing through a marshy country: though the main current be clear, impetuous, and strong, the bounds and banks are shoaly, sedgy, unequal, irregular, and undefined.

Wolsey, as lord chancellor, had often as much occasion to observe the ignorance of the lawyers, as in his episcopal capacity that of the clergy; and he has been described as often interrupting the pleadings of the barristers, and bitterly animadverting on their want of knowledge. To remedy an evil which troubled the public jurisprudence at the fountain-head, and made its necessary ramifications only so many distributors of disorder and vexation, he projected an institution, to be founded in London, in which the study of law should be efficiently cultivated. The scheme was consonant to the general liberality of his view, and perhaps is still requisite. The architectural model for the building was considered a masterpiece, and remained, long after his death, as a curiosity, in the palace at Greenwich.

In the prosecution of these munificent purposes, the cardinal was obliged to contend with the opposition, and to endure the obloquy of every rank and class of the nation. The courtiers, whom his lordliness mortified into enemies, lost no opportunity of repeating to the king every omission, however trivial, in the multitude of the affairs which he undertook to direct; and insinuated, that he excelled the other ministers only in the boldness of his pretensions. But on such occasions Henry always vindicated the sincerity of his own character, and repressed with becoming manliness the intrusions of envy. The censorial court which Wolsey had instituted by virtue of his commission as legate, was an intolerable and continual offence to the priesthood. Allen,* his chaplain, whom he had appointed the judge, and who was afterwards bishop of Dublin, exercised his functions with harshness, and sometimes with partiality. His conduct gave warranty to discontents which had originated in the jurisdictions of the office; and old Warham, who was greedy of accusations against the cardinal, availing himself of some particular instance of impropriety on the part of Allen, complained to the king of the legatine court. Henry observed to him, that "No man is so blind as in his own house; but for you, father, I should not have heard of this matter; I pray you, therefore, go to Wolsey, and tell him, if there be any thing amiss in these proceedings, to amend it." The malicious love of justice which dictated this complaint, was probably, for that time, frustrated; but an occasion soon after occurred of making a special charge against the conduct of the cardinal himself. He advanced a lady who had sullied her youth by carnal indiscretion, to be abbess of the nunnery

---

* John Allen. He was appointed to the bishopric of Dublin in 1528. "The five persons employed by the cardinal to take measures for the demolition of the monasteries, quarrelled among themselves. One killed another, and was hanged for it; the third drowned himself in a well; the fourth was reduced to beggary; and Allen, afterwards a bishop, was cruelly maimed in Ireland."— *Stow.*

of Winton. Henry was speedily informed of the appointment, and immediately expostulated with Wolsey, mentioning, at the same time, that the gifts which were bestowed by the monasteries to promote the building of his colleges, were suspected of being corruptly given, in order to save themselves from the visits of the legatine officers; remarking, that this was the more probably true, as they had never shown any such generosity to the necessities of their sovereign; and, with the frank earnestness of friendship, he entreated him to rectify such abuses. Fortunately for the cardinal, the appointment of the prioress was subject to the approbation of the king; and he submitted himself so humbly, in consequence of the severity of the rebuke, that Henry immediately and kindly reassured him of his entire confidence; at the same time, he still seemed to doubt the propriety of appropriating the funds of the monasteries to the purposes of learning; and he informed him, that it was generally murmured throughout the nation, that the colleges but furnished a cloak to cover the misdemeanours of avarice. The conduct of Henry on this occasion merits applause, both as a man and as a monarch. He showed himself jealous of his own honour and the rights of public property, but he had confidence in the integrity and high views of his minister. While he therefore informed Wolsey of the complaints against him, he trusted that his discretion would obviate them for the future. The event was of importance to the cardinal. It opened his eyes to the depth and extent of his danger, and showed him that he had no other dependence than the precarious favour of a prince. He saw that the envy of his greatness which had been fomented into malice by the success of his measures, was deadly, and he endeavoured to lessen its virulence by reducing the ostentation that served to augment it. He resigned to the king the palace of Hampton; and in his intercourse with the other members of the council, lowered the superiority with which he had so long dictated the measures of the government. But this alteration was calculated rather to encourage the hopes of his enemies than to lessen the avidity with which they desired his destruction. The king, it is true, after the affair of the prioress of Winton, continued to evince the same unlimited friendship as formerly, but the irritation of that occasion unconsciously predisposed him for similar impressions.*

* Storer, from whose beautiful and very scarce poem I have already made several extracts, gives the following picturesque description of the cardinal as a patron of literature :—

> " Look how the God of Wisdom marbled stands,
> Bestowing laurel wreaths of dignity
> In Delphos isle, at whose impartial hands
> Hung antique scrolls of gentle heraldry,
> And at his feet ensigns and trophies lie :
> Such was my state, whom every man did follow,
> A living image of the great Apollo."

BOOK VI.

THE grandeur of Wolsey continued to increase until he became possessed of greater power than, perhaps, any subject
before his time had ever enjoyed. He was virtually the head
of the church in England; prime political minister; the chief
judge of law and equity; legislator of the two universities;
arbiter of disputes between the king and foreign princes: and
his income was supposed to be equal to the amount of the
royal revenues. But the full and perfect round of reflected
splendour was destined to wane, and to suffer at last a total
extinction. In all the vicissitudes of his master's humours,
he had still preserved the first place in his esteem. The
clamours of the clergy failed to disturb this unlimited confidence. The impartial justice of his conduct as a judge,
though offensive to the pretensions of the nobility, afforded
no plausible ground upon which his integrity could be impeached. His views of foreign policy, reaching beyond the
age in which he lived, and comprehending the interests of
posterity, were never popular; far less the financial measures

which they led him to adopt; but the success of his plans for advancing the political importance of the nation, gratified the ambition of Henry; and in those days public opinion was a trifle in comparison with royal favour. At length, however, the same lofty arrogance of principle which showed itself so proud and stubborn to the clergy, the nobility, and the people, was to be found at variance with the wishes of the sovereign himself; and it was Wolsey's fate to furnish one of the most striking instances of the instability of fortune, and the ingratitude of despotic power, which the whole compass of history affords.

Katharine, Henry's queen, had been previously married to his brother Arthur, the prince of Wales. Arthur was then only in his sixteenth year, but he was a vigorous and healthful youth, and he and Katharine lived more than four months together as man and wife. Their bed on the wedding-night, according to a custom of that age, was solemnly blest; a ceremony which certainly implied confidence in the maturity of the parties. A statement of presumptive evidence in favour of the consummation of the marriage was transmitted by the Spanish ambassador to his sovereign; and hints to the same effect had been given by the prince himself on the morning after the nuptials. In consequence of this, when Arthur died, Henry was not created prince of Wales, until it was ascertained, by time, that the princess was not with child.

The political motives which led to the union of Arthur and Katharine did not terminate with the life of the prince; but although they had ceased to be of primary influence, still the large dowry of the princess, which Henry VII. might have been obliged to refund, was of itself sufficient to induce that avaricious tyrant to devise the plan of marrying her to her husband's brother, then in his boyhood. Against this incestuous expedient archbishop Warham strongly remonstrated; but a bull was, notwithstanding, obtained from Julius II. to authorize and sanctify its accomplishment.* In this bull it was plainly stated that the princess had been lawfully married to prince Arthur, and the marriage probably consummated; but that the prince having died without issue, therefore, in order to preserve amity between the crowns of Spain and England, and peace among catholic kings, the pope

---

* 6th December, 1503. Burnet's Col. Book II. No I.

dispensed with the impediments of affinity between Henry
and his brother's widow, and gave them leave to marry, or
even, if already united, confirmed their marriage. Many of
the cardinals disapproved of this extraordinary concession;
but as it was thought to promote the interests of the papacy,
their opposition was low, ineffectual, and soon hushed. It
was imagined that the future kings of England, descendants
of this marriage, would be induced to maintain that authority
from which their right to the crown was derived. But the
design, in the sequel, proved fatal to the fraudulent system
which it was expected so essentially to support.

Soon after the union of Henry and Katharine, the old king
began to doubt the rectitude of what he had done, and his
conscience grew so irksome and unquiet, that when the prince
attained the age of fourteen, at which period the law allows
the heirs of the English throne to exercise the rights of judgment, he commanded him to protest that, being under age,
he had been married to the princess Katharine, but now he
did not confirm that marriage: on the contrary, that he
intended to make it void. This protestation was made in
presence of many of the nobility and clergy. Not satisfied
with merely obtaining the avowal of an intention, the king,
as he lay on his death-bed, earnestly exhorted the prince to
break off the incestuous connexion. An exhortation in itself
so solemn and penitential, though it might be neglected in the
thoughtlessness of youth, was calculated to return upon the
imagination with increased effect, when recalled by occurrences that might be construed into manifestations of the
Divine displeasure.

One of the first questions which, after the death of Henry
VII., came before the council, was, whether the marriage
should be annulled or consummated. The arguments for the
consummation prevailed; and moral delicacy was sacrificed
to political expediency. The king was again married to his
brother's widow, and their public coronation followed.* From
that time the legality of the connexion remained undisputed,
and several children, of whom the princess Mary alone survived, were the issue.

Katharine having fallen into ill health, Henry had, for

---

* Burnet, 35.

several years deserted her bed.   Seeing no likelihood of her
giving a male heir to the crown, he became restless in mind,
and imagined that the curse pronounced in Scripture against
the man who takes his brother's wife had come upon them,
and that he was fated to die childless.   The marriage having
been hitherto undisputed, he was not led to think of dissolving
it till the year 1527, when, in the progress of the treaty of
affinity negotiated with Francis, the French minister objected
to the legitimacy of the princess, on the ground that the
marriage of which she was the fruit had been contracted in
violation of a divine precept, which no human authority
could impair.*   Some time before, the council of Spain had
made similar observations, and, on the doubtfulness of the
matter, endeavoured to justify the dissolution of the contract
of Charles and Mary.

From all these circumstances, it is evident that Henry's
scruples arose from events which happened before Wolsey's
introduction at court, and were strengthened by occurrences
over which he had no control.   The king first disclosed
them to his confessor, and probably soon after to the cardinal;
but there is no evidence to ascribe their origin to the art of
the one, or the machinations of the other.   Nor with greater
justice can it be alleged that the scruples were forged to
disguise a criminal passion for Anne Boleyn, although it will
appear, in the course of the subsequent transactions, that the
influence of her charms in no small degree added to their
weight.   The controversies relative to the royal marriage
lasted several years; and many circumstances in Henry's
conduct during that time served to show that he was affected
by other motives as well as by his partiality for that lady.
In the early stages of the business he seems to have been
actuated by a real anxiety for his religious welfare.   Before
bringing it into public discussion, he had satisfied his own
mind that the marriage was contrary to the Levitical laws.
The next question which presented itself was, whether the
pope possessed the power of dispensing with a precept of
Divine institution? and it might readily occur to him, that the
observance of any law can only be set aside by an authority
equal to that by which it was at first enacted.   The prero-

* Burnet, 36.

gative of the sovereign pontiff to alter the laws of the church was admitted; but the Levitical laws, being promulgated immediately from Heaven, could not be set aside or suspended by any human decision.

Henry, in this stage of his reflections, communicated to Wolsey his determination to try the question publicly, and requested to know what he thought of it? The cardinal was struck with alarm; and instantly foreboding the dangerous consequences of such a resolution, fell on his knees, and intreated the king to abandon a design so hostile to the faith of which he was the declared champion and defender; especially while the whole structure of the church was rent with schisms, and shaken from roof to foundation by the tempest of the Lutheran controversies. Nor could he omit to point out the political evils of incurring the enmity of the queen's relations, and the certainty that her nephew the emperor would violently endeavour to revenge the insult which the proceeding would be to his family. But Henry was not to be persuaded from his resolution: he insisted upon knowing Wolsey's opinion of the abstract question. The cardinal, in order to gain time, and possibly with a hope that some accident might occur to alter the king's mind, begged that, in a matter of such importance, he might be allowed to confer previously with persons better versed in the divine and civil laws. A request so reasonable was readily granted; and, accordingly, by virtue of his legatine commission, he summoned the bishops, and the learned of the universities and cathedrals, to meet him for that purpose at Westminster.

If the cardinal was of opinion at first that the validity of the marriage ought not to be called in question, the case was materially altered when the king's doubts had become publicly known, and were communicated to his subjects. It then became his duty to bring the matter to a speedy issue, and to hasten proceedings which involved the legitimacy of the royal offspring, and which, in the event of the king's premature death, might again entail on the nation the miseries of a disputed succession. As a prince of the church he was bound to maintain the papal authority, by an undeviating adherence to every canon and formality in the course of a process of such importance. He is therefore, in the progress of the divorce, to be regarded as acting in a double capacity, as the minister of the king and of the pope. To both he was bound to act with fidelity. The service of the one was contrary to the interests of the other. His situation was extraordinary, and his difficulties without a precedent. He was placed in a situation where his honesty had the effect of making him equally offensive to both parties; and integrity, almost necessarily, exposed him to the suspicion of partiality and equivocation. Neither ought the private peculiarities of his condition at this time to be forgotten. He had reached the most enviable place of dignity, where he had not one real friend connected with his fate. His unmitigated perseverance in the reformation of the clerical abuses had filled the great body of the priesthood with implacable resentment; his steady maintenance of the papal pretensions exposed him to the hatred of the Lutheran reformers; his severe administration of justice exasperated the pride of the nobility; his expensive foreign policy made him no less obnoxious to the people; and his successful career provoked that antipathy which contemporaries ever feel against the successful, especially when success is obtruded by ostentation. The queen had long been aware of his great influence over her husband; and, as he appeared active and anxious in the investigation of the validity of the marriage, it was not surprising that she should ascribe the origin of the question in a great measure to him. Even Anne Boleyn, of whom Henry had in the meantime become enamoured, was secretly his enemy, and longed for an opportunity of gratifying her spite.

When the king's sister was married to Lewis XII., Anne Boleyn, then only seven years old, went in her train to Paris; and after the death of Lewis, when her mistress returned to England, she remained behind as one of the attendants at the French court; where her beauty and sprightliness had made her a general favourite. After the death of Claude,* the queen

---

* Hall gives a dark and mysterious hint about the death of this lady. In the year 1525, the earl of Angus came from France to England; and, being at Windsor, he declared, that in the council of France, while he was there, they happened to talk of the wars then raging between Charles and Francis; upon which one lord stood up and said it were better that one person suffered, rather than all the realm should be daily in this mischief. It was asked, what he meant. He answered, that if the queen, who was lame and ugly, were dead, ways might be found for the king to marry the emperor's sister, and to have with her the duchy of Milan; and then with her money the king of England could be paid. But whether this was true or false, certain it is that the French queen died very soon after.

of Francis, she was attached to the household of his sister, the duchess of Alençon, with whom she remained until about the period when the scruples of Henry became publicly known, at which time she came back to England; and was, soon after her arrival, appointed one of the maids of honour to the queen.   Among the young noblemen then retained by the cardinal, was lord Percy, eldest son of the earl of Northumberland, between whom and Anne Boleyn an attachment arose, and it became known that they were actually betrothed.* Henry having begun to entertain a passion for the lady, requested Wolsey, when informed of the circumstance, to remonstrate with the young lord on the impropriety of the connexion. The cardinal accordingly severely reproved Percy for matching himself with one so far below his condition. But the lover defended his choice, maintaining, that in point of lineage and relationship she was not his inferior. Her mother was a daughter of the duke of Norfolk; her paternal grandmother was scarcely less eminent, being one of the daughters of the earl of Wiltshire and Ormond; and her grandfather, though himself only a lord mayor of London, had married a daughter of lord Hastings. The cardinal, seeing Percy so fixed in his attachment, sent for the earl of Northumberland, by whose decisive interference the alliance was dissolved. Percy was enjoined to avoid the lady's company, and she was discharged from court. Nor was she recalled until after his marriage with a daughter of the earl of Shrewsbury. She was then not long in discovering that the king viewed her with eyes of admiration; but she never forgave the cardinal for depriving her of Percy.† She considered the banquets of which she partook with the court at his palace only as offerings to propitiate her rising influence, and the idea increased her resentment. But it was still necessary that she should dissemble; and, to ingratiate herself the more with the

* " Lord Herbert, in his Life of Henry VIII., has published an original letter from lord Percy, written in 1536, a short time before queen Anne's execution, in which he denies any such contract in the most solemn terms."—*Wordsworth.*

† "Yet nothing can be stronger than her expressions of gratitude and affection to the cardinal at this period, in letters published by Burnet. (See Appendix.) It should seem, unless we suppose her to have been altogether insincere, that her animosity proceeded from causes later than the affair of Lord Percy."—*Singer.*

king, she treated the cardinal with the utmost external respect. Her vanity grew giddy with the expectation of the crown, long before it was likely that she could receive it; and, enriched by the profusion of her royal lover, she assumed an immodest ostentation of finery.

The queen, dejected by infirm health, beheld with humility the indecorous advancement of her gentlewoman; and with ineffectual meekness endeavoured to win back the affections of her husband. She even seemed to be pleased with her rival, bewailing only in secret that unhappy destiny which, in a foreign country, had reduced herself so low.* The generosity of the people was awakened in her favour, and they quickly found out sufficient reasons to account for the conduct both of Henry and his minister. They observed that the emperor was no longer treated as a friend; and without troubling themselves to appreciate the events which, from the battle of Pavia, had changed the political interests of England, they accused Wolsey of being actuated against Katharine by revenge for slights and disappointments received from her nephew. The notoriety of the king's affection for Anne Boleyn was no less a satisfactory explanation of his motives; although he had before violated his conjugal fidelity, and afterwards returned to the queen, whose virtues and chaste demeanour he had never ceased to esteem.† That Anne Boleyn was frequently seen at those entertainments where the cardinal delighted to exhibit his magnificence, is rather a proof of the lax morality common to the circles of courtiers, than evidence of any deliberate design on his part either to aid her promotion, or to mortify the queen. Towards her, indeed, he appears never to have entertained any particular partiality; and it has been alleged, that one of the causes which hastened his ruin was her apprehension that, in the event of the marriage being annulled, he would exert his influence to provide a more honourable match for the king.‡ She vindictively remembered the frustration of her first love, and dreaded the disappointment of her ambition.

While the cardinal was in France on his great embassy, the first messenger on the subject of the marriage was sent

* " Declaring herself to be a perfect Griselda."—*Cavendish.*
† He had a son by a daughter of sir John Blount.
‡ Lord Herbert, 244.

to Rome. It is not very clearly ascertained whether the message related to the king's scruples, or only to procure such a legitimation by the pope of the princess's birth as should obviate the doubts which had been suggested. The earliest regular despatch written on the subject of the divorce is dated* five months posterior. By it the king's agents at Rome appear to have been previously informed of the state of their master's mind, for in reporting the opinion of the learned as to the illegality of dispensations granted contrary to the divine laws, the cardinal urges the expediency of allowing a divorce to pass, not only to avert the future miseries of a disputed succession, but to appease the inquietude of the king's conscience. Nor were bribes omitted to procure the compliance of his holiness, who granted, in consequence, a commission to investigate the case, and to proceed with the business in England. Before it arrived, Henry transmitted an application for a special legate to be sent to London for the purpose.† This new request was communicated by the pope to two of the cardinals, and in a conference held with them in presence of the English agents, he expressed himself to the following effect: " Wolsey, by the commission already issued, or by his extraordinary general legatine authority, is, I conceive, fully empowered to proceed in this affair. If the king in his own conscience be convinced of the rectitude of his intentions—and there is no doctor in the world more able to settle the point than himself —he should accelerate judgment, and then send for a legate to confirm what he has done; for it will be easier to ratify what cannot be recalled, than to terminate such a process in the court of Rome. The queen may protest against the place and the judge, by which, in the course of law, I shall be obliged to prohibit the king from marrying while the suit is pending, and must revoke the trial to Rome. But if judgment were given in England, and the king married to another wife, very good reasons might be found to justify the confirmation of a decision that had gone so far."‡ This equivocal mode of proceeding was not agreeable to Henry, and Wolsey informed the pope that the king was resolved that the busi-

* 5 December, 1527.
12 January, 1528.   ‡ Burnet, 48.

plexed. We then had recourse to the pope, and procured the venerable legate who has lately arrived from Rome to investigate the case. For the queen, whatever may be the detractions of women and tattlers, we willingly and openly profess, that because in nobleness of mind she far transcends the greatness of her birth, were we now at liberty and free to choose among all the beauties of the world, we would not, as we take God to witness, make choice of any other. In mildness, prudence, sanctity of mind and conversation, she is not to be paralleled. But we were given to the world for other ends than the pursuit of our own pleasure. We therefore prefer the hazard of uncertain trial, rather than commit impiety against heaven and ingratitude against our country, the weal and safety of which every man should prefer before his life and fortune."* This oration affected the audience in different ways: some lamented the king's anxiety, but many more the situation of the queen, and all doubted and feared the result. The boisterous generosity of the people, decidedly in her favour, was not easily controlled; and the declaration of the king was treated by them as an attempt to conceal a gross and adulterous passion.

In the beginning of the year 1529, the pope was seized with a violent disorder, from which he was not expected to recover. Wolsey, on hearing of this, immediately began to canvass for the papal chair, and the correspondence which he held for this purpose serves to illustrate the bias of his ambition, and to show the objects to which he would have directed his attention in the event of attaining the supreme dignity. In one of his letters he charges his agents to procure access to the pope; and, though he were in the very agony of death, to propose two things to him: first, that he would command all the princes of Christendom to lay down their arms. "His holiness," says he, "can do nothing more meritorious for the good of his soul than to close his life with so holy an act. And, secondly, that he would promote the king's business as a thing essential to the clearing of his conscience towards God."† But the pope recovered, and, offended by the eagerness with which the cardinal aspired to succeed him, was little disposed to take his advice. Pressed on the one hand

* Godwin's Annals, p. 52.   † Bennet, 63.

by the queen's relations, who urged him to avocate the cause to Rome, and on the other by Henry, who was equally solicitous that it should be brought to an immediate decision, he adopted a procrastinating policy; and, by the address of Campeggio, the year was far advanced before the requisite arrangements for the trial were completed.

The sovereign of a powerful kingdom, accustomed to absolute sway, and under no apprehensions from any foreign power, freely submitting to be cited before a tribunal erected within his own dominions, for the purpose of determining a cause in which his own honour and happiness were so deeply involved, was a spectacle equally singular and interesting, and calculated to arrest the attention of all descriptions of men. The thirty-first day of May was fixed for opening the court; and the hall of the Blackfriars' convent in London, where the parliament in those days usually assembled, was prepared for the occasion. At the upper end hung a canopy, under which, on an elevated platform, the king sat on a chair of state. The queen was seated at some distance, a little lower. In front of the king, but three steps beneath him, and so placed, that the one appeared on his right hand, and the other on his left, Wolsey and Campeggio were placed and at their feet several clerks and officers; before whom, and within the bar, were the prelates of the realm. Without the bar, on one side, stood the advocates and proctors of the king; and on the other, those appointed for the queen.* The sides of the hall were occupied with successive tiers of benches, which were crowded to a great height with all the most illustrious and noble persons of the nation.

Silence being proclaimed, the commission of the legates

---

* " The chief scribe there was Dr. Stephen Gardener, (afterwards bishop of Winchester,) the apparitor was one Cooke, most commonly called Cooke of Winchester. . . . The doctors for the king were Dr. Sampson, that was afterwards bishop of Chichester, and Dr. Bell, who was afterwards bishop of Worcester, with divers others. The proctors on the king's part, were Dr. Petit, who was afterwards made the king's chief secretary, and Dr. Tregonell and divers others. The counsel for the queen, were Dr. Fisher, bishop of Rochester, and Dr. Standish, some time a grey friar, and then bishop of St. Asaph, two notable clerks in divinity, and in especial the bishop of Rochester, who afterwards suffered death at Tower Hill; and another ancient doctor, called, as I remember, Dr. Ridley, a very small person in stature, but such a great and excellent clerk in divinity."—*Cavendish.*

was read, and an officer, called the apparitor, cried aloud, "Henry, king of England, come into court."* The king answered, "Here I am." The queen was then also summoned, but she made no reply. Rising from her chair, she descended to the floor, and walked round the court. Not a breathing was heard. When she came opposite to the king, she knelt down, and addressed him† to the following effect:—"Sir, I humbly beseech you for all the loves that hath been between us, and for the love of God, to do me justice and right; for I am a poor woman and a stranger, born out of your dominions, having here no assured counsel, and less assurance of friendship. I flee to you as to the head of justice within this realm. Alas! sir, wherein have I offended you? on what occasion of displeasure have I designed against your will and pleasure, intending, as I perceive, to put me from you? I take God and all the world to witness, that I have been to you a true, humble, and obedient wife, ever conformable to your will and pleasure; never did I contrary or gainsay your mind, but always submitted myself in all things wherein you had any delight or dalliance, whether it were in little or much, without grudging, or any sign of discontent. I have loved for your sake those whom you loved, whether I had cause or no, were they friends or foes. I have been this twenty years or more your true wife, by whom you have had many children, although it hath pleased God to call them out of this world, which hath been no fault in me; and when I first came to your bed, I take God to witness I was a true virgin: whether it be true or no, I put it to your conscience.

* Burnet affirms, that the king did not appear personally, but by proxy; and that the queen withdrew, after reading a protest against the competency of her judges: "and from this it is clear," says the bishop, "that the speeches that the historians have made for them are all plain falsities." But it must be observed, that the testimony for the personal appearance of the king before the cardinals is surprisingly powerful; even though we do not go beyond Cavendish and the other ordinary historians. But, in addition to these, reference may be made to the authority of William Thomas, clerk of the council in the reign of Edward VI., and a well-informed writer, who, in a professed apology for Henry VIII., extant in MS. in the Lambeth, and some other libraries, speaking of this affair, affirms, "That the cardinal (Campegius) caused the king, as a private partye, in person to appeare before him, and the ladie Katharine both." Page 31.—*Wordsworth's Eccl. Biog.* vol. i. p. 423.

† "In broken English."—*Cavendish.*

If there be any just cause that you can allege, either of dishonesty or of other impediment, lawful to put me from you, I am well content to depart with shame and rebuke; but if there be none, then I lowly beseech you, let me have justice at your hands. The king, your father, was, in the time of his reign, of such estimation through the world for his excellent wisdom, that he was accounted a second Solomon; and the king of Spain, my father, who was esteemed one of the wisest kings that reigned in Spain these many years—so they were both wise men and noble princes; and it is no question they had wise counsellors of either realms, who thought then the marriage between you and me good and lawful; therefore it is a wonder to hear what new devices are now invented against me, to cause me to stand to the order and judgment of this new court, wherein I conceive ye may do me much wrong, if ye intend any cruelty; for ye may condemn me for not answering sufficiently, having no counsel but such as you have assigned me. You must consider that they cannot be indifferent counsellors for my part, being your own subjects, and such as you have made choice of out of your own counsels, whereunto they are made privy, and dare not disclose your pleasure. Therefore, I most humbly beseech you to spare me until I know how my friends in Spain will advise me. If you will not extend to me so much indifferent favour, then let your pleasure be done, and to God I commit my cause;" and with that she rose, making a low curtsey to the king, and departed thence. She had not, however, proceeded far, when the king commanded the apparitor to call her back. Without attending to the summons, she still went forward. A gentleman, on whose arm she leaned,* observed, that she was called. "I hear it very well," she replied, "but on, on, go you on. Let them proceed against me as they please; I am resolved not to stay." Nor could she be afterwards persuaded to appear a second time.

"Forasmuch as the queen is gone," said Henry, addressing himself to the audience, "I will, in her absence, declare to you all present, that she has been to me a true, obedient wife, and as comfortable as I could wish or desire. She hath all the virtues and good qualities that belong to a woman of her

* " Her receiver-general, called Master Griffith."—*Cavendish.*

dignity, or in any other of meaner estate. Surely she is also a noble woman; if nothing were in her but only her conditions, will well declare the same." Wolsey, conceiving that some of Katharine's insinuations were directed towards him, intreated the king to declare, whether he had either been the first or the chief mover in the business, as suspicions to that effect were entertained. "My lord cardinal," answered Henry, "I can well excuse you herein: Marry, so far from being a mover, ye have been rather against me in attempting thereof. And to put you all out of doubt, I will declare unto you the special cause was a certain scruple that pricked my mind upon divers words spoken by the bishop of Bayonne, the French ambassador, who came here to consult of a marriage between the princess our daughter, the lady Mary, and the duke of Orleans; and upon the resolution and determination thereof, he desired respite to advertise the king his master thereof, whether our daughter Mary should be legitimate in respect of my marriage between the queen here and my brother; which words pondering, begot such a scruple in my conscience that I was much troubled at it, whereby I thought myself in danger of God's heavy displeasure and indignation, and the rather because he sent us no issue male, for all the issue male that I have had by my wife died incontinently after they came into the world, which caused me to fear God's displeasure in that particular. Thus my conscience being tossed on the waves of troublesome doubts, and partly in despair of having any other issue of this lady than I had already, it behoved me to consider the estate of this realm, and the danger it stands in for lack of a prince to succeed me. I therefore thought it good, in release of this mighty burden on my conscience, as also for the great estate of this realm, to attempt a trial in the law herein, I not having any displeasure in the person or age of the queen, with whom I could be well contented to continue, if our marriage may stand with the law of God, as with any woman alive. And it is in this point consisteth all the doubt that we go about to try by the learning and wisdom of you, our prelates and pastors of this realm, to whose consciences and learning I have committed the care and judgment, according to which I will be well contented to submit myself and obey the same. And when my conscience was so troubled, I moved it to you, my lord of

Lincoln, in confession, then being my ghostly father; and forasmuch as you were then in some doubt, you moved me to ask counsel of the rest of the bishops; whereupon I moved it to you, my lord cardinal, to have your licence, as you are metropolitan, to put this matter in question, and so did to all you, my lords, which you all granted under your seals, which are here to show."* The king having delivered this address, the court adjourned.

Katharine persisted in her resolution of never again entering the court. To the monitory letters, citing her to attend, and threatening her with the consequences of contumacy, she replied by appealing to the pope, excepting to the place of trial, to the judges, and to her counsel, and desiring that the cause might be heard at Rome. She was declared contumacious, and the legates proceeded in the process. Notwithstanding her solemn assertions respecting the non-consummation of her first marriage, probability and the testimonies of the witnesses were against her; and the evidence was as distinct as the case admitted, or could have been expected, after the lapse of such a period of time.† Meanwhile she wrote to her nephew, the emperor, and to his brother, the king of Hungary, earnestly entreating them to procure an avocation of the cause to Rome, and declaring that she would suffer anything, even death itself, rather than submit to a divorce. In consequence of these representations, Charles and Ferdinand sent orders to their ambassadors to allow the pope no

* " ' That is truth,' quoth the bishop of Canterbury, ' and I doubt not but all my brothers here present will affirm the same.' ' No, sir, not so, under correction,' quoth the bishop of Rochester, ' for you have not my hand and seal.' ' No, ha !' quoth the king; ' is not this your hand and seal?' and showed to him the instrument with seals. ' No, forsooth,' quoth the bishop. ' How say you to that ?' quoth the king to the bishop of Canterbury. ' Sir, it is his hand and seal,' quoth the bishop of Canterbury. ' That is not so,' quoth the bishop of Rochester; ' indeed you were in hand with me to have both my hand and seal, as other of my lords had done, but I answered that I would never consent to any such act, for it was much against my conscience, and that my hand and seal should never be set to any such instrument, God willing; with many other words to that purpose.' ' You say truth,' quoth the bishop of Canterbury, ' but you were fully resolved at the last that I should subscribe your name, and put your seal, and you would allow of the same.' ' All which,' quoth the bishop of Rochester, ' is untrue.' ' Well,' quoth the king, ' we will not stand in argument with you; you are but one.'—*Cavendish.*

† Burnet, 71, 72.

rest until he consented to the avocation. The emperor threatened that he would regard a sentence against his aunt as a dishonour done to his family, and would lose his throne rather than endure it. At the same time cardinal Campeggio secretly informed his holiness of the proceedings in England, and likewise urged the avocation. The reasons alleged by the queen for appealing were in themselves so just, that the pope was left without any plausible pretext for delaying to comply with the emperor's request. But for some time he was awed by the resolute character of Henry, and the vehement representations of Wolsey. The cardinal warned him, that if the cause was avocated at the suit of Katharine's relations, the king and kingdom of England were lost to the apostolical see; and he besought him to leave it still in the hands of the legates, who would execute their commission justly. "For myself," said he, "rather than be swayed by fear or affection against the dictates of my conscience, I will suffer to be torn in pieces joint by joint."* Clement, however, informed the English agents that the lawyers of Rome were unanimously of opinion, that he could not, in common justice, refuse the avocation; and added, with many sighs and tears, that the destruction of Christendom was inevitable. "No man," he exclaimed, "perceives the consequences of this measure more clearly than I do; but I am between the hammer and the forge, and on my head the whole weight must fall. I would do more for the king than I have promised, but it is impossible to deny the emperor justice. I am surrounded by his forces, and myself and all that I have are at his disposal."† The agents, after this, urged him no further, but only studied to impede the issuing of the bull for the avocation, while they wrote to England, recommending the process to be hurried to a conclusion. Campeggio, on his part, was no less dexterous in contriving expedients to prolong the trial.

The frequent adjournments of the court on frivolous pretences excited suspicions in the breast of Henry; and he began to think that the dispatches of Wolsey‡ evinced a greater degree of anxiety for the interests of the church than

* Burnet's Coll. No. 29, p. 75.
† Burnet, 73. ‡ Burnet's Coll. 29.

M

for those of his sovereign. This idea led him to treat the cardinal with less cordiality, a change which the keen-sighted enmity of the courtiers did not fail to observe and to promote by every art. Wolsey was not blind to the slippery verge on which he stood, nor unaffected by those altered looks which were regarded as the omens of his fall. One day returning in his barge from the trial at Blackfriars to his residence in Westminster, the bishop of Carlisle, who accompanied him, happened to complain of the excessive heat of the weather. "Yea, if ye had been as well chafed, my lord, as I have been to-day, you would be warm indeed," said the cardinal, alluding to a conversation which he had immediately before held with Henry. As soon as he entered his house he undressed and went to bed. He had not, however, lain long down, when lord Rochford, the father of Anne Boleyn, came to him from the king, with a command that he and Campeggio should immediately repair to Katharine, and exhort her to retire into some religious house rather than undergo the disgrace of a public divorce. "You and other lords of the council," exclaimed Wolsey, "have put fancies into the king's head, which trouble all the nation, and for which, in the end, you will receive but little recompence either of God or the world." Rochford, as if conscious of deserving the sternness of the reproaches which the cardinal continued to vent against him as he dressed himself, knelt down at the bedside, and, weeping, made no reply.

The two legates went to the queen, whom they found sitting among her maids at needlework, with a skein of silk hanging about her neck. At their approach she said: "Alack, my lords, I am sorry that you have attended on me so long; what is your pleasure with me?" "If it please your grace," said the cardinal, "to go to your privy chamber, we will show you the cause of our coming." "My lord," said she, "if you have anything to say to me, speak it openly before these folk, for I fear nothing that you can say to me or against me, but that I am willing all the world should both see and hear it." Then began my lord to speak to her in Latin. "Nay, good my lord, speak to me in English," said she, "although I do understand some Latin." "Forsooth," said Wolsey, "good madam, if it please your grace, we come both to know your mind, what you are disposed to do in this matter, and also, to declare to you secretly our counsel and opinion, which we do for very zeal and obedience to your grace." " My lords," said the queen, " I thank you for your good wills; but to make answer to your request I cannot so suddenly, for I was set amongst my maidens at work, little thinking of any such matter, wherein is requisite some deliberation, and a better head than mine to make answer; for I need counsel in this case, which concerns me so near, and friends here I have none; they are in Spain—in my own country. Also, my lords, I am a poor woman, of too weak capacity to answer such noble persons of wisdom as you are in so weighty a matter. And, therefore, I pray you, be good to me a woman, destitute of friendship here in a foreign region. And your counsel I also shall be glad to hear." She then conducted them into an inner apartment, where having attentively heard their message, she addressed herself to Wolsey with great warmth. She accused him as the author of her misfortunes, because she could not endure his excessive arrogance and voluptuous life, and chiefly because she was related to the emperor, who had refused to feed his insatiable ambition with the papal dignity.* Nor would she permit him to reply, but dismissed him with marked displeasure, while she courteously parted from Campeggio.

The trial, as far as respected the examination of evidence, being completed, the court was crowded with spectators, and a general expectation prevailed that sentence would at last be given.† The king himself, impatient for the decision, was

* It is very doubtful if Charles, at any of the elections which happened during the administration of Wolsey, was able to have procured him the popedom ; and I have not found any evidence of the cardinal ascribing his disappointments to remissness on the part of the emperor. The sequel of the queen's affairs shows clearly, that she did Wolsey wrong in considering him as actuated by malice or resentment against her : so far, indeed, was this from being the case, that it may be said he sacrificed himself rather than consent to decide unjustly against her. The dispatches relative to the election after the death of Adrian commence at page 80 of Dr. Fiddes's Collections.

Charles, on the death of Adrian, as well as at the death of Leo, wrote to Rome in favour of Wolsey. I do not see any reason to disbelieve his imperial majesty, especially as we have it certified by himself in a letter to the cardinal, dated at Pampeluna, 16th Dec. 1523.—*Cottonian Library, Vespasian, c.* ii. No. 52.

† July 23, 1529.

M 2

seated in a gallery contiguous to the hall. But, to the surprise of the whole audience, Campeggio adjourned the court, on the pretence, that as it sat as part of the Roman consistory, the legates were bound to follow the rules of that court, which was then in vacation.* And he added, " I will not give judgment herein without the counsel and commandment of the pope, to whom the whole proceedings must be first communicated. The matter is too high for us to deliver a hasty decision, considering the dignity of the persons to whom it relates, the doubtful occasion of it, the nature of our commission, and the authority by which we act. It is, therefore, fitting, that we should consult our proper head and lord. I came not to please, for favour, fear, or reward, any man alive, be he king or subject; I have no such respect to persons that I should offend my conscience; the queen will make no answer, but has appealed to the pope. I am an old man, feeble and sickly, looking every day for death: what will it avail me to put my soul in danger for the favour of any prince in this world? I am here only to see justice administered according to my conscience. The defendant believes we cannot be impartial judges, because we are the king's subjects;† therefore, to avoid all ambiguities and misrepresentations, I adjourn the court, according to the practice of the consistory of Rome, from which our jurisdiction is derived; and that we may not exceed the limits of our commission."‡ The dukes of Norfolk and Suffolk were present, and remonstrated with Campeggio for delaying the sentence; but he replied, that no decision pronounced during the vacation could be legal. Suffolk broke out into a violent passion, and, vehemently striking his hand upon the table, swore by the mass that he saw it was true what was commonly said, that " it was never thus in England till we had cardinals amongst us."§ Wolsey, conceiving the insinuation to be directed against him, said, in a sedate, emphatic manner: " Sir, of all men in this realm you have the least cause to disparage cardinals; for if I, poor cardinal, had not been, you would not now have had a head on your shoulders wherewith to make such report in despite of us, who wish you no harm, neither have given you cause to be

* Burnet, 74.   † He held the bishopric of Salisbury.
‡ Fiddes, 478.   § Burnet, 75.

offended with us.* I would have you to know, my lord, that I and my brother here wish the king as much happiness, and the realm as much honour, wealth, and peace, as you or any other subject whatsoever, and would as gladly accomplish his lawful desires. And now, my lord, I pray you, show me what would you do in such a case as this, if you were one of the king's commissioners in a foreign country, about some weighty matter; would you not advertise the king's majesty before you went through with the same? I doubt not but you would, and, therefore, abate your malice and spite. Consider we are commissioners for a time, and cannot, by virtue of a commission, proceed to judgment, without the knowledge and consent of him from whom our authority is derived. Therefore do we neither more nor less than our commission allows us; and he that will be offended with us therefore, is not a wise man. Pacify yourself, my lord, and speak like a man of honour and wisdom, or hold your peace; speak not reproachfully of your friends; you best know the friendship I have shown you, and which before I never mentioned, either to mine own praise, or your dishonour." The king, in the meantime, comported himself with more moderation than could have been expected from his impetuous temper. He manifested no particular displeasure, but still the ruin of Wolsey was considered inevitable. Campeggio soon after took his leave, and, richly rewarded, departed for Rome; and it was currently reported, that Wolsey also intended to quit the kingdom: so fully convinced was the public mind that he no longer possessed the king's favour. At this crisis, Anne Boleyn, whom a sense of shame had induced to withdraw from court during the trial, was recalled. Regarding Wolsey with fear and aversion, as the determined foe of all her projects of love and ambition, she industriously fostered the suspicions which had grown up in the mind of Henry; and it began to be rumoured, that the cardinal had incurred the

* This great obligation of the duke to the cardinal does not appear, says Fiddes, to be known to the historians. Dr. Pegge, however, in the " Gentleman's Magazine" for 1755, suggests that Wolsey was the means of abating the anger of Henry at the marriage of Suffolk with his sister Mary, queen of France, which might have been a treasonable offence.—*Singer.*

penalties of the statute of premunire.* Although aware of
what was to ensue, and evidently corroded by anxiety and
suspense, a kind of haughty magnanimity would not allow
him to abate, in any respect, his accustomed ostentation and
pretensions. He opened the Michaelmas term at Westminster-

* "In which time cardinal Campeggio made suit to be discharged, and sent
home to Rome ; and in the interim returned Mr. Secretary, and it was concluded that my lord should come to the king to Grafton, in Northampton-
shire, as also cardinal Campeggio, being a stranger, should be conducted
thither by my lord cardinal ; and they came to Grafton upon the Sunday,
in the morning, before whose coming there were divers opinions that the
court would not speak with my lord, whereupon there were many great
wagers laid.

"These two prelates being come to the court gates, and alighting, expected
to be received by the great officers, as the manner was, but they found the
contrary ; nevertheless, because the cardinal Campeggio was a stranger,
the officers met him with staves in their hands, in the outward court, and so
conveyed him to his lodging prepared for him ; and after my lord had brought
him to his lodging he departed, thinking to have gone to his chamber, as he
was wont to do. But it was told him that he had no lodging or chamber
appointed for him in the court, which news did much astonish him.

"Sir Henry Norris, who was then groom of the stole, came unto him,
and desired him to take his chamber for a while, until another was provided
for him ; 'for I assure you,' quoth he, 'here is but little room in this house
for the king, and therefore I humbly beseech your grace accept of mine for
a season.' My lord, thanking him for his courtesy, went to his chamber,
where he shifted his riding apparel. In the meantime came divers noblemen
of his friends to welcome him to the court, by whom my lord was advertised of all things touching the king's displeasure, and being thus informed
of the cause thereof, he was more able to excuse himself; so my lord
made him ready, and went to the chamber of presence with the other cardinal, where the lords of the council stood all of a row, in order in the
chamber, and all the lords saluted them both ; and there were present
many gentlemen who came on purpose to observe the meeting and countenance of the king, to my lord cardinal. Then, immediately after, the king
came into the chamber of presence, and stood under the cloth of state ; then
my lord cardinal took cardinal Campeggio by the hand, and kneeled down
before the king, but what he said to him I know not ; but his countenance
was amiable, and his majesty stooped down, and with both his hands took
him up, and then took him by the hand, and went to the window with him,
and there talked to him a good while ; then, to have beheld the countenance
of the lords and noblemen who had laid wagers, it would have made you smile,
specially those that had laid their money that the king would not speak with
him. They were all deceived ; for the king was in earnest discourse with
him, insomuch that I could hear the king say : 'How can this be ? is not
this your hand ?' and pulled a letter out of his bosom, and showed the same
to my lord, and, as I perceived, my lord so answered the same, that the
king had no more to say, but said to my lord : 'Go to your dinner, and

THE GREAT SEAL DEMANDED OF HIM.

hall, with all his usual pomp and ceremony,* and performed the duties, as if unconscious that it was for the last time. In the course of the evening, it is supposed that he received private information of his disgrace having been decided, for next day he remained at home; but no messenger came from the king. On the following morning, however, the dukes of Norfolk and

take my lord cardinal to keep you company; and after dinner I will speak further with you;' and so they parted; and the king dined that day with Mistress Anne Boleyn in her chamber.

"Then was there set up in the presence chamber a table for my lord, and other lords of the council, where they dined together; and sitting at dinner, telling of divers matters, 'The king should do well,' quoth my lord cardinal, 'to send his bishops and chaplains home to their cures and benefices.' 'Yea, marry,' quoth my lord of Norfolk, 'and so it were meet for you to do also.' 'I would be very well contented therewith,' quoth my lord, 'if it were the king's pleasure to licence me with leave to go to my cure at Winchester.' 'Nay,' quoth my lord of Norfolk, 'to your benefice at York, where your greatest honour and charge is.' 'Even as it shall please the king,' quoth my lord cardinal; and so they fell upon other discourses, for indeed the nobility was loth he should be so near the king as to continue at Winchester. Immediately after dinner they fell to council till the waiters had also dined.

"I heard it repeated by those that waited on the king at dinner, that Mistress Anne Boleyn was offended as much as she durst, that the king did so greatly entertain my lord cardinal, saying: 'Sir, is it not a marvellous thing to see into what great debt and danger he hath brought you, with all your subjects?' 'How so, sweetheart?' quoth the king. 'Forsooth,' quoth she, 'there is not a man in all your whole realm of England, worth a hundred pound, but he hath indebted you to him (meaning of loans which the

* A contemporary poet gives the following description of the style of his procession:—

> "Before him rideth two priests strong,
> And they bear two crosses right long,
>   Gaping in every man's face.
> After him follow two laymen secular,
> And each of them holding a pillar
>   In their hands, instead of a mace.
> Then followeth my lord on his mule,
> Trapped with gold under her cule,
>   In every point most curiously.
> On each side a pole-axe is borne,
> Which in none other use are worn,
>   Pretending some high mystery.
> *   *   *   *
> Then hath he servants five or six score,
> Some behind and some before—
>   A marvellous great company;

Suffolk arrived, and required the great seal to be delivered to them, informing him, that it was the king's pleasure that he should retire to Ashur,* an ecclesiastical seat which belonged to him as bishop of Winchester. With this requisition he refused to comply, saying, that the seal had been given to him personally by the king to enjoy it, with the ministration of

---

king had of his subjects).' 'Well, well,' quoth the king, 'for that there was no blame in him, for I know that matter better than you or any one else.' 'Nay,' quoth she, 'besides that, what exploits hath he wrought, in several parts and places in this realm to your great slander and disgrace? There is never a nobleman but if he had done half so much as he hath done, were well worthy to lose his head; yea, if my lord of Norfolk, my lord of Suffolk, or any other man, had done much less than he hath done, they should have lost their heads ere this.' 'Then I perceive,' quoth the king, 'you are none of my lord cardinal's friends.' 'Why, sir,' quoth she, 'I have no cause, nor any that love you, no more hath your grace if you did well consider his indirect and unlawful doings.' By that time the waiters had dined, and took up the table, and so ended their communication. . . . The king then departed from Mistress Anne Boleyn, and called for my lord, and in the great window had a long discourse with him, but of what I know not. Afterwards the king took him by the hand, and led him into the privy chamber, and sat in consultation with him all alone, without any other of the lords, till it was dark night, which blanked all his enemies very sore,

---

> Of which are lords and gentlemen,
> With many grooms and yeomen,
> 　　And also knaves among.
> Thus daily he proceedeth forth,
> And men must take it at worth,
> 　　Whether he do right or wrong."

The following description of the cardinal's person may be added:—

> A great carl he is and fat;
> Wearing on his head a red hat,
> 　　Procured with angel's subsidy;
> And, as they say, in time of rain,
> Four of his gentlemen are fain
> 　　To hold o'er it a canopy.
> Besides this, to tell thee more news,
> He hath a pair of costly shoes,
> 　　Which seldom touch the ground:
> They are so goodly and curious,
> All of gold and stones precious,
> 　　Costing many a thousand pound.
> And who did for these shoes pay?
> Truly many a rich abbey,
> 　　To be eased of his visitation."

* Esher.

the chancellorship for life, and, as he had letters-patent to that effect, it was necessary that they should produce their commission before he could lawfully deliver it into their hands. A warm debate arose; but the cardinal was firm, and the two noblemen went away without having accomplished their purpose. Next day* they returned with credentials that could not be disputed; and, his power being ended, he prepared for the resignation of his wealth. Inventories† were made of his furniture; and incredible quantities of massy plate, velvets, damasks, and the richest tissues, laid out on

who had no other way but by Mistress Anne Boleyn, in whom was all their trust and affiance, for the accomplishment of their enterprise, for without her they feared that all their purposes would be frustrated.

" Now at night was warning given me that there was no room for my lord to lodge in the court, so that I was forced to provide my lord a lodging in the country, at Euston, one of Master Empson's houses, where my lord came to supper by torch-light, being late before he parted from the king; who wished him to return to him in the morning, for that he would talk further with him about the same matter; and in the morning my lord came again, at whose coming the king's majesty was ready to ride; willing my lord to consult with the lords in his absence, and said he would not talk with him, commanding my lord to depart with cardinal Campeggio, who had already taken his leave of the king.

" This sudden departure of the king's was the especial labour of Mistress Anne Boleyn, who rode with him purposely to draw him away, because he should not return till the departure of the cardinals. The king rode that morning to view a piece of ground, to make a park of, which was afterwards, and is at this time, called Harewell park, where Mistress Anne had provided him a place to dine in, fearing his return before my lord cardinal's departure.

" So my lord rode away after dining with cardinal Campeggio, who took his journey towards Rome, with the king's reward; but what it was I am not certain. After their departure, it was told the king that cardinal Campeggio was departed, and had great treasure with him of my lord's, to be conveyed in great tuns to Rome, whither they surmised he would secretly repair out of this realm; insomuch that they caused a post to ride after the cardinal, to search him, who overtook him at Calais [the bishop of Bayenne says, Dover], and staid him until search was made, but there was found no more than was received of the king as a reward."—*Cavendish.*

---

* October 19, 1529.

† In the Harleian Library in the British Museum there is one of the cardinal's inventories. When I opened it, the sand was still sticking on the ink, and it appeared in many places not to have been opened since it was written.

the tables of his different chambers and galleries, were held by his treasurer at the disposal of the king.*

With his train of gentlemen and yeomen he proceeded to his barge, which lay at the Privy Garden stairs, where a vast multitude was assembled, silently waiting, in the expectation of seeing him conveyed to the Tower. One of his domestics,† with much concern, mentioned what the crowd expected. The cardinal reprimanded him for his credulity and officiousness: "Is this the best comfort you can give to your master in adversity? It hath always been your inclination to be light of credit and much lighter in reporting of lies. I would have you, and all such reporters to know it is untrue, for I never deserved to come there, although it hath pleased the king to take my house ready furnished for his pleasure at this time. I would all the world should know, I have nothing but it is of right for him; of him I received all I have. It is, therefore, fit and reasonable to tender him the same again." The barge was rowed to Putney, where he landed, and mounted his mule. The servants followed; but they had not advanced far when a horseman was discovered riding down the hill towards them. It was a messenger from the king,‡ sent to assure him of unaltered esteem and kindness, and to say that the severity which he suffered was caused more by political

---

* " Then my lord called all his officers before him, and took account of all things they had in their charge. And in his gallery were set divers tables, upon which were laid divers and great store of rich stuffs, whole pieces of silk of all colours, velvets, satins, damasks, taffetas, grograms, sarsnets, and divers rich commodities. Also, there were a thousand pieces of fine Holland, and the hangings of the gallery with cloth of gold, and cloth of silver, and rich cloth of Baudkin (cloth of silk and gold) of divers colours, which were hanged in expectation of the king's coming. Also, on one side of the gallery, were hanged the rich suits of copes of his own providing, which were made for his colleges at Oxford and Ipswich; they were the richest that ever I saw in all my life. Then had he two chambers adjoining to the gallery, the one most commonly called *the gilt chamber,* the other *the council chamber,* wherein were set two broad and long tables, whereupon were set such abundance of plate of all sorts, as was almost incredible to be believed, a great part being all of pure gold; and upon every table and cupboard where the plate was set, were books importing every kind of plate, and every piece, with the contents and weight thereof."—*Cavendish.*

† " His treasurer, Sir William Gascoigne."—*Cavendish.*

‡ " Sir Henry Norris."—*Cavendish.*

considerations than by motives of anger or resentment.*
" His majesty in this," said the messenger, " only follows the
advice of others; and therefore your grace should not give
way to despondency, but cherish comfortable hopes."   In the
surprise and gratitude of the moment, Wolsey alighted from
his mule, and kneeling down on the spot,† lifted up his hands
to heaven, rejoicing that he still possessed so much of the
king's affection.   He rewarded the bearer of this gratifying
intelligence with a chain of gold and a precious relic from
about his neck;‡ and as a proof to the king of the pleasure
which his message had afforded, he sent him a jester from
among his train, with whose buffooneries Henry had often
been diverted.   It might be inferred from this incident, that
the cardinal's disgrace was only a stratagem to intimidate the
pope; but his enemies turned it to their own advantage, and
he was left deserted at Esher.§

Ruin is doubtless the same to men of all conditions; but
persons in elevated stations, as they fall from a greater height
than men of ordinary rank, perhaps suffer under a more over-
whelming sense of calamity.   Disgrace also is more acutely
felt as it is more generally known, and the interest of a whole
people adds an ideal weight to the misfortunes of fallen greatness.   Wolsey now stood forth to view confessedly a ruined
man.   Sudden adversity had blasted all his blushing honours;

* " In token whereof, he delivered him a ring of gold, with a rich stone,
which ring he knew very well, for it was always the private token between
the king and him whensoever the king would have any special matter despatched at his hands."—*Cavendish.*

† " He would have pulled off his under cap of velvet, but could not undo
the knot under his chin : wherefore with violence he rent the laces, and so
pulled it over his head, and kneeled bareheaded."—*Cavendish.*

‡ " The cardinal presented the messenger with a chain of gold, at which
a piece of the true cross hung; but it troubled him much that he had nothing to send to the king, till at last, having espied in his train a facetious
natural, in whom he took much delight, he desired the messenger to present
him to the king.   The fellow, however, did not much relish his promotion,
for the cardinal was obliged to send six of his tallest yeomen to carry him
to court."—*Lord Herbert,* 293.

§ " Thus continued my lord at Asher, three or four weeks, without either
beds, sheets, table-cloths, or dishes to eat their meat in, or money wherewith to buy any.   But there was good store of all kinds of victuals, and of
beer and wine plenty ; but afterwards my lord borrowed some plates and
dishes of the bishop of Carlisle."—*Cavendish.*

and, as a sure prognostic of approaching decay, the ephemeral swarms which had lived in his shade, disappeared, and left him in solitude. Of all afflictions which assail the human heart, ingratitude has ever given the severest blow; and men who have lost the possession of extensive power are peculiarly exposed to the evil. The official dependants of the cardinal manifested the common baseness of political adherents; and none but his immediate domestics, who partook in the overthrow of his fortunes, remained to console their fallen master. Bodily suffering would have been relief to his proud and fervent mind; but to be left alone to brood over his disgrace; to feel the coldness of deliberate neglect; to be conscious of the insolent triumph of his enemies; and, with so liberal a spirit, to be deprived of the means of rewarding the faithful attachment of his servants, was a punishment, as he observed himself, far worse than death. The agitations of suspense gradually subsided into despondency, and he was seized with that sickness of spirit which is more fatal to the powers of life than the sharpest sorrow. Had he been sent to the scaffold, he would in all probability have met death with firmness; but the course which the king pursued, though dictated, no doubt, by some remains of tenderness, was that of all others against which he was least able to bear himself with fortitude.*

* In the fine moral scene between Wolsey and Cromwell, in Henry VIII., Shakspeare appears to have made use of Storer's poem; at least there is something in the tone of the following stanza that reminds me of several expressions in the cardinal's reflections :—

> " If once we fall, we fall Colossus like,
>   We fall at once like pillars of the sun ;
>   They that between our stride their sails did strike,
>   Make us sea marks where they their ships do run,
>   E'en they that had by us their treasure won."

BOOK VII.

HENRY VIII. had now reigned upwards of twenty years with
great prosperity and renown.   Had he died before the close
of the cardinal's administration he would have been commemorated as one of the best, as he was unquestionably one of the
ablest and greatest monarchs that ever wore the crown of
England.   Much of his celebrity would obviously have been
due to Wolsey; but if princes are individually blamed for
the errors and failures of their ministers, humanity claims
for them the honour of their wisdom and success.   As they
are responsible for the measures of the men whom they employ,
it is but just that they should be allowed the merit of discernment when they promote those who maintain the dignity and
advance the power of their states.   In this respect, Henry is
entitled to great praise; for, except by the mission to Maxi-

milian in the preceding reign, Wolsey was unknown as a public character, and had not, by any series of actions or particular exploit, excited a disposition to believe him qualified for the high offices which he so suddenly obtained. Whatever the motives were which induced the king to confer upon him the chief exercise of the royal prerogatives, the sagacity by which he perceived his fitness would have been admired in the profoundest politician. By presenting the cardinal as the main spring of the government, he screened himself from the clamour against unpopular undertakings; and in interposing occasionally to please the people, he acquired more distinguished applause; while, at the same time, the great talents of Wolsey justified the confidence which he continued to bestow. But from the dismissal of the cardinal, his history exhibits a new character. Unrestrained by deference to the opinion of any other, and no longer fully confiding in the abilities of counsellors, whom he was habituated to regard as inferior men, his arbitrary spirit assumed the mastery of the government; and his natural frankness, unqualified for the practice of the reserve and procrastination which are perhaps essential to the management of public affairs, betrayed him into violent courses, which the ready agency of the priesthood and the complacency of the parliament shamefully facilitated. But such is the system of Providence. The base propensities of individuals yield beneficial results to the species, and particular evils always engender general good. To the caprice of Henry VIII. and the sycophancy of his counsellors, England owes the reformation of religion and the reduction of ecclesiastical power.

The cardinal, for more than seven years, had contrived to manage the government without parliamentary advice. The revenue and ordinary resources were adequate to the expenditure, and therefore it was unnecessary to trouble the peers and representatives, for pecuniary necessities constitute the motive which induces ministers to convene the collective council of the nation. After the dismissal of Wolsey, parliament was assembled, both on account of the state of the exchequer, and the vengeance which the king had vowed against the pope for revoking the process to Rome. Except in the appointment of Sir Thomas More to the chancery, no change had taken place in the administration; yet the counsellors had the effrontery to throw upon the cardinal all the blame of the unpopular proceedings in which they had themselves been previously concerned. It is the frequent recurrence of such examples of public dereliction that sickens to disgust, and sours into misanthropy, the feelings of historians in relating the cabals and conspiracies of courts. But the ministers of Henry VIII. were not influenced by those considerations which induced Wolsey to overlook present obstacles in contemplating the consequences of his undertakings. They felt not the desire of that renown which can only be attained by accomplishing works of utility. They wanted that prophetic anticipation of the effects of existing circumstances, which alone enables statesmen to dignify and even to hallow those acts of temporary injustice which seem so often mysteriously imposed upon their transactions. They were fastened close down to sordid and selfish aims; and their views and faculties were limited to momentary expedients, which disturbed, without altering, the great current of human affairs. They procured from parliament acts which abridged the prerogatives of the clergy, in order to manifest to the court of Rome the resolution of the king to maintain his royal supremacy. The utility of these measures obviates the objection to the morality of the motive; but other laws were obtained that have no such apology. The king had contracted debts, and they had absolved him from the payment; and, as if the letting loose of delinquents on society could have been any compensation to his creditors, or any indemnity to mankind for the public violation of common honesty, a general pardon for all offences, except the crimes of murder and treason, was granted. Articles of impeachment were also drawn up against the cardinal, characteristic of the folly and wickedness of the new administration.* He was charged with superiority of talents, and surpassing assiduity in business; and with being eloquent in discourse, sarcastic to the presumptuous, liberal, lofty-minded, subject to the common frailties of man, and disagreeable when afflicted with disease.†

---

* Lord Herbert, 325.
† *Articles of Impeachment exhibited against Cardinal Wolsey:*

1. Whereas your grace and noble progenitors within this realm of England, being kings of England, have been so free, that they have had in all the world no other sovereign, but immediately subject to Almighty God in

The main strength of his enemies lay in the house of lords, among the nobility, the prelates, and abbots; and the bill of impeachment, in consequence, passed that branch of the legislature. But in the house of commons, Thomas Cromwell, who had been secretary to the cardinal, so manfully exposed the absurdity of the charges, and so powerfully vindicated

all things touching the regality of your crown of England, and the same pre-eminence, prerogatives, jurisdiction, lawful and peaceable possession, your grace and noble progenitors have had, used, and enjoyed, without interruption of business therefore by the space of two hundred years and more; whereby your grace may prescribe against the pope's holiness, that he should not nor ought not to send or make any legate, to execute any authority by a line contrary to your grace's prerogative within this your realm: now the lord Cardinal of York, being your subject, and natural liege born, hath of his high, proud, and insatiable mind, for his own advancement and profit, in derogation and to the great detriment and hurt of your said royal jurisdiction and prerogative, and the long continuance of the possession of the same, obtained authority legatine: by reason whereof, he has not only hurt your said prescription, but also, by the said authority legantine, hath spoiled and taken away from many houses of religion, within this your realm, much substance of their goods, and also hath usurped upon all your ordinaries within this your realm, much part of their jurisdiction, in derogation of your prerogative, and to the great hurt of your said ordinaries, prelates, and religious persons.

2. Also the said lord cardinal, being your ambassador in France, made a treaty with the French king for the pope, your majesty not knowing any part thereof, nor named in the same; and binding the said French king to abide his order and award, if any controversy or doubt should arise upon the same betwixt the said pope and the French king.

3. Also the said lord cardinal, being your ambassador in France, sent a commission to sir Gregory de Cassalis, under your great seal, in your grace's name, to conclude a treaty of amity with the duke of Ferrara; without any commandment or warrant of your highness, nor your said highness advertised or made privy to the same.

4. Also the said lord cardinal, of his presumptuous mind, in divers and many of his letters and instructions, sent out of this realm to outward parts, had joined himself with your grace, as in saying and writing, "The king and I would ye should do thus: the king and I do give unto you our hearty thanks:" whereby it is apparent that he used himself more like a fellow to your highness than like a subject.

5. Also where it hath ever been accustomed within this realm, that when noblemen do swear their household servants, the first part of their oath hath been, that they should be true liege men to the king and his heirs kings of England: the same lord cardinal caused his servants to be only sworn to him, as if there had been no sovereign above him.

6. And also, whereas your grace is our sovereign lord and head, in whom standeth all the surety and wealth of this realm; the same lord cardinal, knowing himself to have the foul and contagious disease of the —— broken

the integrity of his old master, that the commons threw out the bill as unworthy of investigation. This circumstance, considering the times, and the general subserviency of the house of commons to the crown, was the most emphatic eulogium that could be pronounced on the long and various administration of Wolsey.

out upon him in divers places of his body, came daily to your grace, rounding (whispering) in your ears, and blowing upon your most noble grace, with his perilous and infective breath, to the marvellous danger of your highness, if God of his infinite goodness had not better provided for your highness: and when he was once healed of them, he made your grace to believe, that his disease was an imposthume in his head, and no other thing.

7. Also, the said lord cardinal, by his authority legatine, hath given by prevention the benefices of divers persons, as well spiritual and temporal, contrary to your crown and dignity, and your laws and statutes therefore provided : by reason whereof, he is in danger to your grace of forfeiture of his lands and goods, and his body at your pleasure.

8. Also, the lord cardinal, taking upon him otherwise than a true counsellor ought to do, hath used to have all ambassadors come first to him alone, and so hearing their charges and intents, it is to be thought he hath instructed them after his pleasure and purpose, before that they came to your presence, contrary to your high commandment by your grace's mouth to him given, and also to other persons sent to him by your grace.

9. And also, the lord cardinal hath practised so, that all manner of letters sent from beyond the sea to your highness hath come first to his hands, contrary to your high commandment by your own mouth ; and also by others sent to him by your grace : by reason whereof your highness, nor any of your council, had knowledge of no matters but of such as it pleased him to show them : whereby your highness and council have been compelled, of very force, to follow his devices, which oftentimes were set forth by him under such crafty and covert meanings, that your highness and your council have oftentimes been abused, insomuch that when your council have found and put divers doubts and things, which afterwards have ensued, he, to abuse them, used these words, " I will lay my head that no such thing shall happen."

10. And the said lord cardinal hath practised, that no manner of persons, having charge to make espial of things done beyond the sea, should, at their return, come first to your grace, nor to any other of your council, but only to himself : and in case they did the contrary he punished them there for so doing.

11. Also the said lord cardinal hath granted licences under your great seal for carrying out of grain and other victuals, after the restraint hath been made thereof, for his own lucre and singular advantage of him and his servants, for to send thither ; as he bare secret favour, without your grace's warrant or knowledge thereof.

12. Also the said lord cardinal used many years together, not only to write unto all your ambassadors resident with other princes in his own name, all advertisements concerning your grace's affairs being in their

The impeachment having failed, the cardinal was immediately indicted on the sixteenth statute of Richard II., for having exercised his legatine commission without the king's authority.* To the judges who were sent to Esher to receive his answer to this shameless accusation, the reply of Wolsey was proud and melancholy. "My lords judges, the king's

charge: and, in the same his letters, wrote many things of his own mind, without your grace's pleasure known, concealing divers things which had been necessary for them to know; but also caused them to write their advertisements unto him; and of the same letters he used to conceal, for the compassing of his purpose, many things both from all your other counsellors and from yourself also.

13. And where good hospitals have been used to be kept in houses and places of religion of this realm, and many poor people thereby relieved, the said hospitality and relief is now decayed and not used; and it is commonly reported that the occasion thereof is, because the said lord cardinal hath taken such impositions of the rulers of the said houses, as well for his favour in making of abbots and priors, as for his visitation by his authority legatine: and yet nevertheless taketh yearly of such religious houses such yearly and continual charges, as they be not able to keep hospitality as they were used to do; which is a great cause that there be so many vagabonds, beggars, and thieves.

14. And where the same said lord cardinal said before the suppression of such houses as he hath suppressed, that the possessions of them should be set to farm among your lay subjects, at such reasonable yearly rent as they should well thereupon live and keep good hospitality: now the demesne possession of the same houses since the suppression of them hath been surveyed, meted, and measured by the acre, and be now set above the value of the old rent; and also such as were farmers by covent seal and copyholders be put out and amoved of their farms, or else compelled to pay new fine, contrary to all equity and conscience.

15. Also the said lord cardinal, sitting among the lords and others of your most honourable privy council, used himself, that if any man would show his mind, according to his duty, contrary to the opinion of the said cardinal, he would so take him up with his accustomable words, that they were better to hold their peace than to speak, so that he would hear no man speak but one or two great personages, so that he would have all the words himself, and consumed much time with a fair tale.

16. Also the said lord cardinal, by his ambition and pride, hath hindered and undone many of your poor subjects for want of dispatchment of matters, for he would no man should meddle but himself: insomuch that it hath been affirmed by many wise men, that ten of the most wise and most expert men in England were not sufficient in convenient time to order the matters that he would retain to himself: and many times he deferred the ending of matters, because that suitors should attend and wait upon him, whereof he had no small pleasure, that his house might be replenished with suitors.

---

* Burnet, 77.

majesty knoweth right well whether I have offended or no, in using my legatine prerogative, for the which I am indicted. I have the king's licence in my coffer to show, under his hand and broad seal, for the executing and using thereof in most large manner, the which now is in the hands of mine enemies. But, because I will not stand here to contend with

17. Also the said lord cardinal, by his authority legatine, hath used, if any spiritual man having any riches or substance, deceased, he hath taken their goods as his own, by reason whereof their wills be not performed; and one means he had, to put them in fear, that were made executors, to refuse to meddle.

18. Also the said lord cardinal constrained all ordinaries in England yearly to compound with him, or else he will usurp half or the whole of their jurisdiction by prevention, not for good order of the diocese, but to extort treasure; for there is never a poor archdeacon in England, but that he paid yearly to him a portion of his living.

19. Also the said lord cardinal hath not only by his untrue suggestion to the pope shamefully slandered many good religious houses, and good virtuous men dwelling in them, but also suppressed, by reason thereof, above thirty houses of religion. And where, by authority of his bull, he should not suppress any house that had more men of religion in number above the number of six or seven, he hath suppressed divers houses that had above the number; and thereupon hath caused divers offices to be found by verdict untruly, that the religious persons so suppressed had voluntarily forsaken their said houses, which was untrue, and so hath caused open perjury to be committed, to the high displeasure of Almighty God.

20. Also the said lord cardinal hath examined divers and many matters in the Chancery, after judgment thereof given at the common law, in subversion of your laws, and made some persons restore again to the other party condemned that they had in execution by virtue of the judgment of the common law.

21. Also the said lord cardinal hath granted many injunctions by writ, and the parties never called thereunto, nor bill put in against them; and by reason thereof, divers of your subjects have been put from their lawful possession of their lands and tenements. And by such means he hath brought the more party of the suitors of this your realm before himself, whereby he and divers of his servants hath gotten much riches, and your subjects suffered great wrongs.

22. Also the said lord cardinal, to augment his great riches, hath caused divers pardons granted by the pope to be suspended, which could not be revived till the said lord cardinal was rewarded, and also had a yearly pension of the said pardon.

23. Also the said lord cardinal, not regarding your laws nor justice, of his extort power hath put out divers and many farmers of his lands, and also patentees of the archbishopric of York and of the bishopric of Winchester, and of the abbey of Saint Albans, which had good and sufficient grant thereof by your laws.

24. Also the same lord cardinal, at many times when any houses of religion hath been void, hath sent his officers thither, and with crafty per-

his majesty, in his own case, I will here, presently before you, confess the indictment, and put myself wholly to the mercy and grace of the king, trusting that he hath a conscience and reason to consider the truth, and my humble submission and obedience, wherein I might well stand to my trial with justice. Thus much may you say to his highness, that I

suasions hath induced them to compromit their election in him; and before he named or confirmed any of them, he and his servants received so much great goods of them, that in a manner it hath been to the undoing of the house.

25. Also, by his authority legatine, the same lord cardinal hath visited the most part of the religious houses and colleges of this your realm, and hath taken from them the twenty-fifth part of their livelihood, to the great extortion of your subjects, and derogation of your laws and prerogative, and no law hath been to bear him so to do.

26. Also, when matters have been near a judgment by process of your common law, the same lord cardinal hath not only given and sent injunctions to the parties, but also sent for your judges, and expressly, by threats, commanded them to defer the judgment, to the evident subversion of your laws, if the judges would so have ceased.

27. And whereas neither the bishop of York, nor Winchester, nor the abbey of St. Albans, nor the profit of his legation, nor the benefit of the Chancery, nor his great pension out of France, nor his wards or other inordinate taking, could suffice him, he hath made his son Winter to spend seven and twenty hundred pounds by the year, which he taketh to his own use, and giveth him not past two hundred pounds yearly to live upon.

28. Also, whereas the said lord cardinal did first sue unto your grace to have your assent to be *legate de latere*, promising and solemnly protesting before your majesty, and before the lords both spiritual and temporal, that he would nothing do nor attempt by the virtue of his Legacy contrary to your gracious prerogative or regality, or to the damage or prejudice of the jurisdiction of any ordinary, and that by his Legacy no man should be hurt nor offended; and upon that condition, and no other, he was admitted by your grace to be legate within this your realm: this condition he hath broken, as is well known to all your subjects. And when that he made this promise, he was busy in his suit at Rome to visit all the clergy of England both exempt and not exempt.

29. Also, upon the suit of the said lord cardinal at Rome to have his authority legatine, he made untrue surmise to the pope's holiness against the clergy of your realm; which was, that the regular persons of the said clergy had given themselves in *reprobum sensum;* which words St. Paul, writing to the Romans, applied to abominable sin; which slander to your church of England shall for ever remain in the register at Rome against the clergy of this your realm.

30. Also, the said lord cardinal had the more part of the goods of Dr. Smith, late bishop of Lincoln, bishop Savage, of York, master Dalby, archdeacon of Richmond, master Tonyers, Dr. Rothall, late bishop of Durham, and of Dr. Fox, late bishop of Winchester, contrary to their wills, and your laws and justice.

wholly submit myself under his obedience, in all things to his princely will and pleasure, whom I never disobeyed or repugned, but was always contented and glad to please him before God, whom I ought most chiefly to have believed and obeyed, whereof I now repent. Yet I most heartily desire to have me commended unto his majesty, for whom I shall during

31. Also, at the Oyer and Terminer of York, proclamation was made that every man should put in their bills for extortion of ordinaries : and when divers bills were put in against the officers of the said lord cardinal of extortion, for taking twelvepence in the pound for probation of testaments, whereof divers bills were found before justice Fitz Herbert and other commissioners, the said lord cardinal removed the said indictments into the Chancery by certiorari, and rebuked the said Fitz Herbert for the same cause.

32. Also the said lord cardinal hath busied himself, and endeavoured by crafty and untrue tales to make dissension and debate amongst your nobles of your realm, which is ready to be proved.

33. Also the said lord cardinal's officers have divers times compelled your subjects to serve him with carts for carriage, and also his servants have taken both corn and cattle, fish, and all other victual, at your grace's price, or under, as though it had been for your grace, which is contrary to your laws.

34. Also the said lord cardinal hath misused himself in your most honourable court, in keeping of as great estate there in your absence, as your grace would have done if you had been there present in your own person.

35. Also, his servants, by virtue of your commission under your broad seal by him to them given, have taken cattle and all other victual, at as low a price as your purveyors have done for your grace by your prerogative, against the laws of your realm.

36. Also, where it hath been accustomed, that your purveyors for your honourable household have had yearly out of your town and liberty of St. Albans three or four hundred quarters of wheat ; truth it is, that since the lord cardinal had the room of abbot, your said purveyors could not be suffered by him and his officers to take any wheat within the said town or liberties.

37. Also, he hath divers times given injunction to your servants, that have been for causes before him in the Star Chamber, that they, nor other for them, should make labour by any manner of way, directly or indirectly, to your grace, to obtain your grace's favour or pardon, which was a presumptuous intent for any subject.

38. Also the said lord cardinal did call before him sir John Stanley, knight, which had taken a farm by convent-seal of the abbot and convent of Chester, and afterwards by his power and might, contrary to right, committed the said sir John Stanley to the prison of Fleet by the space of one year, unto such time as he compelled the said sir John to release his convent-seal to one Leghe, of Adlington, which married one Lark's daughter, which woman the said lord cardinal kept, and had with her two children :*

---

* I have not been able to learn what became of his son ; but by a letter in the British Museum his daughter appears to have been a nun in a convent in Shaftesbury.

my life pray to God to send him much prosperity, honour, and victory over his enemies."

Mr. Shelley, one of the judges, then said that it was the king's pleasure to demand York Place,* the archiepiscopal residence in Westminster: "And that ye do pass the same according to the laws of this realm, his highness hath sent

whereupon the said sir John Stanley, upon displeasure taken in his heart, made himself monk in Westminster, and there died.

39. Also, on a time your grace being at St. Albans, according to the ancient custom used within your verge, your clerk of the market doing his office, did present unto your officers of your most honourable household the prices of all manner of victuals within the precinct of the verge. And it was commanded by your said officers to set up the said prices both on the gates of your honourable household, and also within the market-place in the town of St. Albans, as of ancient custom it hath been used. And the lord cardinal, hearing the same, presumptuously, and not like a subject, caused the aforesaid prices, which were sealed with your grace's seal, accustomably used for the same, to be taken off, and pulled down in the said market-place where they were set up, and in the same places set up his own prices sealed with his seal, and would, if it had not been letted, (opposed,) in semblable manner have used your seal standing upon your gates : and also would of his presumptuous mind have openly set in the stocks within your said town your clerk of your market : by which presumption and usurpation your grace may perceive, that in his heart he hath reputed himself to be equal with your royal majesty.

40. Also the said lord cardinal, of his further pompous and presumptuous mind, hath enterprized to join and imprint the cardinal's hat under your arms in your coin of groats made at your city of York, which like deed hath not been seen to have been done by any subject within your realm before this time.

41. Also, where one sir Ed. Jones, clerk, parson of Crowley, in the county of Bucks, in the eighteenth year of your most noble reign, let his said parsonage, with all tithes and other profits of the same, to one William Johnson, by indenture for certain years, within which years the dean of the said cardinal's college in Oxford pretended title to a certain portion of tithes within the said parsonage, supposing the said portion to belong to the parsonage of Chichelly, which was appropriated to the priory of Tickford lately suppressed, where (of truth) the parsons of Crowley have been peaceably possessed of the said portion time out of mind ; whereupon a subpœna was directed to the said Johnson to appear before the said lord cardinal at Hampton-court, out of any term, with an injunction to suffer the said dean to occupy the said portion. Whereupon the said Johnson appeared before the said lord cardinal at Hampton-court, where, without any bill, the said lord cardinal committed him to the Fleet, where he remained by the space of twelve weeks, because he would not part with the said portion. And, at the last, upon a recognizance made that he should appear before the said lord cardinal whensoever he was commanded, he was delivered out of the Fleet; howbeit as yet the

* Whitehall.

for all his judges and learned counsel, to know their opinions for your assurance thereof, who carefully resolved that your grace must make a recognizance, and before a judge acknowledge and confess the right thereof to belong to the king and his successors, and so his highness shall be assured thereof. Wherefore it hath pleased the king to send me

said portion is so kept from him that he dare not deal with it.

42. Also, where one Martin Docowra had a lease of the manor of Balsall, in the county of Warwick, for term of certain years, an injunction came to him out of the Chancery by writ, upon pain of a thousand pounds, that he should avoid the possession of the same manor, and suffer Sir George Throckmorton, knight, to take the profits of the same manor to the time the matter depending in the Chancery between the lord of St. John's and the said Docowra was discussed. And yet the said Docowra never made answer in the Chancery, nor ever was called into the Chancery for that matter; and now of late he hath received a like injunction upon pain of two thousand pounds, contrary to the course of common law.

43. Also, whereas in the parliament chamber, and in open parliament, communication and devices were had and moved, wherein mention was by an incident made of matters touching heresies and erroneous sects: it was spoken and reported by one bishop there being present, and confirmed by a good number of the same bishops, in presence of all the lords spiritual and temporal then assembled, that two of the said bishops were minded and desired to repair unto the university of Cambridge for examination, reformation, and correction, of such errors as then seemed, and were reported to reign among the students and scholars of the same, as well touching the Lutheran sects and opinions as otherwise: the lord cardinal, informed of the good minds and intents of the said two bishops in that behalf, expressly inhibited and commanded them in no wise so to do. By means whereof, the same errors, as they affirmed, crept more abroad, and took greater place; saying, furthermore, that 'twas not in their defaults that the said heresies were not punished, but in the said lord cardinal, and that 'twas no reason any blame or lack should be given to them for his offence. Whereby it evidently appeareth, that the said lord cardinal, besides all other his heinous offences, hath been the impeacher and disturber of due and direct correction of heresies, being highly to the danger and peril of the whole body, and good Christian people of this your realm.

44. Finally, forasmuch as by the aforesaid articles is evidently declared to your most royal majesty, that the lord cardinal, by his outrageous pride, hath greatly shadowed a long season your grace's honour, which is most highly to be regarded, and by his insatiable avarice and ravenous appetite to have riches and treasure without measure, hath so grievously oppressed your poor subjects with so manifold crafts of bribery and extortion, that the commonwealth of this your grace's realm is thereby greatly decayed and impoverished: and also by his cruelty, iniquity, affection, and partiality, hath subverted the due course and order of your grace's laws to the undoing of a great number of your loving people.

Please it your most royal majesty therefore, of your excellent goodness hither to take of you the recognizance, having in your grace such affiance that you will not refuse to do so. Therefore, I do desire to know your grace's pleasure herein." "Master Shelley," said Wolsey, "I know the king of his own nature is of a royal spirit, not requiring more than reason shall lead him to by the law. And therefore I counsel you, and all other judges and learned men of his council, to put no more into his head than the law which may stand with conscience. When ye tell him this is law, it were well done were ye to tell him also, this is not conscience; for law without conscience is not fit to be ministered unto a king by his council, nor by any of his ministers; for every council to a king ought to have respect to conscience, before the rigour of the law: *laus est facere quod decet, non quod licet.* The king ought, of his royal dignity and prerogative, to mitigate the rigour of the law where conscience hath the most force; and, therefore, in his place of equal justice, he hath constituted a Chancellor to order for him the same: and, therefore, the court of Chancery hath been commonly called the Court of Conscience; for that it hath jurisdiction to command the law in every case to desist from the rigour of allegation. And now I say to you, Master Shelley, have I a power, or may I with conscience give that away which is mine only for me and my

towards the weal of this your realm, and subjects of the same, to set such order and direction upon the said lord cardinal, as may be to the terrible example of others to beware so to offend your grace and your laws hereafter; and that he be so provided for, that he never have any power, jurisdiction, or authority, hereafter, to trouble, vex, and impoverish the commonwealth of this your realm, as he hath done heretofore, to the great hurt and damage of every man almost high and low, which for your grace so doing will daily pray, as their duty is, to Almighty God for the prosperous estate of your most royal majesty, long to endure in honour and good health, to the pleasure of God, and your heart's most desire.

Subscribed the first day of December, the 21st year of the reign of our sovereign lord king Henry the eighth.

T. More.	T. Rochford.
T. Norfolk.	T. Darcy.
C. Suffolk.	W. Mountjoy.
T. Dorset.	W. Sandys.
H. Oxon.	W. Fitzwilliam.
John Oxenford.	Henry Guildford.
H. Northumberland.	Anthony Fitzherbert.
G. Shrewsbury.	John Fitzjames.
R. Fitzwater.	

successors? If this be law and conscience, I pray you show me your opinion." "Forsooth," returned Shelley, "there is no great conscience in it; but having regard to the king's great power, it may the better stand with conscience, since that he is sufficient to recompense the church of York with the double value." "That I know well," said the cardinal; "but here is no such condition, only a bare and simple departure with others' rights. If every bishop should do so, then might every prelate give away the patrimony of the church, which is none of his, and so, in process of time leave nothing for their successors to maintain their dignities, which would be but little to the king's honour. Howbeit, let me see your commission." Upon its being shown him: "Tell his highness," said Wolsey, "that I am his most faithful subject and obedient beadsman, whose command I will in nowise disobey, but in all things fulfil his pleasure, as you, the fathers of the law, say I may. Therefore, I charge your conscience, and discharge my own. Howbeit, show his majesty from me, that I must desire his majesty to remember, that there is both a heaven and a hell." And therewith the clerk was called in, who wrote the recognizance,* with which the judge returned to London.

The declaration was received as the confession of his offence, and the sentence of the law was pronounced. All his possessions and moveables were forfeited to the crown; but he was

---

* "The bishop of Bayonne, who paid the cardinal a visit of commiseration at this period, gives the following affecting picture of his distress: ' I have been to see the cardinal in his trouble, where I found in him the greatest example of fortune which was ever beheld. He set forth his case to me in the worst rhetoric I ever heard, for heart and tongue both failed him entirely; he wept bitterly, and prayed to God that the king and madame might have pity upon him, if they found that he had kept to them his promise to be their good and true servant, to the utmost of his honour and power ; but, all the while, he said to me, that was of better effect than his poor visage, which has fallen away to half its wonted size. I promise you, my lord, that his fortune is such that his enemies, English though they be, cannot but feel pity for him, though, none the less, they will not fail to persecute him to the end ; he sees no means of safety, nor I neither, unless it please the king and madame to aid him. He asks not either the legacy, or the broad seal, or his old credit ; he is ready to give up everything, even down to his shirt ; and to live in a hermitage, so that the king will not hold him in disgrace. I did all I could to comfort him, but had small success therein.'—*John Debellaz, Bishop of Bayonne.*

not, as the law commands, committed to prison.* The fate of his colleges gave him most pain. He had indulged a fond expectation that they would have been his monuments with posterity, as a patron of knowledge, and a benefactor to his country; but they too were confiscated. He wrote to the king, humbly, as on his knees, and with weeping eyes, to spare the college at Oxford. No answer was returned.†

Cromwell, who, in the house of commons, had so ably defended him, acted with such open and manly intrepidity in the cause of his deserted master, that he won the esteem of all parties. Being on a visit of consolation to him at Esher, he one day took occasion to mention, that no provision had been made for several of the servants who had proved themselves very faithful, and had never forsaken him. "Alas!" replied the cardinal, "you know that I have nothing to give them, nor to reward you." Cromwell then proposed that the cardinal's chaplains, who had been preferred to rich benefices by his influence, should, with himself, contribute a little

---

* " After my lord had supped that night, and all men gone to bed, being All-hallowne day, about midnight, one of the porters came to my chamber door, and knocked there to wake me. And being once awake, and perceiving who was there, I asked him, what he would have at that time of the night? 'Sir,' quoth he, 'there be a great number of horsemen at the gate, that would come in, saying that it is sir John Russel, and so it appears by his voice; and what is your pleasure that I should do?' said he. 'Marry,' quoth I, 'go down again, and make a great fire in your lodge, until I come, to dry them;' for it rained all that night most vehemently, as it did at any time the year before. Then I arose and made me ready, and put on my night-gown, and came to the gates, and asked who was there. With that Mr. Russel spake to me, whom I knew right well, and I caused the gates to be set open, and let them all come in, who were wet to the very skin. I caused Mr. Russel to go into the porter's lodge to the fire to dry him; and he showed me that he was come from the king unto my lord in message, with whom he required me to speak. 'Sir,' quoth I, 'I trust your news be good.' 'Yea, and so I promise you on my fidelity; and so tell him, that I have brought him such news as will please him right well.' 'Well then, I will go,' quoth I, 'and wake him, and cause him to rise.' I went incontinent to my lord's chamber door, and knocked there, so that my lord spake to me, and asked me what I would have. With that I told him of the coming of sir John Russel; and then he called up to him one of his grooms to let me in; and when I was come to him, I told him again of the journey that sir John Russel had taken that troublesome night. 'I pray God all be for the best,' quoth he. 'Yes, sir,' quoth I, 'he showed me, and

---

† Lord Herbert, page 339.

money for the support of the domestics; and it was agreed that, as the return of the king's favour was uncertain, it was necessary to reduce their number. The servants were, therefore, summoned into the hall, at the upper end of which stood Wolsey in his pontifical robes, attended by the chaplains and officers of his household, with whom he continued in conversation till the whole were assembled. Turning to address them, he paused for a moment. The sight of so many faithful, though humble friends, powerfully touched his feelings, and for some time he was unable to speak. The tears started into his eyes, and the servants, perceiving his emotion, gave way to their own sorrows. When he had recovered from his agitation, and silence was restored, he spoke to them in the following manner:—" Most faithful gentlemen, and true-hearted yeomen, I do not lament to see you about me, but I lament in a manner a certain ingratitude on my behalf towards you all, in whom hath been a great default, that in my

so bade me tell you, that he had brought such news, as you would greatly rejoice thereat.' 'Well then,' quoth he, ' God be praised, and welcome be his grace! Go ye and fetch him to me, and by that time I will be ready to talk with him.'

" Then I returned into the lodge, and brought Mr. Russel from thence unto my lord, who had cast about him his night-gown. And when Mr. Russel was come before him, he most humbly reverenced him, upon his knees, whom my lord stooped unto, and took him up, and bade him welcome. ' Sir,' quoth he, ' the king commendeth him unto you ;' and delivered him a great ring of gold with a turquois for a token ; ' and willed me to bid you be of good cheer; for he loveth you as well as ever he did, and is sorry for your trouble, whose mind runneth much upon you. Insomuch that before his grace sat down to supper, he called me unto him, and desired me to take the pains secretly to visit you, and to comfort you the best of my power. And sir, I have had the sorest journey for so little a way, that ever I had to my remembrance.'

" My lord thanked him for his pains and good news, and demanded of him if he had supped ; and he said, ' Nay.' ' Well then,' quoth my lord, ' cause the cooks to provide some meat for him ; and cause a chamber to be provided for him, that he may take his rest awhile upon a bed.' All which commandment I fulfilled, and in the mean time my lord and Master Russel were in secret communication ; and in the end, Master Russel went to his chamber, taking his leave of my lord, and said he would tarry but a while, for he would be at the court at Greenwich again before day, and would not for any thing that it were known that he had been with my lord that night. And so being in his chamber, having a small repast, he rested him a while upon a bed, while his servants supped and dried them ; and that done, incontinent he rode away again with speed to the court."—*Cavendish.*

prosperity I have not done so much for you as I might have done, either in deed or word, which lay in my power then to do: but then I knew not the jewel and special treasure I had in my house of you my faithful servants; but now experience hath taught me, and with the eyes of my discretion I do well perceive the same. There was never thing that repented me more that ever I did, than doth the remembrance of my great and most oblivious negligence and unkind ingratitude, that I have not promoted, preferred, or advanced you all, according to your demerits. Howbeit, it is not unknown unto you all, that I was not so fully furnished of temporal promotions in my gift as I was of spiritual preferments. And if I should have preferred you to any of the king's officers, then should I have run in the indignation of the king's servants, who would not much let to report behind my back, that there could no office in the king's gift escape the cardinal and his servants, and thus should I have run in open slander before all the world. But now it is come to this pass, that it hath pleased the king to take all that ever I have into his hands, so that I have nothing to give you; for I have nothing left me but my bare clothes upon my back, the which are simple in comparison to that I had. Howbeit, if it might do you any good, I would not stick to divide the same among you, yea, and the skin of my back too, if it might countervail any value among you. But my good gentlemen and yeomen, my trusty and faithful servants, and of whom no prince hath the like, I shall require you to take some patience with me awhile, for I doubt not but that the king, considering my suggested offence by mine enemies, which is put against me, to be of small grief or hurt, for so great and sudden an overthrow, will shortly restore me to my living, so that I shall be more able to divide my substance among you, whereof ye shall not lack. For whatsoever shall chance hereafter to be an overplus and superfluity of my revenues, at the determination of my yearly account, it shall be distributed among you. For I will never during my life esteem the goods and riches of this world any otherwise than which shall be sufficient to maintain the estate that God hath and shall call me unto. And if the king do not shortly restore me, then will I write for you, either to the king, or to any nobleman within this realm, to retain your service; for I doubt not but the king, or any nobleman within this realm, will credit my letter in your commendation.

Therefore, in the meantime, I would advise you to repair home to your wives, such as have wives; and some of you that have no wives to take a time to visit your parents in the country.   There is none of you all but would, once in a year, require licence to see and visit your wife, and other of your friends: take this time, therefore, in that respect, and in your return I will not refuse you, to beg with you.   I consider that your service in my house hath been such, that ye be not apt to serve any man under the degree of a king; therefore, I would advise you to serve no man but the king, who I am sure will not refuse you.   Therefore, I shall desire you to take your pleasure for a month, and then ye may come again, and, by that time, I trust the king will extend his mercy upon me."

The apprehension of retaliation often engenders in the minds of aggressors sentiments which resemble the workings of revenge, and base spirits, when they have happened to injure, often deliberately continue to persecute.   The enemies of the cardinal combined to prevent the king from ever seeing him again, and continued to mortify his proud heart in the hope that innocence, provoked by injustice, would betray him into some imprudent expression of indignation. Henry himself has indeed been suspected of sanctioning their cruelty, from a vicious principle of policy, in the expectation, that as Wolsey disregarded popular clamour, he might, for the restoration of his grandeur, not scruple to sustain even the obloquy of the Roman consistory by pronouncing the sentence of divorce.   But he ought to have known his lofty character better, and that the love of fame, which renders public men incorruptible, though nearly allied to the love of power and splendour, never admits rank into comparison with reputation.   The treatment which the cardinal received wounded without irritating.   The eagerness with which his former associates endeavoured to rise on his ruins—the neglect of those who had shared his bounty—the abortive assurances that he had received from the king*—and the con-

---

* Storer, in making him describe his feelings after his fall, uses one of the most pathetic and original images in poetry :

"I am the tomb where that affection lies,
That was the closet where it living kept ;
Yet, wise men say, Affection never dies,
No, but it turns ; and, when it long hath slept,
Looks heavy like the eye that long hath wept."

viction that, without being restored to favour, he never could be able to contradict the wilful misrepresentation which was daily made of his purest intentions, but must transmit a blemished and defaced character to posterity, corroded his feelings to such a degree that his life was despaired of. Henry, being informed of his indisposition, inquired of one of the court physicians,* who had professionally visited Esher, what was the matter with the cardinal, and learning that it arose from dejection, struck the table violently with his hand, exclaiming—" Marry, I would rather lose twenty thousand pounds than that he should die! make you haste, therefore, with as many as are of your profession about the court, and endeavour to recover him."† He then took from his finger a ring charged with a ruby, on which his own head was engraved, and sent the doctor with it and many kindly assurances to the cardinal; and he ordered Anne Boleyn, who happened to be present, to send also some token of her regard; and she submissively obeyed, giving the doctor a golden tablet from her side, which she requested him to deliver from her.‡   Soon after, Wolsey was regularly par-

---

* " Dr. Butts."—*Cavendish.*   † Godwin's Annals, 63.

‡ " At Christmas he fell very sore sick, most likely to die. Whereof the king being advertised, was very sorry, and sent Doctor Buttes, his physician, unto him, to see in what state he was. Doctor Buttes came unto him, finding him lying very sick in his bed ; and perceiving the danger returned to the king. Of whom the king demanded, saying, ' Have you seen yonder man ?' ' Yea, sir,' quoth he. ' How do you like him ?' quoth the king. ' Sir,' quoth he, ' if you will have him dead, I warrant him he will be dead within these four days, if he receive no comfort from you shortly, and Mrs. Anne.' ' Marry,' quoth the king, ' God forbid that he should die. I pray you, master Buttes, go again unto him, and do your care unto him ; for I would not lose him for twenty thousand pounds.' ' Then must your grace,' quoth master Buttes, ' send him first some comfortable message, as shortly as you can.' ' Even so I will,' quoth the king, ' by you. And therefore make speed to him again, and ye shall deliver him this ring from me, for a token,' (in the which ring was the king's image, engraved within a ruby, as like the king as could be devised). ' This ring he knoweth right well, for he gave me the same ; and tell him, that I am not offended with him in my heart nothing at all, and that shall he know shortly. Therefore bid him pluck up his heart, and be of good comfort. And I charge you come not from him, until ye have brought him out of the danger of death.' Then spake the king to Mistress Anne Boleyne, saying, ' Good sweetheart, I pray you, as ye love me, send the cardinal a token at my desire, with comfortable words ; and in so doing ye shall deserve our thanks.' She not being disposed to offend the king, would not disobey his loving request, whatsoever

doned* and replaced in the see of York, with a pension of a thousand marks per annum from the bishopric of Winchester; and Henry, unknown to the privy council, restored to him plate and effects to the value of more than six thousand pounds.† These unexpected testimonies of affection essentially contributed to his recovery; and having been allowed

in her heart she intended towards the cardinal; but took incontinent her tablet of gold, that hung at her girdle, and delivered it to Master Buttes, with very gentle and comfortable words. And so Master Buttes departed with speed to Esher; after whom the king sent doctor Cromer the Scot, doctor Clement, and doctor Wotton, to consult with Master Buttes for my lord's recovery.

"After that Master Buttes had been with my lord, and delivered the king's and Mistress Anne's tokens unto him, with the most comfortable words that he could devise on the king's and mistress Anne's behalf, he rejoiced not a little, and advanced himself on his bed, and received the tokens most joyfully, thanking master Buttes for his pains and good comfort. Master Buttes told him, furthermore, that the king's pleasure was, that he should minister unto him for his health: and to join with him, for the better and most assured ways, he hath sent hither doctor Clement, doctor Cromer, and doctor Wotton. 'Therefore, my lord,' quoth he, 'it were well done they were called in to visit you, and to consult with them, and to have their opinions of your disease, trusting to Almighty God that we shall, through his grace and help, ease you of your pains, and rid you of your infirmities.' To this motion my lord was contented to hear their judgments: for he trusted more to doctor Cromer than to all the rest, because he was the very man to bring him from Paris into England, and gave him partly his exhibition in Paris. Then when they were come into his chamber, and had talked with him, he took upon him to debate his disease learnedly, so that they might perceive that he was seen in that art. After they had taken order for their ministration, it was not long ere they brought him out of danger; and within four days they set him on his feet, and got him a stomach to meat. All this done, and he in a right good way of amendment, they took their leave to depart, to whom my lord offered to each of them his reward; the which they refused, saying, that the king had given them a special commandment, that they should take of him nothing for their pains and ministration; for at their return he himself would sufficiently reward them of his own costs: and with great thanks they departed, and left my lord in good state of recovery."—*Cavendish.*

* Feb. 12, 1530.

† Schedule of the king's presents to the cardinal.

"The money, goods, and chattels, given by the king's grace to the lord cardinal:—

"First, in ready money, £3000.

"Then, in plate, 9565 oz. and ¾, at 3s. 3d. the oz., amounteth to £1752 3s. 8d.

"Then, divers apparel of household, as hangings, bedding, drapery, and

permission, when he resigned the palace at Hampton, to
reside in Richmond castle, he ventured to solicit leave to
remove from Esher to the more cheerful air and scenery of
that mansion, which was readily granted.*   But his enemies,
fearing that if he was permitted to reside long so near the
court, the king might be induced to visit or recal him, recommended, that as he was not now detained by the duties
of the chancery, he should be sent to the government of his
diocese; and he was accordingly banished to York.

Some time previous to his departure, the domestics observed an interesting change in his demeanour. Like many
other great men in adversity, his mind took a superstitious
turn, and seemed to discover in accidents certainly trivial, an
ominous and fatal meaning.†   He grew pensive, wore a shirt

other things, as appeareth by the inventory of the same, amounting in value,
by estimation, £1300.
  " Then, in horses and geldings, 80, with their apparel, valued by esti-
mation, £150.
  " Then, in mules for the saddle, with their apparel, valued by estima-
tion, £60.
  " Then, in mules for carriages, 6, with their apparel, valued by estima-
tion, £40.
  " Then, in ling, 1000, valued by estimation, £40.
  " Then, in cod and haberdine, 800, valued by estimation, £40.
  " Then, in salt, 8 way, valued by estimation, £10.
  " Then, in implements of the kitchen, as pots, pans, spits, pewter vessels,
and other things necessary for the same, valued by estimation, £80.
  " Then, 52 oxen, valued by estimation, £80.
  " Then, in muttons, 70, valued by estimation, £12.
  " Then, the apparel of his body, valued by estimation, £300.
  " Summary, £6374 3s. 7d."—Fiddes.

  * Lord Herbert, 303.   " And also, the counsel, had put into the king's
head that the new gallery at Esher, which my lord had late before his fall
newly set up, would be very necessary for the king, to take down and set it
up again at Westminster, which was done accordingly, and stands at the
present day the next to the first gatehouse. The taking away thereof before my
lord's face, was to him a corrosive, which was invented by his enemies only
to torment him, the which indeed discouraged him very sore to tarry any
longer there."—Cavendish.

  † " As my lord was accustomed to walk towards the evening in his garden there (Richmond), and to say his even-song, and other his divine
service, with his chaplain; and it was my chance to wait upon him; and standing in an alley, whilst he in another alley walked with his chaplain, saying
his service as is aforesaid; as I stood I espied certain images of beasts
counterfeited in timber standing in a corner under the lodge, to the which

of haircloth, and held frequent conferences with a venerable old man belonging to the brotherhood of the Charterhouse at Richmond.*

He commenced his journey towards York about the end of Lent. His train consisted of a hundred and sixty horse, and seventy-two wagons, loaded with the relics of his furniture. How great must have been that grandeur which, by comparison, made such wealth appear poverty. Having stopped at Peterborough to celebrate the festival of Easter, on Palm

I repaired to behold; among whom I saw stand there a dun cow, whereon I most mused, because of the like entailing (*sculpture*) thereof. My lord, being in the further side of the garden, espied me, how I viewed and surveyed these beasts; and, having finished his service, came suddenly upon me or I was aware, and speaking to me, said, 'What have you espied here, that you look attentively upon?' 'Forsooth, if it please your grace,' quoth I, 'here I behold these images; the which, I suppose, were ordained to be set up within some place about the king's palace: howbeit, sir, among them all,‡I have most considered this cow, in which, as me seemeth, the workman has most lively showed his cunning.' 'Yea, marry,' quoth he, 'upon this cow hangeth a certain prophecy, the which is this; because peradventure you never heard it before, I will show you. There is a saying,

When the cow masters the bull,
Then, priest, beware thy skull;

of which prophecy neither my lord that declared it, nor yet I that heard it, understood the effect; although the compassing thereof was at that present aworking, and about to be brought to pass. This cow the king had by reason of the earldom of Richmond, which was his inheritance; and this prophecy was afterwards expounded in this way: The dun cow, because it was the king's beast,† betokened the king, and the bull betokened Mistress Anne Boleyn, who was after queen, because that her father had a black bull's head in his cognizance, and was his beast; so that when the king had married queen Anne, the which was unknown to my lord or to any other that he would do so, then was this prophecy thought of all men to be fulfilled. For what numbers of priests, religious and seculars, lost their heads for offending such laws as were made to bring this marriage to effect, is not unknown to all the world.'"—*Cavendish.*

* "Every day he resorted to the Charterhouse there (*Richmond*), and in afternoons he would sit in contemplation with one of the most ancient fathers of that house in their cells, who converted him, and caused him to despise the vain glory of the world, and gave him shirts of hair to wear, the which he wore divers times after."—*Cavendish.*

† Almost all the signs of the public houses in England were originally the crests or arms of popular public characters. The dun cow of the alehouses probably originated in the reign of Henry VII., who was earl of Richmond. The chequer of the public houses in London was the arms of the earls of Arundel, who had anciently the privilege of licensing them.

Sunday he walked in the procession of the monks to the cathedral; and on the following Thursday kept Maunday, according to the practice of the church, washing the feet of the poor, and bestowing alms and blessings.* From Peterborough he proceeded slowly, exercising his pastoral functions by the way, and halted at Stoby, where he resided till Michaelmas, preaching in the churches of the adjacent parishes, interposing to reconcile the variance of neighbours, relieving the necessitous, and performing many other exemplary acts of piety and benevolence. He then went forward to Cawood castle, one of the residences of the archbishop of York, distant from the city about twelve miles. A great conflux of people, drawn together by curiosity, waited to see him arrive, among whom were the clergy of the diocese, who welcomed him with the reverence due to his pontifical dignity. The castle, having been long untenanted, required extensive repairs, which the cardinal immediately commenced, for nature and habit made him decisive and prompt in all circumstances. The short period of his residence in this ancient mansion was, perhaps, the happiest of his life. He appeared delighted with the composure of rural affairs; and by the equity of his demeanour, and a mild condescension, which belied the reports of his haughtiness, he won the hearts of his diocesans. He professed himself a convert from ambition, and having suffered the perils and terrors of shipwreck, he was thankful that at length he had cast anchor in a calm and pleasant haven, with the expectation of safety and rest.

As he had never been installed in the archiepiscopal see, he gave orders to prepare the cathedral for the ceremony, and a day was appointed for the celebration. On this occasion the arrangements were unusually simple, and indicated the altered frame of his mind. As the day approached, incredible

* " Upon Palm-Sunday he bore his palm, and went in procession with the monks, setting forth the divine service right honourably, with such singing men as he had there of his own ; and upon Maunday-Thursday he made his maunday there in our Lady's Chapel, having fifty-nine+ poor men, whose feet he washed and kissed ; and, after he had wiped them, he gave every of the said poor men twelve pence in money, three ells of good canvas to make them shirts, a pair of new shoes, a cast of red herrings, and three white herrings, and one of them had two shillings."—*Cavendish.*

+ This number denoted that he was then fifty-nine years old.

quantities of provisions were sent to him by the neighbouring gentry and clergy, in order that he might maintain the customary hospitalities in a style suitable to his character; and, in the meantime, he was flattered by several friendly messages from the king. The pleasure which the latter afforded was so obvious and lively, that it was difficult to determine whether it arose from a rekindled hope of restoration, or was only the exulting joy of finding his integrity vindicated. But the triumph or the illusion was of short duration, and only served to inflame the sense of disappointment, and to enhance the shock of a second fall.

The Monday after All-Souls day was fixed for the installation; but on the preceding Friday, as he was sitting at dinner, the earl of Northumberland, who, while lord Percy, had been educated in his house, and whose intended marriage with Anne Boleyn the cardinal had been the means of frustrating, accompanied by a privy counsellor and a large retinue, arrived at the castle. He was received with a paternal and a cheerful welcome, and conducted by Wolsey into his own apartments; where they had not, however, exchanged many words, when the earl became agitated, and in a low and troubled voice declared him arrested for high treason. Astonished by a charge so unexpected, Wolsey, for some time, was unable to speak; but, recovering his spirits, he requested Northumberland to show the warrant, protesting that otherwise he would not surrender himself; for as a member of the college of cardinals he was exempted from the jurisdiction of all secular princes. At this moment the privy counsellor entered the room. Wolsey, on seeing him, observed that, as a counsellor of the king, he was sufficiently commissioned to take him into custody, and immediately intimated that he was their prisoner. "I fear not," added he, "the cruelty of my enemies, nor a scrutiny of my allegiance; and I take heaven to witness, that neither in word or deed have I injured the king, and will maintain my innocence face to face with any man alive."

When it was known in the neighbourhood that he was to be conveyed to London, a great crowd assembled round the castle; and as he came out on his mule, guarded, the people began to exclaim, "God save your grace, and foul evil overtake them that have taken you from us." With these and other testimonies of popular affection, he was followed to a considerable distance. Northumberland conducted him to Sheffield-park, and delivered him to the custody of the earl of Shrewsbury, with whom he resided about a fortnight, until the king's further pleasure was known. Shrewsbury entertained him with the respect that became his own honour, and assured him, that though the king could not satisfy the council without sending him to trial, still he believed him guiltless, and that his enemies dreaded his restoration to favour more than he ought to do their malice. But the cardinal could no longer be cheered. He considered his destruction as irrevocably fixed, and resigned himself to the comfortless thoughts which that gloomy notion inspired. His constitution, impaired by age and the vicissitudes of hope and fear, suddenly gave way. One day, at dinner, he complained of a coldness in his stomach, and was soon after seized with a violent flux, which greatly drained his strength. In this situation he was found by sir William Kingston, constable of the Tower, who, with twenty yeomen of the guards that had formerly been in his own service, came to convey him to London. In the whole of his treatment, from the moment of his arrest, a great degree of respect and consideration was shown to him, and it appears to have been at the special command of Henry. Sir William, on being taken to his presence, knelt down, and assured him, in the king's name, of his majesty's unbroken friendship; adding, that it was not necessary for him to make more haste in the journey than suited his health and convenience. The cardinal, however, thought that delay might be regarded as evidence of conscious guilt, and, declining the indulgence, anxiously proceeded forward. Although he travelled slowly, his illness was increased by fatigue, and he grew weak and feverish. On the evening of the third day after leaving Sheffield-park, he approached Leicester. The appearance of nature accorded with the condition of the prisoner. The end of the year was drawing nigh, and the cardinal beheld for the last time the falling leaf and the setting sun.

When the cavalcade reached the monastery, the day was shut in; and the abbot and the friars, apprized of his coming, waited with torches at the gate to receive him. But the honours of this world had ceased to afford him pleasure, and as he passed towards the bottom of the stairs, he said to the brotherhood, "I am come to lay my bones among you." Being supported into a chamber, he immediately went to bed, and languished, with increasing signs of dissolution, all the next day. The following morning, Cavendish, his usher, and afterwards historian, as he was watching near him, thought that he perceived the symptoms of death. The cardinal, noticing him, inquired the hour, and was told eight o'clock; "That cannot be," he replied, "for at eight o'clock you shall lose your master. My time is at hand, and I must depart this world." His confessor, who was standing near, requested Cavendish to inquire, if he would be confessed. "What have you to do with that?" answered he, angrily; but was pacified by the interference of the confessor. Continuing to grow weaker and weaker, he frequently fainted during the course of the day. About four o'clock of the following morning he asked for some refreshment; which having received, and made confession, sir William Kingston entered his room, and inquired how he felt himself. "Sir," said Wolsey, "I tarry but the pleasure of God, to render up my poor soul into his hands;" and, after a few other words between them, he resumed, "I have now been eight days together troubled with a continual flux and fever, a species of disease which, if it do not remit its violence within that period, never fails to terminate in death. I pray you commend me humbly to the king; and beseech him, in my behalf, to call to his princely remembrance all matters that have passed between him and me, particularly in what respects the business of the queen, and then he must know whether I have given him any offence. He is a prince of a most royal nature; but rather than want any part of his pleasure, he will endanger the half of his kingdom. Often have I knelt before him for three hours together, endeavouring to persuade him from his will and appetite, and could not prevail. Had I served God as diligently as I have done the king, he would not have given me over in my grey hairs."*

* This sentiment seems to be common to fallen ministers. When Samrah, the governor of Busorah, was deposed by Maoujyah, the sixth caliph, he is reported to have said, "If I had served God so well as I served him, he would not have condemned me;" and Antonio Perez, the favourite of Philip II. of Spain, made a similar complaint. [So James V. of Scotland imagined that sir James Hamilton addressed him thus in a dream: "Though I am a sinner against God, I failed not to thee. Had I been as good a servant to the Lord my God as I was to thee, I had not died that death."—*Singer.*]

He then continued for a short time to give sir William some advice, in case he should ever be called to the privy council, and adding a few general observations on the revolutionary temper of the times, concluded by saying, "Farewell, I wish all good things to have success. My time draws fast on. I may not tarry with you. Forget not what I have said; and when I am gone, call it often to mind." Towards the conclusion he began to falter, and linger in the articulation of his words. At the end, his eyes became motionless, and his sight failed. The abbot was summoned to administer the extreme unction, and the yeomen of the guard were called in to see him die. As the clock struck eight, he expired."*

The body, with the face uncovered, being laid out in pontifical robes, the magistrates and inhabitants of Leicester were admitted to see it, in order that they might certify the death. In the evening it was removed into the church; but the funeral service was protracted by unusual dirges and orisons, and it was past midnight before the interment took place.† Such was the end of this proud and famous cardinal.‡ The king, when informed of his death, was touched with sincere sorrow; and, as if it could in any way atone for his own conduct, he seemed anxious to reward all those who had shown any kind-

---

* November, 29, 1530.

† Storer, in allusion to the obscurity of the cardinal's grave, says, in addressing Melpomene,

> "Perchance the tenour of that mourning verse
> May lead some pilgrim to my tombless grave,
> Where neither marble monument nor hearse
> The passengers' attentive vein may crave,
> Which honours now the meanest persons have.
> But well is me, where'er my ashes lie,
> If one tear drop from some religious eye."

Bishop Corbet, in his "Iter Boreale," also, in allusion to the same circumstance, says,

> "Although from his own store Wolsey might have
> A palace or a college for his grave;
> Yet here he lies interr'd, as if that all
> Of him to be remembered were his fall;
> Nothing but earth to earth, nor pompous weight
> Upon him but a pebble or a quoit."

‡ Cavendish's more detailed and deeply interesting narrative of the cardinal's journey into the north, and of his last days, will be found in the Appendix, No. 1. *W. H.*

ness to his old favourite. On Cromwell he bestowed no inconsiderable portion of the power which his master had enjoyed; and Cavendish, whose prudence and fidelity had remained unshaken by the ruin which he had witnessed and shared, was promoted to wealth and situations which enabled him to become the founder of the princely dukedom of Devonshire. Henry, indeed, never ceased to regret the cardinal; and often, in the perplexities which afterwards troubled his reign, lamented the loss of Wolsey, always pronouncing his name with an epithet of respect.

If it be true that no man by less effort ever attained so much dignity as cardinal Wolsey, few have been thrown down from so great a height under the imputation of smaller crimes.* He was undoubtedly a character of the most splendid class. Haughty, ambitious, masterly, and magnificent, he felt himself formed for superiority; and his conduct, if not always judicious, was uniformly great. His exterior was dignified, his demeanour courtly, his discernment rapid, his eloquence commanding, and his comprehension vast and prospective. The number, variety, and magnitude of his public trusts, in all of which he was eminently distinguished, are proofs of the elastic powers of his mind, and the versatility of his talents for business. His avidity to amass wealth was contrasted with an expenditure so generous, that it lost the name of avarice, and deserved to be dignified with that of ambition. His ostentation was so richly blended with munificence and hospitality, that it ought to be ascribed rather to the love of distinction than to vanity; and his pride was so nearly allied to honour and justice, that it seemed to be essential to his accomplishments as a statesman. All his undertakings showed the combining and foreseeing faculties of his genius. The league of London was the grand fundamental charter by which the European nations recovered their independence from the pope; and the change in the alliance of England, after the battle of Pavia, was one of those rare and bold measures which may divide the opinion of the world as to their wisdom, but must command its admiration. The principle of that change, having its foundation in the league of London, was to preserve the equilibrium of Europe; and if consistency be essential to character, and

* Lord Herbert, 343.

character be strength as applied to nations, the dignity of England was obviously more advanced by adhering to her principles, than her power would have been augmented by continuing the partnership of war with Charles. The cardinal's system for the reformation of the clergy, though defective in philosophy, was singularly liberal in policy; for statesmen are often, by official necessity, rather the protectors than the enemies of corruption. It is true that he did not calculate on all that flood of consequences which may be traced to his measures, but it could not have arisen from undertakings more partial. Therefore, whether estimated by his natural endowments, his fortune, or his designs, Wolsey must be considered as one of those great occasional men who, at distant intervals, suddenly appear, surprising the world by their movements and their splendour; and who, having agitated and altered the regular frame of society by their influence, are commemorated as the epochal characters of history.

APPENDIX.

APPENDIX I.

NARRATIVE BY GEORGE CAVENDISH, GENTLEMAN USHER TO
CARDINAL WOLSEY, OF THE CARDINAL'S LAST JOURNEY
INTO THE NORTH, AND OF HIS FINAL DISGRACE AND DEATH.

" Then prepared my lord all things with speed for his
journey, and repaired into the North with all celerity, and
sent to London for livery cloths for his servants, that should
ride with him thither. Some of his servants he refused, such
as he thought were not meet to serve; and some again of
their own mind desired his honour to tarry still in the south,
being very loath to forsake their native country, their parents,
wives, and children, whom he right gladly and with good
will licensed so to do, and rendered unto them his hearty
thanks for their long tarrying with him in his trouble. So
that all things being furnished towards his journey, he took
the same in the beginning of the Passion Week, before Easter;
and so rode from Richmond to a place which was the abbots'
of Westminster, called Hendon; and the next day he removed
to a place where my lady Parry lay, called the Rye; the
next day he rode to Royston, where he was lodged in the
priory there; then went he the next day to Huntington, and
there lodged within the abbey; and the next day he rode to
Peterborough, and there lodged in the abbey, making there
his abode all the next week, where he kept the solemn feast of
Easter, with all his train, (save a few in number, which were

continually attending on him) who were lodged in the town, and had board wages; his train was in number a hundred and three score persons, having with him twelve carts to carry his stuff of his own, which he sent for from his college of Oxenford, that were there provided, besides three score other carts of his daily carriage of necessaries for his buildings. Upon Palm Sunday he bare his palm, and went in procession, with the monks, setting forth the divine service right honourably, with such singing men as he then had there of his own. And upon the Maunday Thursday he made his Maundy there in our Lady's chapel, having fifty-nine* poor men, whose feet he washed, and kissed; and after he had wiped them, he gave every of the said poor men twelve pence in money, three ells of good canvass to make them shirts, a pair of new shoes, a cast of red herrings, and three white herrings, and one of them had two shillings. Upon Easter day he rose to the resurrection,† and that day he went in procession in his cardinal's vesture, having his hat on his head, and sang the high mass there he himself solemnly. After his mass he gave his benediction to

---

* This number denotes that he was now fifty-nine years old.

† The Book of Ceremonies before cited, which was compiled in the reign of Henry VIII. observes: "Upon Easter day in the morning *ceremonies* of the *resurrection* be very laudable, to put us in remembrance of Christ's resurrection, which is the cause of our justification."—Strype's *Eccles. Memorials*, v. i. p. 294. Records. What these ceremonies were we may collect from the Rubrics upon that day, in the *Processionale secundum usum Sarum*, fol. 72, edit. 1555, which are to this effect: On Easter day before mass, and before the ringing of the bells, let the clerks assemble, and all the tapers in the church be lighted. Then two persons shall draw nigh to the sepulchre, and after it is censed, let them take the cross out of the sepulchre, and one of them begin *Christus resurgens*. Then let the procession commence. After this they shall all worship (*adorent*) the cross. Then let all the crucifixes and images in the church be unveiled, &c., &c. In like manner Good Friday also had its peculiar ceremonies. Bishop Longland closes his sermon preached on that day before king Henry VIII, A. D. 1538, in the following manner: "In mean season I shall exhort you all in our Lord God, *as of old custom hath here this day been used*, every one of you or ye depart, with most entire devotion, kneeling before our saviour Lord God, this our Jesus Christ, which hath suffered so much for us, to whom we are so much bound, *who lieth in yonder sepulchre;* in honour of him, of his passion and death, and of his five wounds, to say five paternosters, five aves, and one creed: that it may please his merciful goodness to make us partners of the merits of this his most glorious passion, blood, and death." *Imprinted by Thomas Petyt*. See also Michael Wood's *Dialogue or Familiar Talks*. A. D. 1524. Signat. D. 3.—*Wordsworth*.

all the hearers with clean remission; and there continued he till Thursday next.

"My lord continuing there at Peterborough after this manner, intending to remove from thence shortly, commanded me to ride to sir William Fitzwilliams, knight, who dwelt within three or four miles of Peterborough, to provide him there a lodging, for three or four days, in his journey northwards. And being with this sir William Fitzwilliams, I did my message accordingly; whereof he was, as it appeared by his word and deed, the gladdest man alive, that my lord would so lovingly take his house in his way; saying, that he should be most heartily welcome of any man, the king his sovereign except; saying furthermore that my lord should not need to disload or discharge any part of his stuff and carriage for his own use during his abode there, but should have all necessary stuff of his own to occupy, unless it were my lord's bed for his own person. This, upon report made to my lord at my return, rejoiced him not a little; and he commanded me to give warning unto all his officers and servants to prepare them to remove from Peterborough upon Thursday next, which was in Easter week. Then made every man himself and all things in such readiness, as was convenient, paying in the town for all such things as they had taken; for which cause my lord caused proclamation to be made in the town, that if any person or persons were grieved by any of his servants, they should resort to his officers, and there they should be answered and have due remedy; so that, all things ready furnished, my lord took his journey from the abbey of Peterborough on the Thursday in Easter week, to Mr. Fitzwilliams, where he was joyously received, and had worthy and honourable entertainment at the only cost and charge of the said Mr. Fitzwilliams, all the time of my lord's being there with him.

"The occasion that moved Mr. Fitzwilliams thus friendly to do, was this: he was sometime a merchant of London, and sheriff thereof, and bore the charge of the same in the said city: and after there fell a great debate and grudge between the bench of aldermen and the said sir William, for that he would have a new corporation of Merchant Taylors, contrary to the order of the city, the which caused him to surrender up his cloak, and gave over his freedom of the city, against

whose malice my lord bare him much, and after received him
into his service, whom he made his treasurer, and after that
his high chamberlain, and in conclusion, for his wisdom,
gravity, eloquence, and port, being a comely gentleman, my
lord made him one of the king's council, who so continued
during all his life after. And for the special goodness he
always found in my lord in his trouble with the city, like a
faithful servant he was ready then most joyfully to requite
him with the semblable, and granted to show him any pleasure that lay in him to do.

" Thus my lord continued there from Thursday in Easter
week, at Mr. Fitzwilliam's cost, until the Monday next following; at which time he removed from thence unto Stam-
ford, where he lay all night at the sign of the Bull. And
the next day he removed from thence to Grantham, and was
lodged in a gentleman's place whose name was Mr. Hall.
And the next day he rode to Newark, and lodged in the castle
all that night, and the next day also, which is within four
miles of Southwell, whither my lord intended to ride, and
there to continue, as hereafter you shall hear.

" I cannot choose but to declare unto you a notable communication had at Mr. Fitzwilliam's house, between my lord
and me, which was this: my lord walking in the garden at
Mr. Fitzwilliam's house, saying his even song with his chaplain, and I being there attending upon him, after he had
finished his prayers, he commanded his chaplain that bare up
his gown train to deliver the same to me, and to go aside;
and after the chaplain was gone, he spake to me in this wise,
calling me by my name, ' You have been lately at London,'
quoth he; ' Forsooth, my lord,' quoth I, ' not since I was
there to buy your liveries for your servants.' ' And what
news was there then,' quoth he; ' heard you no communication of me? I pray you tell me.' Then perceiving that I
had a good occasion to speak my mind unto him, I said, ' Sir,
if it please your grace, it was my chance to be at dinner in a
certain place, where I also supped, and many honest worshipful
gentlemen, who were for the most part of mine old acquaintance, and therefore durst the bolder participate with me in
conversation of your grace, knowing that I was still your servant, and they asking of me how you did, and how you
accepted your adversity and trouble, I answered that you did

well, and accepted all things in good part; and as it seemed to me they were your indifferent friends, of whom they said none evil, but lamented your decay and fall very sore, doubting much the sequel not to be good for the commonwealth. Also they marvelled much that you, being of such excellent wit, and of such high discretion, would so simply confess yourself guilty unto the king, as you did. For, as they understood by report of some of the king's counsel, your case being well considered, you have great wrong; to the which I could make no direct answer.' 'Is this,' quoth he, 'the opinion of wise men?' 'Yea, forsooth, my lord,' quoth I, and commonly of all men else.' 'Well then,' quoth he, ' for all their wisdom, they perceived not so much as I. For I considered, that mine enemies had brought the matter so to pass against me, that they conveyed and made it the king's matter and case, and caused the king to take the matter into his own hands; and after he had once the possession of all my goods, being the king's only case, rather than he would have delivered me my goods again, and taken a foil or overthrow therein at my hands, without doubt he would not have missed (by the setting forth and procurement of my evil-willers) to have imagined my undoing and destruction therein; whereof the best had been perpetual imprisonment, or the danger of my life. I had rather confess the matter, as I did, and to live at large, like a poor vicar, than to live in prison with all the goods and honours I then had. And therefore it was for me the better way to yield me unto the king's mercy and clemency, than to stand stiff against him in trial of the wrong, which I sustained; wherein the king would have been loth to have been noted, and in my submission the king, I doubt not, had a conscience, wherein he would rather pity me than malign me. And also there was the night-crow, that cried ever in his ears against me; and if she might have perceived any obstinacy in me, she would not have failed to have set it forth with such vehemence, that I should rather have obtained the king's indignation, than his lawful favour; and his favour once lost (which I then knew that I then had done) would never have been by me recovered. Therefore I thought it better to keep still his favour, with loss of goods and dignity, than to win his indignation with all my wit, truth, and policy.

And this was the cause (which all men know not) that I yielded myself so soon guilty to the *premunire*, wherein the king hath since conceived a conscience; for he knoweth, and always did, more the effect thereof than any other person living, and whether I offended him therein or no, to whose conscience I commit the truth of my cause.' And thus we left the substance of our communication in this matter, although we had much more talk; yet this is sufficient to make you understand, as well both the cause of his confession in the *premunire*, as also the occasion of the loss of his goods.

" Now let us return where we left my lord, being now at the castle of Newark, intending to ride to Southwell, which was but four miles from thence, as I showed you before. He took his journey thither against supper, where, for lack of reparation of the bishop's place, which belongs to the see of York, he was compelled to lie in a prebendary's house, over against the bishop's place, and there kept house until Whitsuntide, against which time he removed into the place, being then newly repaired, and there continued all the most part of that summer, not without great resort of the most worshipful of the country. And divers noblemen, having occasion to repair into the same country there, thought it good to visit my lord, as they travelled through the country, of whom they were most gladly entertained, and had right good cheer, whose noble and gentle behaviour caused him to have much love in the country of all kind of people. He kept there a noble house, where was both plenty of meat and drink for all comers, and also much alms given at the gate to the poor of the town and country. He used much charity and clemency among his tenants, and other of the king's subjects. Although the hearing thereof were not pleasant in the ears of such as bare him no good will, yet the country and common people will say as they find cause; for now he was very much familiar among all persons, who then accustomably kept him company, and glad at any time when he might do them any good. He made many agreements and concords between gentleman and gentleman, and between some gentlemen and their wives, and other mean persons, the which had been long before asunder in great trouble; making for every of them, as occasion did serve, great assemblies and feasts, not sparing his purse, where he might make a peace and amity; which got him much love* and friendship in the country.

"It chanced so that upon Corpus Christi even, my lord gave me warning, after supper, to prepare all things in a readiness, for he intended to sing high mass the next day following, which I did not forget, although it were late; and I gave like warning to the head officers and other of my fellows, to see in their rooms all things furnished accordingly. I was not after that scantly laid in my bed, nor fully asleep, but one of the porters came to my chamber door, calling for me, and said that there were two gentlemen at the gate, that would speak with my lord from the king. I rose up incontinent, and went with the porter to the gate. I demanded who was there without. They made answer and said, that there was Mr. Brereton, one of the gentlemen of the king's privy chamber, and Mr. Wriothesley, who were come from the king in post, to speak with my lord. Then having understanding what they were, I caused the porter to let them in. And after their entry they desired me without delay to speak with my lord, whose request I endeavoured myself to obey, and went to my lord's chamber, who was in his bed asleep. But when he heard me speak, he demanded of me what I would have. ' Sir,' said I, ' there is beneath, in the porter's lodge, Mr. Brereton, of the king's privy chamber, and Mr.

---

* The favourable representation given of this portion of the cardinal's life, notwithstanding what is said by Fox, p. 908, is fully confirmed by an authority which cannot be suspected of partiality to his memory, that of a State-Book, which came out from the office of the king's printer in the year 1536, intitled *A Remedy for Sedition*. "Who was less beloved in the north than my lord cardinal, God have his soul, before he was amongst them? Who better beloved, after he had been there awhile? We hate ofttimes whom we have good cause to love. It is a wonder to see how they were turned; how of utter enemies they became his dear friends. He gave bishops a right good example, how they might win men's hearts. There was few holydays but he would ride five or six miles from his house, now to this parish church, now to that, and there cause one or other of his doctors to make a sermon unto the people. He sat amongst them, and said mass before all the parish. He saw why churches were made. He began to restore them to their right and proper use. He brought his dinner with him, and bade divers of the parish to it. He inquired whether there was any debate or grudge between any of them; if there were, after dinner he sent for the parties to the church, and made them all one. Men say well that do well. God's laws shall never be so set by as they ought, before they be well known."—Signat. E. 2.

Wriothesley, come from the king to speak with you; they will not tarry in any wise, but speak with you, and so depart. ' Well, then,' quoth my lord, ' bid them come up into the next chamber, and I will prepare myself to come to them.' Then departed I from my lord, and went down, and showed them that my lord desired them to take the pains to come up into his dining chamber, to whom my lord shortly came. They seeing him in night apparel, did to him due reverence, whom he took by the hands, demanding of them how the king, his sovereign lord, did. ' Sir,' said they, ' right well and merry, thanks be to God. Sir,' said they, ' we must desire you to talk with you apart.' ' With a right good will,' quoth my lord. Then talked they with him in secret in a great window; and after long talk, they took forth of a little mail a close thing, in manner of a little coffer, covered with green velvet, and bound with bars of silver and gilt, with a lock on the same, having a gilt key, with which they opened the chest, out of the which they took an instrument or writing, containing more than a skin of great parchment, having many seals hanging to the same, whereunto they put more wax for my lord's seal; the which my lord sealed, and subscribed his name with his own hand, and delivered the same again unto them, desiring them (forasmuch as they made haste to depart,) to tarry, and take a bed, for it was very late, about midnight or something past. They thanked him, and said they might in no wise tarry, but said they would straightway ride to the earl of Shrewsbury, and do as much as they could to be there before he should be stirring. And my lord, seeing their speedy haste, caused them to eat such cold meat as there was ready in the house, and to drink a bowl or two of wine. And that done, he gave each of them four old sovereigns of fine gold, desiring them to take it *in gree*, saying, that if he had been of greater ability, he would have given them a better reward; and so taking their leave they departed. And after they were departed, as I heard say, they were not contented with their reward. Indeed they were none of his indifferent friends, which caused them to accept the same so disdainfully. Howbeit, if they had known what little store of money he had at that time, being but his indifferent friends, they would have given him great thanks; but nothing is more lost or cast away, than such things as be given to such persons. My lord went again to bed, and yet, nevertheless, for all his disquietness and small rest that he had that night, he rose in the morning betimes, and sang high mass as he was appointed the night before. There was few or none of all the house, besides myself and the porter, that knew of the going or coming of Mr. Brereton and Mr. Wriothesley, and yet there lay in the house many strangers and worshipful gentlemen of the shire.

" After this sort and manner my lord lay at Southwell, until about the latter end of grass time; at which time he intended to remove to Scroby, which is another house and lordship of the bishopric of York. And against the day of his removing, he caused his officers to prepare all things in a readiness, as well provision to be made for him there, as also for his carriage thither, and other matters concerning the same. His removing and intent was not so secret but that it was abroad known in the country; which was not so much sorrow to all his neighbours there about Southwell, but it was as joyful to all the country about Scroby.

" Against the day of his removing, all the knights and other worshipful gentlemen of the shire of that country came unto him to Southwell, upon Sunday, to dinner, and lay with him all that night, to accompany and attend upon him in that journey the next day, and so to conduct him through the forest country unto Scroby. But he, being of their purpose advertised, and how they intended to lodge a great stag or two by the way, where he should needs ride, purposing to show him all the disport and pleasure that they could devise for him, was very loath to use any such honour and disport, not knowing how the king would take it; being also well assured how his enemies would much rejoice to understand that he would take upon him any such presumption, whereby they might find an occasion to persuade with the king how sumptuous he was notwithstanding his adversity and displeasure, and so to bring the king in a perfect ill opinion of him, and thereby breed small hope of reconciliation, but rather to inform the king, that he sought a mean to obtain the favour of the country than of him, with divers such imaginations, wherein he might rather obtain displeasure than honour. And also he was loath to make the worshipful gentlemen privy of this his imagination, lest they should conceive any toy in their heads

P

by means thereof, and so to leave their accustomed access
unto him, which was much to his comfort. Therefore he
devised another way, which might be taken rather for a
laughing disport, than otherwise. And thus it was: first
he called me unto him secretly at night, going to his rest,
and commanded me that I should in most secret wise that
might be, cause six or seven horses, besides his mule, to be
in a readiness for him by break of the day, and such persons
as he appointed to ride with him to Newstead,* an abbey in
the which he intended to lodge by the way to Scroby, willing
me to be also in a readiness to ride with him, and to call him
so early that he might hear mass or ever he went forward,
and be on horseback by the break of day. What will you
have more? All things being accomplished and finished
according to his pleasure, he, with those small number of persons appointed, mounted on his mule, and set forward by the
breaking of the day, towards Newstead, which was about
sixteen miles from thence, whither my lord and we came
before six of the clock in the morning, and so went incontinent unto his bed, leaving all the gentlemen and his household at Southwell in their beds, not knowing of my lord's
sudden departure, who expected his uprising until eight of
the clock. But after it was known unto them and to all the
rest, there was no more to do, but every man to his horseback, and so galloped after, supposing to overtake him. But
he was at his lodging at rest, ere they set forth out of Southwell, and so was their cerf hunting laid apart, and the great
stags uncoursed. But at their thither repair, sitting at
dinner, the matter was laughed at, and so merrily jested out,
that all was well taken.

"Then my lord intending the next day to remove from
thence, there resorted to him the earl of Shrewsbury's keepers
and gentlemen sent from him to desire my lord, in their
master's behalf, to hunt in a park of their master's, called
Worksop Park, which was even at hand, and the nearest and
best way for my lord to travel through in his journey, where
was much plenty of game, that was laid for him in a readiness
to hunt. Howbeit, he thanked both my lord their master for
his gentleness, and them for their pains; and then said, he

* Mr. Singer's edition reads Welbeck.

was a man not meet to receive any such pleasure: for such pastime was meet for men of honour that delighted themselves therein, for whom he said it was more convenient than for him. Nevertheless, he could do no less than think my lord of Shrewsbury to be much his friend, in whom he found such gentleness and noble offer; and rendered also to him his most lowly thanks, from the very bottom of his heart. But in no wise could they entreat him to hunt, although the worshipful men in his company did much provoke him thereto, yet he would not consent, desiring them to be contented; saying, that he came not into the country to frequent or follow any such pleasures, or pastimes, but rather to attend to a greater care that he had in hand, which was both his study and pleasure. And with such reasons and persuasions he pacified them for the time. Howbeit, as he rode through the park, both my lord of Shrewsbury's servants, and also the aforesaid gentlemen, moved him once again, before whom the deer lay very fair for all purposes of pleasure. But it would not avail; and therefore he made as much speed through the park as he could. And at the issue out he called the gentlemen and my lord of Shrewsbury's keepers unto him, desiring them to commend him to my lord their master, thanking him for his most honourable offer, trusting shortly to visit him at his own house, and gave the keepers forty shillings for their reward in conducting him through the park, and so rode to dinner to another abbey called Rufford Abbey; and after dinner he rode to another abbey called Blithe, where he lay all night. And the next day he came to Scroby, where he continued till after Michaelmas, exercising many deeds of charity. And most commonly every Sunday (if the weather did serve) he would travel unto some poor parish church thereabout, and there would say his divine service, and either say or hear mass, and caused one of his chaplains to preach the word of God unto the people. And that done, he would dine in some honest house in the town, where should be distributed to the people a great alms of meat and drink; or of money to supply the want of meat, if the number of the poor did so exceed in necessity. And thus with other good deeds practising and exercising himself during his abode there, as making of love-days and agreements between party and party, being at variance, he daily frequented himself thereabout.

" Then about the feast of Saint Michael next after, he took his journey to Cawood Castle, within seven miles of York; and passing thither, he lay two nights and a day at St. Oswald's Abbey, where he in proper person the next day confirmed children in the church, from the hour of eight until twelve of the clock at noon; and, making a short dinner, resorted thither again soon after one of the clock; and for weariness, at the last was constrained to call for a chair, and there confirmed more children from the said hour unto six of the clock towards night, or ever he could finish and make an end, the number of the children was such. That done, he went to his supper and rested him there all that night. And the next morning he applied himself to depart towards Cawood; and or ever he went, he confirmed almost a hundred children more, and then rode his way from thence. And in his journey, at a plain green a little beyond Ferrybridge, within a quarter of a mile, there were assembled, at a great cross made of stone, a number of more children, accounted by estimation to be about the number of five hundred, where he was fain to alight, and from thence never removed until he had fully confirmed them every one; and then took his mule and rode to Cawood, where he lay long after with much honour and love of the country, both of the worshipful and of the simple, doing of good deeds of charity, and held there an honourable and plentiful household for all comers; and also built and repaired the castle, which was greatly in decay, having a great multitude of artificers and labourers, about the number of three hundred persons, daily in wages.

" Lying there at Cawood he had intelligence by the gentlemen of the country that repaired unto him, that there was sprung a great variance and deadly hate between Sir Richard Tempest, knight, and one Mr. Brian Hastings, then being but an esquire, between whom was like to ensue great murder unless some mean might be found to redress the inconvenience that was like to ensue. My lord being thereof advertised, lamenting the case, made such means by his wise letters and other persuasions, that these two gentlemen were content to resort unto my lord at Cawood, and there to abide his order, high and low. A day was appointed of their thither resort, at which day they came both to Cawood, not without great number on either part assembled. Wherefore, against that day, my lord had required many worshipful gentlemen to be there present, to assist him with their endeavour to accord these two gentlemen, being thus at deadly feud. First, my lord commanded no more to enter the castle with these gentlemen but six of their menial servants, and all the rest to remain without in the town, or where they listed to repair. And himself issuing forth at the gates, calling the number of both parties together before him, he streightly charged them in the king's name firmly to keep the peace, upon their perils, without either bragging or quarrelling either with other, and caused them to have both beer and wine sent them into the town. And then he returned into the castle, being about nine of the clock in the morning, and because he intended to have both these gentlemen to dine with him at his own table, he thought it good to appease the rumour before dinner. Whereupon, he called them into his chapel, and, with the assistance of the other worshipful gentlemen, he began to fall to communication in the matter, declaring to them the dangers that were like to ensue by their wilful and stout stomachs, with many other good and wholesome exhortations. Notwithstanding, the parties laying and alleging many things for their defence, sometime adding stout and despiteful words of defiance each to other, which my lord and the other there assembled had much ado to qualify, their malice was so great. What will ye have more? With long continuance and deep arguments made unto them by my lord, at last, being there until four of the clock in the afternoon, my lord brought them to a final concord and peace, concluding a certain determinate end between them, the which I do not now remember, and so made them friends. And, as it seemed, they were both contented therewith, and very joyous of the same. And then my lord caused them, after they had shaken hands together, to go arm in arm to dinner, the sight whereof pleased much the beholders, and so went to dinner, although it were too late to dine,* yet, notwithstanding, they dined with the

---

* " With us, (says Harrison, in the description of England prefixed to Holinshed's Chronicle, p. 171,) the nobility, gentry, and students, do ordinarily go to dinner at eleven before noon, and to supper at five, or between five and six at afternoon. The merchants dine and sup seldom before twelve at noon and six at night, especially in London. The husbandmen dine also at high noon, as they call it, and sup at seven or eight; but

other gentlemen at my lord's table, where was drinking unto each other, in great amity as the manner is, and making great semblance of amity and love. After dinner my lord caused each of them to discharge their rout and assembly that remained without, out of the town, and to retain with them no more than they were accustomed to ride withal. And that done, these gentlemen, fulfilling his commandment, tarried with all the rest at Cawood, and lay there all that night; whom my lord entertained in such sort, that they took his gentleness in great nobleness and friendship, trusting to have of him a special jewel in their country; and so it proved after by their demeanour towards him, as it shall appear by their gifts, which they prepared for him against his stallation.

"It is not to be doubted but that the worshipful persons, as doctors, and prebendaries of the close of York, would resort unto my lord according to their duties, as unto the chief head, father and patron of their spiritual dignity, at his first coming into the country so nigh their church, which was but bare six miles. Wherefore ye shall understand that doctor Higden, then doctor of the church of York, a worshipful man and a divine, with the treasurer, and divers other officers of the same college, repaired to my lord, and most joyfully welcomed him into those parts; saying that it was to them no small comfort to see their head among them, who hath been so long absent from them, being all the while like fatherless and comfortless children; but they trusted shortly to see him among them in his own church. To whom he answered, that it was the special cause of his coming, not only to be among them for a time, but also to continue his life among them, as a father and as a natural brother. 'Sir, then,' quoth they, 'ye must understand the ordinances and rules of our church, whereof although ye be head and governor, yet ye be not therewith so well acquainted as we be. Therefore, if it

out of the term in our universities, the scholars dine at ten. As for the poorest sort, they generally dine and sup when they may, so that to talk of their order of repast, it were but a needless matter."

" *Theophilus.* You went to dinner betime, I perceive.—*Eusebius.* Even as I do commonly, when I have no business—between nine and ten. Methinks it is a good hour; for by that means I save a breakfast, which, for such idlers as I am, is most fittest."—Dialogue between Eusebius and Theophilus. Signat. B 4. A.D. 1556.

please your grace, we shall, under supportation of the same, open unto you some part of our ancient laws and customs of our church. Sir, where ye do intend to repair unto us, the old law and custom hath evermore been such, that our head prelate and pastor, as ye now be, could, nor ever might, come above our choir door, nor have any stall in the choir, until he by due order were there stalled. Nor, if you should happen to die before your stallation, ye shall not be buried above in the choir, but in the nether part of the body of the church. Therefore we shall heartily desire, in the name of all our brethren, that ye would vouchsafe to do herein as our honourable fathers your predecessors have done; and that ye will break no laudable custom of our church, to the which we be obliged by oath at our first admittance, to observe that, and divers others, which in our chapter remain in record.' 'Those records,' quoth my lord, ' would I fain see; and this seen and digested, I shall then show you further of my mind.' And thus in this matter they ceased communication, and passed the time with other matters; so that a day was assigned to bring in their records to my lord, at which day they resorted unto him with their register and book of records, wherein were written their constitutions and rules, which all the ministers of their church were cheerly bound to observe on their behalf, and to see them kept inviolable. And when my lord had seen and read those records, and debated the same substantially with them that brought these books, he determined to be stalled there at York Minster, the next Monday after Allhallow day, against which time due preparation was made for the same, but not in so sumptuous a wise as were his predecessors before him; nor yet in such sort as the fame and common report was afterwards made of him, to his great slander, and to the reporters' no small dishonesty, to report such lies as I am persuaded they did, to the which I was made privy. I was sent by my lord to York to foresee things there, that should be ordered and provided for the solemnity, which should have been as mean as could be, considering the former decent honours of the worthy minister of York.

"It came so to pass, that upon Allhallow day, one of the head officers of the church, which should have the most doing in all this stallation, was with my lord at dinner at his house at Cawood; and sitting at dinner, they fell in communication of this matter, and of the order thereof, saying that my lord should go on foot from a chapel (which standeth without the gates of the city, called St. James's Chapel) unto the minister upon cloth, the which should be distributed to the poor after his passage. My lord hearing this, made answer to the same in this wise. 'Although that our predecessors did go upon cloth, so we intend to go on foot from thence without any such glory,* in the vamps of our hose. For I take God to my judge, I do not intend to go thither for any triumph or glory, but only to perform the rules of the church, to the which I am bound. And therefore I will desire you all, and will command other of my servants, to go as humbly thither, without any sumptuous or gorgeous apparel, otherwise than in decent manner. For I do purpose to come unto York upon Sunday next against night, and to lodge in the dean's house, and upon Monday to be stalled; and there to make but one dinner for you all of the Close, and for other worshipful gentlemen that shall chance to come thither to the same; and to sup with some of the residences; and the next day to dine with the mayor, and then to repair home hither again; and so to finish the same, whereby I may at all times resort to York.'

"The day being once known unto all the country, which could not be hid, the worshipful gentlemen and other, as abbots and priors, having notice of the day of my lord's installation, sent in such provision of victual that it is almost incredible, wherefore I omit to declare unto you the certainty thereof. But there wanted no store of great and fat beasts and muttons, wildfowl, and venison, both red and fallow, and other dainty things such as would have plentifully furnished his feast, all which things were unknown to my lord: forasmuch as he being prevented and disappointed of his purpose, by the reason that he was arrested of high treason, as ye shall here-after hear; so that most part of this summer provision, that

* The cardinal, perhaps, remembered the credit which was gained by his successful rival cardinal Adrian, who, being elected to the papacy by the conclave, through the influence of the emperor Charles V., " before his entry into the city of Rome, (as we are told by one of Sir Thomas More's biographers,) putting off his hose and shoes, and, as I have credibly heard it reported, bare-footed and bare-legged, passed through the streets towards his palace with such humbleness, that all the people had him in great reverence."—Harpsfield's Life of Sir Thomas More. Lambeth MSS. No. 827, fol. 12.

I spake of before, was sent unto York the same day of his arrest, and the next day following; for his arrest was kept as close and secret from the country as might be, because they doubted the common people, which had him in great estimation and love for his great charity and liberality, which he used daily among them, with familiar gesture and behaviour, which be the very means to attain the love of the people of the north parts.

"Sir, or ever I wade any further in this matter, I do intend to declare unto you what chanced before his last trouble at Cawood, as a sign or token given by God what should follow; which, at the doing of the very thing, no such sequel was of any man premeditate or imagined. Therefore, for as much as it is a notable thing to be considered, I will (God willing) declare it as truly as my memory can record—the which thing I saw myself being then present.

"My lord's enemies being then in the court about the king in good estimation and honourable dignity, having now my lord in more fear and doubt, than they had before his fall, considering the perfect zeal and secret favour that the king bore always towards him, thought at length the king might call him home again; and then if he so did, they supposed that he would rather imagine vengeance than to remit and forget their cruelty which they wrought against him. Wherefore they compassed in their heads, either by some means to dispatch him by accusation of sinister treason, or to bring him in the king's high indignation by some other means. This was daily their study and consultation, having for their espials as many vigilant eyes attendant upon him, as the poet feigned Argus to have; so that he could neither work or do anything but that his enemies had knowledge thereof shortly after. Now at the last, they espied a time wherein they caught an occasion to bring their purpose to pass, thinking thereby to have of him a great advantage; for the matter being once disclosed unto the king, in such vehemence as they purposed, they thought the king would be against him. And that done, and by them executed, the king, upon other complaints moved with great displeasure, thought it good that he should come up and stand to his trial, which they liked nothing at all; notwithstanding, hereupon he was sent for after this sort.   First, they devised that sir Walter

Walsh, knight, one of the king's privy chamber should be
sent down with a commission into the north, unto the earl of
Northumberland,* (who was sometime brought up in house
with my lord cardinal,) and they twain, being jointly in
commission, to arrest my lord of high treason. This conclusion fully resolved, they caused Mr. Walsh to prepare him
for his journey with this commission, and certain instructions
annexed to the same; who made him ready to ride, and take
his horse at the court gate about noon of All-halloween day,
towards my lord of Northumberland. Now, I am come to
the place where I will declare that which I promised in the
latter end of the last chapter, of a certain sign or token of
this my lord's trouble, which thing was this:

"My lord sitting at dinner upon All-halloween day, having
at his board-end† divers of his worshipful chaplains sitting at
dinner to keep him company, for lack of strangers, ye shall
understand, that accustomably my lord's great cross stood in
a corner, at the table's end, leaning against the tappet or
hanging. And when the board's end was taken up, and a
convenient time for the chaplains to arise, they forced themselves to arise from the table; and even as they rose, one
doctor Augustine, a Venetian and physician to my lord,
rising from the table with the other, having upon him a great
gown of boisterous velvet, overthrew my lord's great cross,
which stood in the way at the board's end, and trailing down
along the tappet, it fell upon doctor Bonner's head, who stood
by the tappet, and the point brake his head a little, that the
blood ran down. The company there standing, according

* In the notes to the Northumberland Household Book, p. 428—431,
Dr. Percy has produced from the letters of this nobleman some curious par-
ticulars illustrative of the harsh and unworthy treatment which he had formerly received from the cardinal, and which, in the doctor's mind, are " a
full vindication of the earl from the charge of ingratitude, in being the
person employed to arrest the cardinal at his castle of Cawood."

† " In the houses of our ancient nobility, they dined at long tables.
The lord and his principal guests sat at the upper end of the first table in
the great chamber, which was therefore called the lord's board-end; the
officers of his household and inferior guests at long tables below in the hall.
In the middle of each table stood a great salt-cellar, and as particular care
was taken to place the guests according to their rank, it became a mark of
distinction whether a person sate above or below the salt."—*Notes on the
Northumberland Household Book*, p. 419.

to their duty, ready to give thanks to my lord for their dinner, were greatly astonished with the chance. My lord sitting in his chair, and perceiving the same, demanded of them being next him, what the matter meant of their sudden amaze. I showed him of the fall of his cross upon doctor Bonner's head. 'Hath it,' quoth he, 'drawn any blood?' 'Yea, forsooth, my lord,' quoth I. With that he cast his head aside, looking soberly upon me a certain space, and said unto me, shaking his head, '*malum omen;*' * and therewith said grace, and rose up from the table, and went into his bed-chamber; but what he did there I know not. Now mark the signification, how my lord expounded this matter unto me at Pomfret, after his fall. First, ye shall understand, that the cross which he bore as archbishop of York signified himself; and Augustine, the physician, who overthrew the cross, was only he that accused my lord, whereby his enemies caught an occasion to overthrow him. It fell upon master doctor Bonner's head, who was master of my lord's faculties and spiritual jurisdictions, and was then damnified by the overthrow of the cross: yea, and moreover, and the drawing of the blood of him betokened death, which shortly after did ensue; about which time of this mischance, the same very day and season, Mr. Walsh took his horse at the court gate,

---

* The enemies of archbishop Laud, particularly in the time of his troubles, were fond of comparing him with cardinal Wolsey; and there is reason to think that this life was first printed in the year 1641, for the purpose of prejudicing that great prelate in the minds of the people, by insinuating a parallel between him and the cardinal. However this may have been, the expression in the text recals to memory an affecting anecdote respecting Laud, which the reader will not be displeased to find in this place.

The year 1639, we all know, was big with events calamitous to Laud, and to the church and monarchy. In the Lambeth library is preserved a small pane of glass, in which are written with a diamond pencil the following words :—

" Memorand : Ecclesiæ de Micham, Cheme et Stone, cum aliis fulgure combustæ sunt Januar : 14, 1638-9, Omen avertat Deus."

On a piece of paper of the same size with the glass, and kept in the same case with it, is written by the hand of archbishop Wake (as my friend Mr. Todd, MS. librarian to his grace the present archbishop, informs me) as follows: " This glass was taken out of the west window of the gallery at Croydon before I new built it; and is, as I take it, the writing of archbishop Laud's own hand."

as nigh as it could be judged. And so it must needs be taken for a sign or token of that which after followed, if the circumstance be equally weighed and considered; wherein, as I suppose, God showed him some more secret knowledge of his latter days and end of his troubles: wherein it was thought that he had further inspiration than all men did know, which appeared right well by diverse special communications that he had with me at divers times of his last end. And now that I have made manifest to you the effect of this prodigy and sign, I will return again to my matter.

"Now, the appointed time drew near of his installation, and sitting at dinner upon the Friday next before the Monday on the which he intended to be installed at York, the earl of Northumberland and Mr. Walsh, with a great company of gentlemen of the earl's house, and of the country, whom he gathered together in the king's name, to accompany them, not knowing to what intent, came into the hall at Cawood, the officers being at dinner, and my lord not fully dined, being then in his fruits, nor knowing of the earl's being in the hall. The first thing that the earl did, after he had set order in the hall, he commanded the porter of the gates to deliver him the keys thereof, who would in no wise obey his commandment, although he were roughly threatened, and streightly commanded in the king's name to make delivery of them to one of the earl's servants; but perceiving that, said then unto the earl, 'Sir, seeing that you do but intend to set one of your servants in my place to keep the gates for your pleasure, I know no servant that ye have but that I am as able as he to do it, and keep the gates to your purpose, whatsoever it be. And also, the keys were delivered to me by my lord my master, who charged me with them, both by oath, and other precept and commandment. Therefore, I pray you, my good lord, to pardon me, though I do not obey your commandment; for whatsoever ye shall command me to do in the ministration of mine office, I shall do it with as good a will and as justly as any other of your servants, whatsoever he be.' With that quoth the gentleman being there with the earl, who heard him speak so stoutly, 'Sir, he is a good fellow, and a faithful servant to his master, and speaketh like an honest man; therefore give him your charge, and let him keep still the gates, whom we doubt not but he will be

obedient to your commandment.' 'Well then,' quoth the
earl, 'hold him a book, and command him to lay his hand
thereon. Thou shalt swear,' quoth the earl, 'that thou
shall well and truly keep the gates, by our commandment, to
the king our sovereign lord's use, being his grace's commissioners; and to do all such things as we shall command, and
as to us shall seem good, for the time of our abode here; and
that ye shall let pass neither in nor out at these gates but
such as you shall be commanded by us, from time to time;'
and with this oath he received the keys at the earl's and Mr.
Walsh's hands.

"Of all these doings knew my lord nothing; for they stopped
the stair, so that none went up to my lord's chamber, and
they that came down could no more go up again. At the
last one escaped, who came up, and showed my lord that the
earl of Northumberland was in the hall; whereat my lord
marvelled, and would not believe him at the first, but commanded a gentleman, being his gentleman usher, to look and
bring him the truth, whether it were he or no; who going
down the stairs, where was a loop with a lattice, where
through he looked into the hall, he saw my lord of Northumberland, and went no further, but returned, and showed my
lord it was very he. 'Then,' quoth my lord, 'I am sorry
that we have dined, for I fear that our officers be not provided
of any store of good fish, to make him some honourable cheer
according to his estate; notwithstanding, he shall have such
as we have, with a right good will. Let the table stand,'
quoth he, 'and we will go down and meet him, and bring him
up; and then shall he see how far forth we be at our dinner.'
With that he put the table from him, and rose up; and going
down the stairs he encountered the earl, whom he met upon
the midst of the stairs coming up, with all his men at his tail.
And as soon as my lord espied the earl, he put off his cap,
and said, 'My lord, ye are most heartily welcome' (and so
embraced each other). My lord cardinal said, 'Although
that I have often desired, and wished in my heart to see you
in my house, yet, if ye had loved me well, ye would have
sent me word before of your coming, to the intent I might
have received you according to your honour. Notwithstanding, ye shall have such cheer as I can make you, with a right
good will, trusting that ye will accept the same of me as of

your very loving friend, hoping hereafter to see you oftener, when I shall be more able to entertain you with better fare.' And this said, my lord took the earl by the hand, and had him up into the chamber; whom followed all the number of the earl's servants. And when my lord came into the chamber, he led the earl to the fire, and said, 'Sir, my lord, ye shall go into my bed-chamber, where ye shall have a good fire until your chamber be made ready for you; and let my lord's mail be brought up: and or ever I go, I pray you give me leave to take these gentlemen, your servants, by the hands.' And when he had taken them all by the hands, he returned to the earl, saying, 'I perceive well, my lord, that ye have not altogether forgot my old precepts and counsel which I gave you, when you were with me in your youth, to cherish my lord your father's old servants, which I see here present with you. Surely, my lord, ye do therein very well and nobly, like a wise gentleman. For these be they who will not only love you, but also live and die with you, and be true to you, and glad to see you prosper in honour; the which I beseech God to send you, with long life.' This said, he took the earl by the hand and led him into his bed-chamber. And they being there all alone, save only I, who kept the door, according to my duty, being gentleman usher, these two lords standing at a window by the chimney, the earl trembling said unto my lord, with a soft voice (laying his hand upon his arm), 'My lord, I arrest you of high treason.' With which words my lord was marvellously astonished, standing both still without any more words a good space. But at the last, quoth my lord, 'What authority have you to arrest me?' 'Forsooth, my lord,' quoth the earl, 'I have a commission so to do.' 'Where is your commission,' quoth my lord, 'that I may see it?' 'Nay, sir, that you may not,' said the earl. 'Well, then, quoth my lord, 'hold you contented; then will I not obey your arrest; for there hath been between your ancestors and my predecessors great contentions and debate of an ancient grudge, which may succeed in you, and grow unto the like inconvenience, as it hath done between your ancestors and my predecessors. Therefore, without I see your authority from above, I will not obey you.' Even as they were debating this matter between them in the chamber, so busy was Mr. Walsh in arresting of Dr. Augustine, at the door of the palace, saying unto him, 'Go in, traitor, or I shall make thee.' And with that, I opened the portal door, perceiving them both there. Mr. Walsh thrust Dr. Augustine in before him with violence. These matters, on both sides, astonished me very much, musing what all this should mean; until at the last, Mr. Walsh being entered my lord's chamber, began to pluck off his hood, which he had made him of the same cloth whereof his coat was, which was of Shrewsbury cotton, to the intent he would not be known. And after he had plucked off his hood, he kneeled down to my lord, to whom my lord said, 'Come hither, gentleman, and let me speak with you,' commanding him to stand up, saying thus: 'Sir, here my lord of Northumberland hath arrested me, but by whose authority or commission he showeth me not; but saith, he hath one. If ye be privy thereto, or be joined with him therein, I pray you show me.' 'Indeed, my lord, if it please your grace,' quoth Mr. Walsh, 'he showeth you the truth.' 'Well, then,' quoth my lord, 'I pray you let me see it.' 'Sir, I beseech you,' quoth Mr. Walsh, 'hold us excused. There is annexed to our commission certain instructions which ye may not see, nor yet be privy to the same.' 'Why,' quoth my lord, 'be your instructions such that I may not see them? peradventure, if I might be privy to them, I could help you the better to perform them. It is not unknown but I have been privy and of counsel in as weighty matters as these be: and I doubt not for my part, but I shall prove myself a true man, against the expectation of all my cruel enemies. I see the matter whereupon it groweth. Well, there is no more to do. I trow ye are one of the king's privy chamber; your name is Walsh. I am content to yield to you, but not to my lord of Northumberland, without I see his commission. And also you are a sufficient commissioner in that behalf, inasmuch as ye be one of the king's privy chamber; for the worst there is a sufficient warrant to arrest the greatest peer in this realm, by the king's only commandment, without any commission. Therefore, I am at your will to order and dispose: put, therefore, your commission and authority in execution; spare not, and I will obey the king's will. I fear more the malice and cruelty of my mortal enemies, than I do the untruth of my allegiance; wherein I take God to my judge, I never offended the king in word nor deed; and therein I dare stand face to face with any man alive, having indifferency, without partiality.'

"Then came my lord of Northumberland unto me, standing at the portal door, and commanded me to avoid the chamber; and being loth to depart from my master, I stood still, and would not remove; to whom he spake again, and said unto me, 'There is no remedy, ye must depart.' With that I looked upon my lord (as who would say, shall I go?) upon whom my lord looked very heavily, and shook at me his head. And perceiving by his countenance it booted me not to abide, I departed the chamber, and went into the next chamber, where abode many gentlemen of my fellows, and other, to learn of me some news, to whom I made report what I saw and heard, which was great heaviness unto them all.

"Then the earl called into the chamber divers gentlemen of his own servants; and after that he and Mr. Walsh had taken my lord's keys from him, they gave the charge and custody of my lord unto five gentlemen. And then they went about the house to set all things in order, intending to depart from thence the next day (being Saturday) with my lord; howbeit it was Sunday towards night or ever they could bring all things to pass to depart. Then went they busily about to convey Doctor Augustine away to London, with as much speed as they could, sending with him divers persons to conduct him, which was bound unto his horse like a traitor. And this done, when it came to night, the commissioners assigned two grooms of my lord's to attend upon him in the chamber where he laid that night; and all the rest of my lord of Northumberland's gentlemen watched in the next chamber; and so was all the house watched, and the gates very surely kept, that no man could either pass or repass, in or out, until the next morning. At which time my lord rose up about eight of the clock, and made him ready to ride; where he was kept still close in his chamber, expecting his departing from thence. Then the earl sent for me into his chamber, and being there he commanded me to go to my lord, and give attendance upon him, and charged me with an oath upon certain articles to observe about him. And going my way toward my lord, I met with Mr. Walsh in the court, who called me unto him, and led me into his chamber, and there showed me how the king's majesty bare towards me his princely favour, for my diligent and true service that I ministered daily to my lord and master. 'Wherefore,' quoth he, 'the king's pleasure is, that you shall be about him, as most chief in whom his highness putteth great confidence and trust; and whose pleasure is therefore, that ye shall be sworn unto him to observe certain articles, which you shall have delivered to you in writing.' 'Sir,' quoth I, 'my lord of Northumberland hath already sworn me to divers articles.' 'Yea,' quoth he, 'but he could not deliver you the articles in writing, as I am commanded specially to do. Therefore, I deliver here unto you this bill with articles in writing; look upon them, whether you can observe them or no; for you shall not receive them of me without an oath for the fulfilling of them.' And when I had perused them, and saw them but reasonable and tolerable, I answered, that I was contented to obey the king's pleasure, and to be sworn to the performance of them. And so he gave me a new oath: and then I resorted unto my lord, where he was sitting in a chair, the tables being spread for him to go to dinner. But as soon as he perceived me to come in, he fell out into such a woeful lamentation, with such rueful tears and watery eyes, that it would have caused a flinty heart to mourn with him. And as I could, I with others comforted him; but it would not be. 'For,' quoth he, 'now I lament, that I see this gentleman (meaning me) how faithful, how diligent, and how painful he hath served me, abandoning his own country, wife, and children; his house and family, his rest and quietness, only to serve me, and I have nothing to reward him for his high merits. And also the sight of him causeth me to call to my remembrance the number of faithful servants that I have here with me; whom I did intend to prefer and advance, to the best of my power, from time to time, as occasion should serve. But now, alas! I am prevented, and have nothing here to reward them; all is deprived me, and I am left here their miserable and wretched master. Howbeit,' quoth he to me (calling me by my name), 'I am a true man, and you shall never have shame of me for your service.' 'Sir,' quoth I unto him (perceiving his heaviness), 'I do nothing mistrust your truth: and for the same will I depose both before the king and his honour-

able council. Wherefore, sir,' (kneeling upon my knee)
' comfort yourself, and be of good cheer. The malice of
your ungodly enemies can, nor shall not prevail. I doubt
not but coming to your answer, my heart is such, that you
shall clearly acquit yourself, so to your commendation and
truth, as that, I trust, it shall be much to your great honour,
and restitution unto your former estate.' 'Yea,' quoth he,
' if I may come to my answer, I fear no man alive; for he
liveth not that shall look upon this face (pointing to his own
face), that shall be able to accuse me of any untruth; and
that know well mine enemies, which will be an occasion that
they will not suffer me to have indifferent justice, but seek
some sinister means to dispatch me.' 'Sir,' quoth I, 'ye
need not therein to doubt, the king being so much your good
lord, as he hath always showed himself to be, in all your
troubles.' With that came up my lord's meat; and so we
left our former communication, and I gave my lord water,
and set him down to dinner; who did eat very little meat,
but very many times suddenly he would burst out in tears,
with the most sorrowful words that have been heard of any
woeful creature. And at the last he fetched a great sigh,
and said this text of scripture* in this wise, 'O constantia
Martirum laudabilis! O charitas inextinguibilis! O patientia
invincibilis, quæ licet inter pressuras persequentium visa sit
despicabilis, invenietur in laudem et gloriam ac honorem in
tempore tribulationis.' And thus passed he forth his dinner
in great lamentation and heaviness, who was fed more with
weeping tears than with any delicate meats that were set
before him. I suppose there was not a dry eye among all the
gentlemen that were there attending upon him. And when the
table was taken up, we expected continually our removing,
until it drew to night; and then it was showed my lord, that
he could not go away that night; but on the morrow, by
God's grace, he should depart. 'Even then,' quoth he, 'when

---

* The words which follow, I apprehend, are part of some ecclesiastical
hymn. It was not unusual to attribute the name of *Scripture* to all such
compositions, and to whatever was read in churches. " Also I said and
affirmed" (the words are part of the recantation of a Wickliffite) " that I held
no Scripture catholic nor holy, but only that is contained in the Bible. For
the legends and lives of saints I held them nought ; and the miracles
written of them, I held untrue."—Fox's Acts, p. 591.

my lord of Northumberland shall be pleased.' Wherefore it was concluded, that he should tarry until the next day, being Sunday.

"On which day my lord rose in the morning, and prepared him ready to ride after he had heard mass; and by that time he had said all his divine service, it was dinner time; and after dinner the earl appointed all things how it should be ordered; and by that time it was near night. There were appointed to wait upon him divers persons, among whom I myself and four more of his own servants were assigned unto him. First his chaplain, two grooms, and his barber: and as we were going down out of the great chamber, my lord demanded where his servants were become; the which the earl and Mr. Walsh had inclosed within the chapel there, because they should not trouble his passage. Notwithstanding my lord would not go down until he had a sight of his servants; to whom it was answered that he might not see them. 'Why so?' then quoth my lord. 'I will not out of this house, but I will see my servants, and take my leave of them before I will go any further.' And his servants, being in the chapel, having understanding that my lord was going away, and that they should not see him before his departure, they began to grudge, and to make such a rueful noise, that the commissioners were in doubt of a tumult to tarry among them; wherefore they were let out, and suffered to repair to my lord in the great chamber; where they kneeled down before him; among whom was no one dry eye, but earnestly lamented their master's fall and trouble. To whom my lord gave comfortable words and worthy praises for their diligence, honesty, and truth done to him heretofore, assuring them that what chance soever should happen him, he was a very true and a just man to his sovereign lord. And thus with a lamentable manner shaked every of them by the hand.

Then he was constrained to depart, the night drew so fast on. And so my lord's horse and ours were brought into the inner court; where we mounted, and coming to the gate to ride out, which was shut, the porter opening the same to let us pass, there was ready attending a great number of gentlemen with their servants, such as the earl had appointed for that purpose, to attend and conduct my lord to Pomfret that night, and so forth as you shall hereafter hear. But to tell you of

Q 2

the number of the people of the country that were assembled
at the gate to lament his departing, I suppose there were in
number above three thousand people; which at the opening
of the gates, after they had a sight of him, cried with a loud
voice, 'God save your grace! God save your grace! The
foul evil take them that have thus taken you from us! We
pray God that a very vengeance may light upon them!' Thus
they ran after him, crying through the town of Cawood, they
loved him so well. Surely they had a great loss of him,
both rich and poor: for the poor had by him great relief;
and the rich lacked not his counsel and help in all their
troubles, which caused him to have such love among the
people of the country.

"Then rode he with his conductors towards Pomfret; and
by the way as he rode, he called me unto him, asking me if I
had any gentleman of mine acquaintance among the number
that rode with him. 'Yea, sir,' said I, 'what is your pleasure?' 'Marry,' quoth he, 'I have left a thing behind that
I would fain have; the which I would most gladly send for.'
'If I knew,' quoth I, 'what it were, I should send one incontinent back again for it.' 'Then,' said he, 'let the messenger go to my lord of Northumberland, and desire him to send
me the red buckram bag, lying in my almonry in my chamber, sealed with my seal.' With that I departed from him,
and went straight unto one Sir Roger Lascelles, knight, and
steward with the earl (being one among the rout), and desired him to cause some of his servants to return to my lord
of Northumberland for that purpose; who granted my request
most gently, and thereupon sent incontinent one of his trusty
servants with all speed back again to Cawood for the said
bag; who did so honestly his message, that he brought the
same unto my lord shortly after he was in his chamber at the
abbey of Pomfret, where he lay all night. In which bag
was no other thing inclosed but three shirts of hair, the which
he delivered unto his chaplain and ghostly father secretly.

"Furthermore, as he rode towards Pomfret, he demanded
of me, whither they would lead him that night. 'Marry,
sir,' quoth I, 'to Pomfret.' 'Alas,' quoth he, 'shall I go to
the castle, and lie there, and die like a beast?' 'Sir, I can
tell you no more,' quoth I, 'what they intend to do; but, sir,
I will inquire of a secret friend of mine in this company, who
is chief of all their counsels.'

" With that I repaired unto the said Sir Roger Lascelles, and desired him as earnestly as I could, that he would vouchsafe to show me whither my lord should go to be lodged that night; who answered me again that my lord should be lodged in the abbey of Pomfret, and in none other place; the which I reported to my lord, who was glad thereof; so that within night we came to Pomfret, and there lodged within the abbey as is aforesaid.

" And my lord of Northumberland continued all that night at Cawood, to see the dispatch of the household, and to establish all the stuff within the same in security.

" The next day my lord removed towards Doncaster, and came into the town by torch-light, the which was his desire, because of the people. Yet notwithstanding the people were assembled, and cried out upon him, 'God save your grace, God save your grace, my good lord cardinal,' running before him with candles in their hands; who caused me to ride by his side to shadow him from the people; and yet they perceived him, and lamented his misfortune, cursing his accusers. And thus they brought him to the Black-friars, within the which he was lodged.

" And the next day we removed and rode to Sheffield-park, where my lord of Shrewsbury lay within the lodge, the people all the way thitherward still lamenting him and crying as they did before. And when we came into the park of Sheffield, nigh to the lodge, my lord of Shrewsbury, with my lady and a train of gentlewomen, and all other his gentlemen and servants, stood without the gates, to attend my lord's coming, to receive him; at whose alighting the earl received him with much honour, and embraced my lord, saying these words, ' My lord,' quoth he, ' your grace is most heartily welcome unto me, and I am glad to see you here in my poor lodge, where I have long desired to see you, and should have been much more gladder, if you had come after another sort.' ' Ay, my gentle lord of Shrewsbury,' quoth my lord, ' I heartily thank you: and although I have cause to lament, yet, as a faithful heart may, I do rejoice that my chance is to come unto the custody of so noble a person, whose approved honour and wisdom hath always been right well known to all noble estates. And, sir, howsoever my accusers have used their accusations against me, this I know, and so

before your lordship, and all the world, I do protest, that my
demeanour and proceedings have always been both just and
loyal towards my sovereign and liege lord; of whose usage in
his grace's affairs your lordship hath had right good experience; and even according to my truth, so I beseech God to
help me!' 'I doubt not,' quoth my lord of Shrewsbury, 'of
your truth. Therefore, my lord, be of good cheer, and fear
not; for I am nothing sorry, but that I have not wherewith
to entertain you according to my good will and your honour;
but such as I have, you shall be welcome to it; for I will not
receive you as a prisoner, but as my good lord, and the king's
true and loving subject; and sir, here is my wife come to
salute you.' Whom my lord kissed, with his cap in his hand,
bareheaded, and all the other gentlemen; and took all the
earl's servants by the hands, as well gentlemen as yeomen.
This done, these two lords went into the lodge, arm in arm,
and so conducted my lord into a fair gallery, where was in
the further end thereof a goodly tower with lodgings, where
my lord was lodged. There was also in the midst of the same
gallery a traverse of sarsnet drawn; so that the one end
thereof was preserved for my lord, and the other for the earl.

"Then departed from my lord all the great number of gentlemen and other that conducted him thither. And my lord,
being thus with my lord of Shrewsbury, continued there
eighteen days after; upon whom my lord of Shrewsbury
appointed divers worthy gentlemen to attend continually, to
foresee that he should lack nothing that he would desire, being
served in his own chamber at dinner and supper, as honourably, and with as many dainty dishes, as he had in his own
house commonly being at liberty. And once every day my
lord of Shrewsbury would repair unto him, and commune
with him, sitting upon a bench in a great window in the
gallery. And although that my said lord of Shrewsbury would
right heartily comfort him, yet would he lament so piteously,
that it would make my lord of Shrewsbury to be very heavy
for his grief. 'Sir,' said he, 'I have, and do daily receive,
letters from the king, commanding me to entertain you as one
that he highly favoureth and loveth; whereby I do perceive
ye do lament more than ye have cause to do. And although
ye be accused (as I trust wrongfully), yet the king can do no
less but to put you to your trial, the which is more for the

satisfying of some persons, than for any mistrust that he hath of your traitorous doings.' 'Alas! my lord,' quoth my lord cardinal, 'is it not a piteous case, that any man should so wrongfully accuse me unto the king, and not to come to the king to my answer before his grace? For I am well assured, my lord, that there is no man alive that looketh in this face of mine who is able to accuse me. It grieveth me very much that the king should have any such opinion in me, to think that I would be false or conspire any evil to his person; who may well consider that I have no assured friends in all the world, but only his grace; so that if I should go about to betray my sovereign lord and prince, in whom is all my trust and confidence before all other, all men might justly think and say, that I lacked both grace, wit, and discretion. Nay, nay, my lord, I would rather venture to shed my heart's blood in his defence, as I am bound, both for my allegiance and for my safeguard; for he is my staff that supporteth me, and the wall that defendeth me against all these my corrupt enemies, and all other who knoweth me, and my true diligent proceedings in all his affairs and doings, much better than any of them. Therefore, to conclude, it is not to be thought that ever I would maliciously or traitorously travail or wish any hurt or damage to his royal person or imperial dignity, but, as I said before, defend it with the very shedding of my heart's blood, and if it were but only for mine own defence, to preserve mine estate and simple life, that which mine enemies think I do so much esteem; having no other refuge to fly unto for protection and defence, but only under the shadow of his wings. Alas! my lord, I was in a good estate now, and lived quietly, being right well contented with the same. But mine enemies, who never sleep, but continually study, both sleeping and waking, to rid me out of the way, perceiving the contentation of my mind, doubted that if I lived, their malicious and cruel dealings would grow at length to their shame, rebuke, and open slander; and therefore would prevent the same with the shedding of my blood. But from God, that knoweth the secret of their hearts, and of all others, it cannot be hid, nor yet unrewarded, when he shall see opportunity. And my good lord, if you would show yourself so much my good friend as to require the king's majesty that mine accusers may come before my face in his presence, and there that

I may make answer, I doubt not but ye shall see me acquit myself of all their malicious accusations, and utterly confound them; for they shall never be able to prove, by any due probation, that ever I offended the king either in thought, word, or deed. Therefore I desire you, and most heartily require your good lordship to be a mean for me, that I may answer unto my accusations before the king's majesty. The case is his, and if their accusations were true, then should it touch him more earnestly, wherefore it were convenient that he should hear it himself. But I fear me that they intend to dispatch me, rather than I should come before his presence; for they be well assured, and very certain, that my truth should vanquish all their accusations and untrue surmises, which is the especial cause that maketh me so earnestly desire to make mine answer before the king's majesty. The loss of goods, the slander of my name, nor yet all my trouble grieveth me anything so much as the loss of the king's favour, and that he should have in me such an opinion, without desert, of untruth, that have with such travail and pains served the king so justly, so painfully, and with so good an heart, to his profit and honour at all times. And against the truth of my doings their accusations proved by me to be unjust, should do me more pleasure and good than the obtaining much treasure; as I doubt not to do, if the case might be indifferently heard. Now, my good lord, weigh my reasonable request, and let charity and truth move your heart with pity to help me in all this my truth, wherein you shall take no manner of rebuke or slander, by the grace of God.' 'Well, then,' said my lord of Shrewsbury, 'I will write to the king in your behalf, declaring to him by my letters how ye lament his indignation and displeasure; and also what request ye make for the trial of your truth towards his highness.' And after divers other communications as they were accustomed daily to have, they departed asunder.

"Remaining there thus with my lord the space of a fortnight, having goodly entertainment, and often desired by the earl to kill a doe or hart in his park there, who always refused to take any pleasure either in hunting or otherwise, but applied his prayers continually with great devotion; so that it came to pass at a certain time, as he sat at dinner in his own chamber, having at his board's end the same day, as he accustomably had every day, a mess of gentlemen and chaplains to keep him company, towards the end of his dinner, when he came to the eating of his fruits, I perceived his colour often to change, whereby I judged him not to be in good health. With that I leaned over the table, and, speaking softly unto him, said, ' Sir, me seemeth your grace is not well at ease.' To whom he answered and said, with a loud voice, ' Forsooth, no more I am; for I am,' quoth he, ' taken suddenly with a thing about my stomach that lieth there along as cold as a whetstone, which is no more but wind; therefore I pray you take up the table, and make a short dinner, and that done, resort shortly again.' And after the meat was carried out of the chamber into the gallery, where all the waiters dined, and every man set, I rose up and forsook my dinner, and came into the chamber unto my lord, where I found him still sitting very ill at ease; notwithstanding, he was communing with them at the board's end, whom he had commanded to sit still. And as soon as I was entered the chamber, he desired me to go to the apothecary, and inquire of him if he had anything that would make him break wind upward. Then went I to the earl, and showed him what estate my lord was in, and what he desired. With that my lord of Shrewsbury caused incontinent the apothecary to be called before him; and at his coming he demanded of him if he had anything that would break wind upward in a man's body; and he answered that he had such gear. ' Then,' quoth the earl, ' fetch me some.' Then departed the apothecary, and brought with him a white confection in a fair paper, and showed it unto my lord, who commanded me to give the saye thereof before him, and so I did. And I took the same and brought it to my lord, whereof also I took the saye myself, and then delivered it to my lord, who received it up all at once into his mouth. But immediately after he had received the same, surely he avoided much wind exceedingly upward. ' Lo,' quoth he, ' you may see it was but wind; and now am I well eased, I thank God:' and so rose from the table and went to his prayers, as he used every day after dinner. And that done there came upon him such a laske, that it caused him to go to the stool; and being there, my lord of Shrewsbury sent for me, and at my repair to him, he said, ' Forasmuch as I have always perceived you to be a man in

whom my lord your master hath great affiance, and also
knowing you to be an honest man (with many more words of
commendation and praise than becometh me here to recite),
it is so, that my lord your master hath often desired me to write
to the king, that he might come before his presence to answer
to his accusations; and even so have I done; and this day
have I received letters from the king's grace, by sir William
Kingston, whereby I perceive that the king hath in him a
good opinion; and by my request he hath sent for him, by
the same sir William, to come unto him, who is in his
chamber. Wherefore, now is the time come that my lord
hath often desired to try himself, I trust, much to his honour;
and it shall be the best journey that ever he made in his life.
Therefore, now would I have you to play the part of a wise
man, to break this matter wittily unto him, in such sort that
he may take it quietly and in good part; for he is ever so full
of sorrow and heaviness at my being with him, that I fear
me he will take it in evil part, and then doeth he not well; for
I assure you, and so show him, that the king is his good lord,
and hath given me most worthy thanks for his entertainment,
desiring and commanding me so to continue, not doubting
but that he will right nobly acquit himself towards his highness. Therefore go your ways to him, and persuade with
him that I may find him in good quiet at my coming, for I
will not tarry long after you.' 'Sir,' quoth I, 'if it please
your lordship, I shall endeavour me to the best of my power
to accomplish your lordship's commandment. But, sir, I
doubt, that when I shall name sir William Kingston to him,
he will mistrust that all is not well; because Mr. Kingston
is constable of the Tower, and captain of the guard, having
with him, as I understand, twenty-four of the guard to attend
upon him.' 'Marry, it is truth,' quoth the earl, 'what thereof,
although he be constable of the Tower? he is the most
meetest man for his wisdom and discretion to be sent about
any such message. And for the guard, it is for none other
purpose but only to defend him against them that would
intend him any evil, either in word or deed; and they be all,
or for the most part, such of his old servants as the king took
of late into his service, to the intent that they should attend
upon him most justly, knowing best how to serve him.'
'Well, sir,' said I, 'I shall do what I can,' and so departed
from him towards my lord.

"And as I repaired unto him, I found him sitting at the upper end of the gallery upon a chest, with his staff and his beads in his hands. And espying me coming from the earl, demanded of me, what news? 'Forsooth, sir,' quoth I, 'the best news that ever came to you, if your grace can take it well.' 'I pray God it be,' quoth he, 'what is it?' 'Forsooth, sir,' said I, 'my lord of Shrewsbury, perceiving by your often communication with him, that you were always desirous to come before the king's majesty, he, as your most assured friend, hath travailed so with his letters unto the king, that he hath sent for you, by Mr. Kingston and twenty-four of the guard, to conduct you to his highness.' 'Mr. Kingston,' quoth he, rehearsing his name* once or twice, and with that clapped his hand on his thigh, and gave a great sigh. 'Sir,' quoth I, 'if it please your grace, if you would or could take all things in good part, it should be much better for you. Content yourself, for God's sake, and think that God and your friends have wrought for you, according to your own desire. Did ye not always wish that ye might clear yourself before the king; and now that God and your friends have brought your desire to pass, ye will not take it thankfully? If you consider your truth and loyalty to our sovereign lord, against the which your enemies cannot prevail, the king being your good lord, as he is, ye know well the king can do no less than he doeth to you, being to his highness accused of some heinous crime, but cause you to be brought to your trial, and there to receive according to your merits; the which his highness trusteth, and saith no less, but that you shall prove yourself a just man to his majesty, wherein ye have more cause to rejoice than thus to lament or to mistrust the favourable ministration of due justice.

* "I know not whether or no it be worth the mentioning here (however we will put it on the adventure), but cardinal Wolsey, in his life time was informed by some fortune-tellers, *that he should have his end at Kingston.* This, his credulity interpreted of Kingston-on-Thames; which made him always to avoid the riding through that town, though the nearest way from his house to the court. Afterwards, understanding that he was to be committed by the king's express order to the charge of sir Anthony Kingston (see Henry Lord Howard in his book against Prophecies, chap. 27, fol. 130), it struck to his heart; too late perceiving himself deceived by that father of lies in his homonymous prediction."—Fuller's *Church History,* book 5, p. 178.

For I assure you your enemies be more afraid of you than you of them; and doubting you so much, they wish the thing that they shall never, I trust, bring to pass with all their wits—the king (as I said before) being your indifferent judge and your earnest friend. And, to prove that he so is, see ye not how he hath sent gentle Mr. Kingston to honour you with as much honour as was due to you in your high estate, and to convey you by such easy journeys as you will command him to do; and that ye shall have all your desires and requests by the way in every place, to your grace's contentation and honour. Wherefore, sir, I humbly beseech your grace to imprint all these persuasions, and many other like, in your high discretion, and be of good cheer, wherewith ye shall comfort yourself, and give all your friends and servants good hope of your good speed.' 'Well, well, then,' quoth he, 'I perceive more than ye can imagine or do know; experience of old hath taught me.' And therewith he rose up and went into his chamber, and went to the stool, the laske troubled him so sore; and when he had done he came out again, and immediately after, my lord of Shrewsbury came into the gallery unto him, with whom my lord met, and then sitting down there upon a bench in a great bay window, the earl asked him how he did, and he most lamentably, as he was accustomed to do, answered him, and thanked him for his gentle entertainment. 'Sir,' quoth the earl, 'if ye remember, ye have often wished to come before the king to make your answer, and I perceiving your often desire and earnest request, as one that beareth you good will, have written especially unto the king in that behalf; making him privy also of your lamentable sorrow that ye inwardly have received of his displeasure, who accepteth all your doings therein as friends be accustomed to do in such cases. Wherefore I would advise you to pluck up your heart, and be not aghast of your enemies, who, I assure you, be more in doubt of you than you would think, perceiving that the king is minded to have the hearing of your case before his own person. Now, sir, if you can be of good cheer, I doubt not but this journey which you shall take up unto his highness shall be much to your advancement, and an overthrow to your enemies. The king hath sent for you by the worshipful knight, Mr. Kingston, and with him twenty-four of your old servants, now of the guard, to defend you against your enemies, to the intent that ye may safely come unto his majesty.' 'Sir,' quoth my lord, 'I trow that Mr. Kingston is constable of the Tower.' 'Yea, what of that?' quoth the earl; 'I assure you he is elected of the king for one of your friends, and for a discreet gentleman, most worthy to take upon him the safeguard and conduct of your person, which, without fail, the king much esteemeth, and secretly beareth you special favour, far otherwise than ye do take it.' 'Well, sir,' quoth my lord, 'as God will, so be it. I am subject to fortune, and to fortune I submit myself, being a true man, ready to accept such chances as shall follow, and there an end. Sir, I pray you, where is Mr. Kingston?' 'Marry,' quoth the earl, 'if you will, I will send for him, who would most gladly see you.' 'I pray you then,' quoth my lord, 'send for him.' At whose message he came; and as soon as my lord espied him coming at the gallery end, he made haste to encounter him. Mr. Kingston came towards him with much reverence; and at his coming he kneeled down unto him, and saluted him in the king's behalf, whom my lord, bare-headed, offered to take up, but he still refused. Then quoth my lord, 'Mr. Kingston, I pray you to stand up, and leave your kneeling unto me; for I am but a wretch replete with misery, not esteeming myself, but as a vile abject utterly cast away, without desert, as God knoweth; and, therefore, good Mr. Kingston, stand up, or I will kneel down by you,' whom he would not leave until he stood up. Then spake Mr. Kingston, and said, with humble reverence, 'Sir, the king's majesty hath him commended unto you.' 'I thank his highness,' quoth my lord; 'I trust he is in health and merry.' 'Yea, without doubt,' quoth Mr. Kingston; 'and he commanded me to say unto you, that you should assure yourself that he beareth unto you as much good will and favour as ever he did, and willeth you to be of good cheer. And whereas report hath been made unto him, that you should commit against his royal majesty certain heinous crimes, which he thinketh perfectly to be untrue, yet, for the ministration of justice, in such cases requisite, he can do no less than send for you to your trial, mistrusting nothing your truth nor wisdom, but that ye shall be able to acquit yourself of all complaints and accusations exhibited against you; and to take your journey to him at your own pleasure, commanding me to attend upon you with ministration of due reverence, and to see your person preserved against all inconveniences that may ensue; and to elect all such your old servants, now his, to serve you by the way, who have most experience of your diet. Therefore, sir, I beseech you be of good cheer; and when it shall be your own pleasure to take your journey, I shall be ready to give attendance upon you.' 'Mr. Kingston,' quoth my lord, 'I thank you for your good news; and, sir, hereof assure yourself, that if I were as able and lusty as I have been but of late, I would not fail to ride with you in post; but, sir, I am diseased with a flux* that maketh me very weak. But, Mr. Kingston, all the comfortable words which ye have spoken unto me be spoken but for a purpose to bring me into a fool's paradise; I know what is provided for me. Notwithstanding, I thank you for your good will and pains taken about me, and I shall with all speed make me ready to ride with you to-morrow.' And thus they fell into other communication, both the earl and Mr. Kingston with my lord, who commanded me to foresee and provide that all things might be made ready to depart the morrow after. Then caused I all things to be trussed up, and made in a readiness as fast as they could conveniently.

" When night came that we should go to bed, my lord waxed very sick with the laske, the which caused him still continually from time to time to go to the stool, all that night; insomuch that from the time that it took him, until the next morning, he had fifty stools, so that he was that day very

---

* In the printed editions the passage stands thus: "But alas! I am a diseased man, having a flux: (at which time it was apparent that *he had poisoned himself*) it hath made me very weak." p. 190, edit. 1706. " It is highly probable (says Dr. Fiddes in his Life of Wolsey, p. 499), this expression ought to be taken in a softer sense, than the words strictly import, and that Cavendish only intended by it, that he was poisoned by taking something prepared for him by other hands." Dr. F. then proceeds to invalidate by reasoning, the story of the cardinal having hastened his own death. But I apprehend it cannot be thought that there is much force in the doctor's arguments. It is more important to observe, that it admits of great question, whether the words in the parenthesis are not altogether an interpolation. They do not occur in any MS. which I have seen. Still it is certain that the charge of his having poisoned himself was repeated by contemporary writers without scruple. See Tindall's *Works*, p. 404. *Supplication to the Queen's Majesty*, fol. 7, A. D. 1555. Fox's *Acts*, p. 959.— *Wordsworth*.

weak. His matter that he voided was wondrous black, the which the physician called coller adustine; and when he perceived it, he said to me, that if he had not some help shortly he shall die. With that I caused one doctor Nicholas, a doctor of physic, being with my lord of Shrewsbury, to look upon the gross matter that he voided, upon sight whereof he determined he should not live four or five days; yet, notwithstanding, he would have ridden with Mr. Kingston that same day, if my lord of Shrewsbury had not been. Therefore, in consideration of his infirmity, they caused him to tarry all that day.

" And the next day he took his journey, with Mr. Kingston and them of the guard. And as soon as they espied him, considering that he was their old master, and in such estate, they lamented his misfortune with weeping eyes. Whom my lord took by the hand, and many times, as he rode by the way, he would talk, now with one, then with another, until he came to a house of my lord of Shrewsbury's, called Hardwick Hall, where he lay all that night very evil at ease. The next day he rode to Nottingham, and there lodged that night, more sick, and the next day he rode to Leicester Abbey, and by the way he waxed so sick, that he was almost fallen from his mule, so that it was night before we came to the abbey of Leicester, where at his coming in at the gate, the abbot with all his convent met him with divers torches light, whom they right honourably received and welcomed with great reverence. To whom my lord said, ' Father abbot, I am come hither to leave my bones among you,' riding so still until he came to the stairs of his chamber, where he alighted from his mule; and then Master Kingston took him by the arm, and led him up the stairs, who told me afterwards he never felt so heavy a burden in all his life. And as soon as he was in his chamber, he went incontinent to his bed very sick. This was upon Saturday at night; and then continued he, sicker and sicker.

" Upon Monday, in the morning, as I stood by his bedside, about eight of the clock, the windows being close shut, and having wax lights burning upon the cupboard, I beheld him, as me seemed, drawing fast towards death. He perceiving my shadow upon the wall by the bedside, asked who was there? ' Sir,' quoth I, ' I am here.' ' How do you?' quoth he to me. ' Very well, sir,' quoth I, ' if I might see your grace well.' 'What is it of the clock?' said he to me. 'Sir,' said I, 'it is past eight in the morning.' 'Eight of the clock?' quoth he, 'that cannot be,' rehearsing divers times, 'eight of the clock! eight of the clock! nay, nay,' quoth he at last, 'it cannot be eight of the clock, for by eight of the clock shall you lose your master; for my time draweth near, that I must depart this world.' With that one doctor Palmes, a worshipful gentleman, being his chaplain and ghostly father, standing by, bade me secretly demand of him if he would be shriven, and to be in readiness towards God, whatsoever should chance. At whose desire I asked him that question. 'What have you to do to ask me any such question?' quoth he, and began to be very angry with me for my presumption, until at the last Master Doctor took my part, and talked with him in Latin, and so pacified him.

"At afternoon Master Kingston sent for me into his chamber, and at my coming there said to me, 'So it is, that the king hath sent me letters by Master Vincent, one of your old companions, who hath been in trouble in the Tower for money that my lord should have at his last departing from him, which cannot now be found. Wherefore the king, at this Vincent's request, for the declaration of his truth, hath sent him hither with his grace's letters, that I should examine my lord in that behalf, and to have your counsel herein, to the intent my lord may take it well and in good part. This is the cause of my sending for you; therefore I pray you of your counsel, what way is best to be taken therein, for the true acquittal of this poor gentleman, Master Vincent.' 'Sir,' quoth I, 'as touching that matter, after mine advice, you shall in your own person resort unto him to visit him, and in communication break the matter unto him. And if he will not tell the truth, there be that can satisfy the king's mind therein. But in any wise mention not nor speak of my fellow Vincent. And also I would advise you not to tract the time with him; for he is very sick, and I fear me he will not live past a day.' Then went Master Kingston to visit him; and asked him first how he did, and so forth proceeded in conversation, wherein Master Kingston demanded of him of the said money, saying, 'that my lord of Northumberland hath found a book at Cawood, that reporteth that you had but late fifteen hundred pounds, and it will not be found, not so much as one penny thereof, who hath made the king privy of the same. Wherefore the king hath written unto me, to demand of you where it is become; for it were pity that it should be embezzled from you both. Therefore I shall require you, in the king's name, to tell me the truth, to the intent that I may make just report unto his majesty of your answer therein.' With that my lord paused a little, and said, ' Oh, good Lord ! how much doth it grieve me that the king should think in me any such deceit, wherein I should deceive him of any one penny that I have. Rather than I would, Master Kingston, embezzle, or deceive him of one penny, I would it were moulten, and put into my mouth;' which words he spake twice or thrice very vehemently. ' I have nothing, nor never had (God be my judge,) that I esteemed so much my own, but that I took it ever to be the king's goods, having but the bare use thereof during my life, and after my death to leave it wholly to him; wherein he hath but prevented my intent and purpose. And for this money that you demand of me, I assure you that it is none of mine, for I borrowed it of divers of my friends to bury me, and to bestow among my servants, who have taken great pains about me, like true and faithful servants. Notwithstanding, if it be his pleasure to have this money from me, I must hold me content. Yet I would most humbly beseech his majesty to see that satisfied, for the discharge of my conscience unto them that I owe it.' ' Who be they?' quoth Mr. Kingston. ' That shall I show you,' said my lord. ' I borrowed two hundred pounds thereof of sir John Allen of London; and another two hundred pounds of sir Richard Gresham of London; also other two hundred pounds of the master of the Savoy, also two hundred pounds of Doctor Hickden, dean of my college in Oxford; and two hundred pounds of the treasurer of the church of York; and also two hundred pounds of parson Ellis, my chaplain; and another one hundred pounds of a priest, that was then his steward, whose name I have forgotten; to whom I trust the king will restore the same again, forasmuch as it is none of mine.' ' Sir,' quoth Mr. Kingston, ' there is no doubt in the king; whom you need not to mistrust in that, but when the king shall be advertised hereof, as I shall report at my return, of your earnest request therein, his grace will do as shall become him. But, sir, I pray you, where is this

money?' 'Mr. Kingston,' quoth my lord, 'I will not conceal it from the king, but will declare it unto you, or I die,
by the grace of God. Take a little patience with me, I
beseech you.' 'Well, sir, then will I trouble you no more at
this time, trusting that you will tell me to-morrow.' 'Yea,
that I will, Mr. Kingston, for the money is safe enough,
and in an honest man's keeping, who will not keep one penny
thereof from the king.' And then the abbot of Leicester
sent for Mr. Kingston to supper, who then departed for that
night.

"Howbeit my lord waxed very sick, most likely to die that
night, and often swooned, and as methought drew on fast to
his end, until it was four of the clock of the morning; at
which time I spoke to him, and asked him how he did.
'Well,' quoth he, 'if I had any meat; I pray you give me
some.' 'Sir, there is none ready,' said I. 'I wis,' quoth
he, 'you be the more to blame; for you should have always
meat for me in a readiness, to eat when my stomach serveth
me; therefore, I pray you, get me some; for I intend this
day to make me strong, to the intent that I may occupy myself in confession, and make me ready to God.' 'Then, sir,'
quoth I, 'I will call up the cooks to provide some meat for
you; and will also, if it be your pleasure, call for Mr. Palmes,
that ye may commune with him, until your meat be ready.'
'With a good will,' quoth he. And therewith I went fast,
and called up the cooks, bidding them to prepare some meat
for my lord. Then went I to Mr. Palmes, and told him
what case my lord was in, willing him to rise and resort to
him with speed. And then I went to Mr. Kingston, and
gave him warning, that, as I thought, my lord would not
live: advising him that if he had anything to say to him, he
should make haste, for he was in great danger. 'In good
faith,' quoth Mr. Kingston, 'you be to blame, for you make
him believe that he is sicker and in more danger than he is
indeed.' 'Well, sir,' quoth I, 'you shall not say another
day but I have given you warning, as I am bound to do, and
discharge myself therein. Therefore, I pray you, whatsoever
shall chance, let no negligence be ascribed to me herein; for
I assure you his life is very short. Do, therefore, as you
think best.' Yet, nevertheless, he rose, and made him ready,
and came to him. After he had eaten of a cullace made of

chicken a spoonful or two, at the last quoth he, 'Whereof was this cullace made?' 'Forsooth, sir,' quoth I, 'of a chicken.' 'Why,' quoth he, 'it is fasting day,' (being St. Andrew's even). 'What though it be,' quoth Doctor Palmes, 'you be excused by reason of your sickness?' 'Yea,' quoth he, 'what though? I will eat no more.'

" Then was he in confession the space of an hour. And when he had ended his confession, Master Kingston came to him, and bade him good morrow, for it was about six of the clock, and asked him how he did. 'Sir,' quoth he, 'I tarry but the pleasure of God, to render up my poor soul into his hands.' 'Not so, sir,' quoth Master Kingston, 'with the grace of God, you shall live, and do very well, if you will be of good cheer.' 'Nay, in good sooth, Master Kingston, my disease is such that I cannot live; for I have had some experience in physic. Thus it is; I have a flux with a continual fever; the nature whereof is, that if there be no alteration of the same within eight days, either must ensue excoriation of the entrails, or frenzy, or else present death; and the best of these three is death. And, as I suppose, this is the eighth day; and if you see no alteration in me, there is no remedy, save that I may live a day or two after, but death, which is the best of these three, must follow.' 'Sir,' said Master Kingston, 'you be in such pensiveness, doubting that thing that in good faith you need not.' 'Well, well, Master Kingston,' quoth my lord, 'I see the matter maketh you much worse than you should be against me; how it is framed I know not; but if I had served God as diligently as I have done the king, he would not have given me over in my grey hairs. But this is the just reward that I must receive for my diligent pains and study that I have had to do him service; not regarding my service to God, but only to satisfy his pleasure. I pray you have me most humbly commended unto his royal majesty, and beseech him in my behalf, to call to his princely remembrance all matters proceeding between him and me from the beginning of the world, and the progress of the same; and most especially in his weighty matter;' (meaning the matter between good queen Katharine and him,) 'and then shall his grace's conscience know whether I have offended him or no. He is a prince of royal courage, and hath a princely heart; and rather than he will miss or want

R 2

any part of his will or pleasure, he will endanger the loss of one half of his realm. For I assure you, I have often kneeled before him the space sometimes of three hours, to persuade him from his will and appetite; but I could never dissuade him therefrom. Therefore, Master Kingston, I warn you, if it chance you hereafter to be of his privy council, as for your wisdom you are very meet, be well assured and advised what you put into his head, for you shall never put it out again.

" ' And say, furthermore, that I request his grace, on God's name, that he have a vigilant eye to depress this new sort of Lutherans,* that it do not increase through his negligence, in such a sort as he be at length compelled to put on harness upon his back to subdue them, as the king of Bohemia did, who had good game to see his commons infected with Wickliffe's heresies, to spoil the spiritual men of his realm, who at the last were constrained to call to the king and his nobles for succour against their frantic rage; of whom they could get no help nor refuge, but they laughed and had good game, not regarding their duty. But when these erroneous heretics had subdued all the clergy, both churches and monasteries, and all other spiritual things, then having nothing more to spoil, they caught such a courage of their former spoil, that then they disdained their prince with his nobles, and the heads and governors of the country, and began to spoil and slay them. Insomuch as the king and other noblemen were constrained to put harness upon them, to resist the power of those traitorous heretics, and to defend their lives; who pitched a field against them, in which field the conflict was so vehement and cruel on the rebels part, that, in fine, they slew the king, the nobles, and all the gentlemen of the realm, leaving not one person that bare the name of a nobleman or gentleman, or any person that bare rule in the commonwealth

---

* In the year 1521, the cardinal, by virtue of his legatine authority, issued a mandate to all the bishops in the realm, to take the necessary means for calling in and destroying all books, printed or written, containing any of the errors of Martin Luther: and further directing processes to be instituted against all the possessors and favourers of such books, heresies, &c. The mandate contained also a list of forty-two errors of Luther. See Wilkins's *Concilia*, vol. iii. p. 690—693; and Strype's *Ecclesiastical Memorials*, vol. i. p. 36—40.—*Wordsworth*.

alive; by means of which slaughter they have lived ever since without a head, being brought into such poverty and misery that they be abhorred of all Christian nations. Let this be to him an example to avoid the like danger, I pray you. There is no trust to routs or to unlawful assemblies in the common people; for when they be up, there is no mercy with them. Let him consider the story of king Richard the Second, one of his progenitors, who lived in that same time also of Wickliffe's seditions and erroneous opinions. Did not the commons, I pray you, in his time, arise against the nobles and head governors of this realm of England; whereof some they apprehended, whom without mercy or misery they put to death? and did they not fall to spoiling and robbery, which was their only pretence to have all things in common; and at the last took the king's person perforce out of the Tower of London, and carried him about the city presumptuously, making him obedient to their lewd proclamations? Did not, also, the traitorous heretic, sir John Oldcastle, lord of Cobham, pitch a field with heretics against king Henry the Fifth, where the king himself was personally, and fought against them, to whom God gave the victory? Alas! if these be not plain precedents, and sufficient persuasions to admonish a prince to be circumspect against the semblable mischief, then will God strike, and take from us our prudent rulers, and leave us in the hands of our enemies; and then shall ensue mischief upon mischief, inconvenience upon inconvenience, and barrenness and scarcity for lack of good order in the commonwealth, to the utter ruin and desolation of this realm, from the which God of his tender mercy defend us.

"'Master Kingston, farewell. I can no more say; but I wish, ere I die, all things to have good success. My time draweth on fast. I may not tarry with you. And forget not what I have said and charged you withal; for when I am dead, ye shall peradventure remember my words better.' And even with those words, he began to draw his speech at length, and his tongue to fail—his eyes being presently set in his head, whose sight failed him. Then began we to put him in remembrance of Christ's passion, and caused the yeomen of the guard to stand by secretly to see him die, and to be witness of his words at his departure, who heard all his said communication; and incontinent the clock struck eight, and then gave he up the ghost, and thus he departed this present life.* And calling to remembrance how he said the day before, that at eight of the clock we should lose our master, as it is before rehearsed, one of us looking upon another, supposing that either he knew or prophesied of his departure; yet, before his departure, we sent for the abbot of the house to annoyle him,† who made all the speed he could, and came to his departure, and so said certain prayers before the breath was fully out of his body.

"Here is the end and fall of pride and arrogancy of men, exalted by fortune to dignities; for I assure you, in his time, he was the haughtiest man in all his proceedings alive; having more respect to the honour of his person, than he had to his spiritual profession, wherein should be showed all meekness, humility, and charity; the discussing whereof any further I leave to divines.

"After that he was thus departed, Mr. Kingston sent a post to the king, advertising him of the departure of the cardinal, by one of the guard that saw and heard him die: and then Mr. Kingston and the abbot, calling me unto them, went to consultation of the order of his burial.

"After divers opinions, it was thought good that he should be buried the next day following; for Mr. Kingston would not tarry the return of the post. And it was further thought good, that the mayor of Leicester and his brethren should be sent for, to see him personally dead, to avoid false rumours that might happen to say that he was still alive. Then was the mayor and his brethren sent for; and, in the meantime, the body was taken out of the bed where he lay dead, who had upon him, next his body, a shirt of hair, besides his other shirt, which was of very fine holland, which was not known to any of his servants being continually about him in his chamber, saving to his ghostly father; which shirts were laid

---

* He died Nov. 29, 1530. Le Neve's *Fasti*, p. 310.

† To administer the *extreme unction.* "The *fifth sacrament* is anointing of sick men, the which oil is hallowed of the bishop, and ministered by priests to them that be of lawful age, in great peril of death : in lightness and abating of their sickness, if God will that they live ; and in forgiving of their venial sins, and releasing of their pain, if they shall die." *Festival*, fol. 171.—*Wordsworth.*

in a coffin made for him of boards, having upon his dead corpse all such ornaments as he was professed in when he was made bishop and archbishop, as mitre, cross, ring, and pall, with all other things due to his order and dignity. And laying thus all day in his coffin, open and barefaced, every man that would might see him there dead, without feigning, even as the mayor, his brethren, and others did.

"Lying thus until four or five of the clock at night, he was carried down into the church with great solemnity by the abbot, and conducted with much torch-light and service song, due for such funerals. And being in the church, the corpse was set in our Lady chapel, with divers tapers of wax, and divers poor men sitting about the same, holding torches in their hands, who watched about the corpse all night, while the canons sang dirge and other devout orisons. And about four o'clock in the morning, Mr. Kingston, and we his servants, came into the church, and there tarried the executing of divers ceremonies in such cases used about the corpse of a bishop. Then went they to mass, at which mass the abbot and divers others did offer. And that done, they went about to bury the corpse in the midst of the said chapel, where was made for him a grave. And by that time that he was buried, and all ceremonies ended, it was six of the clock in the morning.

"Then went we and prepared ourselves to horseback, being Saint Andrew's day, the apostle, and so took our journey to the court—riding that same day, being Wednesday, to Northampton, and the next day to Dunstable, and the next day to London, where we tarried until Saint Nicholas even, and then we rode to Hampton Court, where the king and council lay, giving all our attendance upon them for our dispatch.

"And the next day, being Saint Nicholas day, I was sent for, being in Mr. Kingston's chamber there in the court, to come to the king, whom I found shooting at the rounds in the park, on the back side of the garden. And perceiving him occupied in shooting, thought it not good to trouble him; but leaning to a tree, attending there until he had made an end of his disport. And leaning there, being in a great study what the matter should be that his grace should send for me, at the last the king came suddenly behind me, and clapped me upon the shoulder; and when I perceived him, I fell upon my knee. And he, calling me by name, said unto me, 'I will,' quoth he, 'make an end of my game, and then will I talk with you;' and so departed to the mark where he had shot his arrow. And when he came there, they were meting of the shot that lay upon the game, which was ended that shot.

" Then delivered the king his bow unto the yeoman of his bows, and went his ways inward, whom I followed; howbeit, he called for sir John Gage, then his vice-chamberlain, with whom he talked, until he came to the postern gate of his garden, the which being open against his coming, he entered, and then was the gate shut after him, which caused me to go my ways.

" And ere ever I was past half a pair of butt-lengths, the gate opened again, and Mr. Norris called me again, commanding me to come unto the king, who stood behind the door in a night-gown of russet velvet, furred with sable, before whom I kneeled down, being there with him all alone the space of an hour or more, during which season he examined me of divers weighty matters concerning my lord cardinal, wishing rather than twenty thousand pounds that he had lived. He examined me of the fifteen hundred pounds which Mr. Kingston moved to my lord before his death, as I have before rehearsed. 'Sir,' said I, 'I think that I can tell your grace partly where it is, and who hath it.' 'Yea, can you?' quoth the king; 'then I pray you tell me, and you shall do me much pleasure, and it shall not be unrewarded.' 'Sir,' said I, 'if it please your highness, after the departure of David Vincent from my lord at Scroby, who had the custody thereof, leaving the same with my lord in divers bags, he delivered the same unto a certain priest, safely to keep to his use.' 'Is this true?' quoth the king. 'Yea, sir,' quoth I, 'without all doubt. The priest shall not be able to deny it in my presence, for I was at the delivery thereof; who hath gotten divers other rich ornaments into his hands, the which be not rehearsed or registered in any of my lord's books of inventory, or other writings, whereby any man is able to charge him therewith but only I.' 'Well, then,' quoth the king, 'let me alone, and keep this gear secret between yourself and me, and let no man know thereof; for if I hear any more of it, then I know by whom it came out. Howbeit,' quoth he, 'three may keep counsel, if two be away, and if I knew that my cap were privy of my counsel, I would cast it in the fire and burn it. And for your truth and honesty ye shall be our servant, and be in the same room with us wherein you were with your old master. Therefore, go your ways unto sir John Gage, our vice-chamberlain, to whom I have spoken already to give you your oath, and to admit you our servant in the said room; and then go to my lord of Norfolk, and he shall pay you your whole year's wages, which is ten pounds, is it not so?' quoth the king. 'Yea, forsooth,' quoth I, 'and I am behind for three quarters of a year of the same wages.' 'That is true,' quoth the king, 'therefore ye shall have your whole year's wages, with our reward delivered you by the duke of Norfolk,' promising me, furthermore, to be my singular good lord whensoever occasion should serve. And thus I departed from the king.

"And as I went to Mr. Gage to receive mine oath, I happened to meet with Mr. Kingston coming from the council, who commanded me in their name to go straight unto them, for by him they had sent for me: 'And in anywise take good heed,' quoth he, 'what ye say; for ye shall be examined of certain words spoken by my lord your master at his departure, the which I know well enough; and if I tell them the truth,' quoth he, 'what he said, I shall undo myself; for in anywise they may not hear of it: therefore be circumspect what answer ye make to their demands.' 'Why,' quoth I, 'how have you done therein yourself?' 'Marry,' quoth he, 'I have utterly denied that I heard any such words; and he that opened the same first is fled for fear,' which was the yeoman of the guard that rode in post to the king from Leicester. 'Therefore go your ways,' quoth he, 'God send you good speed; and when you have done, come to me into the chamber of presence, where I will tarry to see how you speed, and to know how ye have done with the king.'

"Thus I departed, and went directly to the council chamber door; and as soon as I was come, I was called in amongst them. And being there, my lord of Norfolk first spake, and bade me welcome to the court, and said: 'My lords, this gentleman hath served the cardinal his master like an honest man; therefore, I doubt not but of such questions as ye shall demand of him he will make a just and a true answer, I dare be his surety. How say you, sir?' quoth he to me, 'it is reported that your master spoke such words and such, even at his departure from his life; the truth whereof I doubt not but you know, and as you know, I pray you report, and fear for no man. It shall not need to swear you, therefore go to, how say you, is this true that is reported?' 'Forsooth, my lord,' quoth I, 'I was so diligent about him, attending the preservation of his life, that I marked not every word that he spake: and as for my part, I have heard him talk many idle words, as men do in such extremities, the which I do not now remember. If it please you to call Mr. Kingston before your lordships, he will not let to tell you the truth.' 'Marry, so have we done already,' quoth they, 'who hath been here before us, and hath denied that ever your master spake any such words, at the time of his death, or at any time before. 'Forsooth, my lords,' quoth I, 'then I can say no more; for if he heard them not, I could not hear them, for he heard as much as I, and I as much as he. Therefore, my lords, it were folly to say a thing of untruth, which I am not able to justify.' 'Lo!' quoth my lord of Norfolk, 'I told you before that he was a true man, and would tell the truth. Go your ways: ye be discharged,' quoth he, 'and come to my chamber soon, for I must talk with you.'

"I most humbly thanked them, and so departed, and went into the chamber of presence to meet with Mr. Kingston, whom I found standing in communication with an ancient gentleman, one Mr. Radcliffe, gentleman usher of the king's privy chamber. And at my coming, Mr. Kingston demanded of me if I had been with the council, and what answer I made them. I answered, that I had satisfied their lordships' minds with mine answers, and told him even as I have rehearsed before. And then he asked me how I sped with the king; and I told him all our communications, and of his grace's benevolence and princely liberality towards me, and how he commanded me to go to my lord of Norfolk. And even as we were speaking of my lord of Norfolk, he came out from the council chamber, into the chamber of presence; and as soon as he espied me, he came unto the window, where I stood with Mr. Kingston and Mr. Radcliffe, to whom I declared the king's pleasure. And then these two gentlemen made intercession unto him to be good lord unto me. 'Nay,' quoth my lord of Norfolk, 'I will be better to him than he weneth; for if I could have spoken to him or ever he came to the king, I would have had him to my service, and (the king excepted) he should have done no man service in all England but me. And look,' quoth he, 'what I may do for you, I will do it with all my heart.' ' Sir, then my desire is, that it would please your grace,' quoth I, 'to move the king to be so much my good lord as to give me one of the carts and horses that brought up my stuff with my lord's, (which is now in the Tower,) to carry it home into my country.' ' Yea, marry will I,' quoth he, and returned in to the king, for whom I tarried still with Mr. Kingston. 'And,' quoth Mr. Ratcliffe, ' I will go in, and help my lord of Norfolk in your suit to the king.' And, incontinent, my lord came forth, and told me that the king was my singular good and gracious lord, and had given me six of the best horses I could choose among all my lord's cart horses, and a cart to carry my stuff, and five marks for the cost homewards; 'and hath commanded me,' quoth he, ' to deliver you ten pounds for your wages, being behind, and twenty pounds for a reward; and commanded me to call Mr. Secretary unto him, to make a warrant for all these things.' Then was it told him that Mr. Secretary was gone to Hamworth for that night. Then commanded he one of the messengers of the chamber to ride to him in all haste for those warrants; and also willed me to meet with him the next day at London, and there I should receive both my money and my stuff, with the horses and cart that the king promised me: and so I did, of whom I received all those things, and then I returned home into the country with the same. And thus ended the life of the right triumphant cardinal of England, on whose soul Jesus have mercy! Amen.

"Who list to read and consider with a clear eye this history, may behold the mutability of vain honours and brittle assurance of abundance, the uncertainty of dignities, the flattering of feigned friends, and the fickle favour of worldly princes. Whereof this lord cardinal hath felt and tasted both of the sweet and sour in each degree; as fleeting from honours, losing of riches, deposed from dignities, forsaken of friends, and the mutability of princes' favour—of all which things he had in this world the full felicity, as long as fortune smiled upon him; but when she began to frown, how soon was he deprived of all these mundane joys and vain pleasures. That which in twenty years, with great travel and study, he obtained, was in one year, and less, with great care and sorrow, lost and consumed. O, madness! O, fond desire! O, foolish hope! O, greedy desire of vain honours, dignities, and riches! Oh, what unconstant hope and trust is it in the false feigned countenance and promise of fortune! Wherefore, the prophet saith full well, *Thesaurizat, et ignorat cui congregabit ea.* Who is certain that he shall leave his riches which he hath gathered in this world unto them whom he hath purposed? The wise man saith, 'That another, whom peradventure he hated in his life, shall spend it out, and consume it.'"

APPENDIX II.

LETTERS BETWEEN CARDINAL WOLSEY, KING HENRY, THE
EMPEROR CHARLES V., QUEEN KATHARINE, AND OTHERS.

LETTER I.

QUEEN KATHARINE TO MR. ALMONER WOLSEY, WITH THE
NEWS OF THE BATTLE OF FLODDEN.

(From the Cottonian Collection.)

MR. ALMONER,—When the last messenger went I wrote not
to you, because I had not the surety of anything that was
done in the battle against the Scots. Now since that time
came a post from my lord Howard, with a writing at length
of everything as it was, which I now send to the king; and
you shall thereby perceive so great a gift that Almighty God
hath sent to the king; for by me it is thought the greatest
honour that any prince had, his subjects in his absence not
only to have the victory, but also to slay the (opponent) king
and many of his noblemen. This matter is so marvellous,
that it seemeth to be God's doing alone. I think the king
will remember to thank him for it, for so all the realm here
hath done. And because you shall know by my lord Howard's
letter everything better than I can write, it is no need herein
to say any more of it.

Mr. Almoner, the king, when he was in Calais a little
while ago, sent me a letter touching the matter betwixt my
lord of Canterbury and my lord of Winchester. I did after
his commandment, and showed the same before sir Thomas
Lovel and Mr. Englefield, unto my lord of Canterbury; and

I prayed him to give answer shortly after the king's mind, as he knew it; for the matter was so new to me that I would go no further in it.   Since that time I have divers seasons asked him for the said answer, which I could never have till now; and the same in a letter I send you herein also.   I pray you, Mr. Almoner, excuse me to the king for the tarrying of it so long, for I could have it no sooner.   And with this I make an end, praying you to continue your writing, which is to me a great comfort; and methinketh it is a great while ago that I received any from you.   At Holborn, the 16 Sept. 1513.

KATHARINE, THE QUEEN.

Mr. Almoner, I cannot send you now my lord of Canterbury's answer, for the coffer wherein it is, is gone to my next lodging; and therefore I shall this night send it you by post.

LETTER II.

HENRY VIII. TO THOMAS WOLSEY, BISHOP OF LINCOLN, RELATIVE TO THE NEGOTIATION WITH THE DUKE OF LONGUEVILLE, ANNO 1514.

(From Dr. Fiddes's Collection.)

MY lord of Lincoln, I commend me unto you, and let you wit that I have spoken with the duke; who in the beginning was as ill afraid as ever he was in his life lest no good effect should come to pass.   Nevertheless, in farther communing, we went more roundly to our matters; in so much, that I said to him: 'seeing that the king your master hath sought so gently unto us, both amity and marriage, I assure you (our honour saved) we could be well content to give hearkening thereto; and if the offers were reasonable, agree upon those same.   But this is not reasonable, except the amity should no longer continue than the payment of the money; nor yet so, except there were a reasonable sum of money to be paid in hand, by and by.   If your master will have the marriage, I cannot see how it can be conveniently, except the amity be made during our lives, and one year after, to the intent that all suspicion on both sides may be set apart. Which marriage and amity your master may have under this manner; that is to say, paying yearly one hundred thousand crowns; and at his request I not to stick for ready money in hand, but I to stand content therewith, for recompence of all things. Which, if your master consider what heritance he holdeth from me, and what good my amity may do to help forth his matter in Italy, I think he will not greatly stick at.'

This furthermore I said to the duke: ' Surely, I cannot see how the amity made for years can any longer endure than the payment, which expired would be occasion of new breach and demands, whereby neither he nor I should live quietly; which, if there fell alliance, I would be loath to see; wherefore I see no way to eschew all dangers and perils, and to recompense me for withholding of my inheritance (which, if I would be slack in, my subjects would murmur at), but to make this amity during our lives; and one year after, paying yearly as above rehearsed: which amity once granted, the alliance should not be refused, nor no other thing which, with my honour saved, I might do.' Saying furthermore to him, that if I might demand, with my honour, any less, or take any less offer (seeing his master is so well minded to the aforesaid alliance and amity), I would be glad to do that at his request; but less than this it cannot stand with my honour, nor my subjects will not be content that I should take.

My lord, I showed him furthermore, that if he thought we might trust to have this end, I would be content that you and they should commune on all other articles concerning the amity and marriage, till we might have absolute assurance in that behalf for lessening of time. To which he answered, that he could not assure me thereof; but that he trusted, seeing my demands were so reasonable, that his master would agree thereto. On trust hereon we will, that you begin to pen the residue of the articles, as soon as you can. And thus fare you well. Written with the hand of your loving master.

HENRY R.

LETTER III.

MARY, QUEEN OF FRANCE, TO CARDINAL WOLSEY, AFTER
HER MARRIAGE WITH LOUIS XII.

(From the Cottonian Collection.)

I recommend me unto you as heartily as I can, and
. . . . . . as the king and you thought, I should have been;

for the morning next after the marriage, all my servants, both men and women, were discharged; insomuch that my mother Guildford was also discharged, ... whom, as you know, the king and you willed me in anywise to be my counsellor; but for any thing I might do in nowise might I have my grant for her abode here, which I assure you, my lord, is much to my discomfort, beside many other discomforts, that you would but little have thought. I have not yet seen in France any lady or gentlewoman so necessary for me as she is, nor yet so meet to do the king my brother service, as she is; and for my part, my lord, as you love the king my brother and me, find the means that she may in all haste come here again; for I had as lief lose the winning I shall have in France as lose her counsel when I shall lack it; which is not like long to be required, as I am sure the noblemen and gentlemen can show you more than becometh me to write on this matter. I pray you, my lord, give credence further to my mother Guildford, in everything concerning this matter. And albeit my lord of Norfolk has neither dealt best with me, nor yet with her, at this time, yet I pray you always to be good lord unto her; and would to God ———— I had been so fortunate to have had you with me here, when I had my lord of Norfolk. And thus, fare you well, my lord. Written . . . . . the 12th day of October.

My lord, I pray you give credence to me, my lord, in my sorrows . . . . . .

LETTER IV.

MARY, QUEEN OF FRANCE, TO HENRY VIII., AFTER THE DEATH OF HER OLD HUSBAND, LOUIS XII.

(Cottonian Collection.)

I commend me unto your grace, and would be very glad to hear that your grace were in good health, and to write me, the which should be a great comfort to me . . . . that it could please your grace to write more often to me than you do, for as now I am all out of . . . . . . that all my trust is in your grace, and so shall be during my life; for I pray your grace that it could please your grace to be so good lord and brother to me, that you will send hither . . . . . .* as you may possible . . . . . me, for I beseech your grace that you will keep all the promises that you promised me when I took my leave of you; for your grace knows very well, that I did marry for your pleasure that time, and now I trust that you will suffer me to marry . . . . your grace that . . . . . is not there where they would have me, and I ——— trust . . . . . will not do so to me, that has been so glad to fulfil your command as I have been: wherefore I beseech your grace for to be good lord and brother to me for fear of God, if your grace will . . . . . . married in any place . . . . . ever as my . . . . . I will be there ever as your grace knows, no other you shall have joy of me, for I promise your grace you shall hear that I . . . will be in some religious house, the which I think your grace will be very sorry of . . . . . . also fear I . . . . that that king that . . . . shall never be merry at . . . . . . grace for and ever that . . . . . will I live I trow your grace knows as well as I do, and . . . . . . and so I trust your grace will be contented, else I would never marry . . . . . . but be there where never . . . . . where woman shall . . . . . of me, wherefore I beseech your grace to be good lord to him, and to me both, for I know well that he hath not been any hindrance to your grace . . . . him and me both . . . . and your grace be good lord to us both. I will not change for all the world . . . . . . I beseech your grace be good lord and brother to me, as you have been hereaforetime, for Suffolk is all the trust that I have . . . .

By your humble and loving sister,

MARY, QUEEN OF FRANCE.

LETTER V.

MARY, DOWAGER OF FRANCE, TO WOLSEY, AFTER HER MARRIAGE WITH THE DUKE OF SUFFOLK. 22ND MARCH, 1515.

(Cottonian Collection.)

MY very good lord, in my most hearty manner I recommend me unto you, letting you the same for to understand that my lord of Suffolk hath sent me your letter, which lately

---

* Possibly the duke of Suffolk, her lover.

s

he received by Calais; by which I perceive the faithful mind
which you do bear unto us both, and how that you be determined not to leave us in our present trouble; for the which
your most fast and loving dealing, I most entirely thank you;
requiring you to continue towards us as you have begun . . .
shall never before . . . . any of our behalfs . . . . uttermost of our . . . . be always ready to . . . . . faithful kind the
king our lord, my brother written . . . . . my lord, I require
you that I have some counsel and letters from the king my
brother, and . . . . . . I trow there was never a man that had
more . . . . . .

By your loving friend,

MARY, QUEEN OF FRANCE.

LETTER VI.

TO MY LORD CARDINAL, FROM SARAGOSSA, THE 12TH OF MAY, 1518.

(From the Cottonian Collection.)

[This letter is one of those ghosts of public crimes, which,
after many years, reveal the deeds of the guilty, and inform
the world of what despicable and vicious stuff courtiers are
commonly made. Wolsey has been accused by the contemporary historians of being bribed at this time by the court of
France. It appears, however, that there were other members of the English cabinet in the interest of France; but
there is no proof that the cardinal was corrupted. At this
period he enjoyed a pension from Charles, which pension was
equivalent to what he received for the bishopric of Tournay.]

PLEASE it your grace to know, that amongst divers things
debated between the lord Chevers and the chancellor of Burgundy, whereas they showed us, and willed us, to write to
your grace, that they had sure knowledge out of France, that
the French king and his council reputed themselves firm and
fast of divers estates and nobles in England; to the which we
answered, that we are assured it was not so; and no realm in
the world, with all the subjects in the same, high and low,
were more obedient to the prince than the whole realm of
England, in all degrees, to our master.

They yet abided in their foresaid opinions. We answered them, that the Frenchmen, willing to make discord, do imagine this, which never was intended nor thought. Sir Thomas Espinel informeth us, that one of the secretaries privately told him of writings upon a pension for your grace, which writings when the said secretary did bring to be signed and sealed, the lord Chevers said, let it alone, yet all promises be not kept with me; which words to pass so wise a man's mouth, and so bold, we do not believe; we write as we be informed.

We have also with divers thanks, and other good words of the best, for the said lord Chevers' good conduct, and politic government.

The ambassador of Spain, being in England, wrote to the lord Chevers, that he had a present coming from the king, or you by us; the chancellor hearing of this, was not content with the same, as Sir Thomas Espinel informed us.

We think, under your grace's licence, that it was according such they have been promised, as the master of the rolls can tell you ; and do look for it also, that there be sent to each of them some memorial, at the king's pleasure undoubtedly, after our opinion for their better safeguard, and their honesty also; they be both very good English, they willed us to have them both recommended unto your grace.

The lord Fynnes, a much admired young man, and of his years of most reputation in the court, does humbly recommend him unto your grace, your own for ever, he saith.

Of all other causes sir John Styles, the bearer, can well inform your grace; as of the Infant's going into Flanders, of the meeting of the French king and the king . . . . about the borders of . . . . by the French ambassador, and not likely to be of the reception of the king into Saragossa, with the conditions of the deferring thereof . . . of the . . . archbishop's countenance and behaviour at the same reception of all the king . . . . . lovers and friends of the court; and whither the king intendeth henceforward; to whom we beseech your grace to give . . . . . and for his long services to be his good and gracious lord; and we humbly beseech your grace otherwise to have us in your remembrance: which never shall forget you, with God's grace, who ever more keep and preserve you.   From Saragossa, &c.

Letter VII.

TO CARDINAL WOLSEY.

(From the Cottonian Collection.)

[This letter very distinctly proves, not only that Wolsey was not corrupted as the contemporary historians have alleged, but shows that what he received from Charles was in consideration of the pension that was due from France for the bishopric of Tournay. It will appear afterwards, that when circumstances changed, and it became necessary to take the part of Francis against Charles, in like manner the cardinal provided for his own interests, while he attended to those of the nation. To prove his corruption, it is requisite to show, that in seeking his own advantage he sacrificed the interests of the kingdom.]

PLEASE it your grace, I wrote to the same the 8th of April, amongst other things, what conversation I had with . . . Allemain; and now again, in the conversation which I report in our coming letters, he said, the king's highness and your grace, by Don . . . . . by the emperor's commandment, refuseth to take the pension which the emperor offereth, saying, ye will not, but ye will be free, and principally have respect to good cause. And then Don . . . . said, the emperor well knoweth that, and hath great confidence therein; but peradventure his majesty shall think that your grace mindeth not to do any gratitude to him, if you refuse this pension; and then your grace answered, Nay, I refuse not, but peradventure I will take it now. Saith . . . . Allemain, Why should your grace refuse it? in anywise your grace must take it; and I assure you, saith he, the emperor trusteth him much now indeed; awhile he doubted, but now he beareth another mind and confidence towards him. I said, my lord's grace, I know well, beareth his mind towards his majesty; and then I showed him certain clauses in your grace's letters, as to a friend; and then I said, I trust the emperor will have in remembrance your grace's pension of Tournay, and the arrears, for this is good right. He said this, with much more: first, saith he, in the conclusion of this peace, the money paid therefore, shall be made first payment to the king's highness; and then my lord cardinal shall have all the arrears paid out of hand, and a hundred thousand ducats for his labour; and he must help, that the sum of money be great, although it be the less, yet that is all we look for, and yet he shall have six thousand ducats of new pension made sure in Castille, until he have recompence in spiritual lands; as for the nine thousand crowns he would not now tell where they should be answered, either here or in Flanders; and yet in times past, he told me here. Moreover, he said, if he will be good to the duke of Bourbon, he shall be made sure of twenty thousand ducats more, yearly, to him, and to his heirs for ever, out of the duchy of Milan. I told that your grace would have good consideration of all —— takes for the arrears of the pension of Tournay.

LETTER VIII.

CHARLES V. TO CARDINAL WOLSEY.

My lord the cardinal, my good friend, I have received your letter of the 5th of this month, by which, and from what my ambassadors have written to me touching you, I fully perceive the good counsel, the good care and anxiety you bear and feel for the honour and safety of my person, as well as the affectionate interest you take in the treaty and indissoluble union between myself and the king, my good uncle, for the which I thank you most cordially.

And to tell you my resolution as to one whom I hold for my good and loyal friend, and in whom I have full confidence, as you may plainly perceive, I would have you to know, that I have determined, by the aid of God, to proceed with, and to execute that which I have undertaken, and even to set about it in person; for I cannot, out of respect for my own benefit and honour, defer it; and, although I hold as right and wise what you say, and know that whatever you do proceeds from good affection, yet I am sure, when we have discussed the matter together, and you shall have heard my reasons, you will be of my opinion.

I have always preferred the alliance and confederation of the king, my good uncle, to that of all others, and have ever so acted as clearly to show you this, and things have proceeded in such spirit, both on your part and on mine. You have always told me that you would communicate to me, on the part of the said king, my good uncle, things which no man was to know but he, you, and I; which things, I doubt not, are of great importance, and this understanding is calculated to be one of the principal means of the settlement of our affairs; wherefore I, on my part, also told you that I had determined, for the great confidence I have in you, that I would in like manner declare my purpose in the first instance to you, and I am still firm in this intent. The causes for the determination I have made it is impossible to discuss, thoroughly and seriously, without first going into the details of the matters which you know of; I am anxious, therefore, to converse with yourself, and so seek, personally, your advice and counsel, after showing you my reasons, and the great injury it is to me to delay my affairs thus. In a word, matters are such as to endure very little longer delay, and to allow me, being gone thus far, no means of drawing back from what I have undertaken. I would desire to see you at Bruges next Sunday, unto which day I will await you, although the delay is very detrimental, and might be the cause of irreparable damage to me. I have no doubt that we shall have done all that is necessary in two or three days; for you and I together can do more in one day than our ambassadors could do in a month—there being no necessity for sending backwards and forwards . . . . . that the king, my good uncle, and you, are determined to deal frankly with me, which I am, in like manner, with you, as you know by experience. Should it be so that, notwithstanding your good intention, you cannot come on the said day, but will visit me somewhat later, further off in my camp, I will show you my army, by which you will perceive that I have no intention of going to sleep, and relying merely on the aid of God, or of my friends, and you shall be heartily welcomed. As I heretofore sent you word by my ambassadors, I have need to declare and communicate to you all my affairs, the progress of which, I hope, will be from good to better, if it please God, whom I pray to take you into his holy keeping.

Written at Bruges this   of August, 1521.

Your good friend, CHARLES.

Letter IX.

MARGARET, QUEEN OF SCOTS, TO WOLSEY.

My lord cardinal, I commend me heartily unto you, and I have received your writing, with the articles subscribed with your hand; whereunto I have made answer at length in all points, and therefore I will not be long to you in this writing; but I pray you heartily, my lord, to consider well the answer of your said articles, and not to take so great regard as ye do by your writing to my lord of Angus, which an ye do will put great trouble in this realm, and able to put the king my son in his enemies' hands; wherefore, seeing that I and my partakers have put the king my son out of the danger that he was in, I think it should be well considered, and in such a sort, that the earl of Angus should not be sent to this realm, and specially by the king's grace my brother, which must be our defender and helper, and should give occasion to noblemen to take the king my son's part, and mine, believing therethrough to win his grace's favour, and will cause them to be the better minded unto the king my son and me; and if his grace will send me the earl of Angus, that is contrary part to the earl of Arran, it will be occasion to him to leave the good part that he hath reaped, and to labour otherwise for himself, where now he hath put himself and all his friends in danger of their lives, for the weal of the king my son and me. And if this should not be looked upon before the pleasure of the earl of Angus, that did never sit on steed for me . . . to the king my son, nor may not do, suppose ye, my lord, by other ways I informed and gave trust to the same, as the articles bear at length, not the less, my lord, I pray you, as my great trust is in you, that ye will labour in that sort for me, that I and my partakers may be in a surety that the earl of Angus shall not come in Scotland, as at more length the articles bear, and that with diligence I may be advertised of the king's grace my brother's pleasure; for while that I be in surety of such matters as I have written, I trust the ambassadors shall not be sped, for my partakers think that if they labour for the pleasure of the king's grace my brother, that on his side he should show kindness to them afore any Scottishman, after the king my son. Praying you, therefore, my lord, to give good counsel to the king's grace my brother, and to let me have answer incontinently for the furthering of all matters, God have you in his keeping. Written the 6th day of October, at Edinburgh.

LETTER X.

CARDINAL WOLSEY TO THE LORD DACRE, OF THE NORTH.

AFTER right affectionate recommendations, my lord, though I have received no letters from you since my arrival on this side the sea; nor yet, as I am informed, ye have not advertised the king's highness either of the state of his borders, or of the demeanour of the Scots, since my departing out of England; yet the king's highness hath now of late signified unto me, that credible report is made unto him how the Scots have not only made divers and many excursions in Northumberland, by burning certain villages, taking sundry prisoners, and driving away much cattle and sheep, but also that great preparation is made in Scotland for the coming of the duke of Albany thither; and remembering your old accustomed prudent demeanour, as well in the attaining assured knowledge of the intended purpose of the Scots, from time to time, by such good espial and intelligence that ye have had amongst the said Scots, as of the rumours and news current amongst them, it is the more marvelled that if either any such attempts have been made by the said Scots upon the king's subjects, or that any such rumours be in Scotland of the said duke's thither coming, that ye have not advertised the king's highness or me thereof, before this time; wherefore I thought it right expedient, not only to put you in remembrance thereof, so that ye may with all diligence advertise me how everything hath proceeded there during mine absence out of the realm, to the intent I may at my coming to the king's presence, which, God willing, I shall be with in brief time, ascertain his highness therein, whereof to hear his grace is much desirous, but also to notify unto you what I have heard of the transporting of the said duke of Albany into Scotland, with my advice and counsel what is expedient and necessary to do upon the same. Truth it is, that credible report hath been made unto me now of late, that the said duke is not only passed, or shall shortly pass out of France into Scotland, with the number of two or three thousand men of war, but also hath made great and instant labour in the court of Rome, for a divorce to be had and made for separation of the marriage betwixt the queen of Scots and the earl of Angus, intending to marry with the said queen, whereunto it is said she is agreeable, and that the same duke intendeth to aspire to the crown of Scotland, which he cannot attain unless he destroy the young king. And if the premises be of truth, as by many conjectures it.is in great appearance, right necessary it is, that ye not only make diligent espial in Scotland for assured knowledge to be had of the premises, but also notify the same to the earl of Angus, the Homes, and such others as by the coming of the said duke into Scotland shall be put in danger of their lives and lands, so that they may make their party good and puissant to stop and prevent the damnable and abominable purpose of the said duke. It is verily thought, that in case the said detestable intent and mind of the said duke were published in Scotland, it should provoke the nobles and commons against him, whereby he might be put in danger at his first coming; and to the intent the said bruit may be made in Scotland upon true grounds, I ascertain you for a truth, that the French king now of late showed unto the earl of Worcester, the king's chamberlain, and the bishop of Ely, that the said duke not only intendeth in covert manner to pass into Scotland, but also hath laboured to purchase the said divorce for marrying the queen, suspecting thereby the danger of the said young king. And albeit the said duke could not depart out of France without the permission and sufferance of the French king, yet it is in appearance that he dissembleth therein. I am also advertised, by the king's orator, from the court of Rome, that the same divorce is urgently pursued by the duke of Albany there, in consideration whereof ye have good and probable grounds to instruct as well the said earl of Angus, as the Homes, and other nobles of Scotland, such as ye shall think good, that this is the only purpose of the said duke's coming into Scotland. And that he bringeth his men of war with him, not for the defence of that land, but only to destroy the said earl, and other nobles, that would resist and let him in the achieving of this his damnable mind and enterprise, which he knoweth well can never be brought to pass, unless the said earl and his adherents be subdued. Wherefore ye may persuade unto the said earl, the Homes, and others, that if they value the safety of their prince, if they love their lives, lands, and succession, they must, with all diligence possible, like valiant and noble men, put themselves in readiness, with all their friends, strength, and puissance, to preserve themselves and subdue their mortal enemy; for surely if they look not substantially thereunto, both the young king, they, and all the nobility of Scotland, shall be in great danger. And ye may say, that, inasmuch as the king of Scots, being the king's nephew, shall by such practices perish, and his sister, the queen, be dishonoured and lost thereby for ever, ye doubt not but his highness, in this their laudable and virtuous quarrel, will favour, aid, and assist them, encouraging them with such good words, vehement rumours, and comfortable persuasion, to stir and excite not only them, but also all the nobles and commons of Scotland against the said duke, whereby either he shall be in danger at his coming to Scotland, or else be exterminate from thence for ever. And if the sum of 10,000 or 12,000 marks were politicly spent, to set this division in Scotland, and to provoke the indignation of the nobles and subjects against the said duke, in my opinion it should be well employed, considering the great effects and good consequences that thereof may ensue, whereby great sums of money may be saved, as ye well know: the premises considered, I right heartily desire and pray you, after your accustomable prudent and politic manner, not only to set forth these practices with all speedy diligence, but also to advertise me with similar diligence what ye shall and may do therein, whereby ye do marvellous great pleasure and service to the king's highness, much redounding to his honour and the surety of his realm, assuring you that whatsoever you shall promise, lay out, or covenant, with the said nobles, keeping yourself within the bounds of the said sums, till ye may advertise me of your said further advice, it shall be surely contented and paid unto you, requiring you to do effectual diligence therein.

LETTER XI.

ROBERT SHAW, ABBOT OF PAISLEY, TO CARDINAL WOLSEY,
(FOR PROMOTION.)

(From the Cottonian Library.)

MY LORD,—In my most humble manner I recommend my right lowly service to your grace, certifying the same that your king's highness, your sovereign's ambassador, being in the court of Rome, has, at the instance and request of your grace, solicited the pope's holiness for my promotion to the bishopric of Murray, according to my humble prayer made to your grace before . . . . because that the king's highness, my master, has written for the promotion of a son of the earl of Arran to my abbacy of Paisley, he being of tender age and bastard, our holy father the pope, in consideration of your promise, defers promoting of me to the said bishopric; howbeit, as impediments rising on the part of the said earl's son, ought not in reason to defer my cause, therefore it will please your grace to deign to write to the said ambassador, being with our said holy father, for expedition of my matter, letting the promotion stand suspended whilst that better ways be laboured; and, further, give safe conduct to my brother, too, for waiting upon my said business, and give him leave to pass into Flanders to that effect; assuring your grace, that in so far as my poor power may extend, I shall not fail to be ever a faithful and true servant to the king's highness, your sovereign, and your grace—above all others, next my sovereign and master—as of just cause I am.

To do like as Master Magnus, your truest servant can show. Praying God to preserve your grace in prosperity. At Edinburgh, the 8th day of May, by your grace's humble servant and entreator, at his extreme power,

ROBERT, ABBOT OF PAISLEY.

LETTER XII.

THE EARL OF ARGYLE TO CARDINAL WOLSEY, (SOLICITING THE CARDINAL'S INTEREST TO GET THE ABBEY OF CUPAR FOR HIS BROTHER.)

(From the Cottonian Library,)

MY LORD, I commend me in my most hearty and effectual manner unto your good grace . . . . please it to wit that the king's grace, my sovereign, has written to the pope's holiness, and to the king's highness of England, for promotion of a brother of mine to the abbey of Cupar within this realm; and I have written in likewise to his grace, in most lowly and humble manner . . . . . for my lord; and, because I hope in God, that for the love betwixt the king's highness, your master and mine, and amongst the subjects of both your realms, I would be so bold that I would write humbly to your grace.

I beseech you to further the promotion of my said brother in the best manner as your grace thinks expedient; and it would please ye, too, to promote . . . of mine, called Dougal Campbell. And, my lord, if that there be any service or labour that I can do your grace in this realm, truly there shall be none in it that shall accomplish the same with better heart nor mind nor I shall. And farther, I have shown my mind at length to your grace's right trusty and wise . . . . . . Master Thomas Magnus . . . . . to. I pray your grace to give firm credence in all that he shall show your grace . . . . fully in my behalf. And God Almighty have your grace in his blessed keeping. Written, &c. Edinburgh, the 27th day of May. Yours, WILLIAM OF ARGYLE.

LETTER XIII.

GAWIN DOUGLAS, BISHOP OF DUNKELD, TO WOLSEY.

(From the Cottonian Library.)

PLEASE your grace, my chaplain, which was yesterday at your presence, shows me that Galt, the secretary of the duke of Albany, has said to your grace that I promised not to come within this realm; and wherefore, of his master's behalf, beseech your grace to withhold me herein, and let me pass no farther. My lord, I believe your high wisdom will not give credence so lightly against me; and specially to the duke of Albany, or any of his servants, which is capital and deadly enemy to me and all my house. And, therefore, it is no wonder albeit he say such things for my harm, which divers times, and yet daily, hath said and done all that he may or can imagine to my destruction, and extermination of all my kin.

And, as I shall answer to God and your grace, the contrary of it he said, is plain written; for, both by messenger and writing, I declared how plainly I would pass through this realm, and no other way, and showed him what day I had appointed to enter in your ground of England; the which I kept truly. And this your grace may consider what favour he has to me, or how I should be entreated, if I was in Scotland under his subjection; or when, if I passed to France, or any other part where he may solicit anything, when he is so bold within this realm (wherein I trust he has little credence,) as for to solicit your grace to my hurt. Albeit you have granted me the king's highness safe conduct, the which, I trust, I shall not forfeit, nor yet your grace will suffer to be taken from me. Beside this, the matter is precious; if any kirkman should be stopped going to Rome for his lawful defence on summons thither, as, nevertheless, your grace knows full well, I may be lightly entreated to remain here, but no ways at his command nor desire; and full well I wot your high wisdom knows what is to be done on any service to such a pretension much better nor I and many such can imagine. Albeit, if it might stand with your pleasure, I would bespeak your grace to answer to this Galt; that if the duke, his master, will be content my action and matter be remitted forth from Rome to your grace, and before your arbitration, whereof I would be glad, your grace should cause me remain; and, also, why or how should you hold me from my lawful defence, which is of the law of nature; specially I having the king's safe-conduct to pass, as said is? This is my little case, under correction of your grace, whom I beseech to pardon this my so homely writing; and the Holy Trinity have your grace in keeping. At London, this new year's day, subscribed with the hand of your humble beadsman,

GAWN OF DUNKELD.

LETTER XIV.

WOLSEY TO THE KING'S AMBASSADORS IN SCOTLAND.

MASTER Magnus and master Ratcliff I commend me unto you in my right hearty manner. Since your arrival in the court of Scotland, I received sundry of your letters to me addressed; whereof the last beareth the date at Edinburgh, the 10th day of this instant month; wherein ye have full substantially declared, as well the state and disposition in the which ye find the affairs and state of Scotland, as also the substance of such things as ye, following the tenour of your instructions and letters sent unto you have done, with the queen, lords, and others of Scotland, since your coming into those parts.

And, forasmuch as unto all material points contained in your said letters except the last, and such letters and copies as the duke of Norfolk sent with the same, answer hath been made to the said duke, as the case hath required; though things devised here to be written by him, to you and other, have been altered, changed, and not executed as hath been commanded, I shall therefore now make answer unto your said last letters, copies, and writings, the effects whereof consist principally in these things following:

First, albeit the queen of Scots persisteth in her wilfulness against her husband, the earl of Angus; yet, nevertheless, it seemeth, she and the lords of Scotland be determined that ambassadors shall be sent with diligence unto the king's highness; and that the queen, upon your good exhortations, showeth herself conformable to take sad and wise counsellors about her, by consent of the lords of the parliament.

Secondly, that the archbishop of Saint Andrews maketh outward demonstration to be very well inclined unto the amity of England, showing some towardness that he could be content to come in the embassy. Howbeit divers persons have informed you he would change and vary.

Thirdly, that the said queen and lords would not the earl of Angus should be at the parliament, but have made an overture of his return to Berwick, and remaining there during the same; and there the reconciliation of him to the queen, and agreement with the earl of Arran, to be treated.

Fourthly, the queen's desire for continuance of the . . . men in wage, with increase of one hundred more, to the which queen ye have delivered . . . ., intending also to pay the wage of the said . . . men, if it be sent unto you; fearing lest, if ye should not do so, it might be a means to stop the coming of ambassadors.

Fifthly, that for the same doubt and fear, ye kept back and would be well advised, before ye delivered to the lords of Scotland the king's letters lately sent unto them, or to the queen, such letters as the duke of Norfolk then wrote unto her. And finally, the strange dealing of the said queen and lords, not being contented that ye shall much longer reside and remain there, as in your said letters and writings is mentioned more at large.

As hereunto the king's highness, who hath heard and understood the contents of all your said letters and writings, giveth unto you full good thanks for your discreet and diligent acquittal, used in the charge to you committed, ascertaining you, that when his grace, I, and other of his counsel, have, by mature deliberation, well pondered and considered the said material points, we find that the same, with all the residue of these matters and affairs of Scotland, consisteth upon one of the two things following, whereupon all the residue must depend; that is to say, whether the queen and lords of Scotland perceiving and knowing how the king's highness proceedeth with them, be of mind and inclination to train their king and themselves unto the amity of England, intending to establish a perfect confidence and entire love between the two princes and their realms, being glad so to do, for their own ease, weal, surety, and profit; or else continuing in their former jealousy and suspicion of the king's grace and this realm, with strange and contrarious minds from any good concord or unity to be conduced and brought about, they would rather adhere unto France, training their king to the devotion thereof, so to depend upon the line of the French king, as of him in whom they will have their most assured and special trust and confidence, using the king's highness and this realm as though his grace should be glad to seek for their amity, or had any need or necessity thereof, and not to accept and take the benevolence and bounteous goodness of his grace to proceed of the good will and entire affection that his highness beareth to his dearest nephew and sister the king and queen of Scots, as it doth, recognising and acknowledging themselves highly obliged and bounden unto his grace therefore, and using themselves with mutual correspondence of all kindness as to reason and congruence doth appertain. These be the things which are first and prin-

cipally to be noted, being more material than either sending
ambassadors, pacification of particular quarrels and dis-
pleasures, entertainment of guards, and other like things,
which must depend hereupon. And, therefore, in your doings
and proceedings there, though sending of ambassadors is an
appearance of further towardness, yet lacking a determination
in Scotland to seek and desire to live in firm peace and amity
with this realm, it is not the coming of ambassadors with
hollow and strange minds and intentions, that shall principally
contribute to this business; verily the king's highness perceiving by your letters that the queen of Scots, notwithstanding her wilfulness in not following as yet the king's good
advice towards her husband, is minded nevertheless to advance
the sending of ambassadors, thinketh, that if their setting
forth be in apparent towardness, as by your said letters it
seemeth to be, the same is not now by any sharp dealing or
demonstration to be impeded or hindered; but that the said
queen and lords, having intention and mind, by such despatch
of ambassadors, to procure the good of peace, should rather
in their so doing be comforted, and the more kindly and
favourably entreated and handled. So, inasmuch as the
archbishop of Saint Andrews showeth himself outwardly
right loving and conformable to further this amity, and hath
right good and secret conferences with you touching the
same, he is to be entertained with the best words and manner,
and is to be accepted as ye write, according to his demonstrations and surety. If he could be reasonably induced to come
in the embassy himself, it is not to be doubted but that, by
means of his great wisdom and experience, matters should
take much the better effect; for which purpose I have written
a good letter unto him at this time, like as by the copy thereof;
which, with the original to be delivered unto him, I send
you herewith, ye shall perceive more at large. And the said
copy shall be a sufficient instruction unto you how ye may,
as of yourself, secretly and friendly exhort and advise him
so to do, putting him in comfort, that as great honour and
profit is like to ensue unto him thereof, and peradventure
greater than ever had any archbishop in Scotland. Beside
this, the queen of Scots, proceeding lovingly and kindly with
the king's grace in all other her doings, it is not the matter
most material at this time, whether she will yet accept the

earl of Angus to her favour or not. Nor were it wisdom that the king's grace, now that he hath suffered him to enter into his country, which his highness had no honourable colour to deny him, should so stick unto the making up of the differences between the queen, the earl of Arran, and him, that it should seem to be a matter that the king's grace would prefer to be mixed with the affairs and causes of the realm.

Howbeit somewhat it is to be marvelled for what ground or occasion he should be inhibited to come unto the parliament, considering that he is one of the chief noblemen of that realm and a true subject unto his prince, unless the lords of Scotland, not bearing unto him, as it appeareth, so much favour and good will as by many and many letters sent hither from the borders hath been mentioned, would mind in the said parliament to pass something at the queen's request which shall be to his extreme prejudice and detriment; for, since his coming into Scotland, there hath not yet hitherto, as far as is known here, been shown any corroboration that he is so well beloved, or hath such a party in that realm as hath been reported, but rather it is to be thought, that the lords who cannot suffer any great preeminence or superiority to be in one of themselves above the other, doubt that he, being husband unto the queen, whom for that she is a great princess they could suffer to have the shadow or visage of government, should after his reconciliation unto her favour, rule all the residue; and for that cause very like it is that this divorce hath proceeded for training of him unto her will, till such time as the parliament might be finished, and he neither privy to their drifts and compasses, nor present to withstand such things as might sound to his derogation or hindrance, which thing were far discrepant from honour and reason. And right loath would the king's highness be to see or know such effect to be brought to pass, he being by the king's lieutenant advised and desired to repair unto Berwick; wherein one thing is specially to be noted: the said queen allegeth that it is much against her honour that the earl of Angus should thus be sent into Scotland without her consent and agreement; but she nothing regardeth how much it should sound to the king's dishonour either to have detained him any longer here, having no occasion so to do; or now to allure him unto Berwick, as though his grace were constrained to keep

T

him out of Scotland, till the said queen's pleasure were determined. And if any notable thing should be done against him during his abode in Berwick, then should it also much more touch the king's honour. Wherefore his grace, and other of his counsel, do not a little marvel that either my lord of Norfolk, or you, would consent to such overture, or write therein to the said earl, unless ye might first have had some evident appearance upon what ground the same should have been done, and have well known that it must be for some great or good effect. But if ye may perceive the queen and the lords so to proceed with you that the king's honour be not herein touched, and the matters to be in train, according to the king's mind and desire; then, though the said earl were absent from the parliament, so his presence there should do hurt neither to the assembly of the lords or sending of ambassadors, it is not the thing which the king's grace would ye should stick at.

And likewise the money that ye have given unto the queen, and the payment of the . . . men for one month, if it be done already, may be suffered; ye finding the queen and lords in such good disposition as is aforesaid.

As to delivery of the king's letters to the lords, it is not to be a little marvelled that ye would respite or defer the doing thereof, considering that the matter therein contained is thankful and acceptable, and nothing in the same letters mentioned which soundeth to the said queen's dispraise or dishonour, but rather for the preservation of the same; assuring you, that these letters were devised not without mature deliberation of said counsel, knowing that if, upon particular displeasure, there should be surmise made to the lords of Scotland of any unreasonable demand required by the king's highness, the said letters should be a sufficient declaration unto them, whereby they might know the king's good meaning and intent; but when things be devised here for conducting of the king's matters, and the same by some shall be changed and altered to their device and fantasy, and by others pretermitted, and not delivered, or not put in execution, according to the commandment given in that behalf, it is no marvel though matters many times perish and have adverse success, the experience whereof partly may appear in the delivery of my letter unto the archbishop of Saint Andrews, which much confirmed him in his devotion towards the king's grace; if all other had been delivered in time, and all instructions followed with such sentences, clauses, and manner, as they were here couched, it is not to be doubted but better effect would have ensued thereof; and therefore if the king's said letters be not yet delivered, there is no cause why ye should not, without further delay of time, give the same, considering that they shall rather advance the coming of the ambassadors, and confirm the lords in the king's devotion, than otherwise.

So as for this point, ye do perceive that, finding the queen and lords in such good mind and towardness as is aforesaid, and the ambassadors determined to be sent without further delay, it were not convenient to hinder or disturb the same, but rather to advance it with as good and convenient ways, without suit or desiring them thereunto, as ye can devise.

On the other part, it is to be considered what hath, at and since your departure from hence, been notified to the duke of Norfolk and you, by instructions, letters, and otherwise, touching the plan, form, and manner of the king's intent and meaning in these matters of Scotland, not being grounded upon other thing, but only upon the benevolent and loving mind that the king's grace beareth unto his said dearest nephew and sister, for the proximity of blood and possibility of succession that the said young king is in to the king's highness, and the other good virtues and qualities reported to be in his person; as ye have been largely advertised of the king's mind in that behalf, by you well pondered and regarded, ye may finally perceive that, when the queen of Scots, and lords of that land, shall make strange and high demonstrations unto you in their doings, without due respect had unto the king's gratuities and kindness, but rather use themselves as though the king's highness were fain to seek upon them for amity and friendship, the more ye show yourself inclinable to their demands and requests, and the more they shall perceive you to insist for their good wills, the prouder and more arrogant they shall be; and therefore in this case it were not convenient that, for sending of their ambassadors, which shall be most to their profit and surety, ye should too much follow the queen's mind and desire, or forbear plainly and roundly to open and declare unto her such things as ye have in commandment to do; for by that means

T 2

she shall perceive that only for the weal of her son and herself, the king's grace doth show himself thus benevolent unto them, and not for anything that his grace looketh to win thereby, or to lose by the contrary; whereas, if the plan be not declared unto her, she shall think that the king's highness dare not nor will do anything against her mind, but fulfil all her demands and desires, be they reasonable or not, and so she shall remain in overmuch estimation and arrogance of herself, refusing to condescend unto such things as may be most to the honour, weal, and surety of her and her said son, which perchance she will look more substantially unto, if her ingrate unkind and indiscreet demeanour, be in convenient manner declared unto her. Wherein I lately wrote unto my lord of Norfolk the king's pleasure to be signified unto her, as it was couched in my letters; howbeit both he altered and changed the same far from the fashion that it was in; and still the letters which he sent ye forbear to deliver, as though the coming of the ambassadors should be a thing highly to the king's benefit, and the retardment of them in the said queen's default should sound to the king's extreme hindrance or disadvantage, which was never meant or thought on this side; or that the queen and lords of Scotland, having such fantasy imputed in their mind, should be procured, solicited, or provoked on the king's behalf thereunto. And unless ye have found them of other mind than this, the king's highness doth not a little marvel, that either ye would deliver unto the queen one groat of money, or be of the opinion that the wage of the . . . men should be paid or advanced for the said queen's pleasure, or at her nomination or desire, considering that, by means of the same, she may, if she do not intend and mind to follow the king's ways, make herself and party strong both against the earl of Angus and all other that should be averse to the French faction and pleasure: and therefore if ye have not already made payment for the said . . . men, it shall be wisdom ye be not over hasty in the doing thereof; specially, without ye see the queen in such good train, that the said payment may greatly confer to the furtherance of the king's intent, and do no damage or hindrance to the same.

Finally: whereas there hath been motion made unto you by the queen, by consent and desire of the lords, as she saith, that ye should depart and return home, wherein ye have obtained respite till the coming of the said ambassadors, it is thought very strange that ye, who have been sent thither with such presents, and for demonstration of gratuity and kindness, should be so entreated; whereby there is great appearance that neither the queen nor the lords that make motion of your departure bear any great favour towards the king's grace, but that they have you in suspicion and jealousy, not willing that ye should be privy of their doings and proceedings, unto which matter due regard would be had, for many respects and causes. And if, by good and politic ways, without great pursuit or instance to be made, ye could find the means that, with their good contentation, ye might remain there for a longer season; saying, that when the ambassadors shall be arrived, there may insurge and happen some things wherein it shall be requisite and necessary plainly to explain unto the said queen and lords the king's intent and meaning by mouth, better than can be done by letters of their ambassadors, or by any the king's letters unto the said queen and lords; it is thought your presence and remaining there for a season should do great good; and therefore ye shall, by good dexterity, find the means so to do, if conveniently and honourably, without showing any great desire or fervour on your side thereunto, ye can bring it to pass: but if ye shall perceive that they will be much contrary from it, making great difficulty in the same, then the king's highness is contented that, after the coming of the said ambassadors into England, ye shall take your leave and depart at your pleasure, whereof I doubt not but ye will advertise me before that time, so that I may instruct you of the king's mind and pleasure how ye shall order yourself with the queen and others at your departure after, as it shall be seen, that the said queen and lords shall proceed, and as the case and matters then shall require.

Letter XV.

WOLSEY TO THE KING'S AMBASSADORS WITH THE EMPEROR.

Mr. Sampson and Mr. Jernyngham, I commend me unto you in my most right hearty manner. Since the arrival here of Mr. Boleyn, by whom the king's grace hath been advertised of the state wherein the emperor's matters and affairs stood at his departing, is also come hither Monsieur de Beaurein, sent by the said emperor with letters to the king's grace and me, and also with two instructions; one concerning such matters as he had to be spoken of here, and the other touching certain benefices to be by him done with the duke of G . . a . . e; the effect of both which instructions were taken out and translated into English, and the abstracts of the same, for your better knowledge and understanding, I send unto you herewith. I received also, by the said Beaurein, the letters of you, Mr. Sampson, to me directed, the effect whereof I showed unto the king's grace, who, as well for your diligent writings at that time, as for other your former advertisements, giveth unto you special thanks, like as I do for my part. And forasmuch as by the said two abstracts ye shall amply and fully understand the charge which was committed to Monsieur de Beaurein by the two instructions, I shall therefore refer you thereunto for your knowledge in that behalf, advertising you that, inasmuch as the said Beaurein might not make any abode here, saying that he must be with the said duke at the place prefixed by the latter end of this month; a memorial, therefore, was given unto him of certain things which he should do there on the king's behalf, till such season as Dr. Knight, being ambassador with the lady Margaret, and consequently well on his way, might with commission and instruction sent unto him in diligence, repair also to the same place, there to be present at the diet and treaty with the said duke for the king's part; which commission and instruction, incontinently after the departure of the said Monsieur de Beaurein, were made and sent unto Dr. Knight; the copy whereof and also of the memorial in Latin, given to Beaurein, ye shall receive at this time, so that by all the said copies ye shall know and understand the whole process of everything which hath been devised, concluded, and done by the king's grace and his counsel in this behalf, and how ready and inclined his highness is to every such thing as may sound to the furtherance, benefit, and advancement of the common enterprises and affairs. And in case either the said Monsieur de Beaurein, or the emperor's ambassador here resident, had had any commission or instruction to have treated and concluded with the king's grace, upon the numbers, place, time, and other specialties concerning the advancement of armies, on either side, against France this summer, and for the putting over of the personal invasion, the same had also been fully concluded and agreed; nevertheless, all possible diligence is used here for preparation and putting everything in perfect readiness, that shall be requisite for the army to be sent out of this realm into France, so as, incontinently upon knowledge had from you that the emperor hath concluded a treaty for that purpose, and that ye see real and effectual execution of the same, and advancement forward on that side, the king's army, without delay of time, or delay, shall be in diligence transported, so to proceed according to the conventions and agreements which shall be passed by you in that behalf. Wherefore, ye shall diligently procure and solicit the emperor to accelerate his resolution therein, if it be not done already, as I trust verily it is before this time, and your letters despatched hitherwards, containing answer of the same, which for the more surety ye may duplicate, so as, for lack of knowledge from thence, if any misadventure should happen to your first letters, the king's grace should not remain destitute and unprovided of answer touching the emperor's mind in the premises, without which no fruitful thing, except preparation, can be done, either concerning invasion to be made this year, as is aforesaid, neither also the effectual execution of the treaty to be passed with the said duke. And what the king's grace hath resolved and done touching the charge of Beaurein, ye being now sufficiently instructed by the said copies, shall, with the king's most cordial and my most humble recommendations, show and declare unto the emperor, with such doubtful points as concern de la Moer, and other suspicions which might arise in this matter, as the thing which, though it be not very apparent, yet the king's grace, who tendereth the emperor's honour and weal as much as his own, would not pretermit to advertise his majesty of any matter that might be doubtful and dangerous unto his affairs.

* Over this ye shall show unto the emperor that, upon safe conduct desired by the king of Denmark, and to him granted, he, with the queen his wife, and one hundred persons in their company, be lately arrived here; when the king's grace, as

---

* The following contains the opinion of the cardinal and the English government on one of the most remarkable incidents of the age of Henry VIII.

well for the honour of his highness and of this his realm, as
for the alliance which is with the said king, by reason of the
queen his wife, hath, for the emperor's and her love and honour,
more than for any demonstration of kindness heretofore
showed by the king of Denmark towards the king's grace and
this realm, received and entertained in the best manner, at
the king's charges and expenses, from their arrival at Calais
forward; since whose coming to the king's presence at Greenwich, where they were for a season lodged and feasted, and
also since their coming to London, where they now be, at
Bath place, all at the king's cost as aforesaid, I have, on the
king's behalf, had sundry conversations with the said king of
Denmark, upon the cause and occasion of his coming hither,
perceiving, in effect, by him, that the crown of the realm of
Denmark is not descended unto him by rightful succession of
inheritance, but by election, as it hath always been accustomed,
the prerogative and jurisdiction of which election resteth in
certain special persons of the same realm, who, at the request
of the late king of Denmark, father to this man, passed the
election of him, in his father's days, to succeed in the said
kingdom after his time, with certain conditions whereunto
they astringed and bound him, for the nonobservance and violation, it should be lawful to the same elisors to depart from his
obeisance: which election so passed, the late old king of Denmark, having at that time another son, and being, this king,
at the time of his said election, but of twelve years of age,
was, by the father's persuasion, after the death of the said
other son, ratified and confirmed. Howbeit the said king
affirmeth, that the conditions were more strange than had
been accustomed to be used in other princes' days, whereunto
he, in that minority, was nevertheless obliged and bounden,
and that, for such matters as the said elisors, with other his
subjects, do allege against him, sounding to the rupture and
breach, as they say, of the said conditions, albeit he was and
is contented if he can be found defective in the same, to
reform and amend anything by him passed; yet, nevertheless,
partly by counsel of the duke of Holstein, and partly by the
instigation of the Steds, enemies to the said king, the said
elisors have abandoned him, and elected his uncle, the said
duke of Holstein, who, with the puissance of his adherents,
so proceeded against the said king, that, if he had not fled

with his wife and children, he and they should (as he saith) not only have been put in danger of their persons, but also he had lost his ships, ordnance, goods, and substance, for which cause he withdrew himself, first towards the emperor's said Low Countries, and now into England, to require, demand, and ask of the emperor, and the king's grace, as well help and assistance, as also advice and counsel. And this is the very cause and manner of his repair hither at this time. Whereupon the king's highness, for the near connexion which the said king of Denmark hath with the emperor by marriage of his sister, who is a princess full of good virtues and manners, and whom the king's grace, as well for the emperor's sake as for her noble qualities, right much doth tender and regard, hath at good length debated and devised upon this matter with me, and other of his counsel, to whom it is thought right strange that the king of Denmark (as he affirmeth) having divers other great patrimonies, countries, and places of his inheritance, and otherwise faithful, sure, and true to him, who will at all times take his part, and receive and obey him as their sovereign lord (the names of which countries and places be mentioned in a bill here inclosed), would thus suddenly depart into remote and strange parts, whereby the more courage and boldness might be given to his adversaries and enemies, both to persist in their displeasant minds towards him, and also to provoke other of his loving subjects to their devotion and party: whereas, by his presence and ostentation of himself, they might perchance with good policy and aid of his loving subjects, have been the more facily vanquished and subdued, or, at the least, induced to have changed their purpose. For which cause, upon good deliberation, and often conversations by me had with the said king of Denmark, I have advised and counselled him in anywise to repair again, with diligence, to such of the said countries and places remaining in his obeisance, as he shall think expedient, making his stay and continuance there, for procuring and labouring such things as may be most beneficial to the recovery of the good wills and minds of the said elisors, lords, and subjects of Denmark, and the reconciliation of him unto his enemies. To the furtherance whereof, it is thought that the emperor, of good congruence and kindness, and the king's grace, for gratuity and love, shall put their hands by good mediation, sending ambassadors and letters, both unto the said elisors, duke of Holstein, and other lords of Denmark, which may labour them to resume and take again their said king, who is contented not only to reform all such things, if any be, as they think him to have done contrary to the said conditions, wherein the king's grace will take upon him and be bound as his surety that he should so do; but also will utterly remit and forgive any displeasure or attempt which they or his subjects have enterprised, done, or committed against him in this his expulsion and new election. And furthermore, means may be made to the said Steds, who have great privileges and liberties in the emperor's and king's regions, that at their contemplation, and for their sakes, they will cease from any hostility, war, or rancour, against the said king, and some amicable composition to be made in the differences depending between them. All which devise the king's grace will cause his ambassadors, resident at the court of Rome, to show unto the pope's holiness, to the intent that the same also may send his briefs and writings, both to the said duke of Holstein, elisors, and others of Denmark, and also to the Steds, for this purpose; with which ambassador expedient it shall be that the emperor's ambassador do also join therein; so that it is verily trusted that the emperor putting his hands effectually hereunto, as of reason and kindness he must needs do, the proximity of blood and fair succession descended between the said king and queen considered, this matter may yet be reduced and brought with labour, help, and policy, into good train, and the said king, with God's grace, by loving and fair means restored to his kingdom without further violence, war, or effusion of blood, which way is meet and expedient to be first attempted, and no further hostility to be raised or stirred, in expendure if it be possible. Nevertheless, if the same shall in nowise do profit or avail unto him, but that the Danes and Steds shall remain obstinate and in pertinacity, without conforming themselves to good order and reason, then further direction may be taken for assistance to be given unto the said king, as well by the king's grace and the emperor, as by such other princes of Germany, and elsewhere, as be his confederates, lovers, and friends. Wherefore ye, showing and declaring the premises, shall procure and solicit despatch of such personages and writings as he will send for this purpose, with commandment to be given to his orator at Rome to join with the king's ambassador as is aforesaid; in which mean time as much shall be done by the king's grace as may be possible, for it is a thing far discrepant from good order, reason, or congruence, that a prince shall thus, by the wilfulness of his lords and commons, be expelled and put from his crown, upon any grievances by them pretended, specially not being the matters first showed and objected unto him, and his answer heard upon the same; ascertaining you that the said king, accepting marvellous thankfully, and in good part, this good advice and counsel, the circumstances whereof I have caused to be put in articles in Latin, which he singularly liketh, is minded, within four or five days to depart with the queen his wife, towards Flanders, where his ships be rigging, so to proceed further according to the said device; praying you, therefore, to ascertain me of the emperor's answer and resolution herein, and in all other the premises, with diligence, as the king's special trust is in you.

Post scripta.—Letters be arrived, as well from the bishop of Bath, being the king's ambassador at Rome, dated there the third day of the last month, as also from Mr. Pace, dated at Venice the first day of the same, the copies of which letters, for your better knowledge and information, I send you with these presents; by tenour whereof you shall, among other things, perceive how, upon the attachment of the cardinal Sodormo, the French king hath revoked his ambassadors, which were on their way towards the pope's holiness, and that in the court of Rome is neither commission nor person deputed for the said French king, to treat either of peace or truce; so as there is no manner, likelihood, appearance, or towardness, that anything may or shall at this time be further done therein, or that the emperor and the king's grace shall ground or establish their common matters thereupon, but substantially to foresee and provide for all such things as may concern the most effectual annoyance of the common enemy. Ye shall further perceive by the said copies, that expectation is to be had of the pope's holiness, who in no wise will be induced to condescend unto any treaty offensive against France, respiting also upon the success of the affairs at Venice, to declare and show his resolute mind, touching his entering into a league defensive, which will be the most that he can be induced unto, and that not without difficulty; for which cause, expedient it shall be that the king and the emperor, without further

delay of time, do with diligence furnish, provide, and look
unto their business, and in such wise press the French king
earnestly, and not with small prickings, which as it appeareth
he doth little esteem, that he may be constrained and enforced
otherwise to himself than hitherto he doth begin. In which
matter ye shall declare and show unto the emperor the king's
opinion, consisting in two material points. The first and
greatest thing considered by his grace and his counsel is,
that, remembering the untowardness and obstinacy of the
said French king, it is now thought expedient, by all the
means and ways possible, to accelerate the personal invasion,
and for that purpose to devise how in anywise it may be
feasible, as well by forbearing and sparing other particular
charges, which might sound to the delay and impeachment
thereof, as otherwise; for better it shall be once to annoy the
common enemy with great puissances which he should not be
able to resist, whereby he may be driven to offer and come unto
reasonable conditions, than thus, by driving the time by little
and little, to waste and consume treasure, and in conclusion no
good effect to come thereof: wherefore, if the emperor and
king's grace might be furnished with money, treasure, and
other requisites for a main and great invasion to be made in
their own persons, the sooner the same were done and put in
execution, the rather the common enemy should be brought
and compelled to speak of another time, and perchance some
great and notable victory might thereof ensue, to their great
honour and profits. Nevertheless, if for lack of furniture of
money and treasure, the emperor and the king's grace should
not now do the same in their own persons till the next
summer in the year next following, by which time it shall be
seen what the French king will further do touching peace,
then it is thought a way might be taken for making of an
expedition by lieutenants, the same to invade in such places,
taking the year before them, and with such force and puissance
as some notable effect might ensue thereof, and the enemy
enforced to know himself: the debating and devising of which
matters, by common consent, might, in the residue of this
summer and the next winter, be practised, commenced, and
concluded, so that at the beginning of the next year the same
might be executed accordingly, which is thought a more discreet and prudent way, and better effect shall ensue thereof,
than to defer the enterprises till the summer be almost spent,

as hath been this present year, and as they shall and may be
furnished with money on both sides for the performance of
the premises, either by invasion in person, or by lieutenants.
Necessary shall it be that mutual frank and plain advertisement be made thereof, from time to time, to the intent that
everything may proceed to the honour of both princes, annoyance of the common enemy, and eschewing of superfluous and
vain expenses as shall appertain; for, by such dribbling war
as yet hitherto hath been made by the said princes, the common enemy is rather exalted, contemning and little or nothing
regarding them, than driven to knowledge himself, or come to
honest conditions of truce and peace, desiring the continuance
of war in such manner rather than otherwise, supposing
thereby that the said princes shall be impoverished, and he
little or nothing damaged or annoyed. And in case the
emperor and the king's grace cannot be furnished neither to
invade in their persons, nor by their lieutenants, as above,
wherein plainness ought to be used, and all dissimulation or con-
cealment laid apart: then, by mutual counsel it must be devised
how, and by what good means they may come to an honourable peace, for thus to stand and continue so long in war without doing any notable damage to the enemy, can neither be
to their honour, nor endured by their realms and subjects.

The other matter which the king's grace and his counsel
have special respect unto is this: ye know the full resolution
of his grace touching such things as be to be done this year,
for the answer whereof, and knowledge of the emperor's
mind in the same, his highness looketh to be advertised with
such diligence that, giving one month's respite after the time
of the said answer to assemble and transport his army, the same
may be entered into the enemy's countries by the midst of
August at the furthest; for, as the emperor may well consider
if, for lack of such knowledge in time, the whole month of
August should peradventure expire before the king's army
might be in the field, rainy weather then in September
daily running on, and the army intended to be sent unto
Boulogne, as ye well know, it should not be possible either
for the shortness of time to do any good there, or also in that
foul and wet country to convey back again the artillery and
ordnance. Whereof, consequently, should ensue none other
but waste and expenses of money, loss of the artillery, and
great dishonour; for which cause the king's pleasure is, that

ye, showing the premises to the emperor, do substantially note whether as well the armies to be prepared on that side may be advanced and entered into the French king's country before or by the midst of August at the farthest; as also that your advertisement of the same may come in such time as the king's army, with the said one month's warning, may do the like on this side; in which case the king's grace is and will be right well contented to follow and perform the device and agreement had thereupon, for the execution whereof nothing, in the meantime, is here pretermitted. Nevertheless if either the emperor's armies cannot be so soon ready in those parts, or that his resolution be not so soon taken, sent, and here arrived, that, with the said one month's warning, the king's army, and the other assistance to be sent unto them out of the emperor's Low Countries, may be ready in the field before midst of August, which is as much or more necessary to be done at that time hence than on that side—the strength of the country and the great ordnance requisite to be carried considered. Then it is thought unto the king's grace and his counsel, that better it were to leave and forbear the sending of any such armies this summer, and to spare the money that should be spent in the same for the said personal invasion, than out of time to advance them, and with loss, reproaches, and damage, to return them. And, in the meantime, the emperor and the king's grace, standing in mere terms of defence, and providing sufficiently as well for furniture of their towns, fortresses, and places, as for guarding of the seas with some good and meet ships—that is to say, the emperor from the trade along the coast of Spain, and the king from the trade hither, and so to the coast of Flanders, and they to look there to the guarding of the said quarters; sure they may be that not only their countries and subjects shall be well defended, and with small charges in comparison of the other, but also the common enemy, in the mean season, the more wearied, fatigued, and impoverished; whereby, at the time of the said personal invasion, they should be of the much better strength and ability to maintain themselves for a great space, which is requisite to be done, if any fruit or good effect shall ensue thereof; and to begin in the latter end of the year, when no tarrying or abode may be to do any effectual annoyance to the enemy. And if, perchance, it might be thought that this time were most opportune and convenient by reason of the duke of . . . . . I doubt not but by the time that the emperor and his counsel shall have groundly pondered and noted the difficulties contained before in these my present letters, which peradventure before were not thought upon, it shall appear that there is not like to grow so great benefit or commodity thereof as was esteemed. I require you, therefore, circumspectly and discreetly to handle this matter with the emperor, taking such direction, by your prudent demonstrations to be made unto him herein, that neither the time in making these sober wars against the enemy be thus longer consumed, but that by the advancement of the said personal invasion this next year he may be earnestly handled, as is aforesaid; nor also, that the enterprises to be done this summer be so late by you there concluded, that for lack of knowledge in the time before limited, the king's grace be driven to advance his army and people, and spend his money and time in vain, and consequently no good done, but rather reproach, loss, and damage to be sustained. And of the emperor's resolution in all and singular the premises, with such other knowledge and successes as shall occur in the mean season, I pray you diligently to advertise me, from time to time, as the king's grace specially trusteth you.

And whereas in sundry former letters and instructions given unto Mr. Boleyn and you Mr. Sampson, ye were commanded to solicit and procure the speedy sending into these narrow seas of an army of 3000 men; which thing the king's grace moved and desired, only because at that time the French king prepared a great and puissant army to have been set to the sea, intending, if he might, to have been lord of the same; inasmuch as the same French king, upon knowledge had of the king's army by sea put in readiness, which he saw well he was not able to countervail, hath now left off the setting forth and advancement of his said great army, not being minded, as far as the king's grace can learn, to send out the same this year. The king's highness, therefore, having as great respect to the saving of the emperor's charges as of his own, and rather more, being minded to further everything that may be to the determination of the said charges, so as thereby they may be the more able to make the said personal invasion, willeth, that ye shall show unto his majesty, that for the said considerations he shall not need to put himself to charge at this time for sending of the said

3000 men, but only to provide for the guarding of those seas from the trade along the coast of Spain, as is aforesaid, so as the merchants and subjects of both princes and other their friends, may pass to and fro out of danger as shall appertain. And so heartily fare ye well. At my place beside Westminster, the third day of July. Your loving friend.

T. CARDLIS. EBOR.

To my loving friend, Mr. Richard
Sampson, dean of the king's
Chapel, and sir Richard Jerningham, knights, king's councillors, and ambassadors with
the emperor.

LETTER XVI.

THE SAME TO THE SAME.

MR. Sampson and Mr. Jerningham, I commend me unto you in my right hearty manner. Since my last letters to you addressed, sent by the hands of Chatel, secretary to the lord Beaurein, divers alterations, changes, and contrarieties, have, to the king's great miscontentment, regret, and displeasure, happened and ensued in the common affairs and enterprises; the circumstances whereof, ye, avoiding all sinister and feigned reports, which might be caused or contrived, shall plainly show and declare to the emperor and his council at length in manner and form following.

First, whereas the duke of Suffolk, and count de Buren, with the common army, after —— was taken by surrender, the town and passage of Bray by force, were determined to have fortified the said Bray, there to have established their staple of victuals, and so to have marched the right way towards Paris; trusting and supposing by the way to have had some word or knowledge from the duke of Bourbon. Desiring the king's grace, therefore, not only to send unto them, against the beginning of November, new furniture of money, but also, in consideration of the decrease and diminution of their numbers, by reason of death and sickness, to cause the army to be enforced, as well with a competent number of English footmen, as also with the supplement of the Burgundians on the emperor's part, in such wise as they might be the more able to encounter with the enemies, when need should be, and also to leave convenient garrisons in such places as they had taken, and should take, for defence of the same; promising that they who then were passed the river of Somme, would proceed to a great open town, not far distant from thence, called Lihons, to abide the king's answer and resolution in that behalf. So it was that, upon knowledge of the premises, the king's highness, being very joyous and glad of this good commencement, trusting verily that after the long delay of time, and great difficulty which had been in default of their carriages and limoners, they should now prosperously and commodiously pass to the annoyance of the common enemy, not only sent immediately unto the town of Calais sufficient furniture of money to have sufficed the said army till the beginning of January at the least, directing letters to the said duke of Suffolk to send unto Calais conduct for the same; but also, with all possible diligence, raised an army of 7000 men, to have passed with speed unto the said Lihons, there to have joined with the residue. And besides that, his grace immediately wrote unto the lady Margaret and count de Buren, desiring and instantly requiring them, that the Burgundians, which were then evil payed, and in default thereof daily steal away, might from thenceforth be sufficiently furnished of their payment, and also number of them as lacked might be fulfilled and supplied. To which purpose his highness furthermore instructed you by letters, sent by Chatel, to call upon the emperor for commandment and sure order to be given in that behalf. And was utterly resolved and determined, that the said army should have tarried in the enemies' countries all this winter; the Burgundians doing the like, as the letters sent unto the said duke of Suffolk, count de Buren, and also to the lady Margaret, his highness signified unto them at length. Nevertheless, the king's letters so passed, the money also arrived at Calais, and there remaining, for lack of conduct, and the said enforcement being on the way to Dover there to have taken shipping, suddenly came new letters from the said duke of Suffolk and count de Buren, showing how that Bray was not nor could not be made in short space strong or tenable; and that, as well for more commodious saving of victuals, as for conveyance of money to the Burgundians, and the better joining with the duke of Bourbon, they discharging the garrisons of Amere and Bray,

U

and throwing down the walls, gates, and bulwarks of them
both; destroying also the strength of the said passage; were
fully minded and determined to march towards a place in the
confines of Champaigne, far distant from the said Bray, called
Lanlemoys, trusting there, or by the way, to have some knowledge from the said duke of Bourbon where they might best
join with him, making in those letters neither mention of
money or reinforcement; but only that for the space of twelve
days they could neither send nor receive any letters to or
from the king's grace, showing how they had countermanded
their victuals, great ordnance, and all other things, which
was coming towards them from St. Omers; giving an order,
that as well the same as letters and other requisites to be
sent unto them, should be conveyed unto Valenciennes.   Of
which news and alterations, seeming to precede of the Burgundians, the king's highness not a little marvelled; trusting,
nevertheless, that upon receipt of his former letters, received
with more additions requisite to the purpose, the said duke
and count would have changed this their new deliberation
and intent.   Howbeit the king's hope and expectation therein
was wholly frustrate; for they had so secluded, stopped, and
broken the passages behind them, that not only in twelve days,
but in sixteen, no word, messenger, or letter, did or could
arrive or be sent from the one to the other.   In which
time sundry reports were raised of divers great exploits
done by the said army, whereof no certainty could be had;
whereby the king's grace was still in good hope, advancing
and setting forward the reinforcement, with all other things
requisite for continuance of his army, except only that,
upon this new knowledge, the reinforcement was stayed
at the sea side, till advertisement might be had to what
place they should be sent.   In the mean season letters were
brought from the lady Margaret, declaring resolutely that
she could not, nor might, make any provision for continuance of the said Burgundians, desiring the king therefore to
furnish the same, or at the least till the first day of January
next ensuing.   Of which tidings his grace, who then had an
army of 6000 men against the duke of Albany and the Scots,
besides his armies on the sea, to his grace's extreme charge,
was right heavy and sorry; whereunto, after the said twenty-
one days expired, was added new discomfortable matter, when

his grace, by letters of the said duke of Suffolk and count de
Buren, understood that they in this mean season had taken
Montidier, one of the strongest towns of France, situate six
miles beyond the river of Somme, right meet for the duke of
Bourbon, if need had been to have lain in this winter. And
that, after a right good feat done upon Pontremy and a certain band of French horsemen, whereof sixty at the least
were taken, and among them some good personages, and as
many slain, they had also defeated the strength of the said
Montidier, taken and pillaged Roi, abandoned them both, and
were again returned on this side of the river of Somme;
affirming, that unless they should so have done, the money
of the Burgundians, which as they said was then at Valenciennes, could not in surety come unto them; saying, nevertheless, that after the same, and also the king's said money
being at Calais (for the which they had then sent) received,
they were in as good place to follow their former journey
towards Lan le Lannoys, as they were on the other side of
the said river. And the said duke of Suffolk promising that,
having continuance of the Burgundians, he would not fail to
observe and accomplish the same; of which news concerning
this the said duke's former intent, the king's grace take right
good comfort, and should have taken much more, if his
highness had not been advertised, as well of the said answer
and express refusal made by the said lady Margaret, as also
that the 10,000 lance-knights, which were under the leading
of the count Felix, after their wages paid by the king's grace,
and a great booty taken, the rest of the 100,000 crowns also
arrived for the king's part, were totally retired and gone
home; and the duke of Bourbon utterly resolved to pass with
diligence to the emperor. Which news, all accounted together,
showed in manner a mere impossibility that the king's army
could continue this winter, specially lacking their horsemen,
without whom they could do no good. And being now no
time to make provisions of men in this realm or elsewhere,
considering also that the duke of Bourbon, who at the last,
with the horsemen which he had levied, might have joined
with the king's army, though he lacked his lance-knights,
had also discharged them; all which things did put the king's
grace in some discontent, abiding daily more knowledge of
the certainty. Nevertheless, the said duke of Suffolk and

count de Buren, understanding by this time, from the lady
Margaret and otherwise, that she could not nor might furnish
to the further entertainment of the said Burgundians; perceiving also how their horses and people of both companies,
daily and nightly died in great numbers for cold; and that
if the same should so continue they could not convey their
ordnance from the place where it then was, being within the
enemy's countries, without any knowledge, consent, or commandment of the king's grace; other strong place taken,
which his highness is minded to keep with a good garrison,
repaired and retired wholly and entirely unto Valenciennes;
where the king's army still remaineth, abiding knowledge of
the king's pleasure. Albeit the Burgundians be a good
season passed, departed every one to his own dwelling-house.
Whereupon the king's grace, having knowledge thereof, and
considering in what state be the present affairs of Italy, the
emperor being also, as it is here supposed, in the field in
person, hath given order and commandment unto his said
lieutenants and army, that if in anywise they can have continuance of the said Burgundians, either for the whole winter
or at the least for a season, they shall endeavour themselves
by redoubling of their limoners, and otherwise in anywise to
remain, proceeding again to the enterprises as long as may
be possible; and at the least to resort again to the places at
this side the river of Somme, taking Doulens and Corbe if
it may be; and to establish garrisons in the same, in such wise
as it may evidently appear unto the French king that the
king's grace is not minded to leave his enterprises; nor that
his army shall be discharged from those parts, if in anywise
the same may be continued by garrison or otherwise. And that
the Burgundians will join with them again for that purpose.
Of whom, nor also of the complement of carriages promised
by the lady Margaret to have been provided, they could never
be fully furnished by a great deal; which, besides the long
retardment of the king's army at Calais, the Burgundians
then also not being ready, hath been a marvellous hindrance
unto the common affairs, that else had been much further advanced in the commodious time of the year, and perchance
the enemy by this time have been brought thereby unto right
base and low state. All which premises you shall at length
show and declare unto the emperor, being the very truth and

plainness of the matter, least that perchance the lady Margaret, knowing by report of the count of Buren and other Burgundians, that the duke of Suffolk consented to retire on this side of the river of Somme, and so to Valenciennes, before answer received from the king's grace touching entertainment of the said Burgundians, or before knowledge had there of skaling of the said lance-knights, shall, for her justification to the emperor, make demonstration unto his majesty that there was nor should have been any lack in the entertainment of the Burgundians in case the king's army would have tarried; and for that cause I send unto you, herewith, not only the copies of certain clauses, written at sundry times, by the duke of Suffolk, showing and declaring the great lack of payment of the said Burgundians, which caused them to fall unto spoil, besides the diminution of their numbers, but also copies as well of the count of Buren's letters, written to the king's grace and to me; wherein he showed the non-likelihood of their said entertainment, which was the total cause of the first intended way from Bray abandoned and forsaken; as also of the lady Margaret's letters, written to the emperor's ambassadors here resident, mentioning how she could not nor might furnish money for continuance of the Burgundians as is aforesaid; which things plainly notified unto the emperor, shall put his majesty out of any doubt that the dissolving of the said army was not in the king's fault, or by his will or consent; but is, I assure you, as highly to the displeasure and miscontent of his highness as can be possibly devised or imagined. Nevertheless, since there is now no remedy, his grace will, as well by keeping garrison in the said ——, if it be tenable, and also, if it be possible, in the said towns on this side of the river of Somme, as by all other means, plainly show and prove his assured and perfect mind and intent not to desist from his enterprises in France, but effectually to continue the same, according to the emperor's desire and contemplation. For the better performance whereof his grace hath sent in post after the duke of Bourbon, desiring him, if he be not too far past in his journey, to pass by this the king's realm, as well for his more surety, commodity, and brief expedition, as also to the intent that, upon communication and device, to be had between the king's highness and him, of such further things as be now to be done and enterprised touching the common affairs, the emperor may at his coming and repair unto him, be the more perfectly ripe therein; and the same more directly, by mutual understanding and knowledge from the one to the other, be put in execution, than should be if the said duke passed by Genoa first into Spain, and then thither, as he affirmeth he is minded to do. Howbeit, by such knowledge as is had from sir John Russell, who lieth at Besançon, with the king's money last sent, for payment of the said lance-knights, it should seem that the said duke is already very far on his journey towards Genoa, so as it is thought it shall be too late to send any knowledge to him of the king's said mind and desire. And much it is to be feared least his passage by that way shall be very dangerous. Wherefore, if he shall happen safely to arrive by that way with the emperor, the matter must be taken as it now may be, and the more speedy diligence is to be used, for advertisement to be given unto the king's highness of every thing accordingly.

[Here follow two pages in cypher.]

Over this ye shall show unto the emperor how that, after the great preparations, brags, and boasts made by the duke of Albany, with his Frenchmen and Scots, to invade this the king's realm, and the number of . . . . Scots, at least, assembled and raised for that purpose, he marching with them towards this the king's said realm, furnished right plenteously of ordnances, victuals, and other necessaries, did set forth a truce or peace, to have been treated or communed of by the mean of the king's sister, the queen of Scots, with comprehension of France. Whereunto, besides his hope, answer was made, that as long as he and his Frenchmen were in the realm of Scotland, or the Scots given to the party of the French king, they should never have peace, truce, or other appointment, with many other clauses mentioned in letters of the earl of Surrey, the king's lieutenant for the time in the north parts of this realm, to the reproach and pricking forth of the said duke; whereupon he, after long demurring and lingering upon the borders, trusting that he would come unto Berwick, Carlisle, Norham, or some other strong place, which all were sufficiently furnished for his resistance, came at the last before a poor castle, not yet fully builded and finished, called Wark, wherein were only 100 soldiers,

with a captain named sir William Lislé, unto which place he
bent, and two whole days shot all his great ordnance right
fiercely, being right well, manfully, and valiantly defended;
the third day, early in the morning, he sent over the river
unto this English side, where the base court of the castle was,
3000 Frenchmen and 1500 Scots to give the assault on this
side, while the battery endured on the other, who, being the
base court too large to be with all the rest defended with 100
persons, in process entered the same, giving the assault to
the innerward so eagerly, that, partly by sufferance of the
captain and soldiers, they also entered the same, being slain
with fighting at hard strokes, as fast as they came in, in
suchwise that, after the captain of the French footmen, with
twenty of his company were slain, the rest were driven out
of the inner ward, and by the captain and Englishmen so
freshly pursued, that they, with above 1500 footmen, French
and Scots, then being in the base court, were totally driven
and expelled out of the same, and with loss of above twenty
of them, compelled to flee again over the water, where not a
few were drowned for haste. The castle being thus, for that
time, delivered from the danger of that assault, the captain
gave knowledge of the premises to the king's said lieutenant,
who, with his army, was in sundry places in and near Berwick, lodged in the country in three wards and sundry wings,
as commodity of victuals would suffer, and, incontinently
after his army assembled, marched towards Wark, whereof
the said duke being by espial advertised, immediately levied
his siege, and in the night with all celerity returned, as far
as for the time he might, into Scotland, lodging himself and
whole army at an abbey called Eales. Howbeit, being advertised that the king's said lieutenant was arrived at Wark, and
passing the river with his ordnance and army, intending to
pursue the said duke, he the night following, at midnight,
causing the retreat to be formed, in despite of all the Scottish
borderers, who exhorted him to tarry and revenge the dis-
pleasures done unto them, shamefully and cowardly fled and
ran away, marching continually, with small pauses and rests,
till he came to Edinburgh, where, after his army, to his
perpetual shame, skaled, he called a council, and since that
time hath made new overtures of peace or truce, which be
answered as the former were. Whereupon the king's grace,

inasmuch as for the unseasonableness of the time, sterility, barrenness, and softness of the ground there, no main invasion can as yet be made into Scotland, hath established great garrisons on those borders, who do and shall make continual excursions and roads into that land, devasting and destroying the same, till such time as the commodious time of the year shall come for further annoyance to be made unto them, of which good successes, without loss of any Englishman or hurt of one, may be done to this realm. Albeit the said duke, by his journey, in manner hath destroyed Scotland for many years, the king's grace doubteth not but the emperor will be very joyous and glad, trusting in Almighty God that, by continuance of the wars this spring of the year, and the summer coming, the Scots shall be compelled to know themselves, and either abandon the said duke and faction of France, or else to be of little ability to do any annoyance unto this the king's realm, in presence or absence of his grace, for a long time to come.

Finally, I send unto you, here enclosed, copies of the king's and my letters to the duke of Bourbon, sent by his servant, bearer hereof; after whose arrival to the emperor, ye shall, on the king's and my behalf, salute him with cordial recommendations, rehearsing unto him by mouth how displeasant it was to the king's highness and me to hear and understand of the retirement of the said lance-knights, by whose continuance, after the said duke once joined with them, the king's army, who, ensuing the emperor and the said duke's advice and counsel, left all sieges, and, marching into the bowels of France, and of travers of the same, only to join or be near unto the said duke, and he, with his horsemen and lance-knights, were like to have utterly caused a clear mutation in France, to the high renown of the emperor, the king's grace, and the said duke, whereas by the said retirement matters be now greatly hindered and changed. And nevertheless, if the said duke, after the lance-knights departed, had yet drawn with his horsemen towards the king's army, they should have been puissant enough to have kept the field; and at the least the said duke might have kept Montidier, strengthening the same for his abode there this winter, which would have been a notable countenance against the common enemy. Howbeit, since there is now herein no remedy, ye shall say unto him that the king's grace and I shall think long to hear of such farther ways as be to be devised for the redubbing thereof, and the farther pursuing of the common enterprises, wherein, neither with the rest of the 100,000 crowns, nor with any other thing that may be done on the king's part, and for the honour and weal of the said duke, shall be any lack or default on this side; with such other good words as ye may perceive shall sound to the confirmation of the things mentioned in the said copies; saying furthermore, both unto the emperor and unto him, that, upon knowledge of their minds what way shall now farther be taken, afore the king's grace will send unto you commission for conclusion of all matters with the said duke accordingly; and of his answer herein I pray you to advertise me with diligence, as well of all such things as ye do, can, or shall know touching the intent of the emperor, and of the said matters, concerning practices or appointments, and other the premises, as also of the good news, successes, and speed of the emperor's army, whereof to hear the king's grace thinketh very long; and also of such occurrences as shall happen them from time to time; signifying unto you, sir Richard Jerningham, that the king's highness, in consideration of your travails and pains sustained there, hath appointed you to be his vice-chamberlain, and the same office doth keep and reserve for you purposely, till your coming and return, praying you both not to be slack in often advertisements, considering how much damage and hindrance the lack thereof doth unto the common causes and affairs, which his highness and I both trust ye will ponder and consider, supplying hereafter the far distance of the places by your diligent dispatches and writings, wherein ye shall administer unto his grace very thankful and acceptable service to be considered and remembered accordingly. And fare ye heartily well. At my place besides Westminster, the fourth day of December, 1523.

Your loving friend,

T. CARDLIS. EBOR.

To my loving friends, Mr. Richard Sampson, doctor of the law, and dean of the king's chapel; and sir Richard Jerningham, knight; the king's counsellors and ambassadors to the emperor.

Letter XVII.

LORD SURREY TO CARDINAL WOLSEY.

PLEASE it your grace to be advertised, that upon Friday, at ten o'clock at night, I returned to this town, and all the garrisons to their places assigned, the bishopric men, my lord of Westmoreland, and my lord Dacre, in likewise every man home with their companies without loss of any men, thanked be God, saving eight or ten slain, and divers hurt at skirmishes and assaults of the town of Jedburgh and the fortresses, which town is so severely burnt that no garrisons nor none other shall be lodged there unto the time it be new builded; the burning thereof I committed to two sure men, sir William Bulman and Thomas Tempest.

The town was much better than I wot it had been, for there were twice more houses therein than in Berwick, and well builded, with many honest and fair houses therein sufficient to have lodged . . . horsemen in garrison, and six good towers therein, which town and towers be clearly destroyed, burnt, and thrown down. Undoubtedly there was no excursion made into Scotland in no man's day living with so few a number, that is recounted to be so high an enterprise as this, both what these countrymen and Scottishmen, nor of truth so much hurt done; but in the end a great misfortune did fall only by folly that such order as was commanded by me to be kept was not observed; the manner whereof hereafter shall ensue.

Before my entry into Scotland I appointed sir William Bulmer for the vanguard, and sir William Evers for the rearguard. In the vanguard, I appointed my lord of Westmoreland, as chief with all the bishopric, sir William Bulmer, sir William Overs, my lord Dacre, with all his company, and with me remained all the rest of the garrisons and the Northumberland men. I was of counsel with the marshals at the ordering of our lodging; and our camp was so well environed with ordnance, carts, and dikes, that hard it was to enter or issue but at certain places appointed for that purpose; and assigned the most commodious place of the said camp for my lord Dacre's company, next the water, and next my lord of Westmoreland; and at such time as my lord Dacre came into the field, I being at the assault of the abbey which continued unto two hours within night, my said lord Dacre would in nowise be content to lie within the camp, which was made right sure, but lodged himself without, wherewith at my return I was not content; but then it was too late to remove.   The next day I sent my lord Dacre to a stronghold called Fernherst, the lord whereof was his mortal enemy, and with him sir Arthur Daren, sir Marmaduke Constable, with 700 of their men, one cotont, and divers other good pieces of ordnance for the field.   The said Fernherst stood marvellous strongly within a great wood.   The said two knights, with the most part of their men, and Strickland, your grace's 4000 with 300 Kendal men, went into the wood on foot, with ordnance, where the said Kendal men were so handled, that they found hardy men that were not foot back for them.   The other two knights were also so sharply assailed that they were enforced to call for more of their men, and yet could not bring the ordnance to the fortress, unto the time my lord Dacre with part of his horsemen lighted on foot, and marvellously hardly himself handled; and, finally, with long skirmishing and much difficulty, got forth the ordnance, won the house, and threw down the same; at which skirmish my said lord Dacre, and his brother sir Christopher, and sir Arthur, and sir Marmaduke, and many other gentlemen, did marvellously hardly, and found the best resistance that hath been seen since my coming to this part, and above 300 Scots slain, and not passing four Englishmen, but about forty hurt.   After that, my said lord returning to the camp, would in nowise be lodged in the same, but where he lay the first night; and he being with me at supper, about eight o'clock, the horses of his company broke loose and suddenly ran out of his field, in such number that it caused a marvellous alarm in our field; and our standing watch being set, the horses came running along the camp, at whom were shot above one hundred sheaf of arrows and divers guns, thinking they had been Scots that would have assaulted the camp; finally, the horses were so mad that they ran like wild deer into the field, above twenty at the least in divers companies; and in one place fifty fell down a great rock and slew themselves, and above fifty-two ran into the town, then being on fire, and by the women taken and carried away right evil burnt, and many were taken again; but finally by that I can esteem by the number of them that I saw go on foot the next day, I think there is lost above 200 horses, and all with folly, for lack of not lying within the camp. I dare not write the wonders that my lord Dacre and all his company do say they saw that night six times of spirits and fearful sights; and universally all their company say plainly the devil was that night amongst them six times, which misfortune hath blemished the best women that was in Scotland many years. I assure your grace I found the Scots at this time the boldest and the hottest that ever I saw any nation. And all the remainder, upon all parts of the army, kept us with so continual skirmish, that I never saw the like, if they might assemble . . . as good men as I now saw . . . or . . . it would be a hard encounter to meet them. Pity it is of my lord Dacre's loss of the horses of his company: he brought with him above 300 men, and came and lodged one night in Scotland, in his most mortal enemy's country. There is no harder nor better knight; but oftentimes he doth not use the most sure order, which he hath now paid dearly for. Written at Berwick, the twenty-seventh of September.   Yours, most bounden,

                                             T. SURREY.

LETTER XVIII.

WOLSEY TO THE KING'S RESIDENT MINISTER IN ROME.

MY LORD,—I commend me unto you, in my most hearty manner, perceiving, by tenour of your letters, bearing date at Rome, the . . . and . . . days of December, that my letters to you, addressed by two special couriers, the one the . . . day, and the other the . . . day of November, were safely, after some difficulty in the way, arrived, and come to your hands, with the state and disposition wherein the affairs then were and stood at that time; for the which your diligent advertisement, the king's highness, unto whom I have shown and read your said letters, and also your others of the . . . . . and I, both give unto you our hearty thanks; assuring you, that as well your sundry devices and discourses had with the pope's holiness to very good purposes, as also your discreet order taken for certain of the king's money, with other your doings, there be much to be liked and commended, wherein more and more ye daily show the manifest proof of your wisdom and great zeal to do unto the king's highness and his realm acceptable service, which ye may be assured shall be remembered accordingly, ascertaining you that the king's grace sundry ways hath lately been advertised that the French king, lying himself with the most part of his army still at the siege of Pavia, hath sent and advanced, or intendeth shortly to send forth once again the duke of Albany towards Naples; after whom it was first said, that the said viceroy of Naples and other the emperor's folks, leaving Lodi, passed and took their way thitherward for defence of the same; and that the French king had thereupon sent after them count St. Pol, with other good companies and band of men, thinking to interclude the emperor's folks between both companies; afterward by letters sent from the duke of Milan, of the twenty-second of December, to his ambassador resident with the king's highness, the same among other news perceived, that in case the French king should send any power toward Naples, or make visage so to do for any policy or craft, thinking thereby to cause the said viceroy to abandon Italy, and to attend the defence of Naples, the said French king should be greatly frustrate of his opinion, for the said viceroy would in nowise leave Italy; but as soon as he should have his power, unite experiment battle with the said French king, which thing to hear and understand the king's highness was very joyous and glad, commending and lauding greatly the said viceroy's great virtue, wisdom, and good conduct, in this behalf. This matter, not unlikely to be true, is of great importance and consequence, having many things in it necessary substantially to be considered; for, remembering the common fame, which upon sundry advertisements out of Italy, hath long continued here, that there is a privy part, treaty, and agreement, concluded between the pope's holiness and the French king, both for alliance and other great matters; and seeing that the French king dare take upon him this enterprise, which, without the pope's favour, he could never think to bring unto good purpose; the demonstrations also, which, at the former time, were showed for passage of the Frenchmen through Placenza, with other great arguments and

apparent conjectures, sounding to that purpose; it is verily
to be thought that the pope's holiness, be it that the same be
induced thereunto by fear, affection, ambition, or otherwise,
proceedeth not so sincerely with the emperor and the king's
grace in this behalf, as was supposed; and therefore, that the
king's highness, for his part, upon such assurance as always
I have made unto his grace on the pope's behalf, hath hitherto
grounded his affairs upon an entire confidence towards his
holiness, persuading unto himself, as indeed hath been written
from thence, that neither fear of adversity, though his holiness
should be compelled to fly out of the city of Rome, nor desire
of exaltation of his country, friends or kinsfolks, lucre of
goods, possessions, or other things, should move his holiness
from the constant mind which the same had unto the king
and the emperor; but that if it should come unto the uttermost, he would take such part in peace or war against the
French king as they should do, which thing seemeth not to
be observed so constantly as was written and affirmed. It is
now time to be somewhat more plain with his holiness than
before needed or was intended; for surely if it be true that
is divulged and reported abroad, where it was supposed that
his holiness, for his great virtue, wisdom, experience, perfect
zeal unto Christ's religion, and other his qualities, was like
by his high policy to have done as great good and furtherance
to the weal, quiet, and exaltation of Christendom, and to the
honour and dignity of the see apostolic, or more than any
his predecessors have done of a great season. This manner
of proceeding is evidently apparent to be the high and plain
way to lead straight unto continual and incessant war, to the
hindrance, damage, and diminution of the Christian religion,
and to the great impairing of the dignity of his holiness, and
the said see apostolic; which eminent dangers being so notorious as they be, I cannot, nor may, with my duty towards
his holiness, forbear to signify and cause to be declared unto
the same, with due humility, obedience, and reverence, as one
of the unworthy members of that church whereof his holiness
is the head, praying you therefore that, taking a convenient
time for this purpose, and making unto his holiness my most
lowly recommendations, ye shall begin first with the rumour
and fame divulged here, as is aforesaid; proceeding also to
the firm opinion conceived in him by the king's highness and

me, with other the premises; making also, in my name, protestation, that I specially and entirely for the fervent zeal that I have towards the honour, weal, and surety, of his holiness, and of the quiet and repose of Christendom, am desirous to notify unto the same my poor advice and opinion in this weighty matter. Enter the overture thereof in as good, pleasant, and loving manner, as ye can devise.   Saying, furthermore, that since the time that the king's highness received his crown and dignity royal, the very intent and purpose of his grace hath always been affixed to do his best endeavour to help, further, and conduce universal peace in Christendom, and to repress or bring unto good reformation those that be disturbers of the same.   To the intent, that such peace once had, his highness, whom it pleased Almighty God to constitute in the rule of his people in his flourishing and growing years, might in his life (God so willing,) see the time to do some notable service unto Christ's religion against the infidels, for a general expedition by all princes to be made against the same.

And upon this virtuous purpose his grace hath principally grounded the cause and occasion of his wars against those that daily do impeach the quiet of Christian princes, showing himself always inclinable to that thing which might conduce unto good, sure, and general peace; and what rejoice his highness took, what perfect trust, and confidence, and expectation his grace also had to hear and understand, that the pope's holiness after his assumption to the papal dignity was, and showed himself most entirely minded to this purpose, no man can be better witness than I, who always ceased not to imprint in the mind of his highness that this was the principle and in manner the only intent and meaning of the pope's holiness, whom God had ordained to have correspondence of convenient youth, entire zeal, and singular affection hereunto.

Secondly, when any notable thing hath insurged, which might be to the impeachment of this so virtuous a purpose, as hath been damnable heresies suscitate and brought up by the friar, Martin Luther, how his highness, minding to the uttermost of his power and cunning to repress, both by his sword and also his pen, all things sounding to the division of the holy church, needeth not to be rehearsed.

Thirdly, his grace hath not a little taken to heart and mind the great enterprises now lately, these intestine wars in Christendom enduring, attempted by the Turk, as well against Belgrade, and other parts of Hungary, as against the city and isle of Rhodes; wherein what jacture, loss, detriment, and peril, ensueth, and is apparent to the rest, is facile, and easy to be considered, being one of the things most highly hath moved his grace partly to withdraw the uttermost rigor of his wars, and rather with his own extreme detriment, loss, and prejudice, to condescend unto some way conducing towards peace, whereby the Christian princes unity the malice of the infidels might the better be resisted, than leaning unto his own particular titles, quarrels, and pretences, to enforce the extremity of his wars to the continuance of discord in Christendom, and to the advantage of the enemies of Christ's religion. And in what danger not only the realm of Hungary, but also the realm of Naples, with the rest of Italy, and consequently his holiness, the city of Rome, and generally the state of all Christendom, standeth in, if the Turk in this his pride finding such opportunity, shall attempt to invade the same, there is no wise man but he can well consider.

Besides this, it is notorious, and sorrowful to be remembered, how largely the said Lutheran heads do spread through all Germany, the pestiferous sect whereof is not so kept out of France, Spain, Flanders, Denmark, Scotland and, perchance, many parts of England and other regions, but it hath partly penetrated the same, the remedy whereof is only the expectation that the good people, being members of Christ's church, have had to hear and understand, that the head thereof in this his beginning tended all such things as might sound to the reformation of enormities, the observance of due order, and the following of Christ's laws. And if it shall chance, as God forbid, that they might perceive themselves frustrate of this opinion, it is hard to know how much the malice of the ghostly enemy might work or have power in them.

These things well pondered and remembered, it is hard for the king's highness and me to think or believe that the pope's holiness whom God hath endowed with so great virtue, wisdom, and other notable qualities, doth, or will, for any earthly cause, cease or pretermit to have principal or vigilant respect hereunto, before the fear or dread of any prince, whatsoever he were, and before any desire of exaltation of his house, country, family, or kinfolks, but rather to expend his substance, goods, authority, person, and life, to the maintenance of Christ's religion, than for any particular cause to put the same in hazard and danger.

But if his holiness, who hitherto hath showed himself so studious of universal peace, and to advance the said expedition against the infidels, should now (as God forbid) be moved or induced to lean unto any such thing as might sound to the furtherance and advancement of the prince's cause, which is the only disturber of the tranquillity of Christendom, these things following be undoubtedly evident, and likely to ensue.

First, where there was good hope and appearance of peace to have been composed by mediation of his holiness in brief time, the same may well be assured that the realm of Naples and duchy of Milan both taken from the emperor, he shall never nor will condescend unto peace, truce, or appointment, they being out of his hands, for recovery of which Naples, in that case, the king's highness were bounden to give the emperor assistance, inasmuch as it was in his possession at the time of making the treaty; which were a means that the wars should be more hot and cruel than ever before, without any hope or appearance that they should have any brief end, but long to continue. Of the which war, the pope's holiness, favouring the French king, or not earnestly resisting him in the said enterprise of Naples, might and should be accounted to be the principal author and occasion, to the high displeasure of God, the great inquietation of Christendom, his own dishonour, and the occasion of infinite hurts, damages, and inconveniences in our time, and after our day, to ensue.

Secondly, the French king having the duchy of Milan and the realm of Naples both in his hands, and being a prince of such ambition and cupidity of dominion as he is, it is not to be doubted that he would study and compass the ways how he might by little and little allect and draw unto his subjection as many other countries of Italy as he could, acquiring the residue, by dread or otherwise, unto his will and devotion. Whereby, consequently, he might attain ways and means to attempt the empire of Rome; which had or not had, the pope's holiness might be sure that the same, constitute *inter Scyllam et Charybdim*, should be fain to condescend unto all the will and pleasure of the said French king; who, notwithstanding any good countenance that he doth now make, would not then fail to use and dispose of the pope as of his chaplain; whereby the honour, dignity, and preeminence of the see apostolic should, from the high state of the same, be brought into base and exile reputation, and what dishonour for ever should be spoken and written of a pope, which in his time and default had not only suffered, but in manner given the occasion hereof, I doubt not but his holiness can well consider.

Thirdly, if perchance, as some men say, the pope were minded to erect a kingdom in Etruria, which being feudatory to the see apostolic, might be thought to be a defence unto the same, his holiness may well be assured, that though, perchance, for this time the greatest inconvenience that might ensue thereof, should not appear, yet, nevertheless, it were the next and most plain way after his days, if it be not done in his time, to bring the said see apostolic into extreme danger; for how other princes, being vassals of the church, do use themselves towards the same, is daily in experience; and whether the church be strengthened or defended, or weakened or annoyed by them, is well known. And if the pope's holiness for any particular affection to his own family, should, for exaltation thereof, impair and extremely endamage the see apostolic to the high prejudice of all his successors, and of the dignity of Christ's church, how far such an act were discrepant from the expectation and good opinion which all folks have had that his holiness in his time should not only preserve, but greatly amplify the same to him and his successors, may be well considered.

Over this, there is great respect and consideration to be had unto the frail state wherein a great part of those which should be members of the church of Rome now stand in; for it is not unknown that the Lutheran heresies have, as is aforesaid, infected all Germany, a great part whereof is in the emperor and his brother's dominions; who finding extreme ingratitude in the pope's holiness, a great occasion may be given to their subjects the rather to fall unto such ways as may tend to the pope's displeasure, whereby the whole country, now proud and ready to hearken unto the said heresies, may happen to withdraw themselves from the obedience to the church of Rome. And what Spain shall do is hard to know; nor also whether France shall be as ready thereunto as any other, though the pope's holiness do never so much for it. And, to say the truth, I see such inclination in many of the clergy and people of this realm, that I fear an evil example given by other might soon do much hurt in the same. Which things well considered, it were rather convenient that the pope's holiness should now study ways and means, by his direct and indifferent proceeding with the princes, to confirm and amend the reputation of the dignity papal, than by losing and amitting the benevolence of the emperor, being the greatest prince in Christendom, and having most countries and possessions in his hands, to give occasion whereby the obedience to the church of Rome should be notably diminished. And this matter, among other, is not the least to be regarded and looked unto, for surely the dangers thereof be more eminent than I now do write, like as I am sure the pope's holiness doth perfectly perceive and know. Which thing was in good train of reformation and remedy, by such prudent and virtuous ways as the pope's holiness hath taken, as well in sending my lord cardinal Campeggio into Germany as otherwise; who, by his great dexterity, hath there so much profited in the charge to him committed, that there was apparent and good hope, by little and little to extinct the said infection. Whereas, if this new manner of proceeding should be used, not only the said lord cardinal standeth in extreme danger to be destroyed in Germany, but also there is great appearance that the dignity papal, by declining of Germany and other countries from the obedience thereof, shall suffer and take the greatest detriment and hindrance that ever came thereunto.

Besides this, it is notorious with what cruel mind and intent the Turk infesteth Christendom, studying nothing so much as how to extinguish Christ's faith; for which purpose he hath first won and acquired the two propugnatious and most defensible and strong places of the same, converting all his doing to find the means and ways, by sundry regions and places, to enter Christendom at one time. Who, being a prince of so great a power as he is, thinketh himself puissant enough to subdue all the whole princes and realms of Christendom, though they were never so well united. And what opportunity shall be given unto him finding the same in total division, is easy to be known; for first, in Hungary shall be found small resistance in comparison of his power, the princes most vicinous of the same being the emperor's subjects and allies, and occupied in the defence of his cause; Naples and Sicily being countries of no great strength, and occupied with wars intestine, shall not be able to make against him any resistance; the city of Rome, and the rest of Italy, Naples lost and the Turk's power entered, be of small power to do themselves or any other good or furtherance. Hungary lacking assistance, what way Germany shall be inclined unto, who now so much favours the Lutheran sect, is deeply to be pondered. And then, whether the French king, having war and hostility with England and divers other countries, shall be able, with his alliance made in Italy, to put remedy unto these inconveniences, the pope's holiness, by his great wisdom, can soon judge and discern. Therefore if his holiness, like a gracious father, head and governor of Christ's church, do mind the surety, weal, and preservation of the same, and will, in these tempestuous and troublesome storms, be the very medicine and leech to the diseases and infirmities presently reigning in Christendom, it is no time now to look unto particularities and private affections; but, substantially regarding the supreme dignity that God hath called him unto, and finding affairs in the state that they now be, to intend, with all effect, unto such ways and means as shall tend to the increase of Christ's religion, rather than to give cause or occasion to the manifest impairing of the same. And herein, to say the very truth, and acquit myself with my duty and most tender zeal towards his holiness, I cannot see how it may stand with the law and pleasure of Almighty God that the heads of the church should involve and initiate themselves and their state by their conjunction unto temporal princes in the wars; but that, as I verily suppose, since these leagues offensive or defensive, or both, have been used to be made in the name of any pope, God hath stricken and sent affliction unto the whole church and generality of Christendom for the same. And these contracts and conventions used for the enhancing of particular families and countries, have not hitherto proved either to endure or to do good and furtherance to the papal dignity; but all that one pope hath gone about in such affairs, with much travail, labour, cost, and difficulty, hath, either in his own time, or soon after, been disappointed; and always with the detriment and damage of the see apostolic, and which hath been of the chief causes to provoke such damnable sects against the pope's authority as hath of late days been raised in sundry parts of Christendom. And though I suppose and think verily, that the premises be right well considered and pondered by the pope's holiness, and that the same, any bruit raised to the contrary, is of so high wisdom and virtue that he would never condescend to such things in the favour of the French king as is reported; yet nevertheless being matters of so great importance, I thought convenient, in accomplishing of my duty as a most humble creature of his holiness, to declare unto the same the danger and peril which I see and perceive in these affairs; whereunto I doubt not but his holiness can and will adhibit and put better remedy than here can be studied or devised. Nevertheless, to declare the king's and mine opinion herein, I advertise you, that there be three ways by the which it is thought here that a convenient remedy may be found for disappointing the French king's purpose, the enterprise of Naples, and consequently to eschew the said great dangers and inconveniences apparent to ensue of the same; which three things ye shall declare and show unto the pope's holiness, on the king's and my behalf, as by way of friendly counsel given to the same, in case affairs stand in such case as the king's grace is advertised.

The first and principal is, that the said viceroy persist firmly in this his intention now with diligence to enforce himself to present give and strike battle with the French king before he may enforce his power; for the king's highness, by espial and otherwise, is advertised that the French king hath sent for Monsieur de Lautrec, and all the captains and men of war, from his frontiers, as well on the side of Spain as in Picardy, Burgundy, and elsewhere, to repair unto him, being in likelihood in fear and dread of such battle. And therefore now is the time for the viceroy to accelerate the same, before the French king can be able so to reinforce himself, and thereby to put perfect surety, God willing, both unto the duchy of Milan and to the realm of Naples; for such battle, stricken with advantage, as it now may be, neither the duke of Albany can prosper in Naples, but shall with his army come to extreme ruin; nor also the French king can be of power to do anything in the duchy of Milan, but at the least shall be compelled to abandon the same; whereby he shall be afterwards constrained to come unto reason. And albeit this matter touch not the king's highness, nor any capitulations be passed between the emperor and his grace for the same, yet nevertheless for the tender love that his grace beareth unto the emperor, in case the said viceroy will really and actually strike the said battle with the French king, his grace will, the same done and performed, give unto that army a reward of 50,000 crowns. And in this case of battle stricken, the king's grace is contented that ye not only convert the residue of the 50,000 crowns yet remaining in sir John Russell's hands, and not made hither by exchange, unto this use, for the reward and toward the entertainment before specified, after the battle stricken, and not before; but also that, as well with that which ye have taken, and the residue delivered to my lord of St. John's folk and other, as otherwise ye by your wisdom and policy find the means without any great loss or interest to supply and make up the residue of the said 50,000 crowns. Howbeit, if for lack of good resistance to be made in Naples, or for fear of affection of the people to the French party, or other cause, to the king's highness unknown, this thing, so much profitable to the surety of Italy, cannot be performed and achieved; but that the said viceroy will and shall think good in anywise to follow the French king's army marching towards Naples, then the king's highness thinketh good that they in no wise leave Lodi, Cremona, and other fortified places unfurnished, but surely to provide for defence of the same. And then the pope's holiness who, upon the sudden descent of the French king into Italy, and the lack of sufficient furniture of the emperor's folk, was peradventure the rather induced and inclinable, for his own surety, and fear of the French power, to fall into some practice with the French king, may nevertheless upon these your instructions, exhort the Venetians to advance and set forth their army with all diligence in assistance of the emperor's folk; and his holiness, either openly, or at the least secretly, may give effectual aid unto the same, by such good ways and devices as to his holiness shall be thought expedient; and among other, *conniventibus oculis,* to suffer or cause the peasants and villeins of the territory of Bologna, being, as it is said, churlish people, as well by fortifying and defence of the passages, which be very narrow and dangerous for the marching of an army, as by withholding victuals from them, so to impede the Frenchmen there that they shall not be able to pass that country. Who, either overthrown, or by these means repelled and put back, the French king shall be so discouraged, and his power so enfeebled, that there shall need no fear to be had of any feats by him to be done in Italy at this time. And this device, the Frenchmen passing towards Naples, and being but a small number to speak of, shall be the thing, if the former way be not feasible, that may put surety to the realm of Naples; and consequently the French king's power and estimation so much diminished, to give the emperor's folk a marvellous advantage for the utter defeating of the French king, and the driving of him out of Lombardy; for there is neither of these two ways but, if they may be duly followed, the Frenchmen be like, God willing, to be repressed, and either totally subdued there, or at least compelled by force to abandon Italy. Which shall be the next and most sure means for conducing of peace, without such obstinate refusal and high demands as hitherto hath been showed and required on the French part.

The third way devised and thought good here, if neither of these ways can be brought about, or, the same attempted, shall not fortune to take good effect is, that whereas there was lately overture made unto the viceroy of Naples, on the pope's behalf, that he, and other the emperor's folk there, should condescend to put as much part of the duchy of Milan as yet is in their possession into the pope's hands, *per modum depositi*, for a certain time, within the which communication and treaty may be had for an agreed peace, showing that the French king was contented to do the like for such towns and places within the said duchy as remained in his hands, and thereupon to conclude a truce to depart out of Italy with his army, the pope's holiness should now soon set forth that overture with all effect; which being admitted and accepted, the realm of Naples shall be out of the Frenchmen for this time, and the duchy of Milan, nevertheless, is not omitted nor lost from the emperor, but may perchance either be restored unto him, or ordered unto his contentment; and the French king, not being sure of his successes either in Naples or in the said duchy, condescending hereunto, may save himself and his people, return home with his honour, come unto truce with the emperor and the king; whereof, God willing, may ensue a good peace, and ye be in good appearance to have honourable appointment concerning the duchy of Milan to his contentation hereafter, so as the emperor's folk, in avoiding the danger that may ensue to lose both Milan and Naples, if they take wise ways, ought to condescend hereunto, whereby they may be sure to save the one and not lose the other. And the French king, being not yet sure to acquire either of them, and standing not out of danger of his enemies, never like to enjoy both countries in quiet if he had recovered them, and having his person, honour, army, and reputation at hazard, shall put the same in surety, return with as great honour for the time as can be devised, and yet be in good appearance of the duchy of Milan, or of the disposition thereof to his contentment, as is aforesaid, besides the emolument that may grow unto him by the means hereof to come, God willing, to a good peace. And to the intent it may evidently appear that there shall lack nothing on the king's behalf which conveniently may be done to the furtherance of these matters, his grace hath not only willed his principal secretary, Mr. Ric. Pace, to repair unto the Venetians at this time, to solicit the speedy setting forwards of their army, as is aforesaid, but also sir Gregory Cassillis unto the viceroy of Naples, to exhort him unto the premises, as by the copy of their instructions being herewith ye shall perceive; willing and commanding also, that sir John Russell, for the better advancement of the common affairs, and advertisement to be given of the successes from time to time, shall pass unto the duke of Bourbon, and reside about him for a season; who also, if the case shall so require, and the king's grace is contented, shall repair hither, to the intent, for lacking ways of truce, some annoyance may be done on this side by his means, as shall be thought most convenient. Ascertaining you that Mr. Secretary is commanded among other things to say unto the Venetians, that if the breaking their pacts, bands, and conventions with the emperor, should give unto the French king commodity to attain the realm of Naples, the king's highness cannot repute them as the emperor's friends, but rather his enemies, and will not fail so to accept them also unto his grace. And further he shall secretly say unto the duke and council of Venice, that it is

not known unto the king's highness how inhumanly the
Spaniards have ordered themselves in Italy, giving thereby
cause and occasion to such as favour the emperor's party to
decline from the same; and rather to desire to suffer the
French party there, not being so cruel as the Spaniards. But
he shall say that the matters well proceeding at this time,
the king's highness trusteth to do so much with the emperor
that he shall have the investiture of the duchy of Milan
clearly unto the duke of the same, whereby Italy may be
delivered both from the Frenchmen, and also the Spaniards.
Which thing, if ye also say unto the pope's holiness, it shall
peradventure the more animate and encourage him to put his
hand to the expulsion of the Frenchmen, trusting thereby to
deliver Italy both of them and also of the Spaniards, as is aforesaid. Wherefore, seeing the matters brought to such extreme
hazard as is here reported, if the pope's holiness love God
himself, and the weal of Christendom, now is the time, since
the three things be so feasible, to show the same, which if his
holiness neglect, unless there be other good remedy, or the
matters in other train than is here known, if the inconveniences before specified shall fortune to ensue thereof, the
king's highness, I, and other which thus would give unto the
pope's holiness wholesome admonition and exhortation, be
discharged before God and the world, and the dishonour,
blame, and reproach shall be imputed unto those who have
deserved the same. In declaration of the premises unto
the pope's holiness, ye must use great circumspection; for if
ye shall perceive that his holiness doth no great thing in
favour of the French party, but rather for fear than otherwise, and that ye see no contrary appearance, but that upon
good grounds his holiness may be induced to experiment the
said devices, then shall it be good to open the same unto him;
but if ye do know his holiness totally affectionate unto the
French party, then shall it be dangerous to open unto him
the secrets of the king's mind and opinion, lest he should discover the same unto the Frenchmen; but declaring unto his
holiness the said dangers eminent to the see apostolic, and all
proper done, to keep yourself within good limits in opening
such part of the rest as ye shall think expedient.

And albeit, that by letters sent from the emperor to his
ambassador here resident, whereof ye shall herewith receive

the copy, it is written that he hath sent into Italy the sum of 200,000 ducats; yet, nevertheless, inasmuch as it is not certain whether that money be arrived, or shall come in time or not, the king's highness is content that ye, seeing and perceiving the matters there to be in such train and disposition, that not only the lack of a small sum of money might be the cause or occasion of the ruin of the whole, ye shall in that case rather than all good opportunity should be omitted, advance unto the said emperor's army, before battle stricken, as much part of the said 50,000 crowns as upon your last exchange made remained behind, wherein the king's highness and I trust your accustomed wisdom and discretion not to be over hasty therein, unless ye may see that the lack thereof may be to the extreme peril, and the having thereof a perfect and high advantage unto the surety of the present affairs in time of extreme necessity.

Ye shall furthermore perceive, by copy of the emperor's said letters, how firmly his majesty is determined to the defence of his causes in Italy, which thing is by the pope's holiness well to be considered, that no despair be taken for his usage to the French king, who hitherto as far as is known here, hath gained neither strong places, nor also any honour by this enterprise, and the emperor, either by himself or by his friends, shall not be unpurveyed to defend and maintain his right, honour, and reputation, whatsoever success, good or bad, the French king shall have at this time, which thing in good manner ye may extend unto his holiness, as ye shall see the time and opportunity to require.

Finally, I send unto you herewith a copy of such overtures as by the archbishop of Capua, at his coming from the French king to the emperor, were proposed, and of the answer made unto the same, which both of the one party and the other be so slender, and of so small effect, that little regard is to be had thereunto; and among other things ye may well assure his holiness, that whatsoever sinister report may be spread by the Frenchmen or other, of any practice made on this side with France, by reason of the being here of my lady the French king's mother's servant, or by any other person that may be sent hither on the French king's behalf, his holiness shall perfectly trust that nothing is meant, or shall be passed or concluded here, directly or indirectly, but by the emperor's consent, and as the pope's holiness shall be made privy; but that if any reasonable offers shall fortune to be made for the king's behalf, the same shall be intimated both to the emperor for his consent and to the pope's holiness for knowledge, before anything shall be concluded; and his holiness, as I have always written, to have the honour and final doing thereof, as the very author of the same.

Letter XIX.

WOLSEY TO THE KING'S AMBASSADORS AT THE IMPERIAL COURT.

My lord of London and Mr. Wingfield, I commend me unto you in my right hearty manner. Since my last letters written unto you, I have received letters from the bishop of Bath, the copy whereof I send you herewith, perceiving, as well by tenour thereof as by relation of the pope's nuncio here resident, that his holiness is now minded to enter a league, offensive and defensive, with the king's highness and the emperor, as they shall reasonably devise. There is also in the said letters mention made of certain motions, devised by the Venetians and Florentines, for a league defensive to be made between the pope and states of Italy, which, for the considerations specified in the same letters, the pope's holiness, as he affirmeth, doth refuse. It appeareth furthermore, of what towardness the pope was in at the last to have the realm of France diminished of certain great portions, and the French king's eldest son to be admitted unto the crown thereof, with other matters right necessary for you to know before your coming to the emperor; for which cause I thought convenient to send you the said copy, as well to the intent you should know the pope's mind and inclination herein, as also for that ye may, as ye see cause, give more ample knowledge to the emperor, what is spoken of, and may be done and devised in case his majesty should take any other way at this time than were consonant unto the mutual kindness and intelligence between the king's grace and him, which is a thing right meet to be notified unto him, to the intent he may know the king's highness doth not lack ways and overtures enough made unto his grace, which might be to the particular profit of his highness, if the same would, in any part, decline from the emperor ; and shall the rather induce and move his majesty to concur and join in one proceeding and perfect conformity with the king's highness at this present time.

Ye may perceive also what was reported to the pope's holiness, touching the intent of my lady the French king's mother to repair unto the emperor, which thing I can right well believe, ascertaining you that in case the emperor do admit her unto his presence, and that she come with power of the estates of France to treat, commune, and conclude, it is hard to think that the emperor shall condescend to the personal invasion, or do any great feat of war, till he shall see what fruit shall ensue of the said treaty.

And surely the uncertainty of that matter considered, and that though also the shires of this realm show themselves hitherto as conformable as can be devised to make the contribution unto the king's grace, yet nevertheless it is not certain in how speedy and good manner the same may be levied. Remembering furthermore, that passing into Normandy the king's highness cannot furnish himself of no less victuals than for eight days, which will be very difficult to do, and that victual spent or not spent, it is doubtful how the passage may be had by, which failing, the king's grace should have on his back Montreuil, Hesdin, Terouenne, and Boulogne; I have for these causes, by great persuasions, induced the king's highness to be contented that my lord of Norfolk, with his vanguard, and those appointed in the rearward, which in the whole will amount unto the number of 20,000 men and more, besides the aid of Flanders, shall somewhat in the more diligence pass before, and that his grace shall remain here till such time as more certainty may be had, as well of the emperor's mind and intent how the money may be levied, and also what succeed of taking of the said passage of ——— and thereupon his highness to proceed, after his best commodity and pleasure.

Besides this, I have showed unto the emperor's ambassadors here resident, like as also ye may notify unto the emperor, what divers ways be studied and devised in Italy and other parts to divert the king's good mind and concurrence from the emperor, with the fear conceived by them, that chiefly and principally by means of the first intelligence between the king's grace and him, his majesty having my lady princess in marriage is like to aspire unto the monarchy of Christendom; and among other things, I have declared unto them an offer made unto the king's highness of 50,000 ducats, to be given unto his grace by the potentates of Italy towards the maintenance of his wars against France, with their concurrence that the French king's eldest son may have the crown thereof, the king's highness having right large portions of his patrimonies there, so that the king would give unto the same son my lady princess in marriage, and consequently satisfy their doubt and fear of the said monarchy; so as there lack no ways, if the king's grace would hearken thereunto, how his highness, regarding only his own commodity, might right well do his feat without the emperor; all which things his grace hath utterly refused.

The Scots, also, have now offered that, having my lady princess given in marriage unto the young king, they will deliver him into the king's hands, with certain towns and places on the borders, and utterly abandon France for ever : which thing, also, the king's highness has expressly refused, saying that his grace will never violate or break his promise made unto the emperor, but that his majesty shall have her in marriage.   In such wise as the Scottish ambassadors be departed without any conclusion of peace, truce, or appointment.   Wherefore, all the premises considered, the king's highness specially trusteth that the emperor, showing mutual correspondence of kindness, will in all offers or motions stay himself, not doing or passing any thing without the king's consent, like as his grace, for the emperor's sake, refuseth all the commodities offered for his part.

All which premises shall be good grounds whereupon ye may the more bind upon the emperor to perform such things as on the king's part be desired, not doubting but by your great wisdom and discretion ye will order the same accordingly.

Ye shall understand the king's highness and I be advertised that don Diego de Monçada is sent by the viceroy unto the emperor, and in his company, at the French king's request, be also passed Byron and Montmorenci, who, of likelihood, be sent to make a mean and way for the repair thither of my lady the French king's mother.

I also send unto you herewith a copy of a writing delivered unto me by the pope's orators, and sent to them by the archbishop of Capua, in confirmation of such things as be mentioned in my lord of Bath's letters, and how that John Matthias no more meddleth with the affairs of the state, but that the same be now committed wholly to the said Capuan, so that now John Matthias only meddleth with the dating of bulls; which, if he had so done before, had been to the pope's great honour and reputation. At my place beside Westminster, the 7th day of April, 1525. Your loving friend,

C. Card^{lis}. Ebor.

> To my loving brother in Christ the bishop of London, and my loving friend sir Richard Wingfield, knight, the king's ambassadors to the emperor.

Letter XX.

WOLSEY TO MR. SAMPSON.

Mr. Sampson, I commend me unto you in my right hearty manner. By the hands of Monsieur de Rieux, who as I understand lay a long season in the west countries upon his passage, for default of a convenient wind, I wrote unto you my last letters,* wherein I advertised you such overtures as were made here by the said De Rieux on the duke of Bourbon's behalf, and of the answer given unto him upon the same, with such other matter as was then occurrent; declaring, among other things, the king's firm deliberation nothing to pretermit on this part which might confer unto the advancement of the common affairs, with the great desire of his highness and of me to know and understand the emperor's mind, what his majesty intendeth or thinketh good to be done or set forth against the common enemy this year, in case some honourable appointment do not succeed to their reasonable satisfaction and contentment. In all which matters, and other then written unto you, the king's highness and I attend with great desire to have answer, considering that the spring of the year, convenable for preparations, passeth fast on, and that so great matters as these be should be foreseen and pro-

---

* The intention of Henry to prosecute the war vigorously.

vided in time. In the mean season, the king's highness putteth as good order as may be to the forwardness of his preparations at home, and doth not cease, by all ways and means that can be studied or devised, as the emperor's affairs do succeed in Italy, to further, help, and advance the same; and much the rather, because his highness, supposing before that the emperor had given assured order unto the matters of the duchy of Milan, was nevertheless, long since the despatch of my last letters to you, advertised out of Italy that no letters, word, or knowledge, was then arrived there from the emperor, since the descent of the French king into that duchy; which thing the king's grace and I thought verily to proceed either of contrariety of wind or by reason of the emperor's late sickness of a fever, or of some other adverse chance or misfortune; and his highness, minding, like a most loving and tender father and perfect friend, to supply the default with as much help as then could be done on this side, being advertised that the French king made sundry demonstrations and visages to send the duke of Albany with a power into the realm of Naples, and that the pope's holiness began to run in suspicion that he inclined overmuch to the French party, doubting, also, least the Venetians and others might do the like, after divers letters at sundry times, written both to the pope's said holiness, the infant don Ferdinando, the viceroy of Naples, the duke of Bourbon, and other, comforting and exhorting them to all such things as might sound to the benefit of the emperor's causes and the surety both of Naples and Milan, not only despatched his trusty servant, sir Gregory de Cassillis, to pass in diligence unto the said Infant, duke of Bourbon and viceroy of Naples, but also sent his trusty counsellor, Mr. Richard Pace, then lying at Trent, unto the signory of Venice; wrote furthermore unto the bishop of Bath, the king's orator in the court of Rome, and appointed sir John Russell to repair and reside with the duke of Bourbon, to such intent, effect, and purpose, as by the instructions and letters, the copies whereof I send you herewith, ye shall perceive at great length, being so devised, ordered, and couched in every point, that by the same may evidently and largely appear how like an assured friend and most kind father the king's highness, as well in adversity as in prosperity, doth tender the honour, causes, and matters of

the said emperor; wherein, as may appear, his grace pretermitted nothing that might be thought to confer or conduce to
the weal thereof, and to put remedy to all inconveniences, if
any were, as by the information and advertisement had out of
Italy, there was assuredly before the despatch of the said sir
Gregory an appearance of some danger like to ensue to the
emperor's said matters, if speedy remedy were not adhibited
and provided; for by letters of the bishop of Bath, it appeared
that the pope's holiness, in his conferences with him, showed
himself in much more fear and doubt of the French king,
alleging sundry reasons and introductions whereby might
arise some scruple or suspicion that his holiness was not so
stedfast in the emperor's cause as was supposed; and, besides, that it was reported that the duke of Albany was set
forth towards Placenza, making a countenance to pass into
Naples. Whereupon the king's highness, doubting least some
inconvenience might arise unto the emperor's said matters for
lack of knowledge had in Italy from his majesty, and being
advertised that the Frenchmen, under colour of the being here
of John Joachim, made their vaunt that they were well assured
of the king's grace, made the said despatches not only thereby
to stay the pope, Venetians, and other potentates of Italy
from concluding of anything with the French king, or, at
the least, upon the great and weighty considerations mentioned in the said copies, to withdraw and allect them from
doing anything passed or premised to the same French king,
if any such were; but also to show unto them and all other a
manifest comprobation of the king's firm and deliberate mind
assuredly to lean with all effect unto the defence and maintenance of the said emperor's affairs, and to remove all such
opinion as upon report of the Frenchmen they might conceive
to the contrary.

Ye shall, either by translation of the said copies into
French, or Latin, or otherwise, after the king's most cordial,
and my due and humble recommendations made unto the said
emperor; and after declaration made of the premises, show
and notify at full length unto his majesty and counsel, the
very effect, order, form, and manner of the same; which, if
misinterpretations and sinister reports do not take more place
than the truth, must needs of congruence be in the most
thankful and agreeable part by them accepted, wherein there

is one matter of great and weighty importance, that of very necessity in avoiding sundry inconveniences, which else might ensue to the hindrance of the rooted love and perfect intelligence being between the king and the emperor; I am of force, and in manner against my will, compelled to cause at this time plainly to be signified unto the said emperor; for if I should any longer hide the same from his majesty, I doubt that there might great hindrance and detriment grow thereby, unto his own cause and affairs, like as it is to be supposed, that by reason that the matter was not till now here perfectly and thoroughly comprehended and known, no little damage hath hitherto ensued to the common enterprises.

It hath been of a long season, and from sundry parts, reported unto the king's highness, and to me at divers times, that Monsieur de Praet, who resideth here ambassador for the emperor, hath continually been a man disposed and inclined to make in his letters and writings both to the emperor and the lady Margaret, seditious and sinister reports; saying many times, upon his own fantasy, suspicion, and conjecture, things clearly untrue, and compassing at other times, when things have been done, said, or set forth friendly, kindly, and lovingly, so to couch his reports and the circumstances of the doings thereof, as though the gratuities showed by the king's highness have from time to time been conduced by the industry, policy, and labour of the said ambassadors; ascribing therefore the laud and thanks thereof unto himself, whereby he might acquire the more grace and favour of the said emperor and lady Margaret. To these things the king's highness and I were not over hasty to give soon credence; but, supposing the said ambassador to be a personage of more virtue and inclination to good than now he proveth to be, I would sometimes admonish him, in general words, of such advertisement; exhorting and advising him to be well wary how he, being a minister between two princes so nearly conjoined in intelligence, should attempt or do any thing to the hindrance thereof; but rather, regarding the office of a good ambassador to do that in him is for the nourishing and increase of the same. Wherein he always made me such answer that I conceived no further suspicion or jealousy towards him in that behalf; being therefore the more frank

y

and plain with him in all my conferences, as he, that for the
singular good mind which I have always borne unto the
emperor's honour, weal, and surety, would proceed with his
majesty sincerely, plainly, and truly. And as familiarly,
kindly, and lovingly, hath the king's highness and I admitted,
entertained, and used, the said de Praet, at all times, as the
most hearty love between the king's highness and his majesty
doth require, making him privy and having him present at
all such conversations and accesses have been of other princes,
ambassadors, or of any matter worthy of advertisement or
knowledge; to the intent that he, unto whom the king's highness and I have referred the reports of the same, should
make most credible and plain relation thereof unto the emperor and other to whom it appertained.

Among other, after my accustomable manner, when I had,
the eleventh day of this instant month, received letters from
Mr. Pace, bearing date at Trent the twenty-sixth and twenty-
eighth days of January, the copies whereof I send you here
inclosed, specifying such news of Italy as then were come to
his knowledge, and understanding by the relation of Brian
Tuke, that had sent unto the said ambassador a packet of
letters that had come from my lady Margaret, I sent a servant of mine to the said ambassador, desiring him to take the
pains in the afternoon to repair unto me, as well to the
intent I might make him participant of such news as the
king's highness and I had received, as also to understand
whether he had any good news in confirmation of the same.
Unto whom, on his coming in the presence of the duke of
Norfolk, and some others of the king's counsels, and also of
the ambassador of Milan, who came with him, I read the said
letters and news, declaring the same unto them formally in
the Latin tongue; wherewith, for as much as there was matter therein of right good tenour and effect, we all rejoiced and
were glad. And, proceeding unto the peculiarities, we devised and conjectured upon the making of the three bridges
by the French king over the river of ——————, which we
interpreted to be done rather for his better commodity to flee,
seeing his carriages that might full well have served to the
fortifying of his camp were already transported, than otherwise. We spake also of the doubts that might be, least the
emperor's army, continuing long in the field, should lack

money, wherein the said ambassador inferred, that those which had already helped the French king with money and victuals, naming the pope, the duke of Ferrara, the Florentines, and other, ought also of good congruence to help unto the continuance of the emperor's army. Hereunto I answered, that the coming of sir Gregory de Cassillis should highly confer unto those affairs; for as much as not only he should bring unto the army some comfort of money, and other good knowledge of the king's fast mind, which might the rather encourage them unto the battle; but that also, by the sending of Mr. Pace to Venice, and of my letters to Rome, I trusted the Venetians should be the more glad to continue fast unto the emperor, and that the pope's holiness, of likelihood, upon the great considerations of me alleged, would change his copy; saying, as truth was, that the said sir Gregory, who departed from hence upon the emperor's affairs, as far as could be known here, the distances of the places considered, were in most appearance of despair, should by his coming, God willing, revive the same, having always special trust that the pope's holiness would change his copy as is aforesaid; which, the state of Christendom well considered, appertain unto his holiness to do, if he would be a good father and head of Christ's religion. And if, neglecting the same, his holiness would not do the office of a common father, but rather as a private person or a chaplain, as adhering unto France, the French king would not fail to make him like as I also plainly wrote to be showed unto his holiness on my behalf by the bishop of Bath, as by the copies ye may perceive, then he must be taken according to his acts and merits. Finally, it was devised among us, and I showed my opinion what were expedient to be done, in case the French king, as the chance of battle is uncertain, should either be overthrown in the same, or be compelled to retire, and flee unto France. And in this matter I said expedient it were that the emperor and the king's highness should take substantial ways and means for pursuing of the victory, wherein I doubted not but the king's highness, my master, would do for his part as much as should be requisite; saying, that I would, with all diligence, cause an expedition to be made into Spain for this purpose, and other matters, wherein it is necessary to know the emperor's mind with diligence. These and other like devices, we had to this effect; and with the same the said ambassador, seeming to be joyous and well contented, giving unto me thanks on the emperor's behalf, departed.

Three days before that, as many times is here accustomed, it was appointed that, as that night following, which was the 11th day at night, a privy watch should be made in London, and by a certain circuit and space about it: in the which watch was taken, passing between London and Brentford by certain of the watch appointed to that quarter, one riding towards the said Brentford, who, examined by the watch, answered so closely, that upon suspicion thereof they searched him, and found secretly hid about him a little packet of letters, subscribed in French, which the said watch perceiving, brought the letters unto a man of law's clerk, being of the same company; who supposing the bearer of them to be either a spy or a messenger from some merchant, stranger, or other, intending to disclose things unto the emperor, and perceiving the said packet to be in the taking of it by the unlearned men of the watch broken and evil handled, looked in the letters. And thinking the same by reason of the ciphers more suspect, brought it unto the king's solicitor, being in the same watch; who, not acquainted with the name of the said de Praet, brought the letters so opened unto sir Thomas More, being in another watch near unto the same; and he presented them in the morning following, unto me, being in the Chancery at Westminster; which, when I had read, knowing how far the effect of them was discrepant from the truth, anon I conceived the former advertisements made unto me touching the said ambassador's accustomed usage in making sinister reports to be true. And perceiving by the said letters, that albeit the usage is not here that strangers should pass through the realm without a passport, yet one of the folks was despatched by the said ambassador the day before with letters towards Spain, wherein it was like there might be as evil or worse report than in these, I with all diligence sent to countermand the said former letters, or any other despatched at that time by the said ambassador. And so was taken also a packet of his letters directed to my lady Margaret. Which original letters, directed unto the emperor, with copies of those addressed unto my lady Margaret, viewed and overlooked, and the untruth mentioned in them deprehended, I send unto your hands herewith, as well because the emperor may know such things as his folks on this side do advertise his majesty of, which may confer to the furtherance of his affairs, as also, because the same may hereby the more assuredly and perfectly understand and perceive that the said de Praet hath of likelihood contrived no few matters untrue and feigned in his letters sent of a long season, as well into Spain as into Flanders, whereof there is much appearance by reason of such proceeding, strange demeanour, and suspicion, as hath seemed to have been had towards the king's grace, both on that side and in Flanders of a good season, so that it is evident to be conjectured that the said de Praet hath done more hurt, detriment, and damage, by his evil reports in the common affairs, than ever he can be able to redouble or amend; and surely has by the same deserved much more blame than I will rehearse. And what the king's grace and his counsel may think by the words contained in the said ambassador's letters directed to Mr. John Allemain, finding exception in the king's amity and friendship, as though the same hath been either nothing or very faint and slender, I remit to the emperor and his council, after sight of the same letters, to judge and consider; thinking very strange that the said ambassador would or durst so write unto Mr. John Allemain, being so well acquainted with the emperor's secrets as he is, unless he had before this time perceived like opinion to be imprinted in some of their minds on that side; which if it so be, there is as great injury done unto the king's highness as ever was to noble and gracious prince in this world; who, for the emperor's sake, and to do unto his majesty all honour, gratitude, and pleasure possible, hath done more than in time of man's memory can be found, that ever one prince hath done for another. The particularities whereof shall not need to be rehearsed, forasmuch as they be well known by friends and enemies through all Christendom; and that such rehearsal should be in manner but an exprobation, seeing also that the king's firm trust and confidence is, the emperor of his great wisdom, and the virtuous and discreet men of his counsel, have large experience, and do right well know and consider the same; any such reports, feigned or contrived tales, devised by such indiscreet and inexpert persons as the said de Praet is, notwithstanding. And surely, if it had not been that the king's grace, of his goodness, did benignly and lovingly accept such ministers as

the emperor would depute to do his business here, without
making exception at any of them, his grace long before this
time would have advertised the emperor that the said de
Praet hath always showed himself a man of insufficient qualities, inexpert, and far unmeet to such a province as is committed to him from so great a prince. Nevertheless, for the
emperor's honour and pleasure, the king's grace hath lovingly
tolerate his inability, and studied to supply the same the best
that might be, as he that would not too soon reprove the thing
which by the emperor and his council was thought good and
approved. But if the emperor, knowing the untrue and most
perilous demeanour of the said de Praet, who cannot be taken
here but for a suspect and indign person, will still continue
him here as his ambassador, not only the king's highness and
I shall be in great dread to call him to any matters of importance, but also of all likelihood he shall, as far as in him may
be, do great damage to the common affairs, causing the entire
confidence that hitherto hath been, and as I trust (his sinister
reports notwithstanding,) yet is between the two princes,
rather to decrease and diminish than to be augmented.
Which sort of ministers is necessary to be removed, and
other, minding the furtherance of good amity and good intelligence, to be subrogate in their places. The ordering
whereof the king's highness remitteth to the great wisdom of
the said emperor and his council.

And as to my part, though it pleased him to write, that in
sending for him to me, as is aforesaid, I did more honour
unto him than I had done in the three years that he hath
been here, I am the less miscontented with his untrue report,
forasmuch as the contrary is so evident and well known, and
can be as plainly testified by other of the emperor's councillors and servants which hath been present with him, not only
at many conferences of importance, but also at other times,
when I might show unto him honour, cheer, or demonstration
of love for his master's sake, that I doubt not as little credence
shall be given thereunto as to the rest of his ciphers and open
writing, showing and approving manifestly his untruth, overmuch trust in his own wit, and evident dissimulation. And
in like manner the obscure and dark words conveyed in his
letters to full malicious purpose concerning the pope's holiness, be as little to be regarded. Which words, because he

could not dilate by any specialties to be of other sort than good and honourable, he would conveniently cloak to be interpreted, understood, and taken to some perverse sense and purpose. Nevertheless for my part it sufficeth, and I repute it as a thing which was God's will, that by a misfortune his perilous demeanour is at the last deprehended; whereby the emperor may have cause to remove anything that might perchance be imprinted in his conceit or mind, touching such other evil reports as the said de Praet hath made heretofore, either of the king's highness or of my proceeding, and provide by his wisdom for avoiding of such inconveniences hereafter.

You shall show unto the emperor, that soon after I had deprehended these matters, I desired the said de Praet to come and speak with me; where were present the duke of Norfolk, my lord marquis of Dorset, the bishop of London, sir Richard Wingfield, and other of the king's privy council, of whom many had heard my conference the day before with the said ambassador; to whom in good and plain manner I declared the manner, form, and chance of taking the said letters in the watch, and by what means they came open first to those of the watch unlearned, and after broken and opened unto sir Thomas More's hands, and so unto mine. Which occasion moving me, upon knowledge of the contents therein, to stop and intercept his other letters, proceeding particularly unto some special causes mentioned in the same, wherein methought the said ambassador had done unto the king's highness and to me express injury and wrong, and of likelihood had by many former writings imprinted in the emperor's, my lady Margaret's, and other their counsellors' minds, some sinister opinion far discrepant from the truth, considering that in one and in other of these letters now intercepted, he mentioned divers seditious words and clauses, as followeth.

First, in his letters to the emperor he writeth, this clause depending upon the matters touching the pope's holiness, the Florentines and other, and moreover they are singularly minded to deprive the holy father of his dignity and power. Wherein I said he imputed unto me, being a cardinal and the pope's legate *de latere*, in manner no less offensive then is *crimen lesæ majestatis*. And next he hath couched feigned words touching the despatch of sir Gregory, as though I should vaunt or think the victory, if any be, to proceed only upon the despatch of the same sir Gregory, which was never by me thought, nor the one or other of the said matters otherwise by me spoken, meant, or uttered, than is before touched in the beginning of this letter. And, though it were not convenient that any labour should be used for translation of the clauses, being in cipher, yet the open letters preceding might, and following the same do, give a great light and argument to what evil end the ciphers do tend, special being in his letter to Mr. John Allemain these words inserted, " If we can gain the battle, it will be well for him to remove himself from the danger of such confederates and friends as he has had hitherto. Need is that I say he has no ground for faith in any of the whole set." These words, by marvellous strange, touching, as well by the special words, "confederates," as by the general words "in any of the whole set," not me, but the king's highness, to whom he would affirm the emperor were little beholden. Besides that in his letters to the count of Hoogstraaten, he writeth these words, "when things go well with our people he says nothing about them; when they go ill he vaunts marvellously, as though the success of everything depended on him and his people, and that all of you were nought, I hope ere long to see our master revenged for all these things." How these words sound, and whether in my proceedings I have deserved such thanks of the emperor, or that his majesty should be once revenged upon me, which may be taken by those words, I refer me to all wise men. Over this what a suspicion he would my lady Margaret should conceive, by the king's coming to Bridewell, because John Joachim was lodged near to the same, his letters directed to Monsieur de Thoulouse do declare. And, as well by other his letters directed to the same de Thoulouse, as by those written partly in ciphers to Monsieur de Hoogstraaten, appeareth how evil pleased the said de Praet is with the coming hither of the ambassadors now as is it said despatched from my lady Margaret, fearing of likelihood that they should deprehend some part of his untrue and perilous dealing. Wherefore, after objection unto him of the premises, I desired him to show by what means he could pretend to justify any part of the said reports, and to put in writing such things as he affirmed in his said letters

to Monsieur de Hoogstraaten he had in his memory to be
showed unto the king's highness my master.

Saying furthermore, that his grace is a prince of such great
wisdom, knowledge, and experience in his affairs, that I,
whom his highness doth put in so singular a trust and special
confidence, would be loth to say or do any thing in so great
matters as these be, before I had first well and substantially
known the mind and pleasure of his grace, and been by the
same commanded so to do; nor I may or will of myself take
upon me, without the authority, knowledge, or express commandment of his highness, either to do or undo, whereby the
said ambassador or any other might take ground to write or
report that I could be the cause of any evil that his majesty
hath at this present time; but rather it should seem that the
said ambassador would think or mean that either my master is
a prince of so small knowledge or counsel, that I may do in his
great affairs what I will, or else he would impute covertly
unto his highness that thing which openly he arrecteth unto
me; for what fervent and tender zeal and affection I have in
all my proceedings and doings with his highness borne at all
times unto the emperor's cause and matters, no person living
can better judge than the king my said master can.   Concluding, therefore, that since the king's acts and merits
towards the emperor have been of such sort as is not unknown through all Christendom, the said ambassador could
do no worse service to his master, than thus to study, conspire, and imagine how he may sow jealousy, suspicion, and
unkindness between his majesty and his best friends, seeming to be a thing proceeding of an untrue disposition of the
said de Praet towards the emperor, whose affairs cannot
more be hindered by the greatest enemy, than by such means
rather than of any good mind that he hath to concern and
increase good love and intelligence between both princes.
And whether the king's excellent gratuities showed unto the
emperor's majesty be to be recompensed either with one's deliverance of him from such friends and confederates as the
king's grace is, or with trust once to be revenged as the said
ambassador writeth he doth hope, I refer me to the judgment
and discretion of all good and wise men.   And, for my part,
I had well trusted, and yet do (the seditious reports of the
said de Praet notwithstanding) that the emperor's majesty

had and doth otherwise interpret and accept my acts and proceedings, than it seemeth the same de Praet would they should be accepted, or else I might have cause to think many labours, travails, studies, and pains, taken with most glad heart to do unto his majesty all honour, service, and pleasure to me possible, not so well collocated as I supposed and in manner think and firmly believe them to be, wherein the order to be used by his majesty for punishment of this great error and offence committed by the said ambassador, shall be a great demonstration, light, and appearance hereafter.

Hereunto the said de Praet being not a little abashed, nor without cause, made first exception at the intercepting of his letters, as he that would not give credence to the manner of their interception, and the opening of them, by a fortunate error, as is aforesaid, saying that ambassadors do write unto their princes that which in their conceit is thought good, referring the judgment unto others. He affirmed also, that till this time it could not, nor should be ever found in any of his letters that he hath made any evil report, either of the king's highness or of me, as by his original letters, which he said he desired and would be glad should and might be showed, he would be judged, and that the cause and occasion moving him thus to write at this time, was only the being here of John Joachim eight months, the difficulty made to condescend unto the truce proposed at Rome, the not advancing of an army on this side as was spoken of, and the refusal of the king's highness to contribute anything to the defence of Italy. To this I answered, I could not a little marvel, that he, whom the king's highness and I have always made privy of the successes, would or could suspect or judge any evil herein, considering that as to the coming here of John Joachim, I, at the being here of the archbishop of Capua, showed unto the said ambassador and wrote similarly to you, to be declared unto the emperor, that where the pope's holiness made overture of a truce to be taken at Rome, the king my master was not minded to condescend thereunto, but with three things: one is, that the emperor were first agreed and contented with the same ; secondly, that there might be an appearance how in the time of truce might follow a good peace between all three princes; thirdly, inasmuch as hard, and almost impossible it should be to make the pope's holiness so ripe in the king's particular cause as were needful, that one should be sent hither from the French king, or at the least from my lady regent of France, which might make offers for the king's part; and the same found reasonable, to advertise the emperor thereof. To whom the king's and my opinion was, another person should be also sent for making of similar offers unto his majesty for his part; so that, both princes pleased, the peace might be concluded at Rome, by mutual consent; and the pope's holiness to have the honour, as author and conducer of the same. Upon the return of the which archbishop of Capua through France, the said John Joachim, showing himself to be a merchant, and come for his own causes to Boulogne, with mind to repair into this realm for merchandize, desired a safeconduct so to do. And albeit I suspected it might be but a colour, and that he were some personage sent by the French king's consent, for which cause the safeconduct was granted, yet nevertheless in eight days after his coming he never disclosed unto me what he was, but continently showed himself desirous that some good way were taken between the princes. As soon as upon my strait examination he discovered himself, and that he was sent from the lady regent, I made Monsieur de Praet privy thereof, and of his slender charge, with the answer given unto him upon the same, praying him to advertise the emperor and my lady Margaret, as I also would do, and did so. And from time to time since that season, I have not failed to make the said ambassador privy of all that hath been done, spoken, or communed with the said Joachim, who was lodged in a house within the Blackfriars, belonging to a Mr. Lark, whom you know, to the intent I would have an eye upon him, being sent from an enemy, that he should, as he cannot, nor doth send or receive any letters or messages but by my knowledge. Howbeit, against the king's coming to Bridewell he was removed from that lodging. And what I have written unto you herein, to be signified unto the emperor, my sundry letters, if they be safely arrived, can bear witness. The king's highness and I also continually have made in this time the pope's holiness privy to every of the premises, showing always, that for no messenger, ambassador, or other that might come out of France with offers, whatsoever they were, his grace would never conclude any thing with the French king but with the emperor's express knowledge, consent, will, and agreement, being minded rather to continue his enterprises against the common enemy to the uttermost than otherwise. Wherefore, seeing that neither the pope's holiness, nor the emperor, well regarding the premises, could think anything to be done herein but to the best purpose, I marvelled how the said ambassador, to whom the truth and proceeding here is so well known, could take any colour to excuse his said evil reports upon that ground.

As to the not condescending to take the truce proposed at Rome before the decease of Monsieur de la Roche, I was sure there was neither the emperor, nor other that loved the king my master, which reasonably could or would arrest, default, or blame in me therein; though I, like a true servant, gave counsel unto my said master to the contrary, considering how much that truce proposed; for a long season, that is to say, four or five years, *rebus stantibus ut tunc steterunt,* should have been to the extreme loss and prejudice of the king my master's affairs; for albeit I then said and wrote, and as truth was, such a truce, if it were perpetual, might have been most beneficial for the emperor, having in his hands the whole duchy of Milan, the signiory of Genoa, the city and territory of Tournay, with Naples, Navarre, and Fuentarabia delivered from the danger of the Frenchmen, being also discharged of the pension of Naples, of the marriage with the French king's daughter, and of all other inconveniences whereunto his majesty was bounden by the treaty of Noyon; the indemnity also of the king's highness not answered nor paid; yet nevertheless there could nothing be devised more prejudicial and derogatory unto the king's cause and matters; who by that means having then his preparations in readiness for the wars should give the enemy time to respire, had nothing won or recovered of the things belonging to his grace's right and inheritance, had also sustained and spent excessive charges and treasure for the emperor's sake in these wars. There was furthermore no order taken, nor appearance how the said indemnity should be answered. And finally, nothing of promise or goodness might or could arise unto his grace from that truce. Wherefore if I should, for the pleasure of any prince living, have given at the first counsel unto the king's highness to accept and agree to the said truce, it might have been well thought I had been no good servant or counsellor to his grace, nor I should have acquitted myself according to my most bounden duty unto his highness, afore and above all other earthly princes; but rather, it was expedient that the emperor, who, by my master's good help, had attained so many great pieces, should then somewhat train himself in concurring with his highness, or otherwise, so that there might be some likelihood of more equality in the successes of their enterprises, before they should come unto such an unreasonable truce. All this, notwithstanding, when the king's grace was advertised that there was not sufficient furniture of money on the emperor's behalf for the entertainment of the wars, and that there began to be some doubt and peril least the truce not taken, the affairs of Italy should impair, the king's highness by deliberate advice of me and other of his privy council, for the tender zeal and affection borne towards the emperor's causes, all the said inconveniences that should ensue thereby unto his grace notwithstanding, postponing all his own matters, was contented and sent commission to Rome in all possible diligence for concluding of a truce till May come twelve months; which, if it had not been only for the emperor's sake, and for conservation of his honour, his highness would never have condescended unto. And therefore the said ambassador had far overpassed himself, to write, say, or think, that by anything done on this side in refusal of the said truce, the emperor had cause to be revenged.

Over this, as to the not advancing of an army on this side, as was spoken of, it is well known that the king's highness at all times plainly declared and determined, that his grace was not minded nor would send over any such army that time of the year, unless then his grace might be sure of two things: one was, that the army, then being in Provence, were passed the river of Rhone, with intent to pierce the heart of the enemies' countries ; another was, that the captain general of the company of horsemen and footmen to be sent by the lady Margaret would condescend to pass into such part of France as to the king's lieutenant should be thought most convenient. Without which two things the king's grace always expressly declared, none army should be advanced at that time of the year. And over this the king's highness perceived, by relation of the emperor's own folks, that there lacked money on the emperor's part for contribution to the said army in Provence; which was an evident argument, that where it was capitulated that the emperor should bear the whole contribution after an army were once advanced on this side, the whole enterprises should of likelihood perish in default of money in Provence, when the contribution of the half was not performed, and consequently the army on this side should either be in extreme danger, or compelled to return with reproach, loss, and dishonour, besides the wasteful consumption of treasure. Besides that, the army in Provence not passed the river of Rhone, small good or assistance could be given by them unto the army on this side. And the Burgundians, refusing to promise to pass by such ways as the king's lieutenant should devise, if they should continually keep near to their own frontiers, after the accustomable manner, no great good or profit could arise of that journey. Wherefore, seeing that the sending of the said army was never promised or intended by the king's grace but under the form aforesaid, it was thought more expedient for the emperor's benefit that the king's highness should continually contribute unto the army in Provence lacking money, rather than sending another on this side, to put both in appearance of extreme danger. And consequently, the emperor had cause to give most hearty thanks unto the king's highness, which so much tendered his affairs, minding to have contributed unto the sustentation of the army in Provence all this winter; and to set forth some other good enterprises to their comfort, the beginning of the year; and not to be revenged of these good and friendly deeds, as the said de Praet would provoke his majesty to be. And to that intent, after the king's contribution expired, his grace, over and above his convention, sent the sum of 50,000 crowns, appointing that sir John Russell should have received the same at Trent, so to be conveyed straight unto the army in Provence. Which army, by then the money was come so far as Trent, was clearly dissolved, and the money sent into Italy, there to remain in readiness, if any necessity thereof should chance in the emperor's affairs. And albeit the king's highness (as the certainty of things done in Italy cannot be here at the first known) supposed that good order had been given by the emperor for defence of the same, and thereupon commanded the said sum to be returned by exchange. Yet, nevertheless, upon knowledge had that no word was arrived there from the said emperor since the descent of the French king into these parts, the king's highness, of most hearty and tender mind towards the emperor, sent the said sir Gregory de Cassillis, despatched with the charges aforesaid; who had also in commandment, that if he might perceive the emperor's army to lack money, he should employ and deliver them the said 50,000 crowns, by way of loan; and, rather than fail, clearly to give unto them the same. Which sum, any report made to the contrary notwithstanding, is yet remaining there, in such hands that albeit practise was made for exchange thereof, ways be devised how to have the money upon the sight, though the said ambassador, after his accustomable sinister interruption, would affirm that the said money was sent but for a colour, and that it is totally returned by exchange, which is clearly untrue, as shall appear. Wherefore his feigned report herein was and is to be taken as proceeding of his perverse fantasy without ground of reason, truth, or appearance.

And as to the contribution of Italy, albeit he knew well that there was never capitulation passed between the king's highness and the emperor for that purpose, nor his grace knew what the emperor intended to do therein, or whether the imperials solicited by the pope would have come, or yet will come, to a truce or not; and that also Monsieur de Rieux at his being here confessed error and true demeanour to be in the viceroy of Naples; and that the king's grace hath been from many good places advertised that there were and yet be practices between the French king and the said viceroy for appointment to be taken with the emperor, as in my last letters I wrote unto you more at large, so that his highness could not certainly know by what means assistance should be given to the said viceroy; yet what his grace hath done, by his divers and many letters to sundry parts, and now of late to sir Gregory's despatch at such time as the said emperor's affairs in Italy seemed here to be in most despair, no man could better testify and bear record than the said ambassadors. Wherefore, to write that I would ascribe the victory, if any were, only to the king's grace, or that I were the cause of all the evil that the emperor hath, or that his majesty doth all things alone, and hath no cause to give thanks but to God and his own servants; and that no prince can be better served by the viceroy and other than he is; and that his majesty is little beholden to any his friends and confederates all, whatsoever they be; and that he trusteth to see his majesty once revenged, or that there were appearance that the king's highness, for speaking with so simple a person as John Joachim is, or also with the said president, could find none other mean, if his grace were so disposed, but to come unto Bridewell, specially the said president being lodged in a canon's house at Westminster, I could not a little marvel; saying that hereby the said ambassador had showed manifest appearance that he hath a corrupt mind and perverse intent, studying rather to bring these two princes into jealousy and suspicion than to nourish good love and intelligence between them. To this he could make none other answer but that he wrote his fantasy, remitting the judgment to wiser men than he is. And, provoked to put in writing such other things as he affirmed he could produce against me, he answered, that this was the effect of all; and that when the emperor shall command him, he will so do. Hereupon, having respect unto the emperor's honour, I desired him to forbear writing till such time as he might know further the emperor's pleasure, and so his repairing to the king's highness or to me, unless he had new matter by any letters that should come, saying that the king's highness and I would advertise.*

LETTER XXI.

WOLSEY TO THE BISHOP OF LONDON AND SIR RICHARD WINGFIELD, KNT., AMBASSADORS IN SPAIN.

April 7, 1525.

MY lord of London and Mr. Wingfield, I commend me unto you in my right hearty manner. Since your departure from hence arrived here a servant of the emperor, sent out of Spain with letters to ambassador de Praet, having order given unto him, as he affirmed, incontinently to pass unto the lady Margaret. At the despatch of him out of Spain there was no knowledge of the battle stricken in Italy; but, as I may predict by relation of the president of Malams, whom

---

* There is a letter from Margaret, regent of the Low Countries, to cardinal Wolsey, in which she acknowledges his letter of the 10th of February, and says she is sorry for the discontent he had received by Monsieur de Praet, the emperor's ambassador: that if it were in her power she would recal him, and have him punished for the least thing he should do against his honour, which she holds as dear as her own. She fully acknowledges the cardinal's great zeal towards the emperor, and that he is a true and loyal friend to him.

by good means I caused to disclose more of his secrets unto me than the lord Bevers hath or would do. He said letters sent unto de Praet mentioned the emperor's desire, that for as much as the French king at that time was in Italy, and to drive him out of the same, the king's highness would invade on this side, offering to advance into the parts of Narbonne, on the other side, an army which should be of eight hundred of arms, five hundred light horse, seven thousand Spaniards, and four thousand Germans, besides the peasants, with artillery and ordnance requisite for the same. And that he would maintain, entertain, and continue his army in Italy, under the leading of the duke of Bourbon and the viceroy, at his own proper costs and charges; and over the same would give aid to the king of three thousand footmen, and one thousand horsemen, out of his Low Countries. Notwithstanding this the emperor's determination signified to Mons. de Praet, yet I perceive that his ambassadors here resident would first have advertised the lady Margaret hereof, before the king's highness or I should have had any knowledge of the same; to the intent, that whosoever should be concluded herein, she might have all or a great part of the thanks. Which manner of proceeding I by good means have discovered out of the said president apart. To whom I said, that if my lady Margaret will look to have any thank in this behalf, wherein as yet hitherto she hath little or none deserved, but all that is offered is to be ascribed unto the emperor, it shall be well done that she increase the number of three thousand footmen to four thousand, and the one thousand horsemen to three thousand; and, so doing, she shall deserve special thank, advising him and his colleagues, therefore, to solicit the same. And albeit he thought my lady Margaret might at length be induced thereunto, yet he thought it would be difficile for them to pass with their said aid into any part of Normandy, being so far distant from their frontiers. For avoiding of which difficulty I told him, that perchance the king would personally descend at Calais with a right good part of his army, sending the residue by sea, to make them enter into Normandy; and for so doing, methought they could not of reason make any difficulty, but that their said aid should join with the king's highness and army in his marches of Calais; and so to pass into such places as should be thought unto his grace con-

z

venient. Which overture, as I could perceive, not only contented him, but he promised with all diligence to advertise the lady of the same, not doubting but he should have shortly from her upon the premises a good resolution. Of all which the emperor's offers and occasion aforesaid I thought convenient to advertise you, to the intent you might perceive how before the battle stricken the emperor was inclined and disposed.

Over this there was a clause omitted in your instructions, which is to declare the king's mind, in case the emperor, being contented on this resolution to invade Italy in his own person, will say it should be . . . . . from good conscience to charge him also with entertainment of the duke of Bourbon. Nevertheless, you know that by mouth it was agreed and thought good, that in such case, that if the emperor could in nowise be induced to the said entertainment, the duke of Bourbon should repair unto the said aid of the Low Countries, to have the leading thereof; the same to be in that case somewhat reinforced and increased to a greater number, as to good reason and congruence doth appertain. Which matter, in case of the emperor's invasion, ye shall set forth in degrees; that is to say, first, the emperor to contribute half to the entertainment of the said duke, and the king's grace the other half; so as always the moiety to be borne by the king's grace may be defalked of such money as is due by the emperor unto the king's highness. Secondly, this failing, the king's grace, rather than fail, to bear the whole 300,000 crowns last lent unto the emperor, his majesty supporting the rest; and the same to be paid by the emperor in deduction of the said debt. And, finally, none of these then to come unto the repair of the said duke to the army in the Low Countries, as is aforesaid.

Finally, I send unto you herewith all the commissions, letters, and copies, that were devised for your despatch; with those of the king's, the queen's, and mine own hand. And also an emerald, which my lady princess sendeth to the emperor, whose most humble and cordial recommendations made unto the same, you at the delivery thereof shall say, that her grace hath devised this token for a better knowledge to be had when God shall send them grace to be together, whether his majesty do keep himself as continent and chaste as with God's grace she will. Whereby, you may say, his majesty may see that her assured love towards the same hath already such a passion in her, that it is also confirmed by jealousy, being one of the greatest signs and tokens of hearty love and cordial affection. And thus I beseech Almighty God to send you good speed and passage. At my palace beside Westminster, the third day of April, 1525. Your loving friend,

T. Card^{lis} Ebor.

> To my loving friends, my lord privy
> seal, and sir Richard Wingfield,
> knight of the order, the king's
> ambassadors to the emperor.

Letter XXII.

QUEEN KATHARINE OF ARRAGON AND HENRY VIII. TO CARDINAL WOLSEY, A JOINT LETTER, 1527.

My lord, in my most humblest wise that my heart can think, I desire you to pardon me that I am so bold to trouble you with my simple and rude writing, esteeming it to proceed from her that is much desirous to know that your grace does well. I perceive by this bearer that you do, the which I pray God long to continue, as I am most bound to pray, for I do know the great pains and trouble that ye have taken for me both day and night is never likely to be recompensed on my part, but only in loving you, next to the king's grace, above all creatures living; and I do not doubt but the daily proofs of my deeds shall manifestly declare and affirm my writing to be true, and I do trust you do think the same. My lord, I do assure you I do long to hear from you some news of the legate, for I do hope, if they come from you, they shall be very good, and I am sure that you desire it as much as I, and more, if that were possible, as I know it is not; and thus remaining in a stedfast hope, I make an end of my letter, written with the hand of her that is most bound to be—

(Here queen Katharine's part ends; the rest is written by the king.)

The writer of this letter would not cease till she had caused me likewise to set to my hand, desiring you, though it be short, to take it in good part. I ensure you there is neither of us but that greatly desireth to see you, and much rejoiceth

z 2

to hear that you have escaped this plague so well, trusting the fury thereof to be passed, especially with them that keep good diet, as I trust you do. The not hearing of the legate's arrival in France, causeth us somewhat to muse; notwithstanding we trust by your vigilance and diligence, with the assistance of Almighty God, shortly to be eased out of that trouble. No more to you at this time, but that I pray God send you as good health and prosperity as the writer's. By your loving sovereign and friend,   HENRY, R.

LETTER XXIII.

ANNE BOLEYN TO CARDINAL WOLSEY.

MY lord, after my most humble recommendations, this shall be to give unto your grace, as I am most bound, my humble thanks, for the great pain and travail that your grace doth take, in studying, by your wisdom and great diligence, how to bring to pass honourably the greatest wealth that is possible to come to any creature living; and in especial remembering how wretched and unworthy I am in comparing to his highness. And for you, I do know myself never to have deserved by my deserts that you should take this great pain for me; yet daily of your goodness I do perceive by all my friends; and though that I had not knowledge by them, the daily proof of your deeds doth declare your words and writings toward me to be true. Now, good my lord, your discretion may consider as yet how little it is in my power to recompense you, but alonely with my good will; the which I assure you, that after this matter is brought to pass, you shall find me as I am (bound in the meantime to owe you my service); and then, look what thing in this world I can imagine to do you pleasure in, you shall find me the gladdest woman in the world to do it; and, next unto the king's grace, of one thing I make you full promise to be assured to have it, and that is, my hearty love, unfeignedly, during my life; and being fully determined, with God's grace, never to change this purpose, I make an end of this my rude and true meaned letter, praying our Lord to send you much increase of honour with long life. Written with the hand of her that beseeches your grace to accept this letter as proceeding from one that is most bound to be your humble and obedient servant,

ANNE BOLEYN.

Letter XXIV.

ANNE BOLEYN TO CARDINAL WOLSEY.

My lord, in my most humblest wise that my poor heart can think, I do thank your grace for your kind letter, and for your rich and goodly present, the which I shall never be able to deserve without your great help. Of the which I have hitherto had so great plenty, that all the days of my life I am most bound of all creatures next to the king's grace to love and serve your grace, of the which I beseech you never to doubt that ever I shall vary from this thought as long as any breath is in my body; and as touching your grace's trouble with the sweat, I thank our Lord that they that I desired and prayed for are escaped, and that is the king and you: not doubting but that God has preserved you both for great causes known only to his high wisdom; and as for the coming of the legate I desire that much; and if it be God's pleasure, I pray him to send this matter shortly to a good end; and then I trust, my lord, to recompense part of your great pains, the which I must require you in the mean time to accept my good will in the stead of the power, the which must proceed partly from you, as our Lord knoweth, whom I beseech to send you long life with continuance in honour. Written with the hand of her that is most bound to be, your humble obedient servant,   ANNE BOLEYN.

Letter XXV.

ANNE BOLEYN TO WOLSEY.

My lord, in my most humble wise I thank your grace for the gift of this benefice for master Barlow, howbeit this standeth to none effect, for it is made for Tunbridge, and I would have it, if your pleasure were so, for Sunbridge; for Tunbridge is in my lord my father's gift, by a vowson that he hath, and it is not yet void; I do trust that your grace will grant him Sunbridge, and considering the pain that he hath taken, I do think that it shall be very well bestowed; and in so doing, I reckon myself much bounden to your grace. For all these that hath taken pain in the king's matter, it shall be my daily study to imagine all the ways that I can devise to do them service and pleasure; and thus I make an end, sending you again the letter that you sent me, thanking your grace most humbly for the pain that you take for to write to me, assuring you that, next the king's letter, there is nothing that can rejoice me so much. With the hand of her that is most bounden to be

Your humble and obedient servant, ANNE BOLEYN.

My lord, I beseech your grace, with all my heart, to remember the parson of —— for my sake shortly.

LETTER XXVI.

THE KING TO WOLSEY.

MINE own good cardinal, I recommend me unto you with all my heart, and thank you for the great pain and labour that you do daily take in my business and matters, desiring you, that when you have well established them, to take some pastime and comfort, to the intent you may the longer endure to serve us, for always pain cannot be endured. Surely you have so substantially ordered our matters, both of this side the sea and beyond, that, in mine opinion, little or nothing can be added; nevertheless, according to your desire, I do send you mine opinion by this bearer, the reformation whereof I do remit to you and the remnant of our trusty councillors, which I am sure will substantially look on it. As touching the matter that sir William Says brought answer of, I am well contented with what order soever you do take in it. The queen my wife hath desired to make her most hearty recommendations to you, as to him that she loveth very well; and both she and I would know fain, when you will repair to us. No more to you at this time, but that, with God's help, I trust we shall disappoint our enemies of their intended purpose. Written with the hand of your loving master,

HENRY.

To my lord cardinal.

LETTER XXVII.

WOLSEY, IN HIS DISTRESS, TO THOMAS CROMWELL.

MINE own entirely beloved Cromwell, I beseech you as you love me, and will ever do anything for me, repair hither this

day as soon as the parliament is broken up, laying apart all
things for that time; for I would not only communicate things
unto you, wherein for my comfort and relief I would have
your good and discreet advice and counsel, but also upon the
same commit certain things requiring expedition to you on
my behalf to be solicited. This I pray you, therefore, to
haste your coming hither as afore, without omitting so to do,
as ye, under my succour, relief and comfort, and quietness of
mind; and thus fare ye well. From Esher, in haste, this
Saturday in the morning, with the rude hand and sorrowful
heart of your assured lover,   T. CARD^{LIS} EBOR.

I have also certain things concerning yourself, which I am
sure you will be glad to hear and know. Fail not, therefore,
to be here this night; ye may return early in the morning
again if need shall so require. *Et iterum vale.*

Mr. Augustin showed me how ye had written unto me a
letter wherein ye should advertise of the coming hither of
the duke of Norfolk. I assure you there came to my hands
no such letter.

LETTER XXVIII.

WOLSEY TO DR. STEPHEN GARDENER, SECRETARY OF STATE.

(In the Ashmole Museum at Oxford.)

MY own good master secretary, going this day out of my
pew to say mass, your letters dated yesternight, at London,
were delivered unto me; by the contents whereof I understood that the king's highness, of his excellent goodness
and charity, is contented that I shall enjoy and have the
administration of York merely, with the gifts of the promotion, spiritual and temporal, of the same, reserved only unto
his noble grace the gift of five or six of the best promotions,
and that his pleasure is I should leave Winchester and
St. Albans. As hereunto, Mr. Secretary, I cannot express
how much I am bounden to the king's royal majesty for this
his great and bounteous liberality, reputing the same to be
much more than I shall ever be able to deserve. Howbeit,
if his majesty, considering the short and little time that I shall
live here in this world, by the reason of such heaviness as I
have conceived in my heart, with the ruinousness of the old

houses, and the decay of the said archbishopric, at the best to the sum of 800 marks yearly, by the reason of the act passed as to testaments, with also my long painful service and poor degree; and for the declaration of his grace's excellent charity, if his highness be minded I shall leave Winchester and St. Albans, which I supposed, when I made my submission, not offending in my truth towards his royal person, dignity, or royal majesty, I should not now have deserved to have left; and much the more knowing his excellency's propension to pity and mercy, and remembering the frank departing with of all that I had in this world, that I may have some convenient pension reserved unto me, such as the king's highness of his noble charity shall think meet, so ordering his that shall succeed me and my living, that the same may be of like yearly value and extent. Whereat my trust is, and my heart so giveth me that his majesty would make no difficulty, if it may like you friendly to propose the same, assuring you that I desire not this for any mind (God is my judge,) that I have to accumulate goods, or desire that I have for the muck of the world; for, God be thanked, at this hour I set no more by the riches and promotions of the world, than by the rushes under my foot; but only for the declaration of the king's favour and high charity, and to have wherewith to do good deeds, and to help my poor servants and kinsfolk; and, furthermore, that it would please the king's excellent goodness by your friendly mediation, considering how slenderly I am furnished in my house, now especially that the apparel of Winchester and St. Albans shall be taken from me, to give and appoint unto me a convenient furniture for the same, *non ad pompam, sed necessariam honestatem;* and if I may have the free gift and disposition of the benefices, it shall be greatly to my comfort, and yet when any of the five or six principal shall fortune to be void, the king's grace being minded, any of them his highness shall be as sure of the same as though they were reserved, and thus by his noble and merciful goodness delivered out of extreme calamity, and restored to a new freedom, I shall, with God's mercy and help, so order my life, that I trust his majesty shall take special comfort therein, and be pleased with the same: *spero quod hæc, quæ petò, non videbuntur magna.* Howbeit, I most humbly submit and refer all my petitions, *immo ipsam vitam,* to his grace's ordinance and pleasure, praying you to declare and signify the same, supplying my indisposition and lackness of will, conceived by reason of my extreme sorrowness and heaviness, that the same may be to the king's contentation, wherein I had liefer be dead than to offend in word, thought, or deed, and as touching the granting of the fee of one hundred pounds for Mr. Norris, during his life, for his good service done unto the king's highness, for the which I have always loved him, and for the singular good heart and mind that I know he hath always borne unto me, I am content to make out my grant upon the same; nay, and if it will please the king to enlarge it one hundred pounds more; and in like manner because Mr. Treasurer hath the keeping of the king's game nigh to Farnham; I would gladly, if it may stand with the king's pleasure, grant unto him the reversion of the same things as the lord Sands hath there, with the amplification of the fee above that which is oldly accustomed, to the sum of forty pounds by the year; and also I would gladly give to Mr. Comptroller a like fee, and to Mr. Russell another of twenty pounds by the year, remitting this, and all my suit, to the king's highness, his pleasure, mercy, pity, and compassion most wholly. Beseeching his highness so now graciously to order me that I may henceforth serve God quietly and with repose of mind, and pray, as I am most bounden for the conservation and increase of his most noble and royal state; and thus with my daily prayer I bid you farewell. From Esher, hastily, with the hand and most heavy heart of

Your assured friend and beadsman,

T. Card^{lis} Ebor.

Letter XXIX.

CARDINAL WOLSEY TO DR. STEPHEN GARDENER.

(In the Ashmole Museum at Oxford.)

My own good master secretary, after my most hearty commendations, I pray you at the reverence of God to help, that expedition be used in my pursuits, the delay whereof so replenisheth my heart with heaviness that I can take no rest; not for any vain fear, but only for the miserable condition that I am presently in, and likely to continue in the same, unless that you, in whom is mine assured trust, do help and relieve me therein; for first, continuing here in this moist and corrupt air, being entered into the passion of the dropsy, *Cum prostatione appetitus et continuo insomnio*, I cannot live; wherefore of necessity I must be removed to some other dryer air and place, where I may have commodity of physicians. Secondly, having but York, which is now decayed, by 800*l.* by the year, I cannot tell how to live and keep the poor number of folks which I now have. My house there be in decay, and of every thing meet for household unprovided and unfurnished. I have no apparel for my houses there, nor money to bring me thither, nor to live with till the propitious time of year come to remove thither. These things considered, Mr. Secretary, must needs make me in agony and heaviness, my age therewith and sickness considered. Alas! Mr. Secretary, ye, with other, my lords, showed me that I should be otherwise furnished and seen unto; ye know in your learning and conscience whether I should forfeit my spiritualities of Winchester or no. Alas! the qualities of mine offences considered, with the great punishment and loss of goods I have sustained, ought to move pitiful hearts; and the most noble king, to whom, if it would please you of your charitable goodness to show the premises after your accustomed wisdom and dexterity, it is not to be doubted but his highness would have consideration and compassion, augmenting my living, and appointing such things as should be convenient for my furniture, which to do shall be to the king's high honour, merit, and discharge of conscience, and to you great praise for the bringing of the same to pass, for your old bringer up and loving friend. This kindness exhibited from the king's highness shall prolong my life for some little while, though it shall not be long; by the mean whereof his grace shall take profit, and by my death none. What is it to his highness to give some convenient portion out of Winchester and Saint Albans, his grace taking with my hearty good will the residue. Remember, good Mr. Secretary, my poor degree, and what service I have done, and how now, approaching to death, I must begin the world again. I beseech you therefore, moved with pity and compassion, succour me in this my calamity, and to your power, which I know is great, relieve me; and I with all mine shall not only ascribe this my relief unto you, but also pray to God for the increase of your honour, and as my power shall increase me, I shall not fail to requite your kindness. Written hastily at Esher, with the rude and shaking hand of your daily beadsman, and assured friend, T. CARD^{LIS} EBOR.

To the right honourable and my
assured friend, master secretary.

LETTER XXX.

WOLSEY TO SECRETARY GARDENER.
(From Strype.)

MINE own good master secretary, albeit I am in such alteration and indisposition of my head and body, by the means of my daily sorrow and heaviness, that I am fain omit to write any long letters, yet my trusting friend, Thomas Cromwell, returning and repairing unto you, I could not forbear but briefly to put you in remembrance, how that after the consultation taken by the king's highness upon mine ordering, which ye supposed should be on Sunday was seven-night, ye would not fail to advertise me at the length of the specialities thereof; of the which to hear and have knowledge I have and daily do look for. I pray you, therefore, at the reverence of God, and of this holy time, and as ye love and tender my poor life, do so much as to write unto me your said letters, whereby I may take some comfort and rest; not doubting but your heart is so gentle and pitiful that having knowledge in what agony I remain, ye will take the pain to send unto me your said consolatory letters, whereby ye shall not only deserve toward God, but also bind me to be, as I am, your continual beadsman. Written this morning, at Esher, with the rude hand and sorrowful heart of yours with heart and prayer,

T. CARDINALIS EBOR MISERRIMUS.

To the right honourable Mr. Secretary.

LETTER XXXI.

WOLSEY TO SECRETARY GARDENER.
(From Strype.)

MY own good master secretary, after my most hearty recommendations, with like thanks for your goodness towards me, these shall be to advertise you that I have been informed by my trusty friend, Thomas Cromwell, that ye have signified unto him to my singular consolation how that the king's highness, moved with pity and compassion, and of his excellent goodness and charity, considering the lamentable condition and state that I stand in, hath willed you, with other lords and masters of his honourable council, to intend to the perfecting and absolving, without further tract or delay, of mine end and appointment, and that my pardon should be made in the most ample form that my counsel could devise.

For this the king's most gracious remembrance, proceeding of himself, I count myself not only most bounden to serve and pray for the preservation of his most royal majesty, but also thank God that ye have occasion given unto you to be a solicitor and setter forth of such things as do and shall conserve my said end; in the making and compounding whereof, mine assured trust is, that ye will show the love and affection which ye have and bear towards me, your old friend and lover; so declaring yourself therein that the world may perceive that by your good means the king is the better good lord unto me; and that now, newly in manner coming to the world, there may be such respect had to my poor degree, old age, and long continued service, as shall be to the king's high honour, and your great praise and laud, which undoubtedly shall follow if ye obtained your benevolence towards me, and men perceive that by your wisdom and dexterity I shall be relieved, and in this my calamity helped. At the reverence, therefore, of God, mine own good Mr. Secretary, and refuge, now set to your hand, that I may come to a laudable end and repose, seeing that I may be furnished after such a sort and manner that I may end my short time and life to the honour of Christ's church and the prince; and, besides, by daily prayer and true heart, I shall so requite your kindness, as ye shall have cause to think the same to be well employed, like as my said trusty friend shall more amply show unto you. To whom it may please you to give firm credence and loving audience, and I shall pray for the increase of your honour. Written at Esher, with the trembling hand and heavy heart of your assured friend and beadsman,

T. CARD^{LIS} EBOR.

To the right honourable and my singular
    good friend, master secretary.

Letter XXXII.

WOLSEY TO SECRETARY GARDENER.

(From Strype.)

MINE own gentle master secretary, after my most hearty recommendations, these shall be to thank you for the great humanity, loving and gentle reception, that ye made unto the poor Provost of Beverly; and especially for that ye have in such wise addressed him unto the king's highness' presence; that his grace not only hath showed unto him that he is his good and gracious lord, but also that it hath pleased his majesty to accept him as his poor orator and scholar. Whereby both he and I account ourselves so bounden unto you, that we cannot tell how to requite this your gratitude and kindness; most heartily praying you to continue in your good favour towards him, and to take him and his poor cause into your patronage and protection; and as mine assured expectation and trust is, to remember the poor state and condition that I stand in, and to be a mean to the king's highness for my relief in the same. In doing whereof ye shall not only deserve thanks of God, but also declare, to your perpetual laud and praise, that ye, being in authority, have not forgotten your old master and friend; and in the way of charity, and for the love that you bear to virtue, and *ad bona studia*, be means to the king's highness for my poor colleges, and especially for the college of Oxford. Suffer not the things which, by your great learning, study, counsel, and labour hath been erected, bounden, and with good statutes and ordinances to the honour of God, increase of virtue and learning established, to be dissolved or dismembered. Ye do know —no man better—to what use the monasteries, suppressed by the pope's licence, the king's consent concurring with the same, and a pardon for the premunire, be converted. It is not to be doubted but the king's highness, of his great virtue and equity, being informed how everything is passed, his most gracious licence and consent (as is aforesaid) exhibited thereto, will never go about to dissolve the said incorporations or bodies, whereof so great benefit and commodity shall issue unto his realm and subjects. Superfluities, if any such shall be thought and founden, may be abridged, but to destroy the whole, it were too great pity.

Eftsones, therefore, good master secretary, I beseech you to be good master and patron to the said colleges; " *Et non sinas opas manuum tuarum perire, aut ad nihilum redire.*" Thus doing, both I and they shall not only pray for you, but in such wise deserve your pains, as ye shall have cause to think the same to be well bestowed and employed, like as this present bearer shall more at the large show unto you. To whom it may please the same to give firm credence; and thus, most heartily, fare you well.

From Southwell, the 23rd day of July.

Your loving friend,   T. CARD^{LIS} EBOR.

To the right honourable and my
singular good friend, Mr. Doctor
Stephen, secretary to the king's
highness.

LETTER XXXIII.

WOLSEY TO SECRETARY GARDENER.

(From Strype.)

MINE own good master secretary, after my most hearty recommendations, these shall be to desire, and most effectually to pray you to be good master and friend unto me, concerning the uncharitable suit of Strangways for 700 pounds, which he pretendeth that I should give unto him for the ward of Bowes; and albeit there was at his first coming to my service, by our mutual consent, a perfect end made between him and me for the same, yet now digressing therefrom, perceiving that I am out of favour, destitute of succour, and in calamity, he not only newly demandeth the same 700 pounds, but hath also made complaint unto the king's highness, submitting that I should, contrary to justice, detain from him the said 700 pounds, for the redress whereof, it hath pleased the king's majesty to direct his most honourable letters to me; the contents whereof I am sure be not unknown unto you; and ensuing the purport thereof, and before the delivery of the same three days past, notwithstanding my great necessity and poverty, only to be out of his exclamation and inquietness, I have written to my trusty friend, Mr. Cromwell, to make certain reasonable offers unto him for that intent and purpose; most heartily beseeching you to help,

that upon declaration of such things, as upon my part shall
be signified unto you by the said master Cromwell, some such
end, by your friendly dexterity, may be made betwixt us, as
shall accord with good congruence, and as I may support and
be able (mine other debts and charges considered) to bear.
In the doing whereof, ye shall bind me to be your daily
beadsman, as knoweth God, who always preserve you.   From
Southwell, the 25th day of August.

Yours, with heart and prayer,
T. Card^{lis} Ebor.

To my right entirely well-beloved
   friend, Mr. Stephen Gardener,
     secretary to the king's highness.

LETTER XXXIV.

WOLSEY TO FOX, BISHOP OF WINCHESTER.

AFTER most humble commendations with like desire of your
health and perfect recovery, please it your good lordship to
understand that on Sunday last past the king received letters
from sir Robert Wingfield, dated the 4th of this month, by
the contents whereof he advertised the king that the emperor
had not only word from the court of Rome but from divers
other places, that our holy father the pope should be in such
danger of life that there is no hope of his recovery, for all
the lower parts of his body, from the middle downwards,
were dead mortified, and as cold as any stone; wherefore the
emperor minding and intending to his best the advancement
of the cardinal Adrian *ad papatum*, hath sent the bishop
of —— to Rome effectually to solicit the same; and to the
intent that this his purpose should the better be brought about,
he hath taken with him sir Robert Wingfield, who also at the
instant desire of the emperor intendeth to go to Rome; yesterday at mass I broke with the king in this matter, and
showed unto his grace how much honour, and also furtherance of all his affairs in time to come should ensue to him, if
that by his commendation some cardinal might attain to be
pope, and saying that the emperor was effectually intending
the preferment of the cardinal Adrian, who in manner is as
the king's bounden subject, with his gracious help, the matter

should much the sooner be brought to pass. I found his grace very conformable and agreeable to my saying; howbeit I durst not further wade with his grace as touching your letters of recommendation, as well for the ———— of your other letters and the dates of the same, as also that we have no sure knowledge of the pope's death, otherwise than is before said. Your lordship I trust is nothing miscontent with me that I presumed to break your instructions; for assuredly, except Mr. Treasurer, no earthly man is nor shall be made privy to your letters. I am half afraid that you be displeased, forasmuch I have received no writing from you this long season; I trust you will take my doing to proceed of good will, thinking that it was for the best in good part. My lord, in communication at the large, I have felt how that my lord chamberlain and of Durham be much inclined to the cardinal of Saint George, and in all their talk they cannot speak too much honour of him, dispraising the cardinal Adrian; if your lordship were here this matter would be soon brought to your purpose. And my lord, for divers urgent causes it is thought very expedient that you should repair to the king; for all his great matters be deferred unto your coming, which is daily looked for and desired of all those that would the king's causes should proceed in a good train. The Master of the Rolls is coming to Dover; we look for him daily; he hath written hither that never man had worse cheer than he in France; nothing hath he done further than I wrote on to you in my last letters as touching his charge.

The ambassador of Arragon hath liberally dealt with my lord Darcy;* he hath given to him all he wanted for one whole month after sixpence the day, and for fifteen days after, eight-pence the day, for every soldier more than of very duty he could demand. And the king our master hath for his part given to him the thousand pounds which at his departing his grace lent to him; thus the king's money goeth away in every corner. And as touching the king's abode here, he intendeth not to depart hence till within four or five days before Allhallowtide on Monday next coming, his grace pur-

---

* Sent into Spain with 1500 archers. Upon his arrival, news was brought that a peace was concluded with the Moors. He was liberally rewarded, and dismissed.

poseth to ride to London to see his ship, there to tarry two days, and so return hither again. My lord Stra—— is not yet coming to the court: within three or four days he intendeth to be here. My lord treasurer, at his last coming to the king, which was this day se'nnight, had such manner and countenance shown to him, that on the morrow he departed home again, and as yet is not returned to the court; without little help now he might be utterly, as touching lodging in the same, excluded, whereof in my poor judgment no little good should ensue: the king is minded as yet to send Mr. Deane, of Windsor, to the king of Scots, as well to declare the cause why he hath taken his ships, and thus treated his subjects, as also to bear the queen's bequest, for the which she hath instantly written. Mr. Howard marvellously incenseth the king against the Scots, by whose wanton means his grace spendeth much money, and is more disposed to war than peace: your presence shall be very necessary to repress this appetite. Other news we have none here, but that it is thought that the queen is with child; when other shall occur I shall advertise you of the same, as knoweth God, who preserve your good lordship in good health. At Windsor, in haste, the last day of September, with the rude hand of your loving and humble priest.

As touching the preferment of Mr. Ing, I need not write unto you, for I suppose he hath advertised your lordship at the length in that behalf, and also desired your counsel, now that the king hath showed him his pleasure how far the expedition of his matter shall be further ordered and demeaned. And our Lord send you health and strength.

Thomas Wolsey.

To my singular good lord, my lord of Winchester.

Letter XXXV.

FROM THE SAME TO THE SAME.

After most humble commendations, my lord, I beseech you to attach no blame to me, that since my departing from you I have not written to the same all such news as hath occurred for the time; for in faith unto this day I could attain no time so to do, unless I should have written but half a tale; sure I am hereof you will marvel, but at our next meeting your lordship shall know the cause. And as for the matters of Spain, how the same do go, I am sure you have been advertised by such writings as hath been sent to you from thence. Howbeit, you shall by Mr. Knight's letter, which I now send on to you, know in substance all that is written by my lord marquis John Stile or any other; by the which letters I now perceive your old saying to be true, touching the order and pain which Englishmen will abide, endure; I trow their desire to return home shall be to the hindrance of the enterprise of Guyenne, equivalent to the king of Arragon's slackness, from whom the gentleman which was sent hither in the time of the parliament to view the king's artillery, a man full of words, is lately come to the king, the substance of whose charge resteth only in excusing the king his master, that his army hath not joined with the king's army hitherto, alleging that the danger of Navarre, with the colourable dealing of the king of the same, hath been the cause of this long delay; howbeit now he dare jeopard his life that both armies be joined. The king his master affirmeth by the oath of a prince that he shall neither desist from the war, nor leave the king on to such time as his grace hath recovered and attained to the crown of France, with many other pleasant words; I pray God the deeds may follow and ensue accordingly. And as touching the state of Italy, and how also our ambassadors do in their matters, your lordship shall perceive by such letters as I send to the same in this packet, which when you have read, I beseech you to send again.

And to ascertain you of the lamentable and sorrowful tidings and chance which hath fortuned by the sea, our folks on Tuesday fortnight met with twenty great ships of France, the best with sail and furnished with artillery and men that ever was seen. And after innumerable shooting of guns, and long chasing one another, at the last the Regent most valiantly boarded the great Carrick of Brest, wherein were four lords, three hundred gentlemen, eight hundred soldiers and marines, four hundred cross-bow men, one hundred gunners, two hundred tun of wine, one hundred pipes of other wine, sixty barrels of gunpowder, and fifteen great brazen cortawds, with ten mernelose, a number of siset and other guns of every sort; our men so valiantly acquitted themselves, that within one hour's fight they had utterly vanquished with shot of guns and arrows the said Carrick, and slain most part of the men within the same. And suddenly, as they were yielding themselves, the Carrick was on a flaming fire, and likewise the Regent; within the turning of one hand, she was so anchored and fastened to the Carrick, that by no means possible she might for her safeguard depart from the same. And so both in sight within three hours were burnt, and most part of the men in them. Sir Thomas Knivett, who most valiantly acquitted himself that day, was slain with one gun; sir John Carew, with divers others, whose names be not yet known, be likewise slain; I pray God to have mercy on their souls. And my lord, at the reverence of God; keep these tidings secret to yourself, for there is no living man knoweth the same here, but only the king and I. Your lordship knoweth right well that it is expedient for a while to keep the same secret, to see how the king taketh the matter and behaveth himself. Ye would marvel and much allow his wise and constant manner; I have not, on my faith, seen the like. And thus with heavy heart and sorrowful pen I make an end, beseeching God to preserve your good lordship. From Farnham, this morning, in wondrous haste, the 26th day of August, with the rude hand of your assured chaplain,

THOMAS WOLSEY.

The residue of the French fleet, after long chasing, was by our folks put to flight, and driven off into Brest haven. There were six as great ships of the said fleet as the Regent or Sovereign; howbeit, as cowards they fled; sir Edward hath made his vow to God that he will never see the king in the face till he hath revenged the death of the noble and valiant knight sir Thomas Knivett.

The letters of thanks to my lord cardinal Adrian I send to your lordship in this packet.

LETTER XXXVI.

WAREHAM, ARCHBISHOP OF CANTERBURY, TO WOLSEY.

PLEASE it your grace, I am informed by such credible persons as I have secretly caused to make privy, especially amongst

A A 2

the clergy of my diocese and peculiar jurisdiction, that there is much untowardness in the clergy, which as they say doth greatly grudge to make contribution of the third part of the goods or promotions, saying that now they must pay the subsidy granted at the last convocation, which as yet they have not paid, neither be able to pay, as they say, neither knoweth where or of whom to borrow it. And in case they should now pay the third part of their said goods or promotions, they should live (as they say) in continual poverty, and their chancels, parsonages, vicarages, barns, and other houses, decay and utterly be destroyed; saying also, that if the king's grace should now and also in time to come thus by his grace's letters, missives, privy seals, or other ways, hereafter require aid of the spirituality as oftentimes as it shall please his grace so to do, besides the grants of convocations, to which they acknowledge themselves bound, the church and clergy shall at length be put to such insupportable charges, as they shall not be able to bear, to the utter undoing and destruction of the same, as they say it is almost already, and so hospitality should cease.

It is reported to me also, that divers of the clergy say some of them do support their fathers, some their mothers, and some both, which as they say, they be bound to do by laws of God. And in case now they should be compelled to put them out of their houses, they say they should be compelled to do against charity, the laws of nature and laws of the church, and so their fathers and mothers should be constrained to go a begging, to their utter shame, and they themselves to live in misery.

Item, it is reported that if the clergy had money or knew how to come by it, they would right gladly contribute according to the king's grace's demand; saying that for the time they had money they were as glad to depart to their prince as ever was clergy, but they have so long paid that they be utterly undone and can pay no more; adding, if the king's highness knew their poverty, his grace would not demand the third part of the goods of the church, or yet any part more than they have already paid and granted to pay.

It is reported also that the king's grace have had already of them in tenths, in loans, in subsidies, and other payments, to the sum, every year of his grace's reign, of a tenth, which is sixteen tenths, and reported that the church was never so continually charged in no king's days; and if there should now be any new contribution demanded, the church should be utterly destroyed.

Also I am informed that the clergy do commune amongst themselves, that considering that laymen which standeth only forth keeping of their own goods, and finding of their wives and children, will nothing grant, they were much to be blamed if they would not stand for the defence of the goods of the church, which they allege to be *Bona pauperum et non regum neque nobilium.*

Your grace may perceive by these reports made to me, if they be true, that there is a great untowardness in the clergy, for the which I am right sorry. In case these reports be true, as peradventure a great part be, I beseech your grace that I may know your best advice and counsel how I may best order myself in this behalf. And that knowing, I will help to the best of my power (as I would God should help my soul) to induce the clergy to advance according to the king's grace's instructions.

Upon Thursday next ensuing, divers of the clergy within my jurisdiction be assigned to appear before me here at Otford, and then I shall perceive whether I shall find true or no such reports beforesaid as have been made unto me. And as I shall then find, so will I certify your grace.

As touching the demeanours of the king's grace's subjects, sent unto me by his grace's commissioners of this county, which partly knoweth the demeanour of them, I have written my letters to sir Thomas Boleyn and sir Henry Guildford, knights, which letters I doubt not but your grace have either seen or else shall shortly see. If at any time any of the said laymen should be sent unto the king's grace or yours, in case they should be there well and favourable entreated, they that doth abide at home will think that they should be as favourable entreated. And so they would little regard this demand. And in case they that shall come to the king's grace and yours should be hardly entreated, they that be at home will think they shall be as ill entreated, and peradventure might cause them to make more business at length to their own pains than the king's grace would be contented withal. And what shall be best done in this matter I commit it to your grace's wisdom. At Otford, the 15th day of April.

At your grace's commandment,

WILLIAM CANTUAR.

To the most reverend father in
God, and my very singular good
lord, my lord cardinal of York,
legate *de latere*, his good grace.

LETTER XXXVII.

THE MAYOR AND ALDERMEN OF YORK TO WOLSEY.

MOST reverend father in God and our most singular good and gracious lord, in our most humble manner, with due reverence we commend us unto your grace, to thank your grace, of your most gracious kindness and goodness of late showed unto us, as touching the diminishing of our fee farm enenst the lord of Rutland, wherein we think that your grace was a very good and gracious lord unto us, and in all other causes and businesses concerning the commonweal of the king's grace and your grace's poor city of York, beseeching your said grace of continuance. And for the tender zeal and favour that your said grace hath ever borne to the increase of the poor citizens of the said city that pleased your grace to obtain the king's most gracious letters patent under his grace's broad seal, whereby we and they of late shipped both wool and fell, likewise as the inhabitants of the town of Newcastle now doth. And by reason thereof the said citizens did daily increase in getting of goods as long as they continued such shipping, the which grant so obtained by your grace was the highest and most especial commodity and jewel that ever came to the aforesaid city for the preferment and enriching of the citizens thereof, and also greatly refreshing to all the country about the same ; albeit, that that was otherwise reported by certain persons that did murmur and grudge with your gracious good act and welfare of their poor neighbours. And at such time as we did use and exercise the shipping of the said wool and fells by virtue of the said grant, then we were so glad thereof that we did little regard our old commodity in buying of lead. And at that time the rich merchants of London got the trade of lead as we had before, and so since that time they have had the trade and most part thereof in their hands, and hath enhanced that to so high a price, that we can get but little of that, wherefore, most gracious lord, the premises considered, we beseech your grace in our most humble manner, that we may have and continue the shipping of the said wool and fell, according to the king's grant, and also free passage beyond the sea, with the little substance of lead that we have now ready to be shipped, notwithstanding the restraint thereof made to the contrary, or else we are like to be utterly undone, being poor men, as knoweth the blessed Trinity, who ever more continue your grace in honour. At the city of York, under the seal of office of the mayoralty of the same, the 24th day of June.

By your grace's most bounden and daily beadmen,

THE MAYOR OF THE CITY OF YORK, AND HIS BROTHER ALDERMEN OF THE SAME.

To the most reverend father in
    God, and their most singular
    and gracious lord, the lord le-
    gate, his grace, chancellor of
    England.

LETTER XXXVIII.

WOLSEY TO THE AMBASSADORS OF FRANCE.

My lords, I commend me unto you in right hearty manner. And by the contents of your letters to me addressed, bearing date the 28th of December, I not only understand the good diligence and effectual devoir that you have done, and put you in for the substantial soliciting and fruitful expedition of the king's cause and matter to you committed, but also the great conformity and towardness of the French king in the furtherance of the same; who, as it appeareth by the writing, is right applicable to the accomplishment as well of the conventions, whereunto he is bound by the treaties, as also to amoving all impediments that might impede or let the perfecting thereof: manifestly declaring thereof not only by the answer given to the lord Ligny, but also by making his submission and oaths benevolently as a virtuous prince; and accounting and accepting upon him the restitution to be made to the king's subjects for despoils done upon the seas, and taking the charge upon him for recovering of Mortaign, wherein he hath partly declared his mind, in his loving letters to the king's highness addressed, but not so amply as your letters purport.

Whereupon the king's highness, as well for the great honours and comfortable cheer to you showed and made, since your arrival in that realm, as for the towardness the said king showeth himself to be of, not only in the entertainment of firm love and amity between the king and him, but also to do unto his grace such honour and pleasure as he can, his highness hath now at this time by his right kind and loving letters given unto him right special and cordial thanks, like as by a copy of his said letters here inclosed, you shall perceive more at length. And well assured you may be, the king's highness upon sight of these your said letters, not only much commended your great diligence and provident dexterity, in the wise conducing of these his weighty matters, whereby you have deserved his singular favour and thanks, but also took great rejoicing, consolation and comfort, in this honourable, princely, and loving demeanour of the said French king: having good hope and confidence, that by this his constant dealing at the beginning, the amity and alliance, to the great comfort of their friends, and discomfort of their enemies, honourably and kindly commenced and begun between them, shall not only proceed from good to better, but finally attain the desired end and universal weal of all Christendom.

And as touching the king's mind and pleasure in the difficulties touched in your former letters, concerning the qualities of the hostages, I doubt not but ye have perfect knowledge by the king's letters, to you lately sent, containing ample instructions how to order yourselves in so great a matter, as that is; not doubting but that after your accustomed wise and provident manner, you will so circumspectly order yourselves therein, that the best hostages as may possibly be gotten, may be had. Or at the least, the final resolution of the king's said letters shall be attained; wherein, as heartily as I can, I require and instantly desire you to apply yourselves with all effect. For to this point all other princes take special regard; whereupon not only dependeth the surety of the conventions, but also the stopping of dishonourable bruits, which by acceptation of insufficient hostages might be spread over all, which is more to be pondered than the importance of Tournay, or any other thing thereupon depending.

And as unto the personal meeting of both princes, the viewing of the place, and appointing the number to come with the said princes, in mine opinion ye have taken a right substantial and discreet way; praying you effectually to follow the same, always foreseeing that the number be not too great, in avoiding sundry incommodes and inconveniences that might follow thereof, as I doubt not you can right well consider.

Finally, as touching the monthly wages appointed to the soldiers of Tournay after their discharge to be paid at their arrival in Dover; forasmuch, as ye my lord chamberlain for sundry causes and considerations, and especially for such payments of debts as be owing by many of the said soldiers in Tournay. . . . . . .

LETTER XXXIX.

WOLSEY TO THE KING, (CONCERNING THE FRENCH KING, AND CERTAIN MARITIME AFFAIRS.)

SIR, I perceived by such writings as lately came to my hand from your secretary, that your grace hath received three or four letters from me, of sundry dates. And forasmuch as in some of them nothing was contained but only news, it is not thought requisite any special answer be made thereunto, but only your gracious thanks to me to be given; which I would be right and glad to deserve, by all the industry, labour, and policy that I can use.

And, sir, as touching those news, which at that time were written by your ambassador, sir William Fitz-Williams, touching the promise made by the French king, on his honour, that he would give battle to the emperor's army within brief time, I think, verily, that your said ambassador, as a faithful gentleman, reported no less than the French king spake; howbeit, by the contents, as well of such other letters as I have received this day from your said ambassador, as by the news come from the emperor to his heir, inclosed, your grace shall well perceive that neither the French king is in such a readiness within so brief time to give battle, though he promised on his honour so to do, nor yet that the news written on either party be so true that firm credence ought at all times to be given unto them. Nevertheless, by provident foresight, more credence is to be given to writings of such as most commonly make true reports, than of others, which accustomably use to contrive news upon untrue grounds for the advancement of their own affairs. Whereunto your grace having good experience, as well in times past, as by the experience now occurrent, can best judge, especially when the loss and damage of the French king be by him causelessly to your grace arrected. So that I suppose neither this cruel battle is so near at hand, nor yet such reports, though they be spoken, upon his honour, be always to be believed.

Over this, sir, whereas your grace, foreseeing the dangers, damages, losses, and prejudice that might ensue to your navy, and the subjects of your realm, if, in this suspect and casual time, they should resort to Bordeaux for this vintage, like as they have been accustomably used to do heretofore, desired and commanded me to declare unto you my poor advice and opinion what was most expedient to be done therein; I calling unto me the whole number of such your councillors as be here with me, after long reasoning and debating of the said matter, finally concluded by one assent, that such remedies as were expressed in my letter then to your grace sent, were most convenable provisions to remedy the said danger, loss, and damage. And surely, sir, if by our wits and intendments, better remedies could have been foreseen, the same should have been notified, and intimated unto you. But inasmuch as your grace pondereth the danger and casualties that may ensue, by repairing of your navy and subjects to Bordeaux, that you count none assurance by treaties, placards, proclamations, or articles, to be confirmed by the princes on all parts, to suffice for that indemnity, and presuppose such writings and promises to be fraudulent and evasive allectives, to bring your said navy and subjects to danger; thinking also, that the sending of a convenient number of your small ships to Bordeaux or Leghorn, to be given for bringing Gascony wines into your realm, should raise a murmur among your subjects, &c.

LETTER XL.

WOLSEY TO THE KING, (ABOUT THE DANGER OF HIS SHIPS.)

SIR, whereas your grace, most prudently and providently considering the imminent dangers that may ensue, as well by

taking of your navy and subjects, with such goods and substance as they have, and shall bring with them to Bordeaux,
if they should thither repair this year for vintage, as they
have been heretofore accustomably used to do; as also pondering the suspicion that might be impressed in the French
king's mind, by the abstaining of your said navy and subjects
from thence; which jealousy might perchance cause him to
restrain and stop your pension, payable unto you within brief
time; ye not only desire me maturely to debate and consider
what is best to be done therein, but also to advertise your
grace with diligence of my poor advice and opinion upon the
same, like as in your secretary's letters by your command-
ments unto me addressed, it is contained more at length:

Sir, when I groundly considered your provident forecast,
as well for the conservation of your navy from damage, as
the princely zeal that ye bear to preserve your subjects and
their goods, with the substantial regard that ye take to your
honour and surety, in foreseeing politically before hand, the
danger and damages that in this suspect time may ensue to
your highness, your realm and subjects, it is unto me one of
most singular consolation and comfort that ever I had,
whereby I evidently perceive that no man can more groundly
consider the politic governance of your said realm, nor more
assuredly look to the preservation thereof, than ye yourself.
And therefore, though your grace of your goodness require
my poor advice, yet well assured I am, ye can better provide
remedy for the same than I can imagine or devise.

Nevertheless, to accomplish your noble pleasure and commandment, I shall declare my poor opinion, though remitting
always the same to your reformation and correction.

And first, sir, albeit I suppose and think that the French
king, troubled and infested with so many enemies and armies
on every side, as well within his own realm, as in the duchy
of Milan, and upon the borders of Navarre, will be well
aware how he attempt anything, either by land or sea, whereby
he should give occasion to provoke you to break with him,
and join with any of his enemies, by means whereof he might
fall to many dangers; yet upon that ground will I not take my
foundation.   Though this day the chancellor of France, after
he had dined with me alone, without any of his colleagues,
declared expressly, that not only the king, his master, hath in

you his most affiance, before all other princes, but also plainly showed that though such advice and counsel, as I in your name, and as your lieutenant, should show unto him, for the firm entertainment of the good amity between your grace and him, he had commandment to be conformable; and that both his said master and he was as good English as any of your subjects; like as it should be well known, by his favourable entertaining of your subjects, repairing to any of the dominions under the obeisance of his said master. Whereby it appeareth, that as yet, for any bruits they have no manner suspicion.

Nevertheless, for the assured remedying of the doubtful dangers by your grace foreseen and remembered, I thought not most surety to lean only to words, unless the same were corroborated by available bonds and writings; wherefore, besides other remedies, which I shall hereafter particularly declare in this my letter, I have taken this order with the said chancellor of France.

First, forasmuch as complaints be here daily made by your subjects, of such depredations as be committed upon them by the Frenchmen, which is manifestly proved before the said chancellor, and not only no redress made to some of your subjects upon the same, but also divers ships have been rescued from them; whereof one, with certain Frenchmen apprised thereof, arrived here in your haven this day; I have, therefore, upon those grounds, without speaking of the matter of Bordeaux, caused the said chancellor to determine that proclamations be made throughout the realm of France and Britain, upon the sea coasts, that no man, under pain of death, shall enterprise to take any English ships or Englishmen's goods; but that all English, both by land, sea, and fresh water, shall have as free course in surety to pass, remain, and return at their liberty, as ever they had heretofore in the dominions of the said French king.

I have also moved the said chancellor to write to the king his master, that, over and beside the said proclamations, an open placard, signed and sealed by the said French king, shall be made and delivered to your grace; making assurance to all and singular your subjects, repairing to Bordeaux, or any other his dominions under his obeisance by sea or land, that they and every of them shall not only be favourably entertained, but also suffered safely to return with their ships, goods, and merchandises, according to the treaties, without any trouble or vexation to any your said subjects. To the granting and expedition of which open placard I find the said chancellor right agreeable. And albeit the French king be bound hereunto by treaty, yet, if contrary to the same treaty, proclamations, and placards, they shall attempt anything against your subjects, it may be more grievously arrected unto the said French king's charge, when ye shall make your declaration against him.

And, sir, during our abode at this diet, having the chancellor of France here, they shall not dare to enterprise anything at Bordeaux against the goods or ships of any subject of your realm. And a truce, or abstinence of war, being taken by the commissioners of this diet, as I trust it shall be, then hostility shall cease on all parts during the truce, whereby your navy and ships shall be in surety.

And yet, sir, for an abundant cartel for the safeguard of your ships and navy repairing this year to Bordeaux, I have devised three ways: whereof the first is, that provision by your grace should be made in your ports, that no ship above the portage of an hundred or six score should pass Bordeaux this year, and that no multitude of ships should consort there together and at once, but such a convenient number as ye shall think good; suffering them first to return, for knowledge how they have sped, before any more ships be sent forth. By which means not only the great ships of your realm shall be in safety, but also the most part of your navy conserved from danger.

The second remedy is this, that in case it may like your grace not only to license your subjects to bring their wines upon strangers' bottoms, but also give liberty to the Frenchmen and Britons to bring Gascon wines to your realms upon their proper ships; ye should not only have right great plenty of wines at better prices than it hath been accustomed to be sold heretofore, with the augmentation of your customs, but also relieve Flanders and the emperor's countries with wines; whereof during the wars they shall be destitute, if they be not relieved by your means. And besides that, sir, there shall so many French and British ships resort to your realm, under colour of your said licence and liberty, that you shall always have a good counter security and pain to take their ships, if they would anything enterprise against you.

Finally, sir, among other devices and capitulations that we be now in making for the safety and surety of the fishers, as well of Flanders as of France, during this herring time, I do intend, beside the aforesaid provisions for the safeguard of the navy, to devise the articles to be concluded by the mutual consent of both parties, that not only your subjects, with their ships, goods, and merchandises, shall surely and safely pass and repass through all harbours under the dominion of the emperor and French king, but also that no manner of ships, strangers or others, shall be taken within their streams. By which articles the liberty of your streams and territories of the sea shall be more largely extended and amplified, as well by the emperor's as the French king's express consents, by special articles, than ever it was before; which articles also shall be a high remedy for the preservation of your navy, and free liberty to be given thereby unto them, freely to pass and repass to all coasts and countries under the dominions and obeisances of the said princes without damage.

Letter XLI.

THE SAME TO THE SAME, ON THE SAME SUBJECT.

And whereas your grace doubted not but that I, with your council here, at Calais, had had so large knowledge of the damage of your subjects, being daily despoiled on sea, as ye have advertised me, since both I and they would have agreed with your grace in one opinion; sir, truth it is, that I had certain knowledge of sundry despoils done upon the sea by Frenchmen, before I advertised your grace of my said poor answer and opinion for this Bordeaux voyage, which, upon their complaints had good redress and restitution, whereby I was moved to have the better trust. And since that time I received another letter from your secretary; wherein he writeth that two hulks, wherein were certain goods appertaining to Englishmen, were lately taken by Frenchmen, the one being conveyed to Boulogne and the other to Frith in Scotland.

And as touching the hulk conveyed to Boulogne, surmised to appertain to Birch, wherein one Roch, of London, pretendeth to have goods, I have caused some of your council here to hear complaints of the said Roch; and albeit the said Roch neither can nor will justify the said hulk to appertain to Birch, yet he challengeth certain goods in her, whereof I doubt not he shall have restitution, if he can duly prove them to be his. And as unto the other hulk carried into Scotland, I see no remedy, but letters to be devised and sped by your grace, to be sent to the council of Scotland, by the parties damnified there to pursue for restitution. And if they be Frenchmen that have taken the goods, then a certificate to be made of their names and dwelling-places, with a specialty of the goods taken, I shall endeavour myself with the chancellor of France for restitution to be made according to justice; and this, in effect, be all the despoils that I know newly done. Howbeit, some other pursuits have been made here, for redress of depredations done upon the sea about Midsummer and before; which shall also be remedied in the countries where the offenders dwell; for which purpose letters be delivered by the chancellor to the parties complainants.

This, sir, like as we heretofore conformed our opinions and mind touching the voyage of Bordeaux, to your high pleasure, so we eftsoon remit the same to your great wisdom.

And, sir, to inquire of the Frenchmen why they take the Easterlings hulk, it appertaineth not to me as your lieutenant. For if they will pretend enmity to be betwixt the merchants of Dantzick and them, your grace may not conveniently let the same; howbeit to restore your subjects' goods being in them, I have and will speak accordingly.

And whereas your secretary further writeth, that this first vintage may be further respited and deferred upon good grounds, without distrust or jealousy, by declaration of this manifold despoil, and cruel intreaty of your subjects upon the sea, as well by Frenchmen as Spaniards, by reason whereof it may be said they abstain from the said venture, like as to good policy it appertaineth, for the servation of themselves, and surety of their goods; I think the same full good and reasonable considerations, if they take it well; howbeit to defer that voyage to the latter vintage at Candlemas, so that by virtue of a truce to be taken here, they may then resort thither in surety; sir, under your favour and correction, your said subjects shall be in more danger going than now; for if some suspicion and distrust be taken now by the French king, as your grace judgeth by the strange entreaty of your ambassador, it is to be supposed that by that time it shall be further spread and increased. And so I say that if the treaty not yet declared broken, the placard, safe conduct, and all the other remedies before touched cannot now stand in stead; then the abstention of war, which may be as soon broken, if there be no truce, as all the other assurance, cannot then prevail; especially considering this amity standing yet unbroken betwixt you and the French king, no truce can be taken betwixt you and him. For taking of a truce, presupposeth rupture of amity. And therefore this truce must be only taken betwixt the emperor and the French king, for the indemnity of their subjects, which cannot help your subjects. In consideration whereof, these remedies now provided may better serve at this time than the abstinence of war then, and especially the safe conduct comprised in the placard for all your subjects resorting to France, which is an abundant cartel, though the same standing the amity needed not.

Sir, if princes accustomably observed their safe conducts to their enemies in time of open war, it is to be supposed they will not break it, standing the colour of peace and amity.

And on the other side, the second vintage is commonly in February, about the Purification of our Lady, in which month it is included by treaty that the emperor shall be with you in England; and then the distrust and jealousy shall be more largely imprest in the Frenchmen's minds than it is now. And albeit your subjects may then go surely without impeachment, yet it were not possible to bring wine of the second vintage to serve the emperor at his coming into your realms.

And whereas it is further written that by this treaty taken with the emperor, it is sufficiently provided for the indemnity in the pension of France to be paid by the emperor, if the French king refuse to pay the same; sir, the matter dependeth upon your declaration; and, therefore, good it were to save the next payment to be made by the French king if it might conveniently be.

And whereas it is alleged, that my doubt is solved by mine own writing, whereas I suppose the French king shall not provoke your enmity, but conserve your amity; sir, if my letter be well regarded, I write that only conditionally, unless he be driven thereunto by distrust and diffidence, and so that doubt remaineth not unabsolved.

LETTER XLII.

WOLSEY TO KING HENRY VIII.

SIR, it may like your highness to understand I have this hour received letters from your orator resident in the court of Rome, mentioning how the thirteenth day of this instant it pleased Almighty God to call the pope's holiness to his mercy, whose soul our Lord pardon, and in what train the matters there were at that time for election of the future pope. Your highness shall perceive by the letters of your said orator, which I send unto the same at this time, whereby appeareth that mine absence from thence shall be the only obstacle, if any be, in election of me to that dignity; albeit there is no great semblance that the college of cardinals shall consent upon my being there present, because of the factions that be among themselves, for which cause though before God I repute myself right unmeet and unable to so high and great dignity, desiring much rather to remain, continue, and end my life with your grace, for doing of such poor service as may be to your honour and wealth of this your realm than to be pope, yet nevertheless remembering what mind and opinion your grace was of at the last vacation to have me preferred thereunto, thinking it should be to the honour, benefit, and advancement of your affairs in time coming, and supposing verily that your highness persisteth in the same mind and intent, I shall devise such instructions and commissions and other writings as the last time was delivered to Mr. Pace for that purpose, and the same I shall send to your grace by the next post, whom it may like to do farther therein as shall stand with your gracious pleasure, whereunto I shall always conform myself accordingly; and to the intent it may appear further to your grace what mind and determination they be of towards mine advancement, which, as your orators write, have now at this present time the principal authority and chief stroke in the election of the pope, making in manner *triumviratum*. I send unto your highness their several letters to me addressed in that behalf, beseeching our

B B

lord that such one may be chosen as may be to the honour of God, the weal of Christ's church, and the benefit of all Christendom, and thus Jesus preserve your most noble and royal estate. At the More, the last day of December, by your most humble chaplain,

T. Card^{LIS} Ebor.

Letter XLIII.

THE SAME TO THE SAME, ON THE SAME SUBJECT.

Sir, it may like your grace to understand that ensuing the tenor of my letters sent unto your highness yesterday, I have devised such commissions and letters to be sent unto your councillors, the bishop of Bath, and Richard Pace, and master Thomas Hannibal, jointly and severally as at the last time of vacation of the papal dignity were delivered unto the said master Richard Pace for the preferment either of me or, that failing, of the cardinal de Medicis unto the same, which letters and commissions, if it stand with your gracious pleasure to have that matter set further, it may like your highness of your benign grace and goodness to sign, so to be sent to the court of Rome in such diligence as the importance of the same with the brevity of the time doth necessarily require, and to the intent also that the emperor may the more effectually and speedily concur with your highness for the furtherance thereof. Albeit I suppose verily that ensuing the conferences and communications which he hath had with your grace in that behalf, he hath not pretermitted before this time to advance the same, yet, nevertheless, for the more acceleration of his furtherance to be given thereunto, I have also devised a familiar letter, in the name of your grace, to be directed unto his majesty, which if it may please your highness to take the pain for to note with your own hand, putting thereunto your secret sign and mark, being between your grace and the said emperor, shall undoubtedly do singular benefice and furtherance to your gracious intent and virtuous purpose in that behalf; beseeching Almighty God that such effect may ensue thereof as may be to his pleasure, the contentation of your highness, the weal and exaltation of your most royal estate, realm, and affairs; and however the matters shall chance, I shall no less acknowledge myself bounden far

above any my deserts unto your highness than if I had
attained the same, whereunto I would never in thought aspire,
but to do honour, good, and service unto your noble person and
this your realm, and thus Jesus preserve your most noble and
royal estate.   At the More, the first day of October, by your
most humble chaplain,

T. Card^{LIS} Ebor.

Letter XLIV.

THE SAME TO THE SAME, (TOUCHING THE ELECTION OF THE CARDINAL DE MEDICIS.)

Sir, after my most humble and lowly recommendations, this
shall be only to advertise your highness, that after great and
long altercation and contrariety which hath depended between
the cardinals in the conclave, they, at the last, resolved fully
and determined, the faction of France abandoned, to elect and
choose either my lord cardinal de Medicis or me; which deliberation coming to the knowledge of the nobles and citizens of
Rome, they alleging that the affairs of Italy being in the train
as they then were, it should be to the extreme danger thereof
to choose a person absent, made sundry great acclamations at
the conclave window, whereby the cardinals being in fear not
only of the inconvenience like to ensue unto Italy, but also of
their own persons, albeit they were in manner principally
bent upon me, yet for eschewing the said danger and murmur
by inspiration of the Holy Ghost without further difficulty of
business, the nineteenth day of the last month in the morning,
elected and chose the said cardinal de Medicis, who immediately was published pope, and hath taken the name of Clement VII., of which good and fortunate news, sir, your highness hath much cause to thank Almighty God. Forasmuch as
not only he is a perfect friend, and faithful to the same, but that
also much the rather by your means he hath attained to this;
and for my part, as I take God to record, I am joyous thereof
than if it had fortuned upon my person, knowing his excellent
qualities most meet for the same, and how great and sure a
friend your grace and the emperor be like to have of him, and
I so good a father, by whose assumption unto that dignity,
not only your and the said emperor's affairs, but also all

B B 2

Christendom, shall undoubtedly come to much better and
more prosperous perfection, like as upon the first knowledge
thereof the Frenchmen be already departed from Milan, and
passed a river towards France, called Ticino. Trusting that
the next news which shall come from thence shall be of their
arrival at home, wherein as I shall have further knowledge,
so I shall advertise your highness thereof accordingly. And
thus Jesus preserve your most noble and royal estate. At
my poor house besides Westminster, the seventh day of
December, by your most humble chaplain,

T. Card^{lis} Ebor.

Letter XLV.

WOLSEY'S LETTER TO ROME, FOR PROCURING THE POPEDOM TO HIMSELF, UPON POPE ADRIAN'S DEATH.

My lord of Bath, Mr. Secretary, and Mr. Hannibal, I commend me unto you in my right hearty manner; letting you
wit, that by letters lately sent unto me from you, my lord of
Bath, and Mr. Hannibal, dated at Rome the fourteenth day
of September, which letters I incontinently showed unto the
king's grace his highness, I have been advertised, to our great
discomfort, that the said fourteenth day it pleased Almighty
God to call the pope's holiness unto his infinite mercy, whose
soul Jesus pardon. News certainly unto the king's grace and
to me right heavy, and for the universal weal or quiet of
Christendom, (whereunto his holiness, like a devout and
virtuous father of the holy church was very studious) much
displeasant and contrarious.   Nevertheless, conforming ourselves to the pleasure of Almighty God, to whose calling we
all must be obedient, the mind and intention of the king's
highness, and of me both, is to put some helps and furtherances, as much as conveniently may be, that such a successor
unto him may now, by the holy college of cardinals, be named
and elected, as may, with God's grace, perform, achieve, and
fulfil the good and virtuous purposes and intents concerning
the pacification of Christendom, whereunto our said late
holy father, as much as the brevity of the time did suffer, was,
as it should seem, minded and inclined; which thing, how
necessary it is to the state of Christ's religion, now daily
more and more declining, it is facile and easy to be considered;

and surely amongst other Christian princes there is none which
as ye heretofore have perfectly understood, that to this purpose
more dedicated themselves to give furtherance, advice, and
counsel than the emperor and the king's grace, who as well
before the time of the last vacation as since, by mouth and by
letters, with report of ambassadors and otherwise, had many
sundry conferences, communications, and devices in that
behalf. In which it hath pleased them, far above my merits
or deserts, of their goodness, to think, judge, and esteem me
to be meet and able for to aspire unto that dignity; persuading, exhorting, and desiring me, that whensoever opportunity should be given, I should hearken to their advice,
counsel, and opinion in that behalf, and offering unto me to
interpone their authorities, helps, and furtherances therein to
the uttermost. In comprobation whereof, albeit the emperor,
now being far distant from these parts, could not, nor might
in so brief time, give unto the king's grace new or fresh
confirmation of his purpose, desire, and intent herein, yet,
nevertheless, my lady Margaret, knowing the inclination of
his mind in this same, hath, by a long discourse, made unto
me semblable exhortation; offering, as well on the emperor's
behalf as on her own, that as much shall by them be done to
the furtherance thereof as may be possible. Besides this, both
by your letters, and also by particular and most loving letters
of the cardinals de Medicis, Sanctorum Quatuor, and Campeggio, with credence showed unto me on their behalf, by
their folks here resident, I perceive their good and fast minds,
which they and divers others their friends owe unto me in
that matter. And finally, the king's highness doth not cease,
by all the gracious and comfortable means possible to insist,
that I, for manifold, notable, urgent, and great respects, in
anywise shall consent that his grace and the emperor do set
forth the thing with their best manner. The circumstances
of whose most entire and most firm mind thereunto, with
their bounteous, godly, and beneficial offers for the weal of
Christendom, which his grace maketh to me herein, are too
long to rehearse. For which causes, albeit I know myself
far unmeet and unable to so high a dignity, minding rather
to live and die with his grace in this his realm, doing honour,
service, good, or pleasure to the same, than now (mine old
days approaching) to enter into new things; yet, nevertheless,

for the great zeal and perfect mind which I have to the exaltation of the Christian faith, the honour, weal, and surety of the king's grace and the emperor, and to do my duty both to Almighty God and to the world, I referring everything to God's disposition and pleasure, shall not pretermit to declare unto you such things as the king's highness hath especially willed me to signify unto you, on his grace's behalf, who most effectually willeth and desireth you to set forth the same, omitting nothing that may be to the furtherance thereof, as his special trust is in you.

First, ye shall understand, that the mind and entire desire of his highness, above all earthly things, is, that I should attain to the said dignity, having his perfect and firm hope, that of the same shall ensue, and that in brief time, a general and universal repose, tranquillity, and quietness in Christendom, and as great renown, honour, profit, and reputation to this realm as ever was; besides the singular comfort and rejoice that the king's grace, with all his friends and subjects should take thereof; who might be well assured thereby, to compone and order their great causes and affairs, to their high benefit, commodity, and most advantage. For this, and other great and urgent causes, the pleasure of his highness is, that like as ye my lord of Bath, and Mr. Hannibal, have right prudently and discreetly begun, so ye all, or as many of you as be present in the court of Rome, continue your practices, overtures, motions, and labours, to bring and conduce this the king's inward desire to perfect end and effect.

And because it is not to be doubted, but that before the receipt of these my letters, ye having former instructions, shall have far entered your devices in this matter, wherein the king's grace trusteth ye do lose no time or opportunity that possibly may be had, I shall therefore, briefly and compendiously touch such these things, as the king's highness would ye should substantially note in this behalf.

One is, that albeit ye both before, and also now, know the king's mind and desire herein, as is aforesaid, taking that for your foundation; yet nevertheless, forasmuch as it appeareth by your said letters, and otherwise, that the cardinal de Medicis, whose preferment (if this may not be had) both the king's grace and I tendereth above all other, mindeth to experiment what may be done for himself, great policy and dexterity is in your labours and communications to be used, so that ye may first, by great ensearch and inquiry, perfectly understand, as nigh as may be, the disposition, mind, affection, and inclination, as well of the said cardinal de Medicis, as of all the residue, if it be possible; which thing well known, well pondered and considered, ye shall thereby have a great light to the residue of your business, wherein always ye must so order yourselves, that the matter appearing unto you much doubtful and uncertain, your particular practices (the desired intent peradventure failing) shall not because of displeasure or unkindness be noted by any that may be elected; and for your introduction herein, the king's grace sendeth unto you at this time two commissions under his great seal, the one couched under general words, without making mention of any particular person; and in the other, his highness hath made mention of me by special name: besides that, ye shall receive herewith two letters from his grace to the college of cardinals, with copies of the same; the one in special recommendation of me, and the other in favour of the cardinal de Medicis; beside such other particular letters in my recommendation to certain cardinals, and other, as by the copies of them herewith inclosed ye shall now perceive. After the receipt thereof, if the cardinals before that time shall not be entered into the conclave, ye taking your commodity, as by your wisdom shall be thought most expedient, shall deliver unto the cardinal de Medicis the king's letters and mine to him addressed, showing unto him, with as good words and manner as ye can, that for his great virtue, wisdom, experience, and other commendable merits, with the entire love and favour which the king's grace and I bear unto him, thinking and reputing him most meet and able to aspire unto the papal dignity before all other, ye have commandment, commission, and instruction, specially and most tenderly, to recommend him unto the whole college of cardinals, having also the king's and my letters to them in his favour; upon which declaration ye shall perceive his answer to be made unto you in that behalf; whereupon, and by knowledge of the disposition of the residue, ye may perceive how to govern yourselves in the delivery of the rest of your said letters, for in case it may evidently appear unto you that any of the cardinals, to whom the king's letters be directed, have firmly established their

minds upon the said cardinal de Medicis, the more circumspection is to be used with any such in the delivery to him
of the king's letters, and overture of the secretness of your
minds touching me; considering that if the king's intent might
in nowise take effect for me, his grace would, before all other,
advance and further the said cardinal de Medicis. Nevertheless, if either by his answer to be made unto you, or by other
good knowledge, ye shall perceive that he hath so many
enemies herein, that of likelihood he cannot attain the same,
ye may be the more bold to feel his mind how he is inclined towards me; saying, as indeed the king's grace hath written unto
him, that in case he should fail thereof, the king's highness
would insist as much as to his grace were possible, for me; which
ye may say were in manner one thing, considering that both the
cardinal de Medicis and I bear one mind, zeal, and study, to
the weal and quiet of Christendom, the increase and surety
of Italy, the benefit and advancement of the emperor's and
the king's majesty's causes; and I being pope, he in a manner
(whom I above all men love, trust, and esteem) were pope,
being sure to have everything according to his mind and desire, and as much honour to be put unto him, his friends and
family, as might be devised in such wise: that by these and
other good words and demonstrations, ye may make him
sure, as I think he be, that failing for himself, he with all his
friends do their best for me; and seeing no likelihood for him
ye may then right well proceed to your particular labour and
practises for me, delivering the king's letters both to the
college of cardinals, and to the other, apart, as ye shall see
the case then to require; and soliciting them, by secret
labours, alleging and declaring unto them my poor qualities, and
how I having so great experience of the causes of Christendom, with the entire favour which the emperor and the king's
grace bear unto me; the knowledge also, and deep acquaintance of other princes, and of their great affairs; the studious
mind that I have ever been in, both to the surety and weal of
Italy, and also to the quiet and tranquillity of Christendom;
not lacking, thanked be God, either substance or liberality
to look largely upon my friends; besides the sundry great
promotions, which by election of me should be vacant, to be
disposed unto such of the said cardinals, as by their true and
fast friendship had deserved the same; the loving familiarity

also which they should find in me; and that in my nature
I am not in great dispose to rigour or austereness, but
can be contented, thanked be God, frankly, pleasantly, and
courteously, to participate, dispose, and bestow such things
as I have, or shall come to my disposition, not having any
such faction, family, or kinsman, to whom I might show
any partiality in bestowing the promotions and goods of
the church; and which is highest to be regarded, that is
likely, and in manner sure, that by my means, not only
Italy shall be put in perfect surety for ever, but also a final
rest, peace, and quiet, now most necessary to be established
betwixt all Christian princes; whereupon the greatest and
most notable expedition might be made against the infidels
that hath been heard of many years. For the king's highness in that case would be contented, and hath fully promised,
God willing, to come in person, when God shall send time,
unto Rome; whither also I should not doubt to bring many
more of the Christian princes, being determined, if God
should send me such grace, to expone mine own person in
God's quarrel; by means of which my presence many things
should be stated, that for superiority and otherwise, in times
past, hath been occasion of disagreement amongst princes;
albeit, peradventure, the greatest respect shall not now be
had hereunto, nor this be the best elective to win the cardinal's favour; wherein you must therefore use yourself by your
wisdoms, as you shall see the time, season, and care to require,
assuring them, for the removing of the doubt in changing
of the see, or not speedy repair thither, that after the election
once passed and notified to me, I would not fail, by God's
grace, within three months to be in Rome; there, and in the
parts thereabout, to remain during my life, whereof ye may
make faithful assurance. By these, and other good means and
promises on the king's behalf of large rewards, which his
highness referreth to your discretion, and is contented to perform that which ye do therein, it is not to be doubted but that
you shall obtain the favours of many of them; so as if respect
may be had to the honour of the see apostolic, and the surety
of Italy, the tranquillity of Christendom, the defence of the
same against the infidels, the exaltation of the faith, the persecution of Christ's enemies, the increase and weal of the college
of cardinals, with their advancement and promotion, gentle,

frank, and liberal entertainment of them, and generally
to the benefit of all holy church. The king's grace supposeth
his mind and desire herein, with all your good means, diligence, and solicitations, is not unlike to take good effect;
wherein, for the more authority, and better conducing of
your purpose, the pleasure of his grace is, that you join with
the emperor's ambassadors, as far as you may see and perceive them to favour this the king's intent, like as his grace
thinketh, that according to the often conferences, communications, promises, and exhortations made by the emperor to
me in this behalf, and according to my said lady Margaret's
desire or offer, they have commandment to do. In the politic
handling of all which matters, the king's highness putteth in
you his special trust and confidence, so to order yourself in
the premises, as you shall perceive to accord with the inward
desire of his grace, and the state and disposition of the thing
there; for which purpose his grace hath furnished you at
this time, jointly or severally, with two sundry commissions,
the one general for me, and in my favour, by the which you
have ample authority to bind and promise, on the king's
behalf, as well gift of promotions, as also large sums of
money to as many and such as you shall think convenient;
and sure ye may be, whatsoever ye shall promise and bind his
grace to do in that behalf, his highness will inviolably
observe, keep and perform; the other special, as afore letters
to the college of two effects, the one for the cardinal de
Medicis, and the other for me, with other particular letters
in my favour; all which his pleasure is, that you shall use in
manner and form aforesaid; that is to say, if you shall perceive the affair of the cardinal de Medicis to be in such perfect train that he is like to have the same dignity, ye then
proceed to that which may be his furtherance, using nevertheless your particular labour for me, if you think it may do
good, after such sort as ye shall not conceive any ingratitude
or unkindness therein. And if you may see that the said
cardinal de Medicis be not in such great likelihood thereof,
then considering that the king's grace and I think verily he
will do his best for me, ye shall effectually set forth your
practices for attaining and winning as many friends for me
as possible may be, delivering your letters for the intent, as
you shall see cause. Wherein you being furnished for both

purposes, and also having one of the commissions general and indifferent, without any person therein specially recommended, things to be done or omitted, as you shall know to stand with the state or commodity of the affairs there, and with the ground of the king's mind to you now declared, which shall be your best and perfect instruction; and as you shall do or know herein, so the king's grace desireth you often and speedily to advertise me, by your letters, having no doubt but that his highness will see your travels, diligence, and pains in this behalf, so to be considered, as you shall have cause to think the same well employed and bestowed.

And my lord of Bath, as you do know well, because Mr. Pace, at the time of the last vacation, was sent purposely from hence with commission and instruction for that matter; the king and I, supposing that upon knowledge of this news, he being at Milan, would incontinently repair unto Rome, hath therefore made the foresaid commissions, and also this letter to be directed unto you, jointly and severally willing you, in such substantial and discreet wise to proceed in that matter, not forbearing any thing that may be to the furtherance thereof, as his grace, and my special trust, is in you: And thus most heartily fare you well. At my manor of Hampton-court, the 4th day of October.

[*The rest is in the cardinal's own hand.*]

My lord of Bath, the king hath willed me to write unto you, that his grace hath a marvellous opinion of you; and you knowing his mind as you do, his highness doubteth not but this matter shall be by your policy set forth in such wise, as that the same may come to the desired effect, not sparing any reasonable offers, which is a thing, that amongst so many needy persons is more regarded, than perchance the qualities of the person; ye be wise, and ye wot what I mean; trust yourself best, and be not seduced by fair words, and specially of those which (say what they will) desire more their own preferment than mine. Howbeit, great dexterity is to be used; and the king thinketh that all the imperials shall be clearly with you, if faith be in the emperor and the young men, which, for the most part being needy, will give good ears to fair offers, which shall be undoubtedly performed. The king willeth you neither to spare his authority, or his good money or

substance.   You may be assured, whatsoever you promise
shall be performed; and our Lord send you good speed.

                     Your loving friend,

                              T. CARD^{LIS} EBOR.

                 LETTER XLVI.

MY lord of Bath, Mr. Secretary, and Mr. Hannibal; I
recommend me unto you in my right hearty manner; since my
writing unto you, I have at sundry times received your letters of the last of October and nineteenth of November,
wherein to the king's and my good and full contentation ye
have right diligently advertised me of such things coming to
your knowledge as have succeeded in those parts, as well concerning the cardinals then being in conclave as otherwise,
and how after long altercations and sundry contrarieties which
seemed to be amongst the cardinals, at last, by the grace and
inspiration of the holy spirit, they agreed and condescended
upon my lord cardinal de Medicis, whom the said nineteenth
day they elected and published pope, taking the name of
Clement the Seventh, with other matters mentioned and comprised in your said letters more at large, for the which
your substantial good and speedy advertisements, by me always showed and declared unto the king's highness, his grace
and I give unto you most special and hearty thanks, namely,
for the desired news of the said election, which I assure you
to be as much to the king's and my rejoice, consolation, and
gladness, as possibly may be devised or imagined; for which
cause his highness and I, in sign, token, and approbation of
the singular comfort which we take in the same, not abiding
or tarrying for any intimation to be made thereof, either by
the pope's holiness now elect, or by the college of cardinals,
thought convenient and requisite with diligence to speed
unto you letters congratulatory directed unto the pope's holiness, whereby the same may perceive the entire love and
most cordial affection that his grace and I continually bear
unto him, which letters congratulatory being herewith, you
the effect shall perceive by the copies of the same here inclosed, the king's mind and pleasure is that ye, taking a con-

venient time for that purpose, shall in due, requisite, and most loving manner present and deliver unto the pope's holiness— that is to say:

First, the king's letters and afterwards mine, making such humble, hearty, filial, and obedient commendations on the behalf of his grace, and of me apart, as to the most entire affection and devout mind which he beareth unto his holiness, you do know to be for either of us meet, convenient, and concordant. After the reading whereof, ye shall show and declare unto his holiness at length, what joy, comfort, and gladness it is both to the king's highness and me to perceive and understand that once in our lives it hath pleased God, of his great goodness, to provide and send such a pastor and governor unto his church, as his grace and I have long and inwardly desired; who, for his virtue, wisdom, and other high and notable qualities, merits, and deserts, we have always reputed the most worthy and able person in this world to aspire and be called to that dignity. And, for my part, I have in this behalf attained that thing which I have entirely and cordially longed for and desired; assuring you that I cannot with my tongue or pen express the inward joy which I have taken and do take to serve; for surely besides the manifold particular causes moving the king's highness, and me most especially, to desire the exaltation, weal, and comfort of so faithful and so constant a friend as his holiness hath been ever unto us, having firm and undoubtful hope, that the sincere love and constant affection heretofore surely established, rooted, and knit, is, and shall be for ever most assuredly permanent and indissoluble on either part. His grace and I consider the present calamities, troubles, dissensions, jars, variances, discords, wherewith Christendom is all over vexed, afflicted, and inquieted, besides many other enormities, perils, dangers, and mischiefs, whereby the state thereof is greatly and piteously compelled to decline; for the succour of which infirmities none so apt and convenient a medicine would have been exhibited in this stormy season, as by the provision of God to have a pope and head, which both may, can, and will endeavour himself to repair and restore the same unto the due perfection; whose assumption is undoubtedly to be reputed a due gift of God only, and an act most fortunate and gracious, and chanced in a most convenable time and season; for which the king's grace and I have given and do give unto the Almighty God as loving thanks as may be. And ye may assure his holiness, that the king's grace, like an obedient and most loving son, and as a most pious and virtuous prince, will not fail effectually, firmly, and constantly to join and concur with him, in all things which may sound to his honour, weal, and surety, the tranquillity, quiet, and repose of Christendom, offering his grace's authority, puissance, relief, and blood, for the furtherance thereof to the uttermost. Like as I also, as a most devout and assured member of his, shall not fail to employ my wit, study, person, substance, and life to do unto his holiness all the service and pleasure to me possible; as, by the continual experience of the same, shall assuredly prove from time to time, whensoever and so soon as the case shall require. All which matters ye shall extend with the best most hearty and loving words and demonstrations that you can devise, in such wise as his holiness may thereby perceive the assured mind and cordial affection which the king's grace and I do bear unto the same. Over this, ye shall show unto the pope's holiness that, albeit the king's highness was resolved and determined that his army, being in France, having there right good success with honourable victory, should have remained there all this winter, having made their way and entry into the bowels of France without resistance; the town of ——, near to the river of ——, taken by dedition, and the castles and walls thrown down; the town of Bray, situate upon the said river, mightily fortified, and by the enemy valiantly defended, by strength gotten and acquired; and the said enemies by their loss profligated; the town of ——, six leagues beyond the said river, after approaches fire and battery made thereunto, wherein were Pontremy and divers noblemen, with five hundred footmen and five hundred spears furnished by them, after a conflict made, wherein were taken Monsieur Dannaville and two other great men of arms, and as many slain, besides sixty footmen, and sixty men-at-arms, and as many slain by the king's lieutenant to the use of the king's highness, as parcel of his inheritance of his realm of France, rendered and delivered the towns of Roy and ——, with other towns and castles also taken. And the said army, being upon way of Travers of the realm of France, towards the town called Larm, in Limoges, where they should be in convenient readiness, both to proceed straight to Paris, also to join with the duke of Bourbon, and such as with the ten thousand lance-knights, being at the king's charge he had with him; for which purpose, also, the number of eight thousand fresh soldiers, horsemen and footmen, were prepared for their inforcement, and passed on their way unto Dover, and other places on the sea coast, ready to take passage; the king's army being also sufficiently and amply furnished of money for their continuance, and the sum of a hundred thousand crowns sent unto Ray Samson for the payment of the lance-knights from month to month, so, as on the king's part, nothing was lost or pretermitted, which ought or conveniently might have been done for the continuance of this winter war, whereby the enemy, disturber of the quiet in Christendom, might the rather be enforced to know and inform himself, or else suffer so largely, that his temerity should thereby be mitigated and repressed; yet such fervent colds reigned at that time, with other divers incommodiate weather, that first the lance-knights, being under the leading of the count Felix, and ready to join with the duke of Bourbon, partly by means thereof, and partly (as is aforesaid) by corruption, abandoned the field, and after a great bounty taken, retired into their countries, and that army thereby at this time clearly dissolved. The duke of Bourbon also passed towards Spain by the way of Italy; and over that, the horses and the beasts which drew the king's and emperor's artillery, and other carriages, died daily and nightly in such number, that there remained not enough in dry weather to remove the same, and, continuing two or three days longer, they should have been fain to leave the said artillery for lack of carriages, which could not then for a long season have been recovered. Men also passing by the way, as well Englishmen as Burgundians, perished for cold in so great number, that a pity it was to see. And, finally, there was such lack and default in payment of the Burgundians that, for that and other considerations before specified, the duke of Suffolk and count de Buren, leaders of the common army for the king and emperor, could see no other remedy but for a time to withdraw themselves in some sure place in towns, for release and succour of their men and beasts, or else utterly to lose the same, leave the artillery, and put the common affair in extreme hazard; like as they by common assent retired unto Valencia, taking also, in their way, certain castles and places of Boyhen and Beonerroy, which, being delivered by the duke of Suffolk to the Burgundians, to be kept to the king's use, were since by the said Burgundians abandoned and forsaken. And finding the time of the year clearly unseasonable, of new to proceed and return unto the enemy's country, they, by mutual accord, agreed to discharge their said armies till the beginning of the next spring of the year, leaving every thing in such state and order as they may then right speedily be ready to proceed again unto their enterprises. And forasmuch as, the said army being beyond the sea, chanced the death of the pope Adrian, and the election of the pope's holiness being unto that dignity, by means whereof it is uncertain what further direction shall be taken for his holiness and states of Italy for the year now ensuing and coming, especially the affairs of the duchy of Milan being in better train than they were. It is thought by the king's highness and his counsel necessary and requisite, that ye, showing unto the pope's holiness the said success, with the firm and constant mind which the king's grace is of to perfect these other victories with, in case other princes, to whom, as well for their particular causes, as the tranquillity of all Christendom it appertaineth, will do the semblable, shall desire his holiness to ascertain his highness of his mind in this behalf, showing unto him not only the virtuous grounds why their common enterprises be attempted against him who, by his inordinate ambition, annoys and affects all Christendom, and how much the repressing of him shall sound to the pleasure of God, the weal of Christ's church, the surety of the pope's holiness, and of all Italy, which have been the principal causes moving the king's grace to express his labour, travail, pain, subjects, and assistance with his substance, for reformation thereof; but also such things as for this present time be thought good and profitable to prosecute war against the common enemy, which be these:—

First, the honourable grounds moving the emperor and the king now last into these wars of France.

Secondly, the firm conjunction which is contracted between the emperor and the king.

Thirdly, the base estate whereunto the French king is brought, being exhaust of money, and his subjects not able to contribute more unto him.

Fourthly, his horsemen greatly diminished, without likelihood how he may repair them.

Fifthly, the revolting from him of the duke of Bourbon, having 500 gentlemen in France sworn unto his part.

Sixthly, the mindful hatred that the French king hath amongst all his commons, the fear that he is in by the distrust of his lords, not knowing which of them are his friends or his enemies; the doubt lest that the French king hath amongst all his commons (not being pressed) may gather friends and fortify places now weak, which afterwards by peace may be impregnable; the dishonour which the French king hath taken in Italy, the consideration between the states of Italy, the abandoning of the French king by the Venetians by reason of the new elected pope, shall declare themselves more sincerely for the emperor and the king's grace than before; the way and means found on this side for entering the bowels of France without besieging any strong places; the example of small resistance against the duke of Suffolk, and semblably against the emperor on that side on Spain, and faculty to win the people's favours; the discourage of the French king by disappointment of the Scottish invasion, and flying of the duke of Albany; the annoyance already done to the Scots not being minded or able to continue their wars; the readiness wherein the emperor and king's ships, artillery, and ordnance is in; the goodly sums of money granted to the emperor and the king by their lords and commons; the likelihood that the French king once pressed shall not be able of a long season to be again so insolent, whereby an end shall be of the wars in Christendom for many a day; and, finally, the great uncertainty which is to be reckoned in obeisance of any conventions to be made by the French king concerning the same peace or truce, which he will no longer observe than shall be for his own benefit.

These things well and substantially considered, the king's special trust is, that the pope's holiness (who hath always had fervent inclination to those matters, as to a virtuous cardinal and honourable member of Christ's church appertaineth) will (now that it hath pleased Almighty God to constitute and ordain him to be head of the same) no less tender the weal and quiet of Christendom than he hath hitherto been most desirous thereof, which shall be the highest merit and honour that in this his beginning his holiness may or can attain. Wherefore the king's instant desire is to know assuredly whereunto his grace may trust, and what expectation his highness may have of perfect favour and effectual assistance from those parts, without any more outward demonstrations to be made therein than shall be entirely and sincerely accomplished, for as yet hitherto the king's grace, for the inward zeal which he hath to the weal of Christendom, hath in a manner borne the most and weightiest burthen of these wars, and most effectually hath proceeded unto the same, observing all promises without variance, delay, or alteration, others have been more slack and remiss than shall be now convenient or needful to rehearse, and hitherto no profit hath come unto his highness, but only honourable renown for his gracious and virtuous mind and intent, though other be in state and condition more meet to their purpose, praise and hearken to a perpetual peace, which in process shall be but a colour and shadow of goodness rather than that thing whereof may come in the issue a perfect and general establishment of rest and peace in all Christendom.

The premises well and substantially considered, it shall not only be a virtuous and meritorious, but also a faithful act, for the pope's holiness to declare his full mind, resolution, and intent, plainly herein to the king's grace (who hath always been inclined to do unto the holy church, and particularly to the pope now being, as much honour as hath been in the faculty and power of his grace) who may by such loving knowledge as shall be given unto him by the pope's holiness, order and train his weighty matters and causes accordingly: for his holiness after so many gratitudes to the holy see apostolic, heretofore most largely extended, is now desirous and minded to experiment and see what correspondency shall be showed unto his grace for recovery of such portions as belong to his most mighty titles and inheritance detained and withholden by the common enemy, like as to policy, wisdom, and good reason doth appertain, and to the intent that semblable knowledge may be had of the minds, intents, and dispositions, as well of the Venetians as also of the duke of

Milan, how they will concur for the annoyance of the enemy; the king's mind is either by your special letters to be sent unto Venice, or by such other good means as you shall think convenient, ye do ensearch, know, and understand the inclination, mind, and resolution of the Venetians, which had, the king's highness is contented that Mr. Secretary and Mr. Hannibal, in consideration of your long demurs in these parts, shall return home, passing by the duke of Milan, for knowledge of his intent and mind in the premises for which purpose letters of credence shall be a sufficient instruction for you in such things as shall be needful to be commanded at this time.

Furthermore, ye shall on the king's behalf show unto the pope's holiness, that if the same be minded to establish and further universal peace in Christendom, none so good or convenient way or means can be devised to compel the common enemy to come unto honourable and reasonable conditions, as at this time to press him earnestly and by all ways possible. Wherefore, amongst other annoyances to be done unto him as well on that side as of the countries of Spain and on this side, it shall be in any ways requisite and expedient, that the duke of Bourbon (wheresoever he be at this present time, either in Italy, Spain, or elsewhere,) shall with all possible and convenient diligence repair straight hither to the king's grace, with whom his highness is minded to conclude on the emperor's behalf and his own such notable things for annoyance of his said enemies as (God willing) shall be for the high furtherance of the common cause and affairs; and for that cause you shall desire his holiness to put his hand and help, that in anywise the said duke of Bourbon may repair hither, (as is aforesaid,) and solemnly, if he remain in those parts, you may confer with him upon his speedy coming, as also to assure that the king's highness will be glad and very joyous to see him within this realm, being minded to accept and entertain him in most kind and loving manner, and to take such way with him by the emperor's consent, concurrence, and agreement for the enterprises to be achieved and done with all diligence, as shall be to his most surety, honour, and weal, whereas, if he should refuse to come unto the king's grace for order to be taken in the present affairs, his highness is not minded to charge himself further than he hath done,

for any assistance to be given unto the said duke; and thus
by all good means to you possible you shall advance and solicit,
as well with the pope's holiness as otherwise, that no tract or
delay be used therein, but that to avoid loss of time (which
cannot be recovered) the said duke may accelerate his coming
into this realm; and in case, after the thing perfected with the
king's grace, he shall think good to pass into Spain, yet the
most requisite way for the substantial promoting of all the
common affairs were to pass by the king's grace, if he be not
passed already out of Italy, ascertaining you that the king's
highness hath semblably written unto the emperor, that if
before the arrival of these letters the said duke shall have
fortuned to take the sea towards Spain, the emperor shall
upon his coming to him cause him to use all possible diligence
in his coming hither, like as I am sure the emperor, knowing
the importunity of the matter, will do accordingly; albeit,
that in the beginning of this letter it is mentioned that the
king's grace, not abiding nor tarrying any intimation to be
made by the pope's holiness of his election, doth send now his
letters congratulatory, (as is aforesaid,) yet nevertheless I advertise you to be kept unto yourself, that I have received with
convenient diligence at several times, not only your letters of
the third day of December, but also of the 18th of the same.

In the first was contained matter of right good effect,
whereat the king's highness and I take singular rejoice and
comfort to hear and perceive the pope's holiness was of so
good mind and inclination towards the emperor and the king's
affairs, minding either to concur with him effectually in case
he may be advertised they intend to continue and prosecute
the wars after this winter, or else, if the emperor be not
able so to do, his holiness doing secretly as much as he should
be bound to do, (if he as pope did enter the league) would
keep himself in such state as he might be mediator.   That
after the French king should offer such peace unto them both
as should stand with their honour, wherein his holiness then
(as ye affirmed) had great hope with other good matters contained in your said former letters, howbeit the last seem to be
of another sort, considering that (as ye write) his holiness
giveth to much hearkening unto the French cardinals with
other matters therein contained sounding rather to an appearance of overmuch inclination to the French party and their

practices and abuses than unto his firm adhering unto the
king and emperor.   Wherefore the king's highness and I not
a little marvel, having made these our special trust and confidence, that upon your declaration unto him of the king's mind
and intent, with the great reasons and urgent considerations
specified before in our letters, why the common enemy shall
be earnestly pressed, without which he will never be induced
to any reasonable point, his holiness ensuing that which he
wrote in your former letters will effectually concur with the
king and the emperor's, either declaring himself to accept the
league, if the emperor and the king will continue the wars,
and making also some new league with the king's grace and the
emperor, (as your said letters purport); or else, if the emperor
shall not be furnished for the said continuance, to produce by
policy an honourable and profitable peace, (as is aforesaid);
for you may say unto his holiness, that, of all persons living
which might have aspired unto this dignity, the king's and
my entire confidence is that none would or could be more
favourable unto the emperor and king's affairs than he.   And
it were not honourable that his holiness (being cardinal of
the league, with other things sounding to the peachment of
the common enemy) should now, being pope, find fault or
exception at the same; and sure may he be, that whatsoever
practice of the Frenchmen shall set forth with him, he shall
find them but abuses, wherein his holiness hath good experience in times past, knowing right well that they will neither
observe nor keep any of their conventions or promises longer
than shall stand with their commodity and profit.   Besides,
his holiness not adhering and concurring effectually with the
king and emperor, it should be an occasion for them to think
no small ingratitude for the same, and, therefore, their causes
and affairs should be greatly hindered, and the reputation of
the emperor furthered greatly, who by that means should be
further from any good or reasonable way to be taken than he
is now; and consequently, the enemy prospering in Italy, and
the king and the emperor despairing of the pope's entire
favour, what a danger as well the state of his holiness as of
all Italy were in, is plain and easy to be considered.   The
French king being also at such sore deal, would think to
have all his pleasures and commands of the pope, which had
or refused, he then having so great a foot, would and might

use his holiness as a chaplain. And, finally, the pope, not
then so well assured of the king's and emperor's assistance as
he now is, should experiment what it were to cast away two
such friends, which be able and minded to maintain, conserve,
and defend his estate to the uttermost. The sect also of the
Lutherans might by means thereof the rather be accepted
by divers subjects of the emperor, as well in Germany as elsewhere, which should hear of the pope's ingratitude and peace;
that might spread so far both in France, and Spain, and
Italy, that the dignity of Christ's church might thereby in
brief time be suppressed, and had in small reputation. All
which dangers, with many more which might ensue for lack
of the pope's effectual joining at this time with the king and
emperor, either for war or conducing of peace, (as is aforesaid,)
ye must instantly beseech his highness virtuously and discreetly to ponder and remember, showing unto the same that
for knowledge what the emperor is minded and able to do
this summer for the annoyance of the enemy. His highness
hath before this by me despatched his especial letters both to
his majesty, and also to the king's ambassador there resident,
with intimation of the king's mind being right well able and
thinking best that the enemy be earnestly pressed on both
sides if the emperor should be furnished to do the semblable
for lack thereof; yet there may be such an enterprise
attempted, and is devised to be done by the duke of Bourbon, with the assistance he shall have from the king and
emperor, without excessive charges, and praise shall as much
and more abase the French king, than if the king's grace and
emperor had invaded France in their own persons with their
armies royal: to which purpose the king's highness hath not only
instructed his ambassadors resident with the emperor looking
right shortly for the emperor's answer and resolution therein,
with repairing hither of the duke of Bourbon, but also hath
written to the lady Margaret, desiring her to call a council
general, like as the king's highness doth here the semblable, and
to know and understand what they will contribute, and what
she and other the emperor's Low Countries be minded to do in
this behalf; wherefore ye shall exhort the pope's holiness in
anywise to leave and forbear any demonstration of favour
and inclination towards the French party, showing himself
firm and constant in his love and affection towards the em-

peror and the king's cause, which shall be the next means and way to make the French king to make overture and offer of reasonable conditions, and much the rather if his holiness will declare himself in the league, whereas by the contrary he shall bring the enemy to such elation, that using first crafty practices and subordinations with the pope's holiness, against whom, undoubtedly, he beareth in his heart an old rooted secret and hidden malice, and setting the less by the emperor and the king's grace, he shall at the last, finding time and opportunity, discover his pestiferous intent to the utter ruin, slander, and oppression, as well of the dignity of the church of Rome, as also of the state of Italy for ever. And therefore, if the pope's holiness be minded to be the author of a good peace and unity in Christendom, and will regard his own weal, honour, and surety, he must effectually adhere to the emperor and king, leaving his familiarity with the French cardinal, and hearkening to the practices of their faction, which will be the immediate way to cause the common enemy to know himself, and either to come to reasonable and honourable conditions, or by the firm concurrence together of the pope and emperor, and the king's grace with the Venetians and other states of Italy, and other their friends, to be brought to such base and low estate as he shall not be able to do annoyance, displeasure, or hurt unto them hereafter. And of the pope's answer herein, with all matters worthy of knowledge which you shall advertise me by your letters in diligence, to the intent the king's grace may train his matters accordingly; and of the coming hither of Mr. Melchior from the pope, and is not yet arrived, nor any knowledge had of him; but by your letters to make unto him such answer as shall appertain.

Letter XLVII.

WOLSEY TO MR. SECRETARY PACE, AT ROME.

Mr. Secretary, I commend me unto you in my right hearty manner. By my other letters to my lord of Bath and Mr. Hannibal, at this time directed, I have written unto you all at length, as well in the king's causes as my own. This shall be only to advertise you, that albeit I am right well assured that ye have to the uttermost and best of your power endeavoured and employed yourself to the obtaining of the bull of legation now granted unto me by the pope's holiness, yet, nevertheless, to be plain with you, as one in whom I have my singular trust and confidence, I esteem somewhat more strangeness to be showed unto me than my merits require, in that there hath been difficulty made to amplify my faculties, (*per non familiares*,) and such other things as be contained in my instructions given unto my lord of Bath. Supposing verily ye having familiar and perfect acquaintance with the pope's holiness, may by your dexterity and wisdom do so much to the remedying thereof, if, as of yourself alone, you sometimes do repair unto his holiness, putting the same by good means and introduction in remembrance of my merits, and faithful mind towards him, as well in *minoribus* as now; showing, furthermore, how by pope Leo's grant and pope Adrian's, who passed my legation with as large faculties as now I have, *ad quinquennium*, and so from five years to five years, during my life. I know right well how that for the prerogatives the king's highness hath in this realm, as for other causes, all the profits that may arise of my legation, having also all the amplification of the faculties aforesaid, will not be worth a thousand ducats by the year, whatsoever report may be made to his holiness to the contrary by some that might suppose and think that great revenues might grow thereof, and ye may say, though ye perceive that I repute and esteem the benevolence as much and as high as the same is worthy to be taken, yet, nevertheless, ye have taken me to be one that can note and consider the causes of the said bull; and what emolument, honour, and benefit shall ensue unto me thereby, more than I had before by the grants of other popes, to whom I was entirely dedicated, as to his holiness. Wherefore, you may say your opinion is, as of yourself, that in sign and comprobation of a special grace, and more large favour towards me than others generally, he should amplify the said bull with the said other faculties, or rather with more, which then shall be a very demonstration and manifest appearance that his holiness singularly tendereth and loveth me, whereof I may take such rejoice and comfort as praise hereafter may be to the contentation of his holiness. And thus, by good manner to use yourself in this matter without knowledge that it proceedeth of me; that by your politic handling not only the said faculties may be extended to my desire, but also the pope's holiness to know what it is that he hath done for me, and what of likelihood is my expectation. In which your doing, you shall administer unto me singular pleasure, to be amongst other remembered accordingly. And heartily fare you well. At my palace besides Westminster, the last of February. Your loving friend,

T. Card^{lis} Ebor.

Letter XLVIII.

WOLSEY TO MR. SAMPSON AND MR. JERNINGHAM, RESIDENTS WITH THE EMPEROR.

Mr. Sampson and Mr. Jerningham, I commend me unto you in my right hearty manner. The last October arrived here a post of the emperor's, with letters to his ambassador here resident, having also your letters to the king's highness and me directed of the 8th and 23rd days of September; with him also arrived a gentleman of the emperor's, sent by this way to the duke of Bourbon, who brought several letters of much fresher date addressed to the said ambassador, and two days following, a servant of yours, Mr. Deane, arrived at Woodstock with the king's grace, to whom he delivered all such letters as ye by him sent unto the king's grace and me; as well those that concerned the king's affairs as mine, which letters his grace received and remitted unto me, with diligence like as I also sent unto the king's highness with like manner all your said former writings coming to my hands. By the which, and also by the copies of the emperor's said letters written to his ambassador, together with the relation of the said gentleman, the king's highness and I perceive in what readiness, state, and disposition the emperor's affairs were at the dates of the said letters, with his intent to proceed with his said army in his own person, and to supply by the longer continuance the tardity and slackness which has been used in the setting forth of the same; having also made provision for the payment of 100,000 crowns, for his portion unto the duke of Bourbon, towards the entertainment of 10,000 lance-knights. And desiring that the king's grace would do the semblable for his part; and to give order that his army, leaving sieges and strong places, and passing into the bowels of France, may continue all this winter with a convenient reinforcement, affirming and promising that the count de Buren with the Burgundians horsemen and footmen being under him, should semblably continue; and finally, his majesty showing the good news of arrival of certain gold from the isles, desires the prisoners of Hanover taken in the king's army may be reserved for the redeeming of the duke of Bourbon's friends, which the French king has taken and achieved, besides other good and discreet advertisement comprised in your said letters as might there come to your knowledge, like as in the same is contained more at large; and hereunto, albeit that the lack of advertisement from thence hath not been a little to the king's marvel and discomfort, and the no less hindrance of the common affairs, if by the great foresight, diligence, and policy used on this side, things had not been prevented, remedied, and foreseen, yet nevertheless it appeareth by the dates of the letters, that the same hath been delayed by reason of contrary and unseasonable winds and weather, which must be suffered and taken in patience. And to the intent that the emperor may be by you perfectly advertised how great diligence hath been used for the furtherance of the common enterprises, as well by sending and advancing the king's army with all effect. The order given unto them at the emperor's former request, not to serve any sieges of strong places and to proceed into the bowels of France, the help, succour, and relief by the king's grace to the duke of Bourbon in extreme necessity, by sending and advancing unto him the king's whole portion, that is to say, 100,000 crowns, towards the entertainment of the said lance-knights, without which (lacking then provision for the emperor's part) they had been scattered and retired, and the said duke utterly lost and destroyed, the benevolent and conformable mind of the king's highness at the emperor's instance, and for the weal of the common affairs, not only to continue the said army this winter, but also to reinforce the same with a number of 4000 men, which ye shall name 7000 men; and finally, the successes and matter of proceedings of the duke of Suffolk and the count de Buren, with the king's and emperor's folks being under their leading, I (for your said advertisement) do send unto you herewith the copies of certain letters lately come at sundry times from the duke of Suffolk, with the answer made unto the same; and semblably, with such letters as upon the arrival of your said letters be now written both unto the said duke of Suffolk and unto Dr. Knight, by tenour of which copy you shall now plainly see and understand not only what hath been done, and what train the matters on this side stand in, but also be sufficiently and amply instructed of such things as shall be needful and requisite to be by you showed and declared, on the king's and my behalf to the said emperor, to whom ye may show that before the arrival of these new letters the king's grace had resolved his continuance and enforcement of his army, ready to be set forth as soon as the king must have word that the emperor's army was really and actually set forwards, and in surety that the Burgundians should be entertained and continue with his army, and the emperor's portion for the entertainment of the duke of Bourbon furnished as well for the surety of the emperor's said army, wherein the king understandeth that his majesty passeth personally, as also for the furtherance of the common affairs, considering by foresight and high providence that the same shall be requisite and expedient; and now much the rather because the emperor doth instance the king so to do, though so be by the capitulations as ye know his grace is not bounden to continue his army longer than the month of October; trust me that since his grace hath done this of special foresight and benevolent mind at the emperor's instance and contemplation, his majesty will (according to his writings) supply the tardity of setting forth by continuance; and also take such assured order that the said count de Buren and Burgundians, without whom it shall not be possible for the king's army, not furnished with horsemen, to continue, may remain still with the same this winter, and have from time to time substantial provision of payment, wherein (as by some of the said copies you shall perceive) there is great lack and default, referring you to the reasons, introductions, and persuasions comprised in the copies for enforcing and agreeing of that and all other matters therein necessary to be known, showed and declared or solicited unto the emperor, which ye shall by your wisdoms and discretions use as ye shall see the case and successes of the affairs necessarily to require, noting especially four material and notable things which in no wise may be omitted. The one is the continuance of the emperor's army on that side so long as shall be possible.

The second is, substantial order to be given for the continuance of the said count de Buren and Burgundians, with assured payment to be made from time to time, for the which you have grounds and considerations enough, comprised in the said copies necessary to be highly pondered and regarded.

Thirdly, that no default be in the advancement of the 100,000 crowns for the emperor's portion to the duke of Bourbon, without which not only the enterprise should be subverted, but also lost and totally cast away.

And, fourthly, if the French king whose army was long ago passed into Italy, and he himself remaining at Lyons, do revoke the same for his own strength, as it is thought and bruited abroad, orders may be given unto Prospero Colonna and others of the armies of Italy to follow them in the tail, by means whereof the enemies pressed thus now at one time on all sides, shall (God willing) with less charge and business be brought to right base and low estate. And the matters being in so good train, a final end much the rather put unto the wars of Christendom, than this thing in any point slacked shall be possible to be again brought about in many years, for the performance whereof you may say the king's grace, for his part, spareth neither labour, study, travel, danger, nor expences. And that withal effect and travel on every side, both by sea and land, to the inestimable charge of his highness; for besides the army by sea and in France, and the great garrisons laid also all this summer on the borders towards Scotland, who have done the greatest destructions in Scotland that hath been seen this two hundred years, his highness hath there attending now hourly the battle (if it be not stricken before this, or the duke of Albany and Scots fled), 50,000 soldiers largely and plentifully furnished, equipped and trimmed of ordnance, artillery, and munition carriages, and victuals and other necessaries, besides 3000 lords, noblemen, and gentlemen; which manner of earnest proceedings on all sides with effect at once, you shall say to the emperor, it is and shall be more beneficial to the common affairs than by little and little to continue and prolong the enterprises many years, whereof ensueth small annoyance or impeachment of the enemy, and to the emperor and the king no profit, but loss, expences, and charges; wherefore his majesty pursuing the matter with all effect (as the king's entire confidence is he will) you may say that neither by the duke of Savoy, nor such indirect means, the French king shall seek his peace, wherein the emperor hath substantial order in retaining the messengers (supposed rather to come for exploration than otherwise), and of his advertisement the king's highness most cordially thanketh him, but God willing shall be at the last, in brief time, enforced and compelled to send unto such princes great and honourable ambassadors, with other manner of overtures and offers than he hath yet done, not doubting but the emperor of his great wisdom and prudence for manifold and notable effects that thereof may ensue, as well to the particular causes of his majesty and the king's grace, as for the universal repose, quiet, and tranquillity of Christendom depending thereupon, will substantially and profoundly consider and regard these matters accordingly. Over this you shall signify unto the emperor that sir John Russell concluded and agreed with the duke of Bourbon, and mutual oaths were made for performance of articles between the king's grace and him to the same effect as was contained in a bill thereof, which I heretofore sent unto you (except every article touching the said duke's recognition of the king's grace as his sovereign lord) was touched, to be referred unto the emperor, which the king's highness and I take to be as well for the king's purpose as can be devised. And, by the next post, I shall with all diligence send unto you a commission for conclusion, capitulation, and perfecting the treaty between the emperor, the king's grace, the Infant, archduke, and the duke of Bourbon, with instructions how to order yourselves accordingly. Finally, the king's grace giving you great thanks for your good endeavours used in his causes there, willeth you to have especial respect and regard that his highness and I may have more often knowledge and advertisements from you of the successes in those parts, for surely the loss thereof is as great an impeachment, prejudice, and hindrance to the common enterprises as may be imagined or devised. And, therefore, his highness trusteth that you will substantially look thereunto, according to the special trust and confidence that his grace hath in you; and fare you heartily well. At my place besides Westminster, the sixth day of November.

Postscript. — Here arrived letters from Dr. Knight, the king's ambassador with the lady Margaret, that by reason of

the mariner sent unto them by the archduchess, he was advertised the French army in Italy had had an overthrow,
with the loss of 22,000 men, which news (if they be true)
are of right good consequence; and also the Swiss had condescended to give unto the French king 6000 of them to
attend upon him for the safeguard of his person, besides that
how the duke of Bourbon (not minding to violate the neutrality of the French count) was departed from Bezançon
unto Lure in the county of Ferebre, and that the lance-
knights being not passed with the count Felix 7000 paces,
were at post Suslesance, with whom the said duke, well provided of a goodly band of horsemen, intending with diligence
to join and so march towards the enemies. Over that, as
well by the relation of the said mariner, as by letters from
Rome, it appeareth that the cardinals entered the conclave
the first day of October, and that the sixth day of the same
arrived there the cardinals of Aux, Lorraine, and Vandosme,
who (booted and spurred, without tarrying) entered the said
conclave, whose coming is like to make somewhat longer
tract in the election.

I, therefore, trusting that his majesty hath, by your good
solicitation, set forth that affair with effect long before this
time, shall make no newer rehearsal thereof to you. And fare
you heartily well. At Westminster, the sixth of November.

LETTER XLIX.

THE SAME TO THE SAME.

MR. SAMPSON and Mr. Jerningham, I recommend me unto
you, in my right hearty manner. I have not only received
your letters, to me directed, dated at Valladolid the third day of
July, but also have seen your letters of the same date addressed to the king's highness, together with the original
treaty by you lately passed there, with the emperor's commissions for such enterprises as are to be made this summer
against France; perceiving also by your said letters the discourse, order, and form which hath been used and observed
since the arrival of sir Richard Jerningham to the court, and
the manner of the declaration of your charge unto the emperor, the answers, debating, and final resolutions made, had,

and taken upon the same. The circumstance whereof the king's grace and I like very well, and as well for your good endeavour used therein as for your speedily advertisements of the same (though your servant by contrariness of wind and other impediments, was very long on his journey), the king's highness and I give unto you hearty thanks. And albeit, that by my other letters, lately to you directed, I trust come unto your hands long before this time, I did advertise you of the matters here at time occurring, namely, that of the arrival here of the lord Beaver with the specialities of his charge, of his departure towards ——, and of the answer had from him of such articles and conventions as he had concluded with the said duke, the copy whereof I send unto you at this time, with the copies also of instructions and articles given unto sir John Russell, to be concluded with the said duke, on the king's behalf; who is contented to contribute the sum of one hundred thousand crowns for entertainment of ten thousand Germans, who shall be sent by don Ferdinando unto the duke, showing unto you, furthermore, the consideration and weighty importance of that matter, with the good opportunity and commodity now given unto the king and the emperor, the semblable whereof is like never to ensue again if the same be permitted; albeit his grace hath no manner of knowledge at this time of the treaty by you passed with the emperor's commissioners, yet for the singular and tender mind which his highness always beareth towards the furtherance and advancement of the common affairs, his grace abiding no answer from you of your said charge, did with all diligence possible set forth a mighty and puissant army, by the twenty-second day of this month, should be at Calais to join near unto the marshes of the same, with four thousand horsemen and four thousand footmen, to be appointed by the lady Margaret on the emperor's behalf, and from thence to pass unto the siege of Boulogne, as in my former letters and copies was mentioned more at large; yet, nevertheless, to the intent that the emperor may from time to time be advertised of the success of his great and weighty affairs, whereby his majesty having knowledge thereof, may the better know how to order his matters on that side. For his part, I assertain you, that ensuing the deliberation and determination taken as before, the king's grace hath levied a puissant army as of

actual and puissant persons, with as expert and good captains
as have passed out of this realm at any time this hundred
years; which army, largely furnished and provided of ordnance
and artillery, and other habiliments of war, and semblably of
victuals in sufficient quantity, is committed unto the king's
entirely-beloved cousin and counsellor the duke of Suffolk,
being his grace's lieutenant-general of the same, in whose
company be also divers lords and other councillors and discreet
captains—as namely, the lord Mountjoy, Montague, Ferrers,
Sands, Berkeley, Herbert, Courson, sir Richard Wingfield,
sir Andrew Windsor, sir John Vere, sir William Stenington,
sir Richard Weston, sir Edward Gilford, sir William Kingston, the lord Cobham's son, sir Anthony Wingfield, sir William Sidney, sir Jeffery Oates, sir Richard Cornwall, sir
William Courlen, sir Gyles Strange, with sir Edw. Digby,
sir Edw. Nevill, sir John Willoughby, brother to the lord
Willoughby, sir Henry Owen, sir Arthur Browne, sir Griffin
Dormer, and many other, besides other good captains being
in the king's crews at Calais, which with their numbers shall
join also with the king's army; and, according to former letters,
such extreme diligence, with great study, labour, travail,
and pain hath been made, that not only the said duke of
Suffolk was transported and arrived at Calais the twenty-
third day of this instant month, but also the said captains
and whole army, with the ordnance, victuals, and baggages,
with other requisites which should be sent from thence, were
before him and since his departure transported and passed,
and remain now at Calais only for horsemen that should come
from the lady Margaret, and for the carriages and draughts as
at the king's costs be provided in the emperor's Low Countries,
which, God willing, shall be at Calais wholly and entirely the
last day of this month, on which day the duke intendeth to
set forward on his journey; trusting by the grace of Almighty
God, and the good, hearty inclination of his people, is in, with
all actual provision to be made, there shall be a long essay
made to attain their purpose; wherein I praise God to send
them good speed. Wherefore, inasmuch as this matter is so
far set forth with effect on the king's party, his grace doubteth
not but as well ensuing the tenour of the said new treaty as
for the taking the occasion of the said duke. The emperor
hath also really sent and advanced his puissant army on that

side unto Guyenne, the diligent proceeding whereof to the most damaging and annoyance of the enemy, ye must instantly procure, solicit, and call upon so as the said enemy, now earnestly pressed on both parts, may thereby be compelled to divide his power, which by that means shall be of less ability to make resistance on either side; and, consequently, the affairs of the said duke well set forth, as the king's grace trusteth it shall be, there shall (God willing) appear, in brief time, high and notable effect to ensue of this enterprise, to the emperor and king's great honour and reputation, the singular benefit and advantage of their common causes, and repressing of the said enemy, being the disturber of the quiet in Christendom. And much the rather this matter ought to be effectually followed, for that Almighty God hath, after the long wars, discords, and dissensions which hath been in Italy, to the great danger of the same putting into the hearts and minds, as well of the pope's holiness as of the Venetians and all other princes and potentates, to unite and knit themselves together in one conformity, like as I doubt not but that the emperor is largely and specially advertised from his ambassadors before this, as well of the treaty concluded at Venice, as of the other passed at Rome; which things concurring so well together must needs give the more occasion to the emperor not to slack any time that may be taken for the advancement, but so to reinforce his said army that some honourable exploit may be done there. For the furtherance whereof, it is the king's pleasure that the said sir Richard Jerningham in anywise proceed with the said army, to the intent that he not only may see and know their manner of doing, but also exhort, encourage, and instil the leaders and captains of the same, valiantly to advance themselves and lose no time. And for such other causes as are mentioned in your instructions, of which success I pray you from time to time advertise me, and to the intent you may be participant of such news and occurrences as have been here since the departure of sir Richard Jerningham, I advise you that, upon such knowledge had by special order or otherwise, that the French king, of his malicious mind, continually made great preparations to send the duke of Albany in Scotland with a good army to do annoyance unto the realm, the king's grace hath not only prepared and put in readiness the north parts to a great number, which, under the leading of the earl of Surrey, may at all times either invade or defend us, as shall be commanded, and victual ordered in staples for that purpose, but also hath greatly enforced his army upon the seas. So as besides the navy under sir Anthony Poyn on the west seas, to whom also are sent one of four hundred and the other of three hundred, and besides those that keep the north seas under Christopher Doe, with his army, ship, and one other, sir Henry Sherborne amongst others assaulted a ship of four hundred, sent two months past out of France into Scotland laden with men, of which men the captain and three hundred of his men were in a long, sore fight, some slain, divers taken prisoners, and the ship sore bruised, with the loss of few Englishmen except the said sir Henry Sherborne, who also was slain with a gun, and besides such men of war as guard the passage between Dover and Calais, and such other as conduct the king's merchants to and from Zealand, sir William is and hath been upon the seas with thirty-six great ships, who, though the weather had been to him somewhat stormy and contrarious, hath not only given the chase unto twelve ships of France sent to convoy the archbishop of Glasgow and other ambassadors from the duke of Albany into Scotland, enforced them to take the havens of Dieppe and Boulogne, in either of which havens two of the French ships perished at their entry, but also by some of his ships left for that purpose doth yet continually keep them in the said havens without suffering them to pass on their ambassage. And, moreover, posteth himself along coast, taking ships and boats, landing in divers places, where he hath burned and done much hurt in such wise that the Frenchmen of the countries further in be all descended unto the sea-side, which they have fortified in all places, and do keep continual watch for fear of the king's said army; nevertheless the   of this month the said sir Wm. Fitzwilliams descended at Treport, where the town is situate upon a high cliff, and to the same one only way of small breadth, which way was strongly fortified with bulwarks, and the town garrisoned with a band of 3000 men. And albeit that fierce shot of guns and quarries was made by the Frenchmen at the landing of sir William Fitzwilliams, yet he, with sir Francis Bryan, sir John Hopton, Cary, and divers other captains, with the number of

15,000 men, landed in the sight of the enemy, and shortly after won the said bulwarks, from whence the Frenchmen fled into the town, which the Englishmen thrice assaulted, and the Frenchmen thrice issued giving battle; nevertheless, they were always put back. But forasmuch as the town was so strongly fortified and manned, and the tide being spent, the king's said folks might not with their boats come again on board if they had made longer demur, they burnt the fauxbourgs of the town, wherein 300 houses and above were, destroyed the bulwarks, and took away all the ordnance of the same, which was much and good; burnt, also, twelve ships of war, and twelve other ships in the haven, taking all the ordnance of the same ships with them; and in the conflicts aforesaid slew above 600 men, with the loss of no more than twelve Englishmen. Whereupon they departed to Finhead, showing themselves before the haven's mouth, where the said duke prepareth his shipping, and perceiving he could not nor durst not issue—albeit, by a messenger they offered them battle, with as many ships and men equal to his as he would appoint; knowing, also, both the wind to be contrary to the said duke either to pass by the west seas or the narrow seas, and for that also a great storm compelled them to leave the coast—returned to the Downs, not only to receive fresh victuals, but also to lodge themselves in the narrow seas, there to lie in wait for the said duke; so as, by these means, the said duke hath been disappointed of that day on which he made faithful promise to return into Scotland, which was the feast of the Assumption of our Lady, and, with God's help, shall not yet very easily find commodity to pass by, one way or other, thither; by means whereof, the Scots, being in despair of his coming, began to abandon him and the Frenchmen cleaving to the queen of Scots, and have accorded that if the said duke arrive not at the last day of this month, (as I trust he shall not,) they will not only take unto them another king, forsake the French faction, and constitute governors about him, but also sue unto the king's grace for peace. On the other part, if this said duke should or might arrive, the said earl of Surrey is in perfect readiness to encounter with him, and hath, what with the roads, before the departure of sir Richard Jerningham and since, so devastated and destroyed all Tweedale and the March, that there is left

D D 2

neither house, fortress, village, tree, cattle, corn, or other succour for man, insomuch that some of the people that fled from the same afterwards returning and finding no sustenance, were compelled to come unto England begging bread, which oftentimes when they do eat, they die incontinently for the hunger passed; and with no imprisonment, cutting off their ears, burning them in the faces, or otherwise, can be kept away. Such is the punishment of Almighty God to those that be disturbers of good peace, rest, and quiet in Christendom.

Finally, the king's grace committeth unto your perfect wisdoms, discretions, and diligence, the due solicitation and furtherance of all such things as may be to the advancement of the common affairs, according unto such instructions as have been given unto you beforetime, and as you shall know to stand with the mind and pleasure of his grace, praying you always to be diligent in advertisements of the successes, which is the thing shall greatly further, profit, and prevail those urgent and weighty affairs; the far distance between the king's grace hath proved much incommodious, their common business considered. And heartily farewell. At Hampton Court, this last of August, 1523. Your loving friend,

T. Card^{lis} Ebor.

Letter L.

THE SAME TO THE SAME.

Mr. Sampson and Mr. Jerningham, I commend me unto you in my right hearty manner. By Lucie, servant to the duke of Bourbon, I writ unto you my last letters, and in the same advertised you the cause, manner, and form why the common army, which was under the leading of the duke of Suffolk and the count de Buren, in France, came and repaired into Valencia; with the intention and mind that the king's grace was of, to cause the said army, for his part, to return, and remain for this winter in the emperor's countries, in case the count of Buren, with the emperor's folks, would do the semblable. Nevertheless, forasmuch as the season of the year was so frequent with extreme cold and other sore weathers, that neither men nor beasts could longer endure marching in the field, but died daily and nightly, on both

parts, in a great number, for cold—and divers lost their
fingers, hands, and feet, being frozen and dead upon their
beds, and some daily cut off; being also no manner of possibility to or likelihood that new limoneers and other horses for
draught and carriage should be recovered in less space than
six weeks, at the least, without which it was impossible to
march or draw forth artillery; and yet, after the same
draught recovered, the army being so far out of the heart of
the enemy's country, when wet weather should come the
great ordnance should in no wise be carried; remembering,
also, that the duke of Bourbon's army was then totally
scattered, without hope of any fruit to ensue of his enterprises at this time: for these respects and considerations,
by common consent of the said duke of Suffolk and the count
de Buren, who, by reason of impediments, were of necessity
forced so to do, the said common army was clearly dissolved
and discharged; and before knowledge given to the king's
grace of the same, not only the Burgundians and lance-
knights returned home to their dwelling-places, but also the
pioneers and carriages were likewise discharged and paid; the
king's folks, also, by little and little, passing from Valencia to
Burgos, and there wholly kept themselves till advertisement
hereof was given to the king's highness, and his pleasure
known upon the same; which matter, at the beginning, forasmuch as the king's grace was not then so plainly advertised
of the impediments and incommodities as since, was to his
grace's by-pleasure and miscontentation, a goodly reinforcement being then ready to be sent out of England to the same
army, as in my last letter I wrote to you at length.   Whereupon commandment was given by the king's highness to the
duke of Suffolk, that in case the said count de Buren, and
Burgundians, and lance-knights, would return into the
enemy's countries, contriving their war evasive for all this
winter, or a good part thereof, he, with the king's army, proceeding and doubling the limoneers, should do the semblable.
Howbeit, in conclusion, it was doubled both by the lady
Margaret and count de Buren ; which their answer undoubtedly proveth it to be true, that it was not profitable for
this time to redouble the limoneers and gather again the
said Burgundians and lance-knights under the space of six
months, nor that any exploit, invasion, or marching, other-

wise than lying in garrisons, could further be done this time
of the year; with many large reasons and demonstrations
justifying, confirming, and approving the same, so as the
king's grace was found to accept and take the same, dissolving, in some sort, the better part, tracting, nevertheless, the
time so long as to experiment whether any good exploit
might be studied or advised, and for other causes hereafter
mentioned.

LETTER LI.

THE SAME TO THE SAME.

THIS letter containeth special instructions to persuade the
emperor to cause the duke of Bourbon to come into England
and speak with the king, and to the intent that the duke
might afterwards from the Low Countries make an entry
into France with an army.

That this day the whole army is not returned as well a
great part of them, as also the duke of Suffolk and principal
lords, councillors, and captains, ye shall find in the said letter
to Bourbon, with all other things worthy knowledge.   So as
the king's highness being with you before the spring and
convenable time of the year advertised of the premises, may
in time train and order his matters and affairs accordingly; in
declaration of the premises unto the emperor, you must use
good circumspection, to the intent you must first perceive
and understand the mind and disposition of him and his
council, as well towards the continuance or not continuance
of the wars, as also to do some effectual and notable thing
for the king's benefit and advantage, whereincase it shall be
expedient that this overture made unto his majesty, he take
some cause to deliberate with his council before he can make
unto you a perfect and direct answer upon the same, though
it is not to be thought but that before the receipt of these
letters, they have there advised or spoken of some enterprise
or some further annoyance to be done this year against the
common enemy, unless they saw other appearance of an
honourable and beneficial appointment, both for the king and
the emperor than is here yet; wherefore the king's pleasure
is that ye discreetly and substantially note, mark, and ensearch what device or overture shall be set forth, to the intent

that such matters as you shall prove them with being hereafter, may come perchance rather to their own motion and
desire, or peradventure some other thing may be by the
emperor offered to be done at this time, to the annoyance of
the enemy and benefit of the king's grace, than that which his
highness will demand; wherefore you must publicly and discreetly handle yourselves in the disclosing hereof, accordingly
ascertaining you, that when the king's highness and I have
groundly noted and considered the contents of your last letter,
making mention of the small appearance which you see that
the emperor shall be furnished with money and treasure to do
any notable act, and having regard on the other side how
far the enemy's overtures be from any honourable or profitable employment; thinking, furthermore, that it shall be no
small danger and peril to the king's and emperor's affairs, in
case either for lack of money on the emperor's part, or otherwise, to continue the wars, they should seem and appear to be
of force and necessity over much desirous of peace or truce,
whereby the enemy, perceiving the same, should be greatly
encouraged, and perchance be more obstinate than before,
having commodity given unto them to gather treasure, puissance, and friends; for these causes the king and I, for good
deliberation, have had sundry devices and communications
together, to study and find way how the enemy, without the
emperor's excessive charge, may be continually annoyed and
compelled to spend his money, kept in business, terror, and
fear, and peradventure some good portion acquired and gotten
for the king's grace; whereby, in the end, the French king
may also be compelled to offer conditions of another sort than
he yet hath done. And, in the meantime, emolument and
profit may arise to the emperor, and finally, the duke of
Bourbon, with other the kings and his friends, considered,
holpen, maintained and defended, which advice, if it may take
effect, the emperor may say, he is not a little bound unto the
king's highness for that conservation of his charge, who thus
continually takes unto him the greater weight and burthen of
the common causes and affairs.

First, it is not unknown to the emperor that as long as the
wars shall continue with France, the king's grace, as well for
the passage into the channel, as also for the surety and defence of his merchants and subjects, and for annoyance of the

enemy, must keep a puissant army on the sea, which ariseth to no small yearly charge and expenses; besides that, his grace must also maintain great garrisons and armies, as well for defence of his borders against Scotland and for withstanding Scottish invasions, as to infest, annoy, and invade them at all times requisite, besides continual enemies to be laid at Calais, and other places of the king's marches, there for conservation, surety, and defence of the same; all which charges arising to right great and notable sums, the king's highness, for the emperor's sake, is contented still to support and bear, rather than to be driven to any peace or truce that should not be to both the princes honourable and profitable; and to the intent the good effects before specified may be brought to pass, his grace is also contented if such honourable and profitable conditions of peace be offered as may commodiously be accepted, over this, to charge himself somewhat further towards an honourable enterprise, or exploit, to be attempted against the said enemy, so that the emperor, for his part, furnishing to his wars at Italy as appertaineth, will be contributary to the said enterprise in manner and form following, viz.: if the duke of Bourbon may with diligence transport himself by this way into Flanders and the emperor's Low Countries, and that order be given by the emperor, with all speed possible, for an army of 3000 Burgundian horsemen, at the emperor's charge only, and 1000 lance-knights to be prepared at the common charges of the emperor and the king's grace, to whom his highness will be contented to send 1000 archers at his own charge, with a convenient captain, having his artillery and ordnance in sufficient readiness at Valence; and that his army, furnished of carriages and other requisites out of Flanders, may pass with the said duke of Bourbon the way of A—, or otherwise, as there is sufficient appearance of Normandy, the said duke of Bourbon hath a right great love, intelligence and acquaintance here to recover some towns and places to the king's use, which shall be more facile for the duke of Bourbon to do than any other person; and the way once open, and entry had, the king's grace finding it so, may perchance, either in person or by lieutenant, advance thither an army which shall descend unto Normandy, for the better attaining of the country. It is thought by the king's highness and his council, that these effects following may thereof ensue.

First, the French shall, by this means, continually be put unto business charges and expenses. The friends and lovers of the duke of Bourbon, seeing him entered with such puissance, shall therefore take courage and be the bolder to declare themselves on his part; divers towns and strong places shall facile be rendered and revolt unto him; the rest of the 200,000 crowns promised by the emperor and the king's grace to the duke of Bourbon, may be converted towards the charge of that enterprise, the same duke shall thus be countenanced and aided without putting the emperor and king to double charges. The emperor, for that year, shall not need to charge himself with any other puissant army to enter into France, but only with the contribution towards the charges of the said army, as aforesaid, which, besides the rest of 200,000 crowns, be no such excessive sum as shall much grieve him; more displeasure and terror shall ensue thereof to the French king, having not only strangers entered into his dominions, but also his own subjects against him, whereby he shall be in continual fear, to exact money, or do other feats for gatheing thereof; then if sundry puissant armies of strange princes only should enter his countries, whose parts none of the lords or commons would so facile incline unto as to the said duke of Bourbon; the French king shall so extremely be extenuate, and his realm brought to such diminution that shall not be able to contain his conquests, or continue his army in Italy, but of necessity must abandon the same for safeguard of his own estate and person, whereby the duchy of Milan shall be truly delivered from all dangers of the Frenchmen, and established in good surety for the time to come. The duke of Bourbon thus notably aided, and being so much esteemed and beloved in France, shall be in appearance to make a great revolution through all that realm to the king's, the emperor's, and his great honour and profit; the emperor's Low Countries, on this side, shall be in good surety, by reason that the French king, so occasioned by his subjects, with the help of the said army, shall not be of hostility to attempt anything against the same Low Countries, the enemy shall be content to submit himself unto reasonable, profitable, and honourable conditions. For the king, the emperor, and the said duke, and, finally, both their majesties, not highly charged thereby with money and expenses, may gather money and treasure, which shall be an increase of terror to the French king. And having such treasure, they may then be able (the enemy exhaust of money,) to do further as the case shall require; this device, if it be duly and speedily executed, seemeth to be of great consequence both for the conservation of the emperor's honour and reputation, the avoiding of superfluous charges, earnest pressing of the enemy, the assistance and relief of the duke of Bourbon, and the demonstration of gratitude on the emperor's part towards the king's majesty, and that, with such other small annoyances as may be done without great charge, as well by the emperor, by the parts towards Spain, as also by the king's grace, with some enterprise or bravery to be made also in Britain, by Monsieur de Pontner, who is here with the king's grace, no other better or beneficial a thing can now be devised, studied, or imagined, for advance of the common affairs, whereby ye shall desire the emperor, on the king's behalf, not only to condescend unto the premises for his part, but also to exert money, and persuade the duke of Bourbon, (whether he be in Italy or in Spain) incontinently, and with all diligence, to transport himself into this realm, to the intent that upon commission given unto the emperor's ambassadors here resident, or other command, to treat and conclude the premises, such device, communication, and resolution, may be taken with the duke of Bourbon, for attaining of this enterprise, as on all parts shall be thought requisite and convenient; and order to be given to the emperor for the due execution thereof, and faithful performance of the same, by his folks on this side, without using such remiss manner, difficulty, and state therein, by colourable excuses, and for lack of furniture or money, as hath been done aforetime; for doubtless the king's grace is not minded further to charge himself for assistance of the said duke of Bourbon than he hath done, unless he will attempt his enterprise on this side, where is more appearance that he shall do good in revenging of himself against the French, and recovering of his estate the better than in any place; like as also ye may show unto the said duke, if he be there, having also communication with him at length in this matter, for he may say *sua res agitur*. And for the emperor's sake, the king doth move these affairs, minding effectually to assist him, if he will enter by these parts, as is aforesaid, and come and speak with the king's grace, for deliberation and perfect knowledge what substantial way and direction are to be taken in the present business, which his highness would not only be joyous and glad to see with his realm, but also he may be well assured in friendly manner, to be accepted, used, and entertained, during his abode in the same; thus ye shall instantly and effectually solicit, procure, and advance the speedy coming hither of the duke with commission and instructions to be sent by the emperor, as well to his ambassadors here resident, for conclusion of the said matters with the king and the duke of Bourbon, as to the Lady Margaret, and others to whom it shall appertain, for preparation of horsemen, and footmen, and other things requisite as is aforesaid, so as no time be lost, but the spring of this year taken, whereby, in a commodious season, may be achieved and performed the enterprises intended, with honour and profit, desiring the emperor in any wise to give substantial orders for furniture of money on his part, and that the Burgundians, leaving their accustomed delays and colours to be always near unto their borders, proceed with effect to the execution of the enterprises, as the same shall be intended, concluded and devised. Thus heartily fare you well. At my manor at Hampton Court, this 15th day of January. Your loving friend,

CARD^{LIS} EBOR.

LETTER LII.

WOLSEY TO SECRETARY PACE AND TO SIR JOHN RUSSELL.

THIS is to advertise you only Mr. Secretary and sir John Russell, with hearty commendations, that finding nor here nor at Antwerp to send money to that army by exchange at convenable time, knowing that Mr. Weston, turcupleer of the order of St. John, with divers others of their brethren, do now depart towards the court of Rome, for matters concerning that religion, I have taken order with the same Turcupleer, who shall have in his company above forty persons, Englishmen, to convey unto such convenient places as shall be meet, in, or not far out, of his way towards Rome, and meet for you and sir John Russel, the sum of ten thousand sterling, in crowns of the same, which being secretly carried, shall not be known, but as sent by the prior of St. John's in this realm, to the great master of that religion, for the necessary affairs of the same. And it is devised that Turcupleer, at his coming unto Antwerp, shall have communication with Dr. Knight, who is commanded to repair hither unto him, from the Lady Margaret's court, to the intent, by his advice and consent, he may understand what place may be most convenient whereunto sir John Russell may come to receive the same money, and thereunto to advertise some special man that shall show unto you the said place, and if that of likelihood ye may be there; nevertheless, insomuch as it is not here known whether between you and Dr. Knight be a cipher, and that there may peril and danger ensue, in case the letters should chance to be intercepted, making mention of the premises, ye and Dr. Knight will and be ordered to call the name of the said Turcupleer, Christopher Barker; and by the name of Christopher Barker, ye shall always understand the said Turcupleer. And when sir John Russell shall dispose you to repair to the said place where the said Turcupleer and Dr. Knight shall appoint you, there to hearken of his coming, at which time ye shall receive of him the said 10,000*l.*, and the same ye shall convey with you, by some sure and safe means, unto such place as ye shall think convenient to have it in good surety and readiness for the duke of Bourbon, when the case shall require. Nevertheless, if you would use such diligence that the said Turcupleer in his own way towards Trent, which he is most minded to take, may know by your letters at what place he shall repair unto you, and being convenient for you and sir John Russell to meet him, it should much prevail to the common benefit, the politic ordering whereof the king committeth to your wisdom and discreet management. And as touching the bestowing of the 10,000*l.*, you shall understand that the king, not knowing how the said affairs of the said duke of Bourbon shall proceed, and (willing rather to have money there in readiness, than to lack when need shall be,) doth send the said 10,000*l.* to be reserved for yourself in some sure place, and not be employed but as you shall see the cause to require of necessity; that is to say, if the said duke proceeding forward, and the emperor contributing for his part as the king doth, ye shall, as ye see cause, employ it upon the entertainment of the said duke and his army; and if any other adverse chance happen (as God forbid) that the same should not be well bestowed, and to the direct purpose, then the king and I trust verily ye will not see it scattered and spent in vain, but to be reserved and kept, or otherwise, as the time and commodity shall, by your good discretion, lead you, whereof I will be loth to give over much instructions, forasmuch as it is doubtful what things shall chance in that part, but by such confirmation as you have heretofore of the king's mind and intent. And by the capitulations which ye know be passed between the king and the emperor, and by the manner of his doings, and the said duke's proceedings, you shall know how to govern the matter to the king's honour, surety, and profit, and to the best advancement of his grace's affairs; assuring ye that it is not a little to the king's marvel and mine, to hear and understand, by your letters of the 27th of June, and others sent by Curson, (who shall be dispatched with all diligence with the answers of the same,) that the payment of the emperor's money for the entertainment of the duke of Bourbon, is thus retarded and slacked, whereby the proceeding forth of that army hath been greatly hindered, the coming, also, of the lance knights to them letted and impeached, besides the danger that ensueth by the long demur of the emperor's ordinary horsemen, contrary to the tenor of the capitulation passed between the king and him; all which things be greatly to the hurt and danger of the common enterprises, sounding also to the great dishonour of them, and to the comfort of the enemy; like as in all other proceedings, the emperor's folks make great vaunts and promises for payment of moneys, but when it cometh to the point, nothing is observed. For which cause, ye must have special regard hereunto, causing the duke of Bourbon to call for the emperor's money, that the king be not driven off thus always with fair words, and the most burden laid upon him. In which times, making computation from the first day of August, which I understand was the first day of your entry into the French ground at St. Lawrence, and being then to account, first, of the emperor's two hundred thousand crowns, and after of the king's, albeit the whole army had been then assembled, yet it should have been the 30th day of July, before any part of the king's money should have begun to run in payment; the 27th of this instant month, before the 20,000*l.* sent by sir John Russell should be expired and spent, though everything were attempted to the uttermost, according to the estimate which we sent, mentioning the rate of these things. After which 27th day, the emperor then beginning anew to contribute 100,000 crowns for his part, it should be the 24th of September before you should occupy any part of the money now sent by Turcupleer, which, with the 10,000*l.* that the king intendeth to send by some other means, with diligence, should serve, though there were no other fardels towards the same entertainment, till the 27th of October next ensuing; so that the emperor observing his promise for the said contribution, as the king doth, the duke of Bourbon may (God willing) make a great alteration in France, having many notable successes and victories before that time, especially finding so small resistance as he is like to find.

LETTER LIII.

WOLSEY TO SECRETARY PACE.

MR. SECRETARY, I commend me unto you in my right hearty manner; the king's highness and I received your letters, dated at Venice, the 17th of this last month, perceiving by the contents of the same, not only the disposition wherein you have found the duke and senate, with the answers by them made unto your charge, but also the expectation may be had of their intents and purposes, declaring finally such news from the camp, and other as then were come to your knowledge, for which your good endeavour and diligent advertisement, the king's highness and I give you most hearty thanks, abiding with great desire to know and understand the further successes of these matters, and whether upon such new things chanced in the camp, you can by good policy and industry profit any better with them for the furtherance of the common affairs, wherein the king's highness and I be well assured that you will pretermit no good occasion that may be taken to induce them to all such things as may confer to the intended end and purpose, signifying unto you by certain letters, received from sundry parts of Italy, the king's high-

ness and I have been advertised, that albeit two armies of the
imperials and Frenchmen were within half a mile the one
from the other, the 7th day of the same last month, so remaining and continuing till the 17th day of the same also, which
is the date of those letters we had from those parts, yet
nevertheless there was at that time no battle stricken, but
rather small appearance thereof for so much as the French
king, strongly encamped in his field, would not issue out, nor
they might without their great disadvantage, assail him and
enter upon his fortifications, so that it was thought that the
French king's intent was only to weary and confine the imperials for lack of money to maintain and keep their army
together; and forasmuch as the king's grace understandeth
that 20,000 ducats sent by the emperor into Italy were not
then arrived, and that a great part of the 50,000 crowns that
were in sir John Russel's hands, which the king's grace ordained to have been given to the emperor's army in reward,
is returned hither by exchange, and not possible to be recovered at Rome, whereby, without other provision speedily
made, the king's and emperor's affairs might be in great
danger, and the French king prosecute his purpose in one
thing of the said imperials; the king's highness minded most
like a loving father, uncle, and loving brother to put succour
unto the lack which there may be on the imperials' side, hath
caused conventions to be made with Anthony Vivaldi, merchant of Sienna, and Anthony Dodo, merchant of Venice, in
such gold and monies had at such time, price, and rate, as you,
knowing the valuation thereof, can best rate and agree with
their agents in the city, to whom promise and assurance is
made, that upon exhibition thereof yours and my lord of
Bath's acquiescence specifying the receipt thereof, the same
price and value aforesaid shall be here paid and contented
for the same; whereupon they write at this time, not only
unto you, but also to their said agents—that is to say, Vivaldi
to his brother, and Dodo to his father, showing themselves
right glad and comfortable to do unto the king's grace,
service and pleasure herein, without any lucre or gain, but
only as they may save themselves harmless with their goods,
if they perform the same, the king's highness will not fail to
have the same in remembrance accordingly; whereof the king's
pleasure is that, incontinently upon receipt hereof, you shall

APPENDIX.

practise with the said agents and bankers, having communication with them upon the certain price, rate, and value of
the said money, and to know how much they will be contented to bargain with you for, upon the commission of the
said Anthony Dodo and Anthony Vivaldi, after the manner
and form as is aforesaid, making your bargain assured with
them for that purpose, so the money upon requisition may be
had and received accordingly, without binding yourself to
take more or less, but as the case and necessity doth require,
which thing well perfected and done, if then my lord of Bath
shall write unto you to send away part of the money unto
him, or other place, to be bestowed according to such instructions as shall be now given unto him in that behalf,
which is to perform and make up the 50,000 crowns, which
was at Rome, by this and other means, and rather than fail,
to employ also more in case of extreme necessity upon the
said emperor's army, before they should be compelled to break
for lack of a competent sum of money, ye shall, in this case,
cause such money to be delivered, giving acquittance unto
the merchant for the same, as my said lord of Bath shall
appoint, wherein the king's mind is that you shall give unto
the bishop of Bath from time to time your good counsel—
that is to say, how he were best to order himself in departing
with more or less of the said money, as is necessary in the
emperor's army, and commodious with the knowledge of the
successes as there shall require, to the intent his and your
good wisdom and discretion may the better concur together
in that behalf; and he having counsel of the king's trusty
friends and servants there, as all wise men be desirous to
have, may with confidence proceed in his doings as shall
appertain, not for that he should not do anything herein
without your counsel, for therein by tracts of time might be
peril, but that he having your opinion might confer the same
with his own, and then do as he shall think most convenient,
for in effect this is the king's mind.

First, to observe his promise made in these and my former
letters for advancement of the 50,000 crowns to the emperor's
army, and secondly, disbursing no money in waste, for five or
sen thousand more, rather then fail, if the same be thought
to convenient; and that lacking other provision, they should
be else compelled to fail and lose their enterprises, or that the

having thereof may save and conserve the same. Wherefore now ye be advertised of the king's full mind herein, knowing also the state of the matters there, better than can be done here, the king's highness and I do require you to order yourself doing diligence herein accordingly so as his grace may, by your good endeavours there, conduce these matters to the desired end to the honour of his highness, and to the benefit of his affairs, as is the king's and my special trust in you; and fare ye well. At the king's manor at Bridewell, the 5th of March, 1549. Your loving friend,

T. Card^{lis} Ebor.

Letter LIII.

WILLIAM, ARCHBISHOP OF CANTERBURY, TO WOLSEY, (IN BEHALF OF HIS JURISDICTION OF THE PREROGATIVE COURT, WHICH THE CARDINAL'S OFFICERS ASSUMED.)

PLEASETH it your grace to understand, that I am informed by the friends of Jane Roper, wife and executrix to her late husband John Roper, that she is called to appear before certain of your grace's commissaries in your chapel at York-place, for to take upon her as executrix, or else to refuse, or to be repelled as non-executrix, and the will of the said John Roper to be taken as no will, nor she to be taken as executrix. So it is, as I am informed, that this testamentary cause was called before such commissaries as were deputed to examine such testamentary causes as concerned the prerogative, where, by your grace's commissaries and mine, the party thinketh that she might have had indifferent justice; and now by special labour and sinister means to be called before other commissaries of the prerogative, she and some other of her counsel writeth to me, that she is otherwise ordered than according to good justice.

It is written to me also, that in case your grace should call all testamentary causes to special commissaries, that finally the jurisdiction of the prerogative should be extinct: and also all testamentary causes shall only depend upon your grace's pleasure, and no man's will to take any effect, but as it shall please your grace.

I take God to be my judge, I write none otherwise unto your grace than others have written or spoken to my face.

E E

Her friends saith also, that she desireth nothing but to be admitted as executrix to her said husband; and in case there be anything to be reformed in the will of the said John Roper, she is therewith contented as the law and good conscience shall require.

I would your grace knew what rumour and obloquy is both in these parts, and also in London, that no testaments can take effect otherwise than your grace is content. And it hath openly been showed me by divers men, that it is a great trouble, vexation and inquieting to be called before your grace's commissaries and mine; and also to be called before your grace's special commissaries in your said chapel, or otherwhere at your grace's pleasure. And many saith, that it is a great oversight in me that I would make such a composition with your grace which should turn so many men to trouble and vexation. I take God to my judge, I write none otherwise unto your grace than it hath been showed to my face, or else written unto me by letters; for I find your grace so loving to me and to mine that I do hide nothing from your grace.

Finally, I beseech your grace as heartily as I can, that it may please you that this matter may be deferred till after Easter; at which time I shall wait upon your grace, and I doubt not that by means of your grace, and my waiting on your grace, all inconvenience in this behalf may be eschewed, and the parties more shortly relieved than by the process of the law. I am and always shall be glad that your grace use all things at your pleasure; but I am sure your grace will do nothing contrary to the composition sealed with your grace's seal, and subscribed with your grace's hand concerning the prerogative, which my church time out of mind hath been in possession of. I write plainly to your grace, for I know right well your grace will be best content with truth and plain dealing, or else I would not be so bold to write unto your grace in this manner, as God knoweth, who ever preserve your grace. From Charing, the 24th day of February. At your grace's commandment,   WILLIAM CANTUAR.

LETTER LIV.

THE SAME TO THE SAME, (OF THE SAME IMPORT.)

PLEASETH it your good grace to understand I am informed that your grace intendeth to interrupt me in the use of the prerogative, in the which my predecessors and I, in the right of my church at Canterbury, hath been possessed by privilege, custom and prescription, time out of mind. And for the interruption of the same, your grace is minded, as I am informed, to depute Dr. Allen; which if your grace should so do, considering that not only all mine officers of my courts of the arches and the audience, but also the commissaries of my diocese of Kent, and I myself, not only in matters of suit of instance of parties, but also in cases of correction depending before me and them be continually inhabited by our officers, I should have nothing left for me and my officers to do; but should be as a shadow and image of an archbishop and legate, void of authority and jurisdiction, which would be to me perpetual reproach, and to my church a perpetual prejudice.

Wherefore, inasmuch as I trust verily in your great goodness, that your grace would not be so extreme against me and the right of my church before named, I beseech your grace, the premises considered, to defer and respect this matter until I may have communication in this behalf with your grace when it shall please you at your leisure. And your pleasure known, I will be ready to give attendance on your grace, beseeching you also to give credence to my chaplain, Master Wellis, this bearer, in such matters he will show your grace on my behalf. At my manor of Croydon, the 18th day of March. At your grace's commandment,

WILLIAM CANTUAR.

LETTER LV.

WOLSEY TO STEPHEN GARDINER, (ABOUT THE POPEDOM.)

MR. STEPHEN, albeit ye shall be sufficiently with your colleges, by such instructions as be given to Monk Vincent, informed of the king's mind and mine concerning my advancement unto the dignity papal, not doubting but that for the singular devotion which ye bear towards the king and his affairs both general and particular, and perfect love which ye have towards me, ye will omit nothing that may be excogitate to serve and conduce to that purpose, yet I thought convenient for the more fervent expression of mine in that behalf to write to you as to the person whom I most entirely do trust; and by whom this thing shall be most rightly set forth, these few

words following of mine own hand. I doubt not but ye do
profoundly consider as well the state wherein the church and
all Christendom doth stand now presently, as also the state of
this realm and of the king's secret matter, which if it should
be brought to pass by any other means than by the authority
of the church, I account this prince and realm utterly undone.
Wherefore, that is expedient to have such one to be pope and
common father to all princes as may, can, and would give remedy
to the premises. And albeit I account myself much unable,
and that shall be now incommodious in mine old age to be the
said common father; yet when all things be well pondered,
and the qualities of all the cardinals well considered, *absit
verbum jactantiæ*, there shall be none found that can and will
set remedy in the aforesaid things but only the cardinal Ebor,
whose good will and holiness not to you of all men unknown;
and were it not for the re-integration of the state of the
church and see apostolic to the pristine dignity, and for the
conducing of peace amongst Christian princes, and especially
to relieve this prince and realm from the calamities that the
same be now in, all the riches or honour of the world should
not cause me *nedum aspirare sed ne consentire* to accept the
said dignity, and although the same with all commodities
were offered unto me. Nevertheless, conforming myself to
the necessity of the time, and the will and pleasure of these
two princes, I am content to appone all my wit and study,
and to set forth all means and ways *et bene faciam rebus
Christianitatis* for the attaining of the said dignity; for the
achieving and attaining whereof, forasmuch as thereupon
dependeth the health and wealth, not only of these two princes
and their realms, but all Christendom, nothing is to be omitted
that may conduce to the said end and purpose; wherefore,
Mr. Stephen since now ye be so plainly advertised of my
mind and intent, I shall pray you to extend *omnes nervos
ingenii tui, ut ista res ad effectum perduci possit, nullis par-
cendo sumptibus, pollicitationibus sive laboribus, ita ut horum
videris ingenia et affectiones sive ad privata sive ad publica
ita accommodes actiones tuas. Non deest tibi et collegis tuis
amplissima potestas nullis terminis aut conditionibus limitata
sive restricta et quicquid feceris, scito omnia apud hunc regem
et me esse grata et rata. Nam omnia, ut paucis absolvam, in
tuo ingenio et fide reposuimus. Nihil super est aliud scriben-*

" Charles, by the grace of God, king of Castille, Leon, Grenada, Arragon, Navarre, the two Sicilies, Jerusalem, Valencia, Majorca, Sardinia, Corsica, &c., archduke of Austria,
duke of Burgundy, Brabant, Styria, Carinthia, Carniola, Lem-
burgh, Luxemburg and Gueldres, count of Flanders, Haps-
burg, Tyrol, Artois, Palatine, Burgundy, and Hainault, landgrave d'Alsace, prince of Suabia, marquis of Burgaw and of
the Holy Empire, of Holland, Zeeland, Ferrette, Friburg,
Namur, and Zutphen, count of Friesland, of the Marches of
Sclavonia, of Portenau, Salins, and Malines, to our trusty
friends and subjects, the treasurer-general and treasurers of
our domains and exchequer, health and goodwill :

" We would have you to know that out of the good and singular affection that we bear to the person of the right reverend
father in God, our dear and especial friend, the archbishop of
York, cardinal and primate of England, and in some small
degree to reward him for the labours, pains, and trouble he
has had and taken in arranging and bringing to pass the
good, firm, and favourable friendship, confederation, and understanding, lately effected between our well-beloved brother
and uncle, the king of England, his master, and ourselves, to
the said lord cardinal, for these causes, and others moving us
thereto, and that he may be the more disposed to retain his
goodwill towards us, and to occupy himself in the maintenance, increase, and firm continuation of the said friendship
and confederation, we have accorded, and do award and accord
to have and to hold from us the yearly sum of three thousand,
livres, forty gros of our Flemish money to the livre.

" We therefore order and direct that there be paid to him,
by the hands of our friend and faithful counsellor, the receiver-
general of our revenues, John Mirecault, or any other receiver-
general for the time being, out of the funds in his possession,
the said yearly pension, in half yearly equal proportions, com-
mencing from the first day of July, the year 1516 last past,
and so on in every future year, during our good pleasure.

" To which said receiver-general, present or future, this
shall be his sufficient warrant for paying the said pension.

" Given at Ghent, this 8th day of June, 1516, the second
year of our reign.   " By the King."

APPENDIX IV.

RIGHT honourable, after most humble commendations, I
likewise beseech you, that the contents of this my simple
letter may be secret, and that forasmuch as I have great
cause to go home, I beseech your good mastership to command Mr. Heritage to give attendance upon your mastership
for the knowledge of your pleasure in the said secret matter,
which is this; my lord cardinal caused me to put a young
gentlewoman to the monastery and nunnery of Shaftesbury,
and there to be professed, and would her to be named my
daughter, and the truth is, she was his daughter, and now
by your visitation she hath commandment to depart, and
knoweth not whither ; wherefore I humbly beseech your
mastership to direct your letter to the abbess there, that
she may there continue, at her full age to be professed.

Without doubt she is either twenty-four years full, or shall
be at such time of the year as she was born, which was
about Michaelmas. In this your doing, your mastership
shall do a very charitable deed, and also bind her and me
to do you such service as lieth in our little power, as
knoweth our Lord God, whom I humbly beseech prosperously and long to preserve you.   Your orator,

                                          JOHN CLUSEY.

To the right honourable and his
   most especial good Mr. Master
   Cromwell, secretary to our sovereign the king.

NOTES.

Note 1, (p. 4.)—Astrology has long, by the absurd pretensions of its professors, been so effectually consigned to oblivious contempt, that the books which treat of its principles are rarely to be found even in libraries of curious literature, and are never inquired for without provoking a sort of compassionate ridicule not easily withstood. And yet the study itself, as professing to discover by celestial phenomena future mutations in the elements and terrestrial bodies,* ought not to be despised. The theory of the tides is altogether an astrological doctrine, and long before the days of Sir Isaac Newton, was as well understood as it is at this moment. The correspondence which the ancient physicians alleged to exist between the positions of the moon and the stages of various diseases, has certainly received a degree of confirmation, auspicious to a modified revival of the doctrine of celestial influences.† It is not a just philosophy which rejects as vain what appears to be improbable. Though many things, of which the astrologers speak, be apparently fanciful, they are not the less worthy of being examined. They have asserted, that the fits of a particular kind of madness are governed by the moon; that her rays quicken the putrefaction of animals;‡ that persons are rendered dull and drowsy who sleep abroad in the moonlight; that vegetables sown in the spring of the moon, differ in flavour from the same kind sown in her wane; that vines pruned during her conjunction with the sun, shoot forth a less rank foliage afterwards; and that timber felled, at the same time, endures longest uncorrupted.§ They have also alleged that oysters, crabs, and all testaceous fish, grow fat and full with the waxing of the moon, and dwindle with her waning. That she has an influence on the procreation of mares and horses; and that children born at the time of new moons are always short-lived. Any man, possessing patience and inclination, might so easily ascertain the fact of these things, that it is surprising they should be still pronounced incredible, and denied rather than contradicted.

> " Yet safe the world and free from change doth last;
> No years increase it, and no years can waste,
> Its course it urges on, and keeps its frame,
> And still will be, because 'twas still the same.
> It stands secure from Time's devouring rage,
> For 'tis a God, nor can it change with age."

---

* Sir Christopher Heydon's Defence of Astrology, 2 Ed. 1603.

† Dr. Mead's Treatise concerning the influence of the sun and moon upon human bodies, &c.

‡ Heydon, 425.   § Ibid. 186.

And, therefore, say the astrologers, a correspondence and coincidence must exist throughout the universal phenomena ; as in the machinery of a clock, in which the state of one part indicates what has passed, or is to happen in another.

The principles of astrology, like those of every other science, must have been founded on some species of experience. The first occurrences that probably attracted observation, would be those that naturally had some apparent concordance with the great luminaries and planets, such as the seasons of the year, &c. The tides, varying with the phases of the moon, would early obtain attention : their regular increase, corresponding to her opposition and conjunction, would lead to the consideration of the solar influence. Thence, perhaps, it was observed, that when certain planets were in particular constellations, and the sun in certain signs of the zodiac, the tides were otherwise affected. Hence the qualities of the planetary influence came to be studied.

A transition from the tides to the variations of the atmosphere, if they did not first attract notice, was very natural ; and as valetudinarians are particularly affected by the weather, the progress towards that branch of astrology which relates to diseases would be the consequence.

If the diseases of man be regulated by the stars, why not his passions also ? And, as his passions govern his actions, making one class of motives more acceptable than another, why not by the means of his passions regulate his fortune ? Fortune is but another name for situation, and men are evidently allured into their various circumstances or situations by their passions. The next inquiry would naturally, therefore, be to ascertain from what particular aspects of the skies the varieties of fate and character proceed. Hence the theory of nativities, and that branch of the study which has brought the whole into such disrepute. Ptolemy had vainly warned his followers not to foretel particularly, but universally, as one that seeth a thing afar off ; but, not content with telling particularly, they alleged, in the very face of their fundamental position, that man possessed a power of altering his destiny, by affirming that his will was free, and that he had the power of choice and election, forgetting that the foreknowledge of an apprehended future evil, generated a motive which might lead to the adoption of the conduct by which it was avoided.

The notion of the *unalterability* of the world, as the atheistical astrologers entertained it, is at once curious and absurd, and warranted inferences which they would not, perhaps, have readily admitted. Proceeding upon the supposition that there does exist such a concordance in the universe as they maintained, it is obvious, from the motions of the earth, and of the system to which she belongs, that no two astrological observations could be found in the course of many ages precisely similar : a general resemblance of effect is the utmost that could be obtained, until, in the progress of the various movements of the whole universe, the earth, in all respects, came again to the situation which she held, in relation to every other part, when the first observation was made. When she has done this, it must be allowed from the premises, that a new series of effects will commence, in everything resembling the past. History having finished her tale, will begin to repeat it ; and persons and events under the same names, and in the same forms, as those of whom we have heard, will appear.

The professors of alchymy have written the records of their processes, in a language of types and symbols as inscrutable as that of the priests of Anubis. Whether they did or did not possess the art of making gold, may be fairly questioned, until the knowledge of their secrets is complete, and their experiments have been renewed; but that no natural impediment exists to the attainment of the art, Mr. Davy has gone far to show. From the reported testimony of one of themselves, it would appear that the hope of making an immortalizing elixir was not seriously entertained by the alchymists. The utmost which they professed to make, was a cordial which should refresh and preserve the animal spirits when the frame was not vitally impaired. Possibly, extricated from the cabalistic technical jargon which they used, their studies may have been both rational and ingenious; at least, an opinion of them ought not to be formed from the ridicule which ignorant pretenders so justly provoked. John Frederick Helvetius, doctor and practitioner of medicine at the Hague, in the year 1666, gives a curious account of a conversation which he had with an alchymist on the subject of the Stone and the Elixir, and which he introduces with a description of the alchymist's person, that, even in the bad translation before me, has the merit of being remarkably vivid and natural.

The doctor inquired whether, by the use of that elixir which Elias affirmed was known to the alchymists, the pristine nature of man may be converted into a new one—the sad into cheerful ? " Not at all, Sir," said the artist, " for so great power was never conferred on any medicament, that it could change the nature of man. Wine inebriating, taken by diverse individual men, in him who is drunk changeth not his nature, but only provokes, and deduceth into act what is naturally and potentially in him, but before was, as it were, dead. Even so is the operation of the universal medicine, which, by recreation of the vital spirits, excites sanity, for a time only suppressed, because it was naturally in him before; even as the heat of the sun changeth not herbs or flowers, but only provokes the same, and from the proper potential nature of them deduceth them into act only : for a man of a melancholy temper is again raised to exercise his own melancholy matters ; and the jovial man, who was pleasant, is recreated in all his cheerful actions ; and so, consequently, in all desperate diseases it is a present or most excellent preservative." Soon after he adds, " But if any prolongation of life by some philosophic medicament could have been induced against the predestination of the omnipotent God, undoubtedly neither Hermes, Trismegistus nor Paracelsus, nor Raymund Lully,* nor count Bernhard, and many more like illustrious possessors of this great mystery, would have yielded to the common death of all mortals, but, perhaps, have protracted their life until this very day. Therefore, it would be the part of a fanatic and foolish man to affirm this—yea, of a most foolish man to believe and assent to the same, touching any one medicament in the things of nature."

Presently the conversation changed to the transmutation of metals, and Helvetius affirms that Elias gave him a specimen of the Philosopher's Stone, with which he performed a successful experiment. Helvetius himself does not appear to have been an alchymist; he was unacquainted with the subjects of which Elias spoke, and had written a book against sir Kenelm

* Raymund Lully is said to have taught Edward III. the art of making gold.—Sinclair, Hist. Revenue, 75.

Digby, who professed to make a sympathetic powder which could cure wounds at a distance. In refuting the pretensions of sir Kenelm, he had made use of some expressions relative to the pursuits of alchymy, which induced Elias to call on him.—Golden Calf, 99, 100, ed. 1670. A good name for such a book!

The Rosicrucians were a particular Order of Alchymists, and professed to be able to transmute the metals. The names of secret substances employed in the process, were communicated to the members at their admission into the society, or, rather, the meaning of the symbolical language by which the materials were described was explained to them, and it was the use of that language which gave rise to the opinion, that the Rosicrucians held particular notions relative to spirits. They were, in fact, a society of experimental philosophers, and used, according to the fashion of the age in which the society was founded—a cabalistic mode of expression, in order to enhance the merits of their knowledge. This society is still supposed to have some sort of an existence ; but whether its members believe they possess the key to the symbolical language, and are able to convert common into precious metals, is not easy to be ascertained. I have met with a gentleman, who said he was a Rosicrucian. There is a dictionary, in French, which says, that Ovid's Metamorphoses describe alchymical processes. I have not been able to meet with it.

. Note 2. (p. 18.)—Pinkerton, whose researches have illustrated the transactions between the courts of England and Scotland, during the reigns of James IV. and his son, more fully than any of the historians who have written of that period, gives an account to the following effect, of the origin of this war. Letters of reprisal had been granted to Andrew, Robert, and John Barton, who in the year 1486, commanded a rich merchant ship, which a Portuguese squadron captured, and for the loss of which the sufferers could not otherwise obtain indemnity. Although the lapse of thirty years might have abated the sense of injury, the Bartons were active in revenging their domestic misfortunes. Emanuel, king of Portugal, remonstrated against their depredations on his subjects, and offered a judicial examination of their claims : but as he neglected a message which, four years before, James had sent, to conciliate the dispute, and to restore the ancient amity of the two nations, his remonstrance and offer were equally disregarded, and the Bartons repaid the loss sustained by their father, from the spoil of the Portuguese trade, which, in consequence of the discovery of the maritime route to India by Gama, was then the richest in the world. Andrew Barton, with two vessels, the Lion, a large ship of war, and Jenny Pirwen, an armed sloop, traversed the narrow seas, to the annoyance of the English vessels, which he molested upon pretence of searching for Portuguese goods. The English merchants complained of this grievance; and, in consequence, lord Thomas Howard and sir Edward Howard, sons of the earl of Surrey, were sent with two ships in pursuit of Barton, whom they met in the Downs. After an obstinate conflict, the Scottish commander fell, and the Howards were victorious. James, exceedingly vexed by the event, and loss of so gallant an officer, despatched a herald to the English court to claim reparation ; but Henry only answered, that the fate of pirates should never occasion disputes among princes.

A more minute cause of enmity arose from another private feud. Sir

Robert Ker, cupbearer to James, and also warden of the middle march, having been severe in the administration of the latter office, was slain by Heron, Lilburn, and Starked, three turbulent English borderers. Henry VII., in whose reign this outrage was perpetrated, gave up Lilburn. Starked and Heron escaped; but Heron of Ford, brother to the murderer, was given up as a pledge for the surrender of the latter, and was imprisoned in Fastcalle, with Lilburn, who died there. Soon after the accession of Henry VIII., Starked and Heron re-appeared, as if conscious that they should be protected. Andrew Ker, son of sir Robert, acquainted with this fact, sent two of his servants to punish the assassins of his father, and they returned with Starked's head, which Ker exposed with impunity in one of the most public places in Edinburgh.

Pinkerton also mentions a domestic provocation which Henry had given to the family of Scotland, by evading the delivery of a legacy of valuable jewels, bequeathed to the queen by her father. The character of Margaret was not unlike her brother's, bold and fiery. In one of her letters to him, she upbraids him for his pitiful conduct concerning the legacy, and desires no more may be said of it, as her husband grew every day more and more kind to her, and would pay the value of the legacy himself. "We are ashamed," she adds, "therewith, and would God never word had been thereof: it is not worth such estimation as is in your diverse letters of the same."

The grand source of the war must still, however, be looked for in the principles which had for many ages induced the government of Scotland to prefer the politics of France to those of England. For, on the 10th July, 1512, James ratified a league, previously arranged, by which he, in fact, united himself to Lewis, although more than another year after was consumed in fruitless and insincere negotiation.

NOTE 3, (p. 19.)—It is somewhat extraordinary that a work so generally read as Hume's History of England, should pass through several editions for the last twenty years, with the omission of the character of pope Julius II. The passage alluded to may be found in the early editions of Hume's England, in the reign of Henry VIII. about the year 1510, and on the subject of the league of Cambray. It exhibits one of those sketches of character for which Hume is justly celebrated, and in his best manner. The style is vigorous, the colouring impressive, and the whole piece indicates the hand of a master. It is as follows:

"Alexander the Sixth was dead; a man of a singular character, and, excepting his son, Cæsar Borgia, almost the only man we read of in history who has joined great capacity with the blackest vices, and the most abandoned profligacy of manners. After a short interval, Julius the Second had succeeded to the papal throne, who, though endowed with many virtues, gave almost as much scandal to the world as his detested predecessor: his virtues were deemed unsuitable to his station of sovereign pontiff, the spiritual judge and common father of Christians. Actuated by an unextinguishable thirst of glory, inflexible in his schemes, undaunted in his enterprises, indefatigable in his pursuits; magnanimous, imperious, domineering; his vast soul broke through all fetters which old age and the priestly character imposed upon it, and, during his pontificate, kept the world in continual agitation."

Note 4, (p. 28.)—General Monk mentions, that Selim was induced to undertake the invasion of Persia by the representation of one of the pashas. The information, however, which the pasha had given as to the state of the country through which his march lay, was so incorrect, that the army lost a vast number of men, and suffered great hardships in those deserts, which had proved so disastrous to the Roman legions. Considering the pasha justly responsible for his advice and information, he ordered him to be put to death, although the enterprise had proved successful.—*Observations on Military and Political Affairs, folio edit., page* 20.—G.

Note 5, (p. 46.)—There is a very pretty monkish morality in the British Museum; the subject of which is the incredulity of Thomas.—*Cottonian (Library) Vespasian, D. VIII.*

The piece opens with a dialogue: Eneas and Cleophas.

> *Cleophas.*—Brother Eneas, I you pray,
> Pleasing to you if that it be,
> To the castle then a little way
> That you vouchsafe to go with me.

> *Eneas.*—Already, brother, I walk with thee
> To yonder castle with right good cheer;
> Run together, anon go we,
> Brother Cleophas, we two, in fear.

> *Cleophas.*—Brother Eneas, I am sore mov'd
> When Christ our master comes in my mind,
> When that I think how he was griev'd
> Joy in my heart I none can find:
> He was so lowly, so good, so kind,
> Holy of life and meek of mood,
> Alas! the Jews eyes they were too blind
> Him for to kill, that was so good.

They continue to discourse on the crucifixion, when Christ joins them, and requests to walk with them in fellowship.

In the same volume, there is another composition still more singular. It is no less than a rude dramatic outline of the subject of "Milton's Paradise Lost." It opens with one Deus giving the following account of himself:—

> "My name is known, God and King,
> My work to make well I wend,
> In myself resteth my reign-ing,
> It hath no 'ginning nor none end,
> And all that ever shall have being
> It is enclosed in my mind:
> When it is made at my liking,
> I may it save, I may it chind,
>   After my pleasure.
> So great of might is my powstie,
> All things that be, belong to me;
> I am a God in person three
>   Knit in one substance.
> I am the true Trinitie
> Here walking in the wone,

> Three persons myself I see.
> Looking in me God alone
> I am the fader of powstie,
> My son with me 'ginneth gone,
> My ghost is grace, in majestie.
> I willeth welth up in heaven's throne.
> One God three I call;
> I am father of might,
> My son keepeth right,
> My ghost hath light
> And grace with all;
> Myself beginning never did take,
> And endless I am through my own might.
> First I made heaven with stars of light
> In mirth and joy ever more to wake,
> In heaven I beheld angels full bright
> My servants to be all for my sake,
> With mirth and melody worship my might.
> I held them in my bliss,
> Angels in heav'n ever more shall be
> With mirth and song to worship me
> And joys they may not wis.

Here angels enter singing Hallelujah. *Lucifer* then says—

> To those who worship sing ye this song,
> To worship God, or reverence me?
> Bot ye me worship ye do me wrong,
> For I am the worthiest that e'er may be.

Angel *Boni.*—We worship God of might most strong,
> Who hath formed both us and thee;
> We may ne'er worship him too long,
> For he is most worthy of majestie.
> On knee to God we fall,
> Our Lord God worship we,
> And in no wise honoureth we thee,
> A greater lord may ne'er now be
> Than he that made us all.

Lucifer.—A worthier lord, forsooth, am I,
> And worthier than he e'er will be.
> In evidence that I am more worthie
> I will go sitten in God's see.
> Above sun, moon, and stars or sky,
> I am now set as you may see.
> Now worship me for most might,
> And for your lord honour now me
> Sitting in my seat.

Angel *Mali.*—God mighty we forsake,
> And for more mighty we thee take,
> Thee to worship honour we make,
> And fall down at thy feet.

Deus.—Thee, Lucifer, for thy mighty pride,
　　I bid thee fall from heaven to hell ;
　　And all who holden on thy side
　　In my bliss never more to dwell,
　　At my commandment anon down them flyde
　　With mirth and joy never more to dwell ;
　　In mischief and movas ay shall they abide,
　　In bitter burning and fire so fell
　　In pain ever to be pight.

Lucifer.—At thy bidding that will I work,
　　And pass from joy to pain so smart.
　　Now I am a devil full dark
　　That was an angel bright.
　　Now to hell the way I take
　　In endless pain into the pight,
　　For fear of fire a faint I crake
　　In hell's dungeon my doom is dight.

Deus.—Now heaven is made for angels' sake
　　The first day and the first night ;
　　The second day water I make,
　　The welkin also so fair and light."

　　The reader, I am sure, will readily pardon the length of this curious quotation.　Before Milton's day, his subject, if not attempted in prose, was, certainly, in rhyme.　I am not aware that either of these two holy operas has ever been printed or quoted.

INDEX.

THE END.

T. C. Savill, Printer, 4, Chandos Street, Covent Garden.